Mathematics of Financial Markets

Mathematics of Financial Markets

*Financial Instruments and Derivatives Modeling,
Valuation and Risk Issues*

Alain Ruttiens

A John Wiley & Sons, Ltd., Publication

Library of Congress Cataloging-in-Publication Data to follow

A catalogue record for this book is available from the British Library.

ISBN 978-1-118-51345-3 (hardback) ISBN 978-1-118-51347-7 (ebk)
ISBN 978-1-118-51348-4 (ebk) ISBN 978-1-118-51349-1 (ebk)

Set in 10/12pt Times by Aptara, Inc., New Delhi, India

MIX
Paper from
responsible sources
FSC® C013604

To Prof. Didier Marteau,
without whom this book would not exist

Contents

Foreword

The valuation and risk dimensions of financial instruments, and, to some extent, the way they behave, rest on a vast, complex set of mathematical models grouped into what is called quantitative finance. Today more than ever, it should be required that each and every one involved in financial markets or products has good command of quantitative finance. The problem is that the many books in this field are devoted either to a specific type of financial instruments, combining product description and quantitative aspects, or to a specific mathematical or statistical theory, or otherwise, with an impressive degree of mathematical formalism, which needs a high degree of competence in mathematics and quantitative methods. Alain Ruttiens' text is aiming to offer in a single book what should be needed to be known by a wide readership to master the quantitative finance at large. It covers, on the one hand, all the financial products, from the traditional spot instruments in forex, stocks, interest rates, and so on, to the most complex derivatives, and, on the other hand, the major quantitative tools designed to value them, and to assess their risk potentials. This book should therefore provide the best entry-level reference for anyone concerned in some way with financial markets and products to master their quantitative aspects, or to fill the gaps in areas with which they are less familiar.

At first sight, this ambitious objective seems hard to achieve, given the variety and the complexity of the materials it aims to cover. As a matter of fact, Alain recognizes that fulfilling such an objective implies sorting among a vast array of topics in a rather subjective way. Fortunately, the author had the chance to at least induce a positive bias in such a subjective selection by relying upon his experience as a market practitioner for more than 20 years. He furthermore treats this material in a clear, pedagogical way, requiring no prerequisites in the reader, except the basics of algebra and statistics.

Finally, the reader should appreciate the overall aim of Alain's book, allowing for useful comparisons – some valuation methods appearing to be more robust and trustworthy than others – and often warning against the lack of reliability of some quantitative models, due to the hypotheses on which they are built. This last point is all the more crucial after the recent financial crises, which were at least partially due to some inappropriate uses of quantitative models.

For all of these reasons, my expectation is that Alain's book should be a great success.

A.G. Malliaris
Loyola University, Chicago

Main Notations

B	bond price
c	coupon rate of a bond
C	convexity, or call price, in function of the context
cov(.)	covariance of (.)
d	dividend paid by a stock
D	duration
D_t	discount factor relative to time t
$E(.)$	expected value of (.)
F	forward price, or future price (depends on the context)
FV	future value
-ibor	generic for LIBOR, EURIBOR, or any other inter-bank market rate
K	strike price of an option
κ	kurtosis
M	month or million, depending on context
MD	modified duration
MtM	"Marked to Market" (= valued to the observed current market price)
μ	drift of a stochastic process
N	total number of a series (integer number), or nominal (notional) amount (depends on the context)
$\mathcal{N}(.)$	Gaussian (normal) density distribution function
$N(.)$	Gaussian (normal) cumulative distribution function
P	put price
$P\{.\}$	probability of {.}
PV	present value
$\mathcal{Q}(.)$	Poisson density distribution function
r	generic symbol for a rate of return
r_f	risk-free return
$\rho(.)$	correlation of (.)
skew	skewness
S	spot price of an asset (equity, currency, etc.), as specified by the context
STD(.)	standard deviation of (.)
σ	volatility of a stochastic process
t	current time, or time in general (depends on the context)

t_0	initial time
T	maturity time
τ	tenor, that is, time interval between current time t and maturity T
$V(.)$	variance of $(.)$
$\tilde{X}(.)$	stochastic process of $(.)$
$\tilde{y}$	stochastic variable
z_t	"zero" or 0-coupon rate of maturity t
Z	standard Wiener process (Brownian motion, white noise)

Introduction

The world is the excess of possible.[1]

The aim of this book is to present the quantitative aspects of financial markets instruments and their derivatives. With such a broad scope, it goes without saying that it remains a "general" book, which is why, at the end of each of the chapters, there is a list of further reading for those who want to expand the topic (this also applies at a global level, *cf.* the end of this Introduction). Ideally, everyone concerned with financial markets – whether a trader, a risk manager, a sales person, an accountant, or managing a fund, an institutional or a bank, and so on, or else a student in finance, of course – should have to be aware of what is happening, quantitatively speaking, behind the financial instruments' behaviors.

In writing this book, my concern was twofold: to sort out what really needs to be mastered, and to write up the text in the most pedagogical way. I hope that with both my 25-year professional experience in financial markets and my teaching activities, this objective will have been reached in a satisfactory way.

As regards the mathematical formulae, they are not proved, except when the proof brings some useful insight. Rather, I have tried to justify as much as possible their importance, and to translate them from algebra into plain English. After all, the vast majority of people involved with financial markets do not compute prices, sensitivities, and so on since they have access to data providers such as Bloomberg, where almost everything is valued. Therefore, it is not a question of replacing the computer but of having some command of these calculations, both for a safety reason – it is better to understand what is behind the data we manipulate – and to be able to appreciate the order of magnitude of the prices we are confronted with. And even sometimes to be capable of drafting some rough calculation aside from the market data.

Also, I have tried as much as possible to avoid excessive formalism – formalism is securing the outputs of research, but may, in other circumstances, burden the understanding by non-mathematicians. This is the case, for example, in Chapter 8, *The Basis of Stochastic Calculus*. Besides the basics of algebra and probabilities and statistics, there is no prerequisite for using this book.

I warmly thank Renaud Beaupain, Christian Berbé,[2] Frédéric Botteman, Marc Buckens, Simon Dablemont, François Delclaux, Jean-Charles Devin, Andrés Feal, Florena Gaillard,

---

[1] (Translated from French) Thomas RIEN, *Cette mémoire du cœur*, 1985.
[2] Who sadly passed away recently.

Michel Godefroid, Christian Jaumain, Mahnoosh Mirghaemi and Angelo Pessaris, who each agreed to proofread one or two of the 15 chapters – they helped me significantly with their remarks and comments. As the saying goes, any remaining errors or deficiencies are my own. In the same way, I welcome readers' comments and remarks at ruttiens@pt.lu.

Two final, practical remarks:

- In the many real market examples, dates are expressed as dd/mm/yy.
- I am using the "-ibor" notation to globally denote any kind of LIBOR as well as EURIBOR interbank interest rate. By the way, to make the reading of formulae easier, I have tried to choose symbols (see *Main Notations*) which are as close as possible to what they represent.

Alain Ruttiens

FURTHER READING

As general references:

John Y. CAMPBELL, Andrew W. LO, A. Craigh MACKINLAY, *The Econometrics of Fnancial Markets*, Princeton University Press, 1996, 632 p.

Sergio M. FOCARDI, Frank J. FABOZZI, *The Mathematics of Financial Modeling and Investment Management*, John Wiley & Sons, Inc., Hoboken, 2004, 800 p.

Lawrence GALITZ, *Financial Times Handbook of Financial Engineering*, FT Press, 3rd ed. Scheduled on November 2011, 480 p.

Philippe JORION, *Financial Risk Manager Handbook*, John Wiley & Sons, Inc., Hoboken, 5th ed., 2009, 752 p.

Tze Leung LAI, Haipeng XING, *Statistical Models and Methods for Financial Markets*, Springer, 2008, 374 p.

David RUPPERT, *Statistics and Finance, An Introduction*, Springer, 2004, 482 p.

Dan STEFANICA, *A Primer for the Mathematics of Financial Engineering*, FE Press, 2011, 352 p.

Robert STEINER, *Mastering Financial Calculations*, FT Prentice Hall, 1997, 400 p.

John L. TEALL, *Financial Market Analytics*, Quorum Books, 1999, 328 p. Presents the maths needed to understand quantitative finance, with examples and applications focusing on financial markets.

Part I
The Deterministic Environment

1

Prior to the yield curve:
spot and forward rates

1.1 INTEREST RATES, PRESENT AND FUTURE VALUES, INTEREST COMPOUNDING

Consider a period of time, from t_0 to t, in Figure 1.1.

$1 invested (or borrowed) @ i from t_0 up to t gives $A. t is the *maturity* or *tenor* of the operation. $1 is called the *present value* (PV), and $A the corresponding *future value* (FV). i represents the *interest rate* or *yield*.

In this basic operation, no interest payment is made between t_0 and t: in such a case, i is called a "0-coupon rate" or "zero" in short. Zeroes are also called "spot rates" as they refer to currently prevailing rates (at t_0). Let us denote z_t the current zero for a maturity t.

In the financial markets, the unit period of time is the year, and the interest rates, or yields, are expressed in *percent per annum* (% p.a.), that is, per year. In the US market, interest rates may also be expressed on a semi-annual basis (s.a.) with respect to the market of US bonds paying semi-annual coupons. Database providers, such as Bloomberg or Reuters, do well in always specifying whether the rates they mention are expressed on an annual or a semi-annual basis.

If the maturity $t = 1$ year, and z_1 the corresponding zero rate expressed in % p.a., the relationship between *PV* and *FV* is

$$PV\,(1 + z_1) = FV \tag{1.1}$$

meaning that the future value *FV* is the sum of the present value *PV* plus the interest computed on *PV* @ z_1, that is, $PV \times z_1$.

If the maturity t is shorter than 1 year, the interest is computed *pro rata temporis*, t being counted as a fraction of a year. Equation 1.1 becomes

$$PV\,(1 + z_t t) = FV \tag{1.2}$$

The time unit period of 1 year is a natural *compounding time unit*, that is, above 1 year, interests must be compounded (see the following). On the US market, the compounding time unit is normally 0.5 years.

If $t > 1$ year for zeroes expressed on an annual basis, or >0.5 year for zeroes expressed on a semi-annual basis,

- ◆ either t is a round number of years (or of half-years in the case of semi-annual basis), Eq. 1.1 becomes

$$PV\,(1 + z_t)^t = FV \tag{1.3}$$

that is, z_t is *compounded t times*. Indeed, suppose that $t = 2$ years. Since for a zero-coupon there are no cash flows (of interest) paid between t_0 and year 2, the interest relating to the

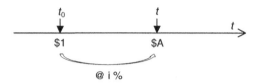

Figure 1.1   Interest on a period of time, from t_0 to t

first year is *compounded* so that, for the second year, the present value at the beginning of year 2 becomes

$$PV(1 + z_2)$$

and earns interest @ z_2 during the second year so that

$$[PV(1 + z_2)](1 + z_2) = PV(1 + z_2)^2 = FV$$

In the case of compounding of s.a. rates, Eq. 1.3 becomes

$$PV\left(1 + \frac{z_t}{2}\right)^{2t} = FV$$

And, more generally, if the zero rates were to be compounded n times a year,

$$PV\left(1 + \frac{z_t}{n}\right)^{nt} = FV \tag{1.4}$$

- ◆ or t is not a round number of years, for example $t = n$ years $+ t'$. In this case the market practice consists of combining both rules (Eq. 1.2 and Eq. 1.3):

$$PV\left(1 + z_t\right)^n \left(1 + z_t \times t'\right) = FV$$

1.1.1   Counting the number of days

The rules for expressing t differ from one market to another: fractions of a year may be counted as a number of days n_d that can be based on the actual (ACT) number of days, or on full months of 30 days plus actual number of days for a fraction of a month, the year being counted as a 360-days or a 365-days year, to follow the most usual conventions.

The market practice uses the following day count conventions:
In USD:

- on the money market (cf. Section 2.1): ACT/360, that is, the actual number of days, divided by (a year of) 360 days;
- on longer maturities: USD swap rates[1]: 30/360 (semi-annual), US government Treasury bonds: ACT/365 (semi-annual).

In EUR:

- on the money market: ACT/360;
- on longer maturities: EUR swap rates: 30/360, EUR sovereign bonds: ACT/ACT.

---

[1] This is to show that day count conventions may vary even in the same currency. Swaps and swap rates are studied in Chapter 6.

The set of z_ts, or $\{z_t\}$, is called the *term structure of interest rates*, or the *yield curve*. Strictly speaking, this wording should apply only to spot or zero-coupon interest rates, and not to usual bond yields.

The set $\{z_t\}$ plays a key role in financial calculus, especially for pricing interest rate products, such as bonds, or instruments such as derivatives. Indeed, these instruments are anything but combinations of cash flows to be paid or received on some future dates, so that to value them at the current time, one needs to compute the present value of any future cash flows involved, by use of zeroes corresponding to their respective maturity dates.

Examples of FV Calculations (Rounded at Four Decimals)

- For a "nominal" amount of $1, if $z_t = 5\%$ p.a. with $t = 4$ months totaling 122 days, ACT/360, Eq. 1.2 gives:

$$FV = 1(1 + 0.05 \times 122/360) = \$1.0169$$

- If $z_t = 5\%$ p.a. with $t = 4$ years, annual 30/360 ($= 1$ per full year), Eq. 1.3 gives:

$$FV = 1(1 + 0.05)^4 = \$1.2155$$

- If $z_t = 5\%$ p.a. on a semi-annual basis, with $t = 4$ years $= 8$ half-years, $z_t = 5/2 = 2.5\%$ per half-year period, and Eq. 1.4 gives:

$$FV = 1(1 + 0.05/2)^8 = \$1.2184$$

  that is, higher than $1.2155 above: the interests are compounded faster.
- If $z_t = 5\%$ p.a. with $t = 4$ years annual 30/360 plus 4 months or 122 days, ACT/360, combining Eq. 1.2 and Eq. 1.3 gives:

$$FV = 1(1 + 0.05)^4 \times (1 + 0.05 \times 122/360) = \$1.2361$$

1.2 DISCOUNT FACTORS

Eq. 1.2 and Eq. 1.3 can be rearranged as follows, introducing the *discount factors* D_t:

$$PV = \frac{FV}{(1 + z_t)^t} = FV \times \text{s.th., called "discount factor" } D_t; \quad PV = \frac{FV}{1 + z_t t} = FV \times D_t$$

Hence,

$$D_t = \frac{1}{(1 + z_t)^t} \text{ or } = \frac{1}{1 + z_t t} \tag{1.5}$$

So that, since t is at the denominator of the fraction, the longer the maturity, the lower the discount factor.

Examples. The discount factors corresponding to the above two first examples are:

- $z_t = 5\%$ p.a. with $t = 4$ months or 122 days, ACT/360:

$$D_t = \frac{1}{1 + 0.05 \times \,^{122}\!/_{360}} = \frac{1}{1.01694} = 0.9833$$

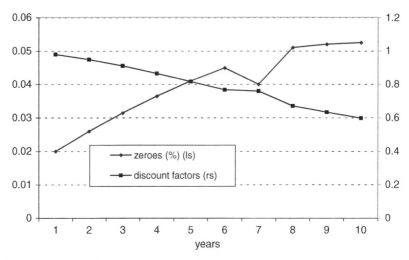

Figure 1.2   Impact of the 7-year zero rate on both curves

- $z_t = 5\%$ p.a., $t = 4$ years:

$$D_t = \frac{1}{(1 + 0.05)^4} = \frac{1}{1.2155} = 0.8227$$

An apparent advantage of the D_ts is that a D curve looks smoother than a zeroes curve.[2]

Example: on a set of fictitious rates, the 7-year zero rate has voluntarily been moved down to compare the impact on both curves – see Figure 1.2.

But in fact, despite the appearance, the interpolation between two D_ts is not more precise (given the importance of the decimals) than between two z_ts.

1.3   CONTINUOUS COMPOUNDING AND CONTINUOUS RATES

Up to now, we have considered discrete compounding only, mainly on annual or semi-annual periods of time. The definition and use of a continuous compounding concept sometimes lead to useful applications (see, e.g., Chapter 8 onwards).

Let us start from Eq. 1.4 applied on $t = 1$ year, using z instead of z_1 for the 1-year zero rate:

$$FV(n) = PV \left(1 + \frac{z}{n}\right)^n \tag{1.6}$$

and take for example $PV = 100$ and $z = 8\%$:

- for $n = 1$ (annual compounding), $FV(1) = 100(1 + 0.08) = 108.0$
- for $n = 2$ (semi-annual compounding), $FV(2) = 100(1 + 0.08/2)^2 = 108.16$
- for $n = 12$ (monthly), $FV(12) = 100(1 + 0.08/12)^{12} = 108.30$
- for $n = 365$ (daily), $FV(365) = 100(1 + 0.08/365)^{365} = 108.3277$

---

[2] Yield curves are studied in Chapter 2. Here we just compare "rough" curves of joined discount factors and of zeroes.

With increasing n, we notice that FV is growing, although at a more and more reducing pace. And what if n continues to grow further, that is, if the periodicity is shorter and shorter,[3] after each hour, each minute, and so on? We may expect that FV will still grow, but less and less, to some "limit". At the extreme, we may compute FV for $n = \infty$, that is, for such a short compounding periodicity that it becomes *continuous*, on the contrary to finite values of n, corresponding to a *discrete compounding*. To obtain this limit, let us use the classic algebraic formula defining the "e" number $(= 2.71828\ldots)$:

$$\lim_{x \to \infty} \left(1 + \frac{1}{x}\right)^x = e$$

By making $x = n/z$ and raising each side to the power z we get

$$\lim_{\frac{n}{z} \to \infty} \left(1 + \frac{z}{n}\right)^{\frac{n}{z}z} = \lim \left(1 + \frac{z}{n}\right)^n = e^z$$

and in Eq. 1.6, by making $n \to \infty$, we get

$$FV(n \to \infty) = PV \times \lim \left(1 + \frac{z}{n}\right)^n = PV \times e^z$$

giving $FV(n \to \infty = 100\, e^{0.08} = 108.3287)\ldots$ (not much more than $FV(n = 365)$). We therefore have the corresponding relationships for $t = 1$ year:

continuous compounding:	discrete (annual) compounding:
$FV = PVe^{z_c}$	$FV = PV(1 + z_d)$

where z_c means the *continuous* (zero) rate while z_d is a discrete (zero) rate. It results from the previous table that the relationship between z_c and z_d is:

$$(e^{z_c} = 1 + z_d \to) \quad z_d = e^{z_c} - 1 \quad \text{or} \quad z_c = \ln(1 + z_d) \quad \text{or} \quad e^{z_c} = 1 + z_d \quad (1.6\text{bis})$$

Note that one also speaks of *continuous time* versus *discrete time* to refer to continuous or discrete compounding.

In practice, one shall consider that z without subscript means z_d, and if there is a risk of confusion one must specify z_d or z_c.

The correspondence

$$FV = PVe^{z_c} \leftrightarrow FV = PV(1 + z_c)$$

may be generalized on t years, and with zero-coupon rates z_{ct} and z_{dt} respectively, as follows:

$$FV = PVe^{z_{ct}t} \quad FV = PV(1 + z_{dt})^t \quad (1.7)$$

In particular, due to its very essence of implying an instantaneous compounding, it appears that the "continuous" formula no longer needs a different formulation whether t is inferior or superior of 1 year (or 0.5 year) as with the "discrete" form. In Eq. 1.7, $FV = PVe^{z_{ct}t}$ holds as well with $t = 3$ months as with $t = 3$ years, for example.

Further on, the discount factors in continuous time become:

$$(PV = FV \times D_t \to) D_t = e^{-z_{ct}t} \quad (1.8)$$

that is, the continuous time equivalent of Eq. 1.5 in discrete time.

---

[3] Although in the practice, the minimum period for an interest period is a day.

Coming back to the previous example of $z_d = 5\%$, $t = 4$ years, $PV = 1$, where D_t was $= 1/1.05^4 = 0.8227$ in discrete time, corresponding to $FV = 1.2155$, we have now, with the same 5% as a z_c rate:

$$FV = e^{0.05 \times 4} = 1.2214$$

and

$$D_t = e^{-0.05 \times 4} = 0.8187$$

But in fact we must take into account that if $z_d = 5\%$ was a discrete rate, its corresponding continuous value is

$$z_c = \ln(1 + z_d) = \ln 1.05 = 0.04879, \text{ i.e. } z_c = 4.879\%$$

giving

$$FV = e^{0.04879 \times 4} = 1.2155$$

and

$$D_t = e^{-0.04879 \times 4} = 0.8227$$

that is, the same results as in discrete time.

1.4 FORWARD RATES

Let's have the following set of spot rates $z_1, z_2, \ldots, z_t$, whatever the corresponding time periods $t = 1, 2, \ldots, t$ are (e.g., years), and define $f_{t,t+1}$ the *forward zero-coupon rate* between time t and time $t + 1$. In particular, 1-period forward after 0-period is the spot-on 1-period, or $f_{0,1} \equiv z_1$. As a first example, we can determine $f_{1,2}$ from the following relationship:

$$(1 + z_2)^2 = (1 + z_1)(1 + f_{1,2}) \tag{1.9}$$

meaning that investing (or borrowing) on 2 periods @ z_2 must be equivalent to investing (or borrowing) on period 1 @ z_1, then investing (or borrowing) the proceeds on period 2, at a 1-period rate $f_{1,2}$ that results from Eq. 1.9 – see Figure 1.3.

In other words, $f_{1,2}$ is such that for a 2-year investment (or borrowing), there should be no reason to favor:

- either, the operation made in one step, @ z_2,
- or made in two steps, first @ z_1, then @ $f_{1,2}$ as determined today.

This approach involves a condition of *no arbitrage*, which will be detailed at the end of this chapter. Also, the way $f_{1,2}$ is determined is such that it cannot pretend to anticipate what will actually be the 1-period z_1 at the end of period 1. Rather, $f_{1,2}$ represents the most coherent rate implied by the current observation of both z_1 and z_2.

By generalizing Eq. 1.9,

$$(1 + z_t)^t = (1 + z_{t-1})^{t-1}(1 + f_{t-1,t}) \tag{1.10}$$

where $f_{t-1,t}$ can be viewed as a marginal rate, that is, the reinvestment rate on a period as implied by the structure of the rates prevailing for the previous periods – see Figure 1.4.

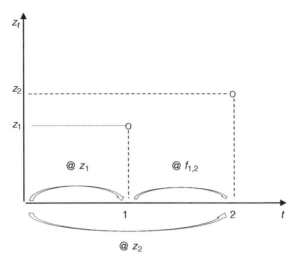

Figure 1.3   The forward zero-coupon rate

From Eq. 1.10:

$$f_{t-1,t} = \frac{(1+z_t)^t}{(1+z_{t-1})^{t-1}} - 1 \tag{1.11}$$

Example: with $z_2 = 4\%$, $z_3 = 5\%$:

$$f_{2,3} = 1.05^3/1.04^2 - 1 = 0.07028\ldots = 7.03\%$$

Note that Eq. 1.10 must be adjusted if any sub-period of time, including the one going from $t-1$ to t, is inferior to the compounding period, by use of Eq. 1.2 instead of Eq. 1.3.

From Eq. 1.11 and from this example, one observes that if the zeroes are growing with t, the forwards are growing higher. Indeed, the rate in the numerator of the fraction is higher than in the denominator, and is affected by a higher power. Conversely, the forwards are lower if the zeroes are decreasing.

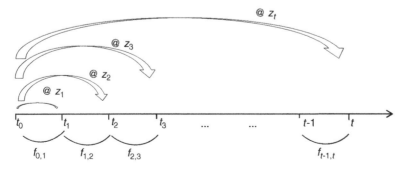

Figure 1.4   Forward rates on successive single periods of time

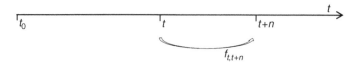

Figure 1.5   Forward rates on n periods after t periods

1.4.1   Generalization: forwards and discount factors

Forward rates on n periods after t periods can be defined by generalizing Eq. 1.10 and Eq. 1.11:

$$(1 + z_{t+n})^{t+n} = (1 + z_t)^t (1 + f_{t,t+n})^n \tag{1.12}$$

$$f_{t,t+n} = \sqrt[n]{\frac{(1 + z_{t+n})^{t+n}}{(1 + z_t)^t}} - 1 \tag{1.13}$$

and by compounding forwards on several unit periods:

$$(1 + f_{t,t+n})^n = \left(1 + f_{t,t+1}\right)\left(1 + f_{t+1,t+2}\right)\ldots\left(1 + f_{t+n-1,t+n}\right) \tag{1.14}$$

$$(1 + z_t)^t = \left(1 + f_{0,1}\right)\left(1 + f_{1,2}\right)\ldots\left(1 + f_{t-1,t}\right) \tag{1.15}$$

Example: $z_1 = 5\% = f_{0,1}$, $z_2 = 6\%$, $z_3 = 7\%$. Let us compute the 2-year in 1-year forward rate:

$$\text{Eq. 1.13} \rightarrow f_{1,3} = \sqrt{(1 + z_3)^3 / (1 + z_1)} - 1 = \sqrt{1.07^3 / 1.05} - 1 = 8.01\%$$

The discount factors earlier defined on zeroes can also be expressed in function of the forwards. From Eq. 1.5 and Eq. 1.15:

$$D_t = \frac{1}{(1 + z_t)^t} = \frac{1}{\left(1 + f_{0,1}\right)\left(1 + f_{1,2}\right)\ldots\left(1 + f_{t-1,t}\right)} \tag{1.16}$$

Example Based on the Above Data

$D_1 = 1/1.05 = 0.9524$, $D_2 = 1/1.06^2 = 0.89999\ldots$, and
$D_3 = 1/1.07^3 = 0.8163 =$ also $1/1.05 \times 1.0701 \times 1.0903$ if we compute $f_{1,2} = 7.01\%$ and
$f_{2,3} = 9.03\%$, by use of Eq. 1.11.
Using the $z_d \leftrightarrow z_c$ equivalence as per Eq. 1.6bis, and omitting the c suffix to the z and f rates, corresponding relationships in a continuous compounding basis are:

$$\text{Eq. 1.10 } e^{z_t t} = e^{z_{t-1}(t-1) + f_{t-1,t}} \quad z_t t = z_{t-1}(t-1) + f_{t-1,t}$$

$$\text{Eq. 1.11 } f_{t-1,t} = z_t t - z_{t-1}(t-1)$$

$$\text{Eq. 1.13 } f_{t,t+n} = \frac{z_{t+n}(t+n) - z_t t}{n}$$

$$\text{Eq. 1.14 } f_{t,t+n} = \frac{f_{t,t+1} + f_{t+1,t+2} + \ldots + f_{t+n-1,t+n}}{n}$$

$$\text{Eq. 1.15 } z_t t = f_{0,1} + f_{1,2} + \ldots + f_{t-1,t}$$

$$\text{Eq. 1.16 } D_t = e^{-z_t t} = e^{-(f_{0,1} + f_{1,2} + \ldots + f_{t-1,t})}$$

1.5 THE NO ARBITRAGE CONDITION

In the previous section, the theoretical value of a forward rate has been deduced from a reasoning based on the absence of arbitrage opportunity. This is the case for almost every kind of forward financial instrument, when it is possible.[4] This will be illustrated many times in the course of this book. The no arbitrage condition turns out to be a very realistic and grounded approach: the theoretical value of an instrument such as a forward, or a future, an option, and so on is indeed dependent on existing spot prices and is therefore coherent with them.

Market forward rates must never be too different from their theoretical calculation or "fair value", to avoid arbitrage operations. By arbitrage operations, one means operations obeying to the three following conditions:

- The operation must give rise to a profit.
- This profit must be (known and) certain from the inception of the operation.
- The operation must not require cash to be entered.

A sure profit means that the profit resulting from the arbitrage operation cannot be wiped out by a loss resulting from market risks arising from the operation. In other words, an arbitrage operation shall always involve two opposite positions. Such opposite positions cancel each other out with respect to their exposure to market prices moves, so that globally the operation implies no net exposure.

The arbitrage operation shall always follow this scheme:

- If the operation applies to prices, the arbitrage opportunity will result from a market price higher or lower than its fair value. The technique consists in buying at a cheaper market price (respectively, selling at an overpriced market price) and selling (respectively buying) something equivalent to the bought position, so that the operation yields a profit, but without being subject to the evolution of market prices, that is, with no net exposure.
- If the operation applies – as here – to interest rate products, the arbitrage opportunity will result from a market rate higher or lower than its fair value. Here, the operation consists in borrowing at a lower market rate or lending at a higher market rate, and lending or borrowing other instruments, achieving no net position in the market rate.

In practice, market prices may differ slightly from their fair, theoretical value, provided that such differences remain smaller than the costs associated with an arbitrage operation, such as bid–offer spreads, to allow for a net profit.

Based on the data from the last example, one can illustrate the principle of arbitrage opportunities as follows (without specifying the type of forward rate used, and deliberately ignoring the bid–ask spread, which should be crucial in the real market life):

- Suppose, first, that the market forward rate $f_{1,2}$ is quoted 6.80%, that is, lower than its fair value of 7.01%. The arbitrageur would:
  - borrow on 1 year at the spot market rate of 5% and borrow on 1 year after 1 year at the abnormally low market forward rate of 6.8%. The cost on 1\$ after the 2 years is

$$-(1 + 0.05)(1 + 0.068) = -1.1214$$

---

[4] In some cases, the reasoning is unfortunately not possible, for example, with credit derivatives. The valuation of such instruments is, therefore, more questionable.

- lend on 2 years at the spot market rate of 6%, which yields

$$(1 + 0.06)^2 = +1.1236$$

Hence a net profit of 0.0022 per \$, known and fixed from the beginning of the operation and without cash need.

- Conversely, suppose now that the market forward rate $f_{1,2}$ is quoted 7.20%, that is, higher than its fair value of 7.01%. The arbitrageur would:
  - lend on 1 year at the spot market rate of 5% and lend on 1 year after 1 year at the abnormally high market forward rate of 7.2%. The return on 1\$ after the 2 years is

$$(1 + 0.05)(1 + 0.072) = +1.1256$$

  - borrow on 2 years at the spot market rate of 6%, what costs

$$-(1 + 0.06)^2 = -1.1236$$

Hence a net profit of 0.0020 per \$.

The more liquid a market, the fewer arbitrage opportunities there are because (mid) market prices turn out to be almost equal to their corresponding fair values. Conversely, if a market is relatively illiquid, there may exist arbitrage opportunities, but since an arbitrage operation needs to be performed with a huge enough size to get a reasonable profit, this lack of liquidity makes the operation actually impracticable. This explains why real arbitrage operations arise so seldom, and may occur in temporary/transitory market situations, in a medium-sized liquidity context.

Besides, one can mention *quasi* arbitrage operations, such as "reverse cash and carry" operations in the futures market (cf. Chapter 7): the profit is still certain, but not really fixed at the inception of the operation.

However, for "marketing" reasons (and misuse of language), it happens that many operations are abusively qualified as "arbitrage", though they are in fact purely speculative; but the speculator is more or less convinced that his operation will give rise to a profit, based on the difference between observed market prices and his own evaluation of an adequate fair value. Typical examples involve some derivatives hard to price theoretically, such as credit derivatives, some exotic options, and so on.

FURTHER READING

Pamela PETERSON-DRAKE, Frank J. FABOZZI, *Foundations and Applications of the Time Value of Money*, John Wiley & Sons, Inc., Hoboken, 2009, 298 p.
Paul FAGE, *Yield Calculations*, CSFB, 1986, 134 p.

2

The term structure or yield curve

2.1 INTRODUCTION TO THE YIELD CURVE

A *term structure* or *yield curve* can be defined as the graph of spot rates or zeroes[1] in function of their maturity. Since most of the time interest rates are higher with longer maturities, one talks of a "normal" yield curve if it is going upwards, and of an "inverse" yield curve if and when longer rates are lower than shorter rates.

Alternatively, the term structure can be built on discount factors, as functions of the zero rates, but this way is less used in practice.

Yield curves can be built with mid rates – the most usual way – or with borrowing or lending rates. The two main uses of a yield curve are:

- to determine the corresponding interest rate for a given maturity, by interpolation on the yield curve;
- to serve as the "spinal column" for the pricing of any kind of financial instruments involving future cash flows, such as bonds, stocks, and all kinds of derivative products. Indeed, derivatives being basically forward products – their valuation is subject to the value of yields relative to the corresponding forward maturities involved.

Before moving on, it is worthwhile mentioning an unsolvable methodological problem: dealing with the yield curve implies using swaps and bonds data. But dealing with swaps and bonds implies using the yield curve. We have opted for starting with the yield curve – given it is a corner stone in financial mathematics of the markets – and refer the reader to the subsequent chapters dealing with bonds (cf. Section 3.2) and swaps (cf. Chapter 6). Fortunately, for the present chapter, it is enough to know that bonds and swaps are used here only as "sources" of interest rates, without being concerned by how they run.

To build a term structure you first need to determine the market and the kind of debtors the curve will refer to. Historically speaking, one determined a yield curve referring to risk-less Organisation for Economic Co-operation and Development (OECD) government bonds,[2] hence using *risk-free* rates. For non-risk-less debtors, of lower rating, a spread was added upon, depending on the maturity and on the degree of risk taken on the issuer's name. This procedure was justified for two reasons:

1. On mature markets, the government counterparty risk is the only fully objective and clearly identified (non-defaultable sovereign risk of OECD countries).
2. Government bonds represented by far the largest issues, and the validity of a price/yield strongly depends on its liquidity.

Today, the first reason holds, but swap markets have become larger than government bond markets. There is actually a homogeneity in swap market rates, although their counterpart risk level – the big banks of OECD countries – remains rather heterogeneous: AAA rates cohabit

---

[1] In practice, curves of coupon rates are also built, and used, but improperly called yield curves.
[2] Today, we should rather speak of "non-defaultable" government bonds.

with various AA sub-classes, or lower. Altogether, this has not prevented the swap market rates from superseding government/risk-free rates as reference or *benchmark* rates, except – up to now – in the US. As a result, except for the USD yield curve, market practitioners prefer to start from a swap yield curve and, for each maturity, deduct some spread to obtain the corresponding risk-free yield curve, or add a spread to quote corporate bonds of other issuers of lower rating, or to penalize a restricted liquidity. However, the market nowadays tends to favor a variant of the swap curve called the OIS swap curve (OIS swaps are explained in Chapter 6, Section 6.7.2).

In addition, we will see that interpolating rates between two points of a yield curve is much easier and grounded on a swap curve than on a government bonds yield curve. We will therefore present the building of both yield curves, but in more detail for the swap curve.

Theoretically, interest rates as data points may form a yield curve in various ways. The key question is: what is the precision of rate determination obtained by interpolating between two points? (We will elaborate on this later.) More fundamentally: are interpolated rates precise enough with respect to their use (for example, for derivatives pricing)? And is this precision sufficient with respect to the precision obtained on the data points used for building the curve?

Whatever the interpolation technique chosen, the precision obtained in interpolating between two points on a yield curve will obviously depend first on the precision obtained in determining these points. A preliminary rule in building a valid yield curve will thus be in selecting the most adequate rates, that is, the rates computed from the most liquid instruments available on the market.

Another key point in selecting market data for a good yield curve is ensuring that these data have been extracted at the same time, to avoid mixing not strictly contemporaneous data. This is in fact easier to say than to do, since among simultaneous data some of them are possibly "refreshed" (updated) less recently – because of a lack of transactions – than others, at the time they are extracted. This is again a market liquidity problem.

Altogether, it is preferable to select fewer rates but the most appropriate ones, even if the distance between the points will make the interpolation more sensitive, than to select more rates but involving some less valid data.

Lastly, in the case of both swap curves and risk-less curves, the building of a yield curve will be different on the short end of the curve (for the *money market* rates) from the long end of the curve (*capital market* rates). Historically, the frontier between these two portions of the yield curve was located on the 1-year maturity, what corresponds to the longest -ibor maturity.[3] Due to the development of instruments such as forward rate agreements (FRAs) (cf. Chapter 5, Section 5.2) and -ibor futures, this frontier has shifted towards the 2-year maturity – for example, FRA and forward exchange rates maturities stretch up to 2 years. A relatively less liquid secondary market for government paper of <2-year maturities has helped in this.

Building a yield curve implies two steps:

- first, to determine, among the various interest rates observed in the market, what set of data will be selected as adequate components of the curve;
- second, to determine to what kind of curve these data will be fitted. This step is distinct from the one consisting of *modeling* a yield curve, that is, determining a theoretical model or process, that would describe how interest rates behave. Models for yields will be presented in Chapter 11.

---

[3] In this book, we call "-ibor" any interbank market rate, such as LIBOR, EURIBOR, and so on.

Let us first consider how to select adequate interest rates as building blocks for the yield curve.

2.2 THE YIELD CURVE COMPONENTS

2.2.1 The money market side

If one wants to build a strictly risk-free yield curve, one can only use risk-free short-term instruments such as Treasury bills, and bonds of <1–2-year maturity. As we have said, for the sake of precision, it is preferable to favor the quality of the selected data over quantity.

Supposing we select good enough data:

- some of them will be "natural" zero-coupon rates, that is, in the US market, rates of ≤half-year maturities (≤1-year maturities in Europe), to be used as such;
- others will be "coupon" rates (i.e., paying intermediate revenues), to be transformed into zeroes.

Practically speaking, however, for such short maturities, the precision required in the rates is less important, since these rates apply *pro rata temporis*, on (very) short periods of time. So, it is not unusual to observe risk-free yield curves involving non-risk-free rates on the short end (such as -ibor rates and futures on -ibor rates), as more liquid instruments, subject to a greater sensitivity to market moves than short-term government paper. This problem does not arise in the case of a swap yield curve.

2.2.2 Capital market side: the case of the risk-free yield curve

Theoretical Approach

Theoretically, building the long-term side of a risk-free yield curve is easy. It suffices to collect a set $\{B_i\}$ of T Treasury bond prices, maturing at $i = 1, \ldots, T$. Let a_{ij} be the cash flow (coupon or principal) of bond i maturing at time j, and D_j the discount factor relative to time j. (The way these bond prices are valued, as in the equations below, is explained in Section 3.2.1). The system

$$\begin{cases} B_1 = a_{11}D_1 \\ B_2 = a_{21}D_1 + a_{22}D_2 \\ \ldots \\ B_i = a_{i1}D_1 + a_{i2}D_2 + \ldots + a_{ij}D_i + \ldots + a_{it}D_t \\ \ldots \\ B_{T-1} = \ldots \\ B_T = a_{T1}D_1 + a_{T2}D_2 + \ldots + a_{TT}D_T \end{cases}$$

can be solved straightforwardly as

$$\begin{bmatrix} a_{11} & 0 & & & & 0 \\ a_{21} & a_{22} & 0 & & & 0 \\ \ldots & & & & & 0 \\ a_{i1} & a_{i2} & \cdots & a_{it} & 0 & \cdots & 0 \\ \ldots & & & & & 0 \\ a_{T1} & \cdots & & & \cdots & a_{TT} \end{bmatrix} \times \begin{bmatrix} D_1 \\ D_2 \\ \ldots \\ D_i \\ \ldots \\ D_T \end{bmatrix} = \begin{bmatrix} B_1 \\ B_2 \\ \ldots \\ B_i \\ \ldots \\ B_T \end{bmatrix}$$

in the D_is, giving the z_i of the yield curve, through Eq. 1.5 of Chapter 1. Practically speaking, since one cannot find a set of Treasury bonds with successive integer years of maturities at any given day of the year, this method is hardly applicable.

Practical Approach

Zero-coupons rates are deducted from relationships given in Section 3.2.1, introducing y, as the "yield to maturity" of each bond, with respect to c, the corresponding coupon rate. These relationships give a set of ys for various bond maturities that are not integers. For integer maturities, one usually uses linear interpolations on these ys and deducts a set of ys on integer maturities. The corresponding z_Ts can be computed from

$$z_1 = y_1$$

assuming the 1-year bond is a zero-coupon bond, and for maturities from $t = 2$ to T:

$$z_t \approx \left[\frac{y_{t-1}(1 + y_t)(1 + z_{t-1})^{t-1}}{y_t - (y_t - y_{t-1})(1 + z_{t-1})^{t-1}} \right]^{\frac{1}{t}} - 1$$

This formula gives approximate values for z_t since it is based on the hypothesis that the ys are equal to the cs. Moreover, this formula is based on a linear interpolation method, which is subject to some criticism (see Section 2.3), especially when bonds maturities are too far from each other, such as for the longest maturities.[4]

2.2.3   Capital market side: the case of the swap yield curve

Since swap rates are quoted for integer maturities in years (or transformed from semi- to annual rates), the above theoretical method for bonds is applicable here. Beside the use of matrix calculus, it can also be solved step by step, as in the following example.

Let the set of annual swap rates $s_1 = 4\%$, $s_2 = 4.20\%$, $s_3 = 4.35\%$, and so on. As we will see in Section 6.2, IRS swaps can be viewed as par bonds so that

$$100 = 104/(1 + 0.04)$$

for the 1-year swap, where $s_1 = 4\%$ is the natural zero z_1; the 2-year swap, viewed as a 2-year par bond of coupon $= 4.20\%$, is such as

$$100 = 4.20/(1 + z_1 \text{ or } 0.04) + 104.20/(1 + z_2)^2$$

then $z_2 = 4.204\%$; then, for z_3,

$$100 = 4.35/(1 + z_1 \text{ or } 0.04) + 4.35/(1 + z_2 \text{ or } 0.04204)^2 + 104.35/(1 + z_3)^3$$

giving z_3, and so on.

---

[4] A very interesting and detailed study on the problem of extracting zeroes from a set of bonds has been published in French: Christian JAUMAIN, Extraction des taux spots d'un marché obligataire. Application au marché des OAT, *Revue Banque*, no. 37, December 2004.

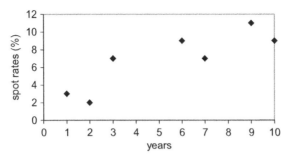

Figure 2.1   Example of a fictitious set of seven spot rates as data points

This recurrent computation is called the *bootstrap* method.[5] The method can also be applied with discount factors, which would of course lead to the same z_is. Example on the 3-year discount factor previously:

$$100 = 4.35^* D_1 + 4.35^* D_2 + 104.35^* D_3$$

Now, let us see how to fit the data into a suitable yield curve.

2.3 BUILDING A YIELD CURVE: METHODOLOGY

To emphasize the strengths and weaknesses of different existing methods, let us apply them to the set of seven data points shown in Figure 2.1 that have been voluntarily chosen as excessively irregular.

Method #1: The Data Points can be Joined by Linear Segments

This is unquestionably the most common method used by practitioners, although the least precise method *per se*. Indeed intuitively, the yield curve should not adequately be made of a succession of linear sections. There is necessarily an interpolation bias between the linear sections and the curvature of the yield curve. As long as this bias is not perceived as excessive, such a straightforward method may be considered as good enough vis-à-vis more elaborate methods, but involving some arbitrary hypothesis, as shown further in this section.

Figure 2.2 shows an example of such a usual yield curve, using linear interpolations.

Applying the linear method to the seven data points in Figure 2.1, one can question the validity of the linear extrapolation, for example between the 3- and 6-year rates (see Figure 2.3).

Method #2: Determining a Polynomial Curve that Exactly Fits Each of the Data Points

Theoretically, the problem is in determining the coefficients of a polynomial of order equal to the number of the data points minus one, that gives a unique solution. At least, the curve is exact with respect to the observed market data points. But their dispersion may lead to an unrealistic curve, of an odd form. Interpolation of rates on the yield can give unreasonable values.

---

[5] The OIS swap curve, mentioned earlier (and explained in Chapter 6, Section 6.7.2) is also built by using the bootstrap method.

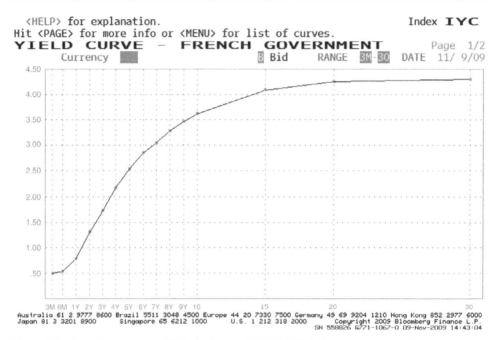

Figure 2.2   French government EUR yield curve (11/09/2009), built on coupon rates beyond 1 year
Source: Bloomberg

Applying the method to the previous example, the seven data points are linked by a six-order polynomial, as in Figure 2.4.

The obtained curve presents unrealistic bumps: for example, interpolating for rates between 3- and 6-year maturities is most probably unrealistic, despite the fact that the curve adequately fits with all the data points.

Method #3: One Can Determine a Polynomial Curve Passing "Through" the Set of Data Points

This method consists in determining a curve of a certain order – usually low – such as the distances between each of the points and the curve is minimized, by means of a non-linear regression. For example, on the set of seven data points, the resulting curve is smoother than

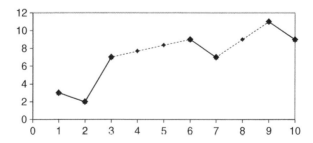

Figure 2.3   Example of the linear method

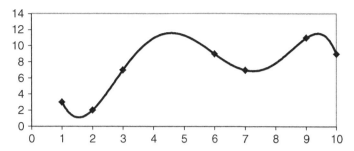

Figure 2.4   Example of a six-order polynomial

by the previous methods (see Figure 2.5) and interpolations are more acceptable since they present a "natural" curvature. Unfortunately, by construction, the curve is almost not passing by the selected data points, so that the most valuable ingredients of the yield curve are not in fact part of it.

Nevertheless, sometimes it is worth using this method, for example when the yield curve can more or less realistically be assimilated to a logarithmic curve. Also, it may prove useful within the context of modeling of derivatives, where the aim is less to draw the most accurate yield curve for market applications than to give mathematical support to a model for interest rates derivatives. But its main *raison d'être* is when a yield curve must be built from a set of untrustworthy data, hence the drawback of a curve not actually passing through these data is less important. This is the case, for example, of illiquid interest rates markets such as emerging markets.

Method #4: Cubic Splines Method

In this method, data points are joined two by two by linked segments or "splines" of polynomial curves, actually *cubic* or order-3 polynomials. The choice of cubic polynomials will be justified by the rationale of the methodology itself, but it is also in the spirit of the *parsimony principle*, contrary to the inefficient too high order of the polynomial of method #2.

Also, order-3 polynomials allow for computing first and second derivatives that are not constants. This copes with the general approach in financial calculus, aiming to work within a framework offering the flexibility of a variable "slope" and a variable "convexity".

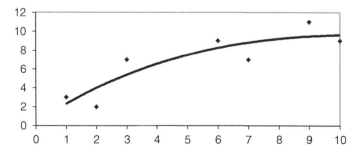

Figure 2.5   A polynomial curve passing through the set of data points

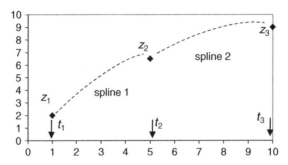

Figure 2.6 Example of two cubic splines linking three zeroes

Let us consider an order-3 polynomial spline i, delimited by two successive data points from the series of zero rates of maturity $t = 1 \ldots i \ldots T$, denoted z_t. It is a function of time t of the form

$$a_i + b_i t + c_i t^2 + d_i t^3$$

determined by the value of its four coefficients a_i, b_i, c_i, and d_i.

To show how this method works, let us consider the simplified but hypothetical case of a yield curve built on three data points only. In such a case, the curve consists of two splines, with $i = 1$ and 2, joining three zeroes, z_1, z_2, and z_3:

$$a_1 + b_1 t + c_1 t^2 + d_1 t^3 \quad \text{and} \quad a_2 + b_2 t + c_2 t^2 + d_2 t^3$$

To determine them, one needs to value eight coefficients, namely, a_1 to d_2. One thus needs eight relations expressing the constraints of building both these splines (see Figure 2.6).

Spline 1 must pass through z_1 and z_2, and spline 2 must pass through z_2 and z_3, that is, four relations:

$$\text{on } z_1, \text{ spline 1: } \quad z_1 = a_1 + b_1 t_1 + c_1 t_1^2 + d_1 t_1^3$$

$$\text{on } z_2, \text{ spline 1: } \quad z_2 = a_1 + b_1 t_2 + c_1 t_2^2 + d_1 t_2^3$$

$$\text{on } z_2, \text{ spline 2: } \quad z_2 = a_2 + b_2 t_2 + c_2 t_2^2 + d_2 t_2^3$$

$$\text{on } z_3, \text{ spline 2: } \quad z_3 = a_2 + b_2 t_3 + c_2 t_3^2 + d_2 t_3^3$$

To assure a smooth junction between spline 1 and spline 2 at their common point z_2, the slopes of spline 1 and 2 must be equal on point z_2, that is one relation of the form

$$b_1 + 2c_1 t_2 + 3d_1 t_2^2 = b_2 + 2c_2 t_2 + 3d_2 t_2^2$$

equalizing first derivatives of splines 1 and 2 at z_2.

Also, for smoothing reasons, the curvature of the yield curve must be the same on both sides of the common point z_2, that is a relation of the form

$$2c_1 + 6d_1 t_2 = 2c_2 + 6d_2 t_2$$

equalizing second derivatives of splines 1 and 2 at z_2.

The last two relations express how the splines behave at the extremities of the yield curve. It may be realistic to consider that the change of slope of the yield curve is zero on its extremities

t_1 and t_3, that is, by having the second derivative of the splines equal zero at the extremities of the curve:

$$2c_1 + 6d_1 t_1 = 0$$

$$2c_2 + 6d_2 t_3 = 0$$

2.4   AN EXAMPLE OF YIELD CURVE POINTS DETERMINATION

Data from the US market (March 1991) on the short maturities are shown below (* refers to following comments).

Days	Dates	"Cash" rates (%)*	Futures prices	90-day fwd (%)*	D at 90 days	D	z (%)
0	01/03/91					1	
7	08/03/91	6.25					6.25
19	20/03/91		94.04	5.96	0.985332	0.996695	6.28
31	01/04/91	6.31					6.31
109	18/06/91					0.982064	6.03*
110	19/06/91		94.63	5.37	0.986753	0.981901	6.03
200	17/09/91					0.968894	5.78
201	18/09/91		94.79	5.21	0.987142	0.968749	5.78
291	17/12/91					0.956294	5.65
292	18/12/91		94.71	5.29	0.986948	0.956155	5.65
382	17/03/92					0.943675	5.62

*"Cash" rates: \$ LIBOR rates, 1 week and 1 month, instead of US T-bills implied futures rates: rule: $rate = 100 - price$, see, for example, Section 7.4.1; NB: futures on LIBOR: 90-days maturities.
spot rate z at day 109: it is computed from the zero z_1 on $n_1 = 19$ days and the future in $n_1 + n_2 = 109$ days after 19 days ($n_2 = 90$ days); we have

$$1 + z \times (n_1 + n_2)/360 = (1 + z_1 \times n_1/360)(1 + f_1 \times 90/360)$$

with z_1 being linearly interpolated the two cash rates in 7 and 31 days respectively (i.e., 1-week and 1-month rates):

$$z_1 = 0.0625 + (0.0631 - 0.0625) \times (19 - 7)/(31 - 7) = 0.0628$$

hence

$$1 + z \times 109/360 = (1 + 0.0628 \times 19/360)(1 + 0.0596 \times 90/360) \rightarrow z = 6.03\%$$

or, alternatively:

$$D_{109d} = D_{19d\ spot} \times D_{90d\ fwd}$$

$$= 1/(1 + 0.0628 \times 19/360) = 0.99669\ldots = 1/(1 + 0.0596 \times 90/360) = 0.9853\ldots$$

$$\rightarrow D_{109d} = 0.99669\ldots \times 0.9853\ldots = 0.98206\ldots$$

$$\rightarrow z \times 109/360 = 1/D_{109d} - 1 \rightarrow z = 6.03\%$$

2.5   INTERPOLATIONS ON A YIELD CURVE

Having built a yield curve $z = z(t)$, from a certain number of adequately chosen points, the question remains as to how to interpolate between these points. With cubic splines, the answer is straightforward, but what if the curve is simply made of linear segments between the points?

One could choose between linear interpolation between the points, or their corresponding discount factors. Both methods have advantages and disadvantages.

Consider the trivial case of interpolating between two zeroes of equal value, here 6%, and let z_1 be the spot rate $= 6\%$ for $t_1 = 180$ days and $z_2 = 6\%$ for $t_2 = 360$ days, to determine z_i for $t_i = 270$ days.

The result of the linear interpolation on the zs is obviously 6%, which is coherent with the data used. Via the discount factors, in continuous time we have

$$D_1 = e^{-0.06*180/360} = 0.9704455,\ D_2 = 0.9417645,$$

$$\text{hence}\, D_i = (0.9704455 + 0.9417645)/2 = 0.956105$$

giving $z_i = 5.98\%$. This seems an unacceptable solution, although this illustrates the fact that – unlike interpolating linearly on the rates – interpolating on discount factors creates some curvature, which is intuitively a normal feature for a yield curve. Note that we would have reached the same conclusions if we had worked in discrete time. To summarize:

Interpolation:	Advantages:	Disadvantages:
on the spot rates:	straightforward, coherent	no curvature
on the discount factors:	OK for curvature	not coherent with data

To bypass this problem, instead of a linear interpolation one can use the *exponential interpolation*, as follows:

$$D_i = D_1^{(1-\lambda)t_i/t_1}\, D_2^{\lambda t_i/t_2}\quad \text{with}\quad \lambda = (t_i - t_1)/(t_2 - t_1)$$

Continuation of the example:

$$\lambda = (270/360 - 180/360)/(360/360 - 180/360) = 0.5$$
$$D_i = 0.9704455^{0.5*270/180} \times 0.9417645^{0.5*270/360} = 0.9559974$$
$$\rightarrow z_i = -\ln 0.9559974/270/360 = 6\%$$

which is in line with the z_1 and z_2 values.

FURTHER READING

Moorhad CHOUDHRY, *Analysing and Interpreting the Yield Curve*, John Wiley & Sons, Ltd, Singapore, 2004, 300 p.
Moorhad CHOUDHRY, *Yield Curve Analytics*, Butterworth-Heinemann, 2004, 352 p.
Carl DE BOOR, *A Practical Guide to Splines*, Springer-Verlag, rev. ed., 2001.
Livingston DOUGLAS, *Yield Curve Analysis*, New York Institute of Finance, 1988, 300 p.

Spot instruments

This chapter deals with spot instruments other than stocks: given the large amount of quantitative material about stocks they are treated separately, in the next chapter.

3.1 SHORT-TERM RATES

With respect to quantitative aspects and calculations, there is almost nothing to add for short-term rates instruments beyond what we considered in Chapter 1 (among others, the calculations relative to present and future values). But we should mention that some of the short-term instruments are generally traded in prices, on a "discount basis", namely in PV prices (e.g., Treasury bills, banker's acceptances and commercial paper), while others are traded in rates, "on a yield basis", that is, in interest percentage (i.e., repo rates, certificates of deposits, bank deposits, interbank rates, etc.).

Short-Term Rates Traded on a Discount Basis

For US T-bills, quoted in PV prices corresponding to a FV as par value of 100 at maturity, to compute the corresponding yield z the US Treasury uses a formula slightly different from the conventional Eq. 1.2 of Chapter 1, as follows:

$$z = \left(1 - \frac{PV}{FV}\right)\bigg/ t$$

on an ACT/360 basis. Let us take, for example, the 180-days US T-bill as traded on 01/04/08, @ 98.39: for $t = 180/360 = 0.5$, it corresponds to a yield of

$$z = \left(1 - {98.39}/{100}\right)\big/0.5 = 3.22\%$$

Using Eq. 1.2,

$$PV(1 + z_t t) = FV$$

we would have obtained

$$z = \left({FV}/{PV} - 1\right)\big/t = \left({100}/{98.39} - 1\right)\big/0.5 = 3.273\%$$

Short-Term Rates Traded on a Rate Basis

These belong to two main categories: they are quoted either in real time or as a unique, daily quotation, called a fixing rate.

Fixing rates will appear as playing a major role in the valuation of many derivatives, such as swaps, options, and so on. They consist of interbank rates, the most used ones being interbank offered rates (i.e., lending rates: the bank lends, corresponding to a borrowing rate for a client). The main -ibor rates are the LIBOR (for London Interbank, etc.) and the EURIBOR, its equivalent in EUR. Later in this book we will use *-ibor* to refer to both EURIBOR and LIBOR rates. The LIBOR rates are quoted once a day, at 11 a.m. London time, for 10 major currencies, as an average of cost borrowing unsecured funds, quoted by major banks and published by the British Bankers' Association. The EURIBOR rates are computed in a similar way and published by the European Banking Federation at 11 a.m. Central European Time (CET). Besides -ibor rates, the market is quoting -ibid rates, for interbank bid rates (i.e., borrowing rates: the bank is borrowing, corresponding to a deposit rate for a client). Both -ibor and -ibid rates give rise to -imean rates, for interbank mean rate, that is, the average between -ibor and -ibid.

3.2 BONDS

3.2.1 Bond pricing

The bond market is dominated by government bonds. Most of the bonds are issued with a fixed (annual or semi-annual) interest payment or "coupon", and as "bullet" bonds, that is, the principal being repaid in one shot at the bond's maturity. We will first deal with fixed-coupon bullet bonds and consider separately the impact of a default risk on bond prices.

The theoretical[1] value of a bond must reflect what this bond will return to its holder. In actuarial words, *the value of a bond is* therefore *the sum of the present values of all its future cash flows*, both in interest and in (reimbursement of its) principle or capital. In this first sub-section, we will consider the case of future cash flows occurring on integer numbers of years (or of semi-annual periods).

Recall that a bond price is expressed as a percentage of the nominal amount issued by the bond issuer. At inception, the bond is generally issued "at par" (or near to the par), that is at 100, meaning at 100% of the nominal amount issued. In absence of any trouble (default), the bond will be reimbursed at par. In the meantime, the bond price will evolve, on the secondary market, due to the changes in the yield curve, affecting the present value calculations (besides possible troubles affecting the issuer's rating).

The price relationship is rather straightforward for a zero-coupon bond of price $B_{0\text{-}cpn}$. As an example, a 5-year zero-coupon bond @ 5% is estimated from Eq. 1.7, that is

in discrete compounding:	in continuous compounding:
$B_{0\text{-}cpn} = 100 / (1 + 0.05)^5 = 78.35$	$B_{0\text{-}cpn} = 100 * e^{-0.05*5} = 77.88,$

supposing the rate is 5% in both cases. These relationships indicate that investing in the bond at its present value brings $100 to the investor at maturity, the return of such an investment corresponding to the interest rate of the zero-coupon bond.

For a classic bullet coupon bond, we can extrapolate the above result by considering that a coupon bond on n installments may be viewed as a sum of a series of n zero-coupon bonds, that is, for a bond involving n semi- or annual coupons:

- one zero-coupon bond for each of coupon payments, until the $n-1$th installment: their maturities correspond to those of the interest payments; each single repayment is equal to the coupon;
- one zero-coupon bond for the last (nth) installment, at maturity, corresponding to the payment of the last coupon plus the reimbursement of the principal.

---

[1] Actually, in normal circumstances, bond market prices are close to their theoretical price.

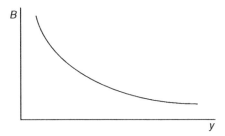

Figure 3.1   Relationship between B and y

Hence, the price B of a bullet bond of maturity T, priced exactly on a coupon payment date,[2] is

$$B = \sum B_{0-cpn} = \sum \frac{a_t}{(1+z_t)^t} \text{ or } = \sum a_t \times e^{-z_t t} \qquad (3.1)$$

where $\sum$ goes from $t=1$ to $t=T$, the a_t being the series of cash flows consisting of coupons or last coupon plus principal payment,[3] or also, by use of the discount factors (see Eq. 1.5 and Eq. 1.8),

$$B = \sum D_t \times a_t \qquad (3.2)$$

For historical reasons as well as for simplicity's sake, the market does not price a bond by using a series of zeroes to compute the present value of each cash flow. Rather, it prefers to use a single discount rate, common for the whole series of a_t. Algebraically speaking, it is not difficult to determine a common discount rate y equivalent of the series of t zeroes. This common rate is called the *yield to maturity* (YTM) or *yield* of the bond, and actually represents the long-term rate implied by a bond price. As such, Eq. 3.1 becomes

$$B = \sum \frac{a_t}{(1+y)^t} \text{ or } = \sum a_t \times e^{-yt} \qquad (3.3)$$

Prices of bonds priced with the YTM will not exactly equal prices obtained from the series of z_ts, but the difference should not be problematic, and cannot give rise to true arbitrages (taking into account the bid-ask spreads involved): after all, for capital market rates, the z_ts are coming from bond prices (cf. Chapter 2, Section 2.2).

Equation 3.3 shows that the higher the YTM y, the lower the bond price B, and conversely. The relationship between B and y is obviously not linear, as shown in Figure 3.1.

Examples

1. Let us verify how the price of a 5-year bullet bond, with an 8% coupon issued at par, is priced at issuance. Equation 3.3 gives[4]

$$100 = 8/1.08 + 8/1.08^2 + 8/1.08^3 + 8/1.08^4 + 108/1.08^5$$

---

[2] The case of pricing a bond at any other date will be considered in the next section.
[3] The formula also goes for non-bullets: then, a_t represents any kind of cash flow, involving or not some principal amortization.
[4] Note that the result of 100 is not grounded. This may seem surprising since it comes from a series of fractions each involving several decimals.

2. Now, let's take a bullet bond issued some years earlier and still having 5 years to maturity, with an 8% coupon and the prevailing 5-year market rate being 6%. Its price should be:

$$8/1.06 + 8/1.06^2 + 8/1.06^3 + 8/1.06^4 + 108/1.06^5 = 108.42$$

3. In the real market life, since bonds are quoted in prices, given a price we should compute the corresponding YTM. Take the same bond as above, and suppose it is currently quoted 104.10. Its YTM y must verify

$$104.10 = 8/(1 + y) + 8/(1 + y)^2 + 8/(1 + y)^3 + 8/(1 + y)^4 + 108/(1 + y)^5$$

Solving this equation in y is not straightforward: we must solve it by successive approximations or use programmed functions in Excel or in pocket calculators. The answer is 7%.

For US bonds, which pay a semi-annual coupon, the adjustment of Eq. 3.3 is straightforward. The a_t involves semi-annual coupons (which is not explicit in the formula below) and y in % p.a. must be divided by 2:

$$B = \sum \frac{a_t}{\left(1 + \dfrac{y}{2}\right)^t} \text{ or } = \sum a_t \times e^{-\frac{y}{2}t}$$

The Case of a Risky Bond

As such, previous relationships do not enlighten the possible default risk presented by the bond issuer. This does not matter if the bond is a risk-less bond, issued by a non-defaultable government. To reveal the impact of a default risk, Eq. 3.3 can be rewritten as

$$B = \sum \frac{(a_t + \text{spread})}{(1 + y + \text{risk premium})^t} \tag{3.4}$$

where a_t is viewed as corresponding to the coupon for a risk-less issuer.

Let us consider two typical situations:

- The case of a high-rating bond, issued at par, whose rating is later downgraded: the initial spread in the numerator of Eq. 3.4 was justified by the initial rating level, and is incorporated in the coupon value, that is more or less higher than the corresponding coupon for a risk-less bond. But if later on, on the secondary market, the risk premium – as perceived by the market – is significantly higher, it pushes the bond price B down, even in the absence of increases in market interest rates (that should affect the y). This is the case of the Greek government bond shown in Figure 3.2 (see the huge downward move from spring 2010).
- Conversely, the case of a bond issued by a poor rated corporation: to be issued at par, the borrower will have to pay some spread over the current coupon level, that would be paid by a risk-less issuer. This spread in the numerator will be needed for compensating the risk premium in the denominator, which is charged by the market. Now, if the borrower's rating is improved later on, the bond price will appreciate above par (in the absence of yield curve impacts on y), due to a reduction of the market risk premium affecting the denominator of Eq. 3.4.

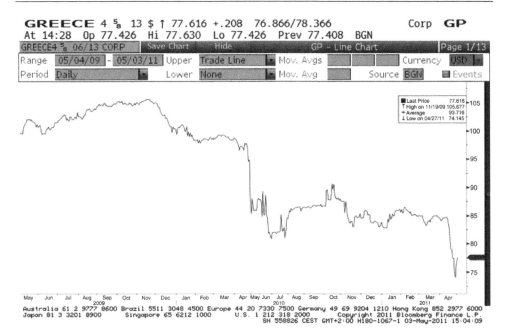

Figure 3.2   Greek government bond 2010–2011
Source: Bloomberg

It is worth noting that both the spread and risk premium result from a mixture of rational – based on an objective valuation of the borrower's financial solvability – and irrational – speculative pressures, or market fears and overreactions – considerations.

The comparison between a $(y + risk\ premium)$ and the yield of a risk-less bond of the same features is called yield spread analysis. Beyond its impact of a risky bond price, the credit default risk will be further developed in Chapter 13.

Clean Price versus Dirty Price

Bond prices are quoted by the market as shown above. But on the secondary market, in the case of a trade between two coupon dates, in addition to the market quoted price the buyer must pay to the seller the portion of the coupon *pro rata temporis*, called *accrued interest*. The same principle is also applied in accounting, between two coupon dates, according to the Mark-to-Market rules imposed by IFRS standards.

The quoted price, ex coupon, is called the *clean price*, while the (full) price actually paid is the *dirty price*. Only the clean price is subject to price changes, due to Eq. 3.3, because of the effect of the discount rate y, subject to market rate changes. The accrued interest is a fixed rate, *pro rata* the time elapsed since the last coupon payment date. As such, it doesn't need a market quotation.

To value a bond on a date comprised of two anniversary dates of coupon payment, let us start from Eq. 3.3, that is, based on the YTM. And let us restrict ourselves to discrete compounding, on an ACT/365 basis. Here, the valuation occurs n_d days after the last coupon date. The next coupon dates will occur $1 - n_d/365$ year later, then $2 - n_d/365$ year thereafter, and so on. From Eq. 3.3 – where a_t is made of coupons c and redemption or reimbursement of the principal P – the bond price of maturity T becomes, for a bullet bond

$$B = \frac{c}{(1+y)^{1-n_d/365}} + \frac{c}{(1+y)^{2-n_d/365}} + \ldots + \frac{P}{(1+y)^{T-n_d/365}}$$

Or, by making $(1+y)^{n_d/365}$ in evidence

$$B = \left[\frac{c}{(1+y)} + \frac{c}{(1+y)^2} + \ldots + \frac{P}{(1+y)^T} \right] (1+y)^{n_d/365}$$

The terms in c inside the brackets form a geometrical progression of T terms, with a common ratio of $1/(1+y)$, a scale factor c and a first-term exponent I, so that the result is

$$B = \left[c\frac{1 - \left(\dfrac{1}{1+y}\right)^T}{y} + \frac{P}{(1+y)^T} \right] (1+y)^{n_d/365} \tag{3.5}$$

Example: let us consider the following 5-year US T-bond:

- issuance date: 15/11/01
- maturity: 15/11/06
- coupon: 3.5%, semi-annual, ACT/ACT.

On 10/12/01 (for settlement date 11/12) it quoted "96-5", that is, "96 and 5/32" or 96.15625% of par, as the market clean price. Buying $1M at this price means paying

$$\$1\,000\,000 \times 96.15625 + \text{accrued interest}$$

In this case, the accrued interest is due for 26 days, that is, from the issue date (corresponding to the anniversary date for coupons) up to the settlement date, *pro rata* the 181 days totaling the first semi-annual coupon payment, @ 3.50% p.a./2 $= 1.75\%$:

$$\text{accrued interest} = 0.0175 \times 26/181 \times \$1\,000\,000 = \$2\,513.81$$
$$\text{Or in percent of the \$ amount}: = (2\,51381/1\,000\,000) \times 100.$$

Hence, the dirty price is

$$96.15625 + 0.25138 = 96.40763 \% \text{ of par}$$
$$\text{corresponding to a payment of } \$964\,076.31.$$

Floating Rate Bonds

Floating rate bonds are also called FRN for floating rate notes or floaters, and pay a coupon that is revised (updated) periodically, with reference to an -ibor rate, usually a 3-month -ibor rate. Because of this periodical update, the bond price is at least every 3 months at par, so that, in between, its price cannot actually move away from par.

Inflation-Linked Bonds

Inflation-linked bonds are sovereign bonds (or bonds issued by institutions) whose interest and reimbursement payments involve some inflation component. They cover a broad maturity spectrum. Their coupon is paid on the inflated nominal amount, so that the fixed coupon is actually accreted by inflation. At maturity, the reimbursed nominal amount is also augmented with the inflation accretion. The inflation reference is in most cases a CPI index.

In their usual form[5] the bond features come in the following form:

- for a nominal amount A, issued at year 0, with a coupon, called "real coupon" c_r and a maturity T, of n years;
- and a reference index going from I_1 to I_n, based on CPI, with some lag (needing the CPI actually published before application: a 3-month yield is common);

so that

- $I_i = CPI_{i-lag} / CPI_{0-lag}$
- nominal amount on year i $(i = 1, \ldots, n)$: $A \times I_i$
- coupon actually paid: $r_c \times A \times I_i$,
- principal paid at redemption: $A \times I_n$.

For some inflation-linked bonds (for example, OATi in France, TIPS in the US), the final redemption is floored at the (initial) nominal amount A.

Inflation-linked bond prices are quoted as a percentage of the (initial) nominal amount A, to cope with vanilla bond quotations. The accrued interest is computed as for a vanilla bond, here based on the coupon actually paid.

The real yield y_r of an inflation-linked coupon is the YTM corresponding to 0% inflation throughout the bond's life. By confronting the real yield and the nominal yield y, we can compute the break-even of inflation level to justify investing in the inflation-linked bond rather than in an equivalent vanilla bond:

$$\text{breakeven inflation} = \frac{1+y}{1+y_r} - 1 \cong y - y_r$$

Examples. On July 7, 2011, let us compare

- US T-bond 3 1/8 05/15/21: mid $y = 3.12\%$;
- US TIPS 1 1/8 01/15/21 (i.e., almost equivalent maturity): mid $y = 0.695\%$.

By application of the above formula, the break-even inflation is $1.0312/1.00695 - 1 = 0.024083 \cong 0.0312 - 0.00695 = 0.02425$ (i.e., an inflation rate of 2.4%).

3.2.2   Duration

The duration of a bond may appear somewhat confusing. First, unlike the vast majority of concepts and measures, the same notion of duration is used to answer two rather different questions:

---

[5] There exist variants, such as on the Korean market, where only the coupons are indexed, and in an additive way.

- How to adequately compare, with a single measure, different bonds having different prices, maturities, coupons and yields?
- What is the sensitivity of a bond price in the case of a yield change?

Second, the formal answer to the second question being a price change/yield change ratio, it may seem surprising that this ratio, namely the duration, is actually expressed in the number of years.

The concept of duration can be introduced practically, "physically" or mathematically.[6]

Practical Approach of the Duration

To introduce the duration practically, let us first compare two 10-year bonds, both issued at par, one bullet and one amortizing bond. From the investor's viewpoint, investing in a 10-year bullet or in a 10-year bond amortized in principal by a tenth at the end of each year is obviously different. Indeed, the invested amount in the second case is reducing with time. The way to compare both investments is by comparing their *average life*. Under its most general formulation, the average life of a bond is

$$\text{average life} = (p_1 \times 1 + p_2 \times 2 + \ldots + p_n \times n)/(p_1 + p_2 + \ldots + p_n)$$

where p_i is the reimbursed amount (amortizing) in principal relative to year i – if any – for an n-year bond, $i = 1, \ldots, n$. Since there are p_is in both the numerator and the denominator, the result of this fraction must be expressed in years (the 1 to n of the numerator). In our example, for the amortized bond we have

$$(10 \times 1 + 10 \times 2 + 10 \times 3 + 10 \times 4 + 10 \times 5 + 10 \times 6 + 10 \times 7 + 10 \times 8 + 10 \times 9 + 10 \times 10)/$$
$$(10 + 10 + 10 + 10 + 10 + 10 + 10 + 10 + 10 + 10) = 5.5 \text{ years}$$

while for the bullet bond the calculation would obviously give $100 \times 10/100 = 10$ years (the average life of a bullet bond is its maturity).

The average life appears to be *the average of time periods weighted by their respective reimbursed amount in principal*. But amounts in principal are only a part of the cash flows paid by the issuer of the bond to the investor. To go one step further, we could compute an average of not only the capital paid (reimbursed) per year but also all the cash flows paid during the lifetime of the bond, that is, including the paid coupons. This should lead to an average that generalizes the above average life formula as follows, where c_i is the coupons paid on year i:

$$\frac{(p_1 + c_1) \times 1 + (p_2 + c_2) \times 2 + \ldots + (p_n + c_n) \times n}{(p_1 + c_1) + (p_2 + c_2) + \ldots + (p_n + c_n)}$$

Another step further, we could take into account that a cash flow paid in year i should not be considered today as equivalent to a cash flow paid on another year j. To cope with this, the cash flows in $(p_i + c_i)$, or a_i, would better be actualized, at the YTM y:

$$\frac{a_1 \times 1/(1+y)^1 + a_2 \times 2/(1+y)^2 + \ldots + a_n \times n/(1+y)^n}{a_1/(1+y)^1 + a_2/(1+y)^2 + \ldots + a_n/(1+y)^n} \tag{3.6}$$

---

[6] In this sub-section, we will perform all the calculations on a current time coinciding with a coupon date. Extension to any other date will be provided later.

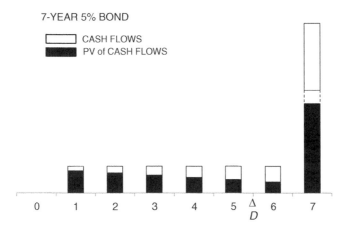

Figure 3.3   A 7-year bond with a 5% coupon

This ratio is called the *duration D*, that is, *the average of the discounted cash flows weighted by their maturities*. The denominator of Eq. 3.6 is nothing other than the bond price *B* (cf. Eq. 3.3), so that *D* can be expressed as

$$D = \frac{1}{B} \sum_{i=1}^{n} \frac{a_i . i}{(1+y)^i} \tag{3.7}$$

Physical Approach of the Duration

A "physical" approach of the duration facilitates the understanding of some of its properties. Let us take a kind of Roberval balance[7] and align small containers on it. Let us work with a 7-year bullet bond, with a 5% yearly coupon. Each of the small containers is equivalent to a yearly coupon cash flow, and the big one represents the final reimbursement in principal. The size of the containers is equivalent to the full (future) value of the cash flows. The containers are filled with water to the extent of the present value of the cash flows. The length of the balance is graduated in years. The balance can be figured as shown in Figure 3.3.

The equilibrium point of the balance is exactly situated on the duration of the bond, here, somewhere between 5–6 years.

Alternatively, let us consider now a similar 7-year bullet bond, but with a 9% coupon. With taller containers (sized to 9% instead of 5% coupon) and water filling adjusted accordingly, the balance now looks like that in Figure 3.4.

We immediately understand that the equilibrium point is nearer: *other things remaining equal, a higher coupon means a shorter duration, and conversely*. As a limiting case, for a zero-coupon there will be one container only, and the equilibrium point – thus the duration – will be at maturity: *the duration of a zero-coupon is equal to its maturity*.

More generally, whatever intermediate cash flows are, as for an amortizing bond, the duration is always shorter than the maturity, *the importance of intermediate cash flows reducing the duration accordingly*.

---

[7] The Roberval balance is a traditional weighing scale, made of two horizontal beams that must be balanced in weight.

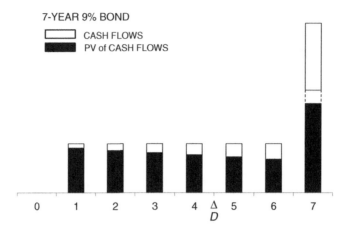

Figure 3.4   A 7-year bond with a 9% coupon

Mathematical Approach of the Duration

The mathematical approach of the duration is, of course, the richest. Let us start from the bond pricing Eq. 3.3, in discrete time:

$$B = \sum \frac{a_t}{(1+y)^t}$$

The bond price being a function of both its time to maturity and its yield to maturity, differentiating B by y gives

$$\frac{\partial B}{\partial y} = -\frac{1}{1+y} \sum t.a_t.(1+y)^{-t} \tag{3.7bis}$$

or, by dividing on both sides by B and rearranging,

$$-\frac{\partial B}{\partial y}.\frac{1+y}{B} = \frac{1}{B} \sum t.a_t.(1+y)^{-t} \tag{3.8}$$

the right side being nothing other than D, as per Eq. 3.7 previously.

Notice that D is a positive number (of years): $\partial B/\partial y$ is the *negative* slope of $B(y)$ (cf. Section 3.2.1), so that $\partial B/\partial y$ is positive.

Equation 3.8 also shows that the lower the y, the higher the slope (and therefore the duration, as shown earlier), and conversely on (B_1, y_1), the slope (and the duration) is smaller than on (B_2, y_2), having $y_2 < y_1$ – see Figure 3.5.

Moreover, because

$$\partial y = \partial(1+y)$$

we can rewrite the left side of Eq. 3.8 as:

$$\frac{-\partial B/B}{\partial(1+y)/(1+y)} = D$$

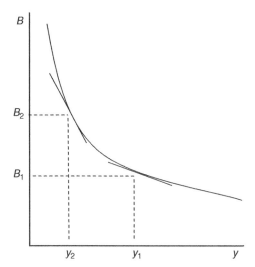

Figure 3.5   The lower the y, the higher the slope and therefore the duration

that is, the relative, or percent, change of B divided by the relative, or percent, change of y. For finite changes instead of infinitesimal ones, we have

$$D \cong \frac{-\Delta B/B}{\Delta(1+y)/(1+y)} \tag{3.9}$$

showing that the duration is the "elasticity" in YTM of the bond price.

Example of Duration Calculation

Let us take the 10-year benchmark German T-bond called Bund (data as of 20/09/10), 2.25%, maturing 04/09/20, and quoting 99.257, with a yield of 2.334%, shown in Table 3.1.

Representing the duration in function of the maturity T of a bond, we may have several typical configurations, as shown in Figure 3.6.

The straight diagonal line represents the duration of a zero-coupon bond, with $D = T$. The three curved lines represent the duration of bullet bonds, respectively at par, at discount and at premium. They all converge towards the horizontal dotted line, representing the duration of a perpetual bond. Indeed, for longer and longer maturities, the last cash flows (including cash flows in principal) weigh less and less in present value (if necessary, use the physical approach

Table 3.1   10-year benchmark German T-bond

	2011	2012	2013	2014	2015	2016	2017	2018	2019	2020
t (years):	1	2	3	4	5	6	7	8	9	10
cash flows:	2.25	2.25	2.25	2.25	2.25	2.25	2.25	2.25	2.25	102.25
YTM:	0.02334	0.02334	0.02334	0.02334	0.02334	0.02334	0.02334	0.02334	0.02334	0.02334
disc. (t^*cash fl.):	2.198683	4.297072	6.298598	8.206589	10.02427	11.75477	13.40111	14.96625	16.45301	811.8276

$D = \Sigma$ disc. (t^*cash fl.)/99 257 = 9.06

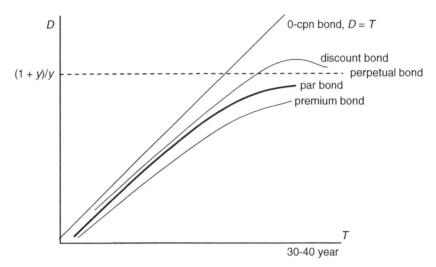

Figure 3.6   Typical configurations of a bond's duration in function of its maturity

to cope with this observation). This horizontal dotted line corresponds to the asymptote of
the various duration curves for coupon bonds. We may compute that its ordinate is equal to
$(1 + y)/y$, that is, a duration value without any term in t.

Figure 3.7 summarizes the properties of the duration.

Modified Duration

The duration D is also called the *Macaulay* duration, from the name of its author. As such, it
corresponds to the actual derivation of the bond pricing formula, but turns out to be not that
practical. Indeed, if a relative change of bond price is straightforward – a bond being priced
in percent of its par value – a relative change in yield rate is not. A relative change of 1% in
a 5% yield means 5% + or – 5bp, and a relative change of 1% in a 7% yield means 7% +
or – 7bp.

What we would like to use is an *absolute* change in yield, so that an absolute change of,
say, 1% in a 5% or in a 7% (or any other) yield always means + or – a fixed 1% on the yield.

The relative change in yield comes from the term

$$\Delta(1 + y)/(1 + y)$$

Bond feature:	Duration:
maturity T ↗	D ↗
YTM y ↗	D ↘
coupon c ↗	D ↘
coupon frequency ↗	D ↘

Figure 3.7   Duration of the bond: a summary

in Eq. 3.9, that can be rearranged as

$$\frac{-\Delta B/B}{\Delta(1+y)} = D \times \frac{1}{1+y} = MD \tag{3.10}$$

that is, the modified duration, or sensitivity of the bond price. Equation 3.10 shows that the modified duration is the measure of the relative change in price of a bond, for an absolute change in yield. MD as per Eq. 3.10 is indicated for quantifying the impact of a small yield change. Indeed, the duration being calculated from the derivative or slope of the bond price curve in function of yields, in the case of y varying by a Δy, the corresponding change in bond price, ΔB, is approximated by the duration only if Δ is small. For a larger Δy, this approximation suffices no more (cf. convexity, Section 3.2.3.2).

Example: Continuing With the Previous 10-year Bund

Having obtained $D = 9.06$ year, with YTM $= 2.334\%$, MD $= 9.06/1.02334 = 8.855$. What would be the impact of a yield increase of $+ \frac{1}{4}\%$?
From Eq. 3.10,[8]

$$-\Delta B = MD \times B \times Dy8 = 8.855 \times 99.257 \times 0.0025 = 2.197$$
$$\rightarrow B = 99.257 - 2.197 = 97.060$$

A particular case of the modified duration is called the *basis point value* (BPV), that measures the bond price change caused by an absolute change in yield *conventionally fixed at 1 bp*, that is:

$$BPV = -\Delta B \text{ for a } \Delta y = 1 \text{ bp}$$

So that, by using Eq. 3.10,

$$\frac{-\Delta B/B}{\Delta\left((1+y)=\right)10^{-4}} = MD - \Delta B = BPV = MD \times B \times 10^{-4}$$

Continuation of the Bund example: the BPV is $8.855 \times 99.257 \times 10^{-4} = 0.0879$
Viewing B as a \$ (or other currency) amount, instead of a percentage of nominal amount, the BPV is equivalent to the "dollar duration".

Effective Duration

If a bond presents some embedded optional component (cf. for example callable and putable bonds), the above formulae cannot apply, given the uncertainty affecting future cash flows. An alternative measure of duration, called effective duration, has to be used. This case is dealt with in Chapter 11, Sections 11.2.1 and 11.2.2 (callable and putable bonds).

---

[8] $\Delta(1 + y) = \Delta y$ of course.

Duration in Continuous Time

By using Eq. 1.7, Eq. 3.7, and Eq. 3.10 become

$$D = \frac{1}{B} \sum t.a_t.e^{-yt}$$
$$MD = D.e^{-y}$$

Duration Between Two Coupon Dates

If the duration is calculated on a period of b – in $n_{days}/360$ or 365, depending on the adequate day count convention – before the next coupon date, Eq. 3.8 becomes

$$D = \frac{1}{B} \sum (b+t).a_t.(1+y)^{-(b+t)}$$

and its equivalent in continuous time,

$$D = \frac{1}{B} \sum (b+t).a_t.e^{-y(b+t)}$$

We should notice a particular behavior of the duration near to a coupon date. Indeed, just before such a coupon date, the first coupon flow weighs very little in the calculation of the duration, since it is multiplied by a very small t. The day after the detachment of the coupon, the sum of present values of remaining coupons in the bond price is proportionally increased since there is one coupon less. Moreover, the detached coupon and the variation in number of days related to remaining coupons have a minor impact on the duration, so that, altogether, the duration is slightly increased in reaching a day of coupon detachment, which could seem paradoxical. Of course, time elapsing further will affect the duration downwards, as usual.

Duration of Bond Forwards, Futures and Options Contracts

The duration D_{fwd} of bond forwards (cf. Chapter 5, Section 5.3) or futures (cf. Chapter 7, Section 7.5) is equal to the duration D_{spot} of the corresponding spot instrument:

$$D_{fwd} = D_{spot}$$

Let us first consider a single cash flow valuing FV after time t. Its corresponding present value is PV. As single cash flows, both FV and PV are valued via a zero coupon. Since the duration of a zero coupon equals its maturity, the duration of FV and PV are respectively t and 0. Let us now shift both cash flows PV and FV by $+$ a time T. Their durations are now valuing T and $t+T$ respectively. Buying a forward or future contract of maturity T on a zero-coupon bond maturing at t after T can be viewed as the combination of one short cash flow PV, corresponding to the payment of the contract at its maturity T, plus one long cash flow FV, at time t later – see Figure 3.8.

Hence, the duration D_{fwd} is the sum of both durations of PV (as a negative cash flow) and FV:

$$D_{fwd} = -D_{PV} + D_{FV} = -T + (T + t) = t = D_{spot}$$

The extension to a coupon bond is straightforward, since a coupon bond can be split into a series of zero-coupon bonds.

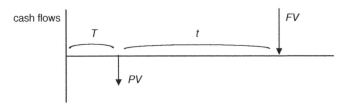

Figure 3.8   A single cash flow valuing *FV* after time *t*

The duration D_{opt} of bond options (cf. Chapter 11, Section 11.2) will understandably involve the duration D_B of its underlying bond, the delta Δ of the option (i.e., the quantity of underlying used to hedge the option position, cf. Chapter 10, Section 10.5), the price B of the underlying and the price O_B of the option (call or put). The calculation gives

$$D_{\mathrm{opt}} = \frac{B}{O_B} \times \Delta \times D_B$$

The presence of the B/O_B ratio, as the leverage offered by the option, shows that durations on options can reach very high values.

Example: Let us use an option premium of 3.5, with a 70% delta, on a par 10%, 10-year bond of duration 6.76 years:

$$D_{\mathrm{opt}} = 100/3.5 \times 0.70 \times 6.76 = 135 \text{ years!}$$

Duration of an FRN

For a floating rate note (cf. Section 3.2.4), the duration is obviously equal to the maturity of the -ibor coupon, that is, 0.25 years if the reference rate is a 3-month -ibor.

Duration of a Swap

Since an IRS swap can be viewed as a bond financed @ -ibor (cf. Chapter 6, Section 6.2), its duration is

IRS rate – -ibor rate

(with the adequate sign, depending on whether it is a payer or receiver swap).

Portfolio Duration

Durations are *additive*: the duration D_P of a bonds portfolio P is a weighted sum of bonds D_i durations, involving the corresponding nominal amounts N_i and bond prices B_i:

$$D_P = \frac{\sum N_i B_i D_i}{\sum N_i B_i}$$

(NB: this can be extended to portfolios also including bonds futures and options.)

Example: Let's consider a portfolio of Belgian T-bonds comprising the following four bonds (data on 10/07/03):

bond	cpn	maturity	price	yield	duration	nominal (EUR millions)
# 1	7 ¾ %	15/10/04	105.490	2.21 %	0.93 year	20
# 2	4 ¾ %	28/09/06	105.147	2.91 %	2.76	20
# 3	4 ¼ %	28/09/13	99.820	4.27 %	7.98	30
# 4	8 %	28/03/15	132.680	4.32 %	7.83	30
Total portfolio:						100

Its duration is

$$D_P = (20 \times 105.49 \times 0.93 + 20 \times 105.147 \times 2.76 + 30 \times 99.82 \times 7.98 + 30 \times 132.68$$
$$\times 7.83)/(20 \times 105.49 + 20 \times 105.147 + 30 \times 99.82 + 30 \times 132.68) = 6.82 \text{ year}$$

This duration is used in portfolio management for adjusting the portfolio content according to the portfolio manager's expectation about possible parallel changes in the yield curve.

Uses of Duration

Comparison Between Bonds Having Different Prices, Coupons, Yields, and Maturities

Without their duration measure, it should be difficult to select among alternative purchases or sales of bonds, besides other considerations (market pricing attractiveness, specific features (callable, etc.), market liquidity).

Example: in the previous portfolio, the duration is a convenient unique measure to compare the four bonds of different features. In particular, having to choose between bonds #3 and 4 – despite the former having a shorter time to maturity than the latter, because of a smaller coupon, its duration is larger than the latter: 7.98 against 7.83 years.

Portfolio Risk Management Tool

Since duration measures the sensitivity of a bonds portfolio to changes in market yields, the portfolio duration is a direct measure of its global exposure to interest rates. Moreover, portfolio managers may act on the duration of their portfolio by purchasing or selling bonds to increase or decrease their global duration, based on their expectation of interest rate movements. In the absence of other considerations such as specific valuation dates or investing horizon, it is usual to increase the portfolio duration if a lowering of interest rates is expected, and conversely.

The duration is also used for bonds VaR calculation (cf. Chapter 14, Section 14.2).

Portfolio Immunization

Immunization has to be distinguished from hedging:

- A position is said to be *immunized* if its value does not change when market conditions (prices or rates) change.

- A position is said to be *hedged* if its value may change but with a (reasonably) *limited* risk of loss.

It is worth noting that in both cases we refer to a market risk; such immunization or hedging does not preclude some counterparty risk.

The return gained or lost on a given portfolio P and a given period of time t to $t+1$ can be defined as

$$\frac{P_{t+1}}{P_t}$$

For a bond portfolio, this return is a function of:

- the return brought by reinvesting coupons between t and $t+1$;
- the change in the portfolio's bond prices.

These variations are two different functions of the yields $\{y_t\}$. Let us consider a portfolio comprising only one bond priced B at time t. This bond currently quotes B above par, with a yield y and a duration D. But because of changes in yield over time, we have:

Portfolio return $= f$ (reinvesting coupons, bond price)

$$\begin{array}{lll} \text{if } y \nearrow: & \nearrow & \searrow \\ \text{if } y \searrow: & \searrow & \nearrow \end{array}$$

$\Rightarrow$ there must be a *compensation* between positive and negative returns at some *time* that corresponds to the *duration* of the portfolio. In other words, a portfolio is immunized (in the sense of a parallel shift in yields) at a horizon of time corresponding to its duration. Earlier and later, the portfolio is in risk – see Figure 3.9.

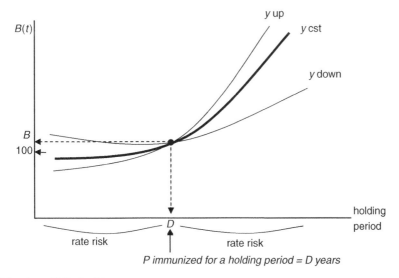

Figure 3.9 A portfolio in risk

The portfolio manager who anticipates a yield increase will therefore feel better with the duration of his portfolio shorter than his horizon of investment, and conversely if he is expecting a decrease in yields. Unfortunately, the duration will also vary over time, so that this holding period remains subject to further changes.

Important Remark About the Duration

Finally, we must also note that all duration calculations, through the derivation, involve a single yield value and therefore ignore that in fact yields are a function of maturities: $y = y(t)$. Hence, by changing y by some Δy, duration calculus assumes that $y(t)$ is moving by a parallel shift of Δy, which is far from the reality. Duration calculus must thus be considered as an approximation to the real phenomenon of bond price changes due to yield curve changes, not only in a parallel shift move but also by steepening or flattening of the curve.

3.2.3 Convexity

The convexity measure goes one step further than duration. To make this concrete, let us start with the derivative of the bond price in y, as done with Eq. 3.7bis:

$$\frac{\partial B}{\partial y} = -\frac{1}{1+y} \sum t.a_t.(1+y)^{-t}$$

The second partial derivative of B in y is

$$\frac{\partial^2 B}{\partial y^2} = \frac{1}{(1+y)^2} \sum (t\,(t+1).a_t.(1+y)^{-t}$$

Notice that the term before the sum sign passed from a negative value $-1/(1+y)$ to a positive one, $1/(1+y)^2$. More generally, the full derivative is

$$dB = \frac{\partial B}{\partial y} dy + \frac{1}{2}\frac{\partial^2 B}{\partial y^2} dy^2 + \frac{1}{3!}\frac{\partial^3 B}{\partial y^3} dy^3 + \ldots \text{terms of higher order}$$

$$\Downarrow \qquad \Downarrow$$
$$\text{slope} \quad \text{curvature}$$

where the second derivative or curvature leads to the convexity term. In practice, the convexity C is determined similarly as the modified duration, from the following relationship, having dB divided by B and ignoring the terms of order > 2

$$\frac{dB}{B} \cong \underbrace{\frac{1}{B}\frac{\partial B}{\partial y} dy}_{\text{- MD}} + \underbrace{\frac{1}{2}\frac{1}{B}\frac{\partial^2 B}{\partial y^2} dy^2}_{\text{convexity } C} \qquad (3.11)$$

(cf. Eq. 3.10)

not forgetting the $\frac{1}{2}$ multiplying factor when computing C.

For a bullet bond with coupon c, principal p and maturity T, the calculation of C can be done by using the following formula:

$$C = \frac{\sum_{t=1}^{T} t\,(t+1)\,c(1+y)^{-t} + T\,(T+1)\,p(1+y)^{-T}}{(1+y)^2 \left[\sum_{t=1}^{T} c(1+y)^{-t} + p(1+y)^{-T}\right]}$$

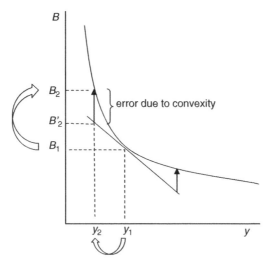

Figure 3.10   Positive convexity

From these calculations, we can see that if the slope of the bond price is negative, the convexity is actually positive[9] – see Figure 3.10.

Practically speaking, for a given Δy, going from y_1 to y_2, to compute the corresponding ΔB the convexity corrects the approximation of the duration in case Δy is too large. Actually, B_1 goes to B_2, and not to B'_1 as obtained from the duration. We can see that the correcting term of convexity is always positive, whether y is moving up or down.

Examples.   Let us go further with the Bund example used for duration, with a $2^1/_4$% coupon, @ 99.257 mid, with a corresponding YTM of 2.334%. Rounded calculations gave MD $=$ 8.855 and $C = 97.79$.

Let us first consider a yield change of -10 bp, that is, YTM becomes 2.234%. For this yield, the corresponding bond price should now be 100.142, by Eq. 3.3 – see Table 3.2.

Here, the duration suffices to explain this price change. Indeed,

$$-\Delta B / B = 8.855 \times (-10 \text{ bp})$$
$$\rightarrow \Delta B = 99.257 \times 8.855 \times 0.001 = +0.879$$
$$\rightarrow B = 99.257 + 0.879 = 100.136 \cong 100.142 \text{ (given rounding)}$$

Table 3.2   A yield change of -10 bp

		2011	2012	2013	2014	2015	2016	2017	2018	2019	2020
	t (years):	1	2	3	4	5	6	7	8	9	10
	yield:	0.02234	0.02234	0.02234	0.02234	0.02234	0.02234	0.02234	0.02234	0.02234	0.02234
Σ of cash fl. $= 100.142 = B$		2.200833	2.152741	2.1057	2.059686	2.014678	1.970654	1.927592	1.88547	1.844269	81.98035

---

[9] Convexity may be negative in some circumstances: see, for example, the case of callable bonds (cf. Chapter 11, Section 11.2.1), also dealing with "effective convexity".

But if we now consider a yield change of –1% instead, with a YTM of 1.334% and a corresponding bond price of 108.522 (computed in a similar way as above), the bond price change "explained" by duration is

$$\Delta B_{duration} = 99.257 \times 8.855 \times 0.01 = +8.789 \rightarrow B = 108.046 \text{ instead of } 108.522$$

To improve this result, we have to add the price change explained by convexity:
by Eq. 3.11, $\Delta B_{convexity} = 99.257 \times \frac{1}{2} \times 97.79 \times (-1\%)^2 = +0.485$

$$\rightarrow B = 99.257 + 8.789 + 0.485 = 108.531 \cong 108.522$$

which is fine. In practice, however, the use of convexity can be more problematic than the use of duration in the case of lack of market liquidity, affecting the market bond price.

Here are some properties of convexity:

- As yields decrease, both duration and convexity increase, and conversely.
- Among bonds with equal duration:
  - the higher the coupon, the higher the convexity;
  - the zero-coupon bond has the smallest convexity.
  This can easily be checked by building (B,y) curves for a zero-coupon bond and for various coupon bonds of same duration: we see that the flattest curve is the one of the zero coupon.
- Among bonds with same maturity, the zero-coupon bond has not only the greatest duration but also the greatest convexity.

Beyond its role of improving the sensitivity calculation from only the use of duration, the convexity may also play some role in selecting bonds for a portfolio. Suppose that a portfolio manager needs to buy a bond with a given duration and has a choice between two bonds, A of lower convexity and B with higher convexity. (We suppose that both A and B present equivalent market characteristics of liquidity, rating, etc.) He would select B, although the market would normally price B slightly higher than A. In the case of slight yield variations, both bonds will vary almost equally in price, but for greater yield changes, the effect of the positive convexity will push the price of B more and more above the corresponding A bond of lower convexity. So if yields decrease, B will increase more than A, while if yields decrease, B will be less affected than A – see Figure 3.11.

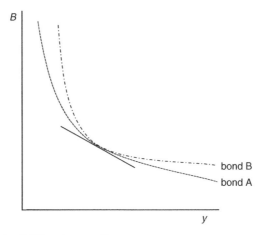

Figure 3.11   Two bonds of different convexity

Figure 3.12   The EUR/USD rate 1992–2009
Source: Traderforce

3.3 CURRENCIES

3.3.1   Introduction to the currencies spot market

The currencies or *forex* market presents some key features:

- Historically speaking, the forex is the oldest interbank market. It remains the biggest in terms of traded volume, and the most liquid among all financial markets.
- Unlike any other commodities, currencies are priced in *relative* value, that is, a currency is quoted against another currency.
- Differently to stocks and stock indexes and bonds, price history on the long run is not globally upward trending or mean reverting. See, for example, Figure 3.12, which shows the EUR/USD rate from 1992 (recomputed) up to 2009.

It is therefore not surprising that the forex market is almost not correlated with other markets. For example, on the 20-year period 1989–2009, the correlation between EUR/USD and the S&P 500 was –0.11! This sounds attractive in terms of portfolio diversification objective, but given its features, a successful forex trading performance remains a challenge.

3.3.2   Spot quotations

Using the universal ISO code for currencies, prices are presented as follows, for example the EUR against USD:

EUR/USD

| on the left side: the market quotes 1 unit of the currency, called the reference currency (ref) | on the right side: the market quotes the corresponding x units of the currency, called the counter-value currency (c/v) |

For each couple of currencies, the role of *ref* and *c/v* currency results from the market practice. In particular, the USD can be used as a *ref* currency – for example, in the case of USD against JPY – or as a *c/v* currency, as in the case of EUR/USD. As a rule of thumb:

- *ref* currencies are GBP, USD, EUR;
- USD is the *ref* currency against Asian and Latin-American currencies;
- EUR is the *ref* currency against North and Eastern European currencies, and CHF.

As for other commodities, currencies are quoted as two-way prices:

ex: on 07/07/09, 6.07 pm: 1unit of EUR (ref) expressed in *x* units of USD (c/v):
EUR/USD 1.3951–52
means

$$1 \text{ EUR} = 1.3951 \text{ and } 1.3952 \text{ USD}$$

↙   ↘

called the *"bid"* price   called the "ask" or *"offer"* price
1.39515 being the corresponding "mid" price.

Also, in such quotations, the rank of decimals (or digits on the right of the dot point) is labeled as follows:
1 . 3 9 5 1

    ↳ "pip"
   ↳ "figure"
  ↳ "big figure"

In this example, the quotation is presented with the usual market *spread* of 1 pip. The width of the bid-ask spread depends mainly on the market volume: the higher the volume, the tighter the spread. For a given forex quotation, the bid-ask spread can vary over time:

- In function of the current market activity: a lower activity will tend to widen the spread (e.g., on the Pacific time zone, or during the weekend, when the market is only active in the Middle East area).
- In function of the volatility: a temporarily higher volatility will tend to widen the spread.
- In function of market circumstances: in the case of temporary greater uncertainties, the spread is widening, for example several minutes before the announcement of important US statistics.

Knowing that banks are playing the role of market makers in the currencies market, the rationale of the bid-ask quotation is such as:

EUR/USD 1.3951–52

bank buys 1 unit of ref @ 1.3951 units of c/v ↵ |
   bank sells 1 unit of ref @ 1.3952 units of c/v ↵

The market is quoting major pairs of currency prices, others being determined by "crossing" quoted pairs. Crossing can imply either a multiplication or a division, effected on mid prices:

• Crossing by multiplication: example (data: June 06):

to quote EUR/JPY: ... .- ... . ?
observing simultaneously
EUR/USD: 1.2620–24   USD/JPY: 116.35–45
⇒   mid: 1.2622   116.40
that is, 1 EUR = 1.2622 USD and 1 USD = 116.40 CHF

hence, 1 EUR = 1.2622 × 116.40 = 146.92 JPY in mid. For a 1-pip spread, it gives either EUR/JPY @ 146.92–93 or 146.91–92 (each market maker will propose its own quotation, more or less in line with these values, with respect to its existing exposure and market expectation).

• Crossing by division: example (data June 06):

to quote USD/CHF: .... .- .... ?
observing simultaneously
EUR/USD: 1.2620–24   EUR/CHF: 1.5625–29
⇒   mid: 1.2622   1.5627
that is, 1 EUR = 1.2622 USD and also = 1.5627 CHF

hence, 1 USD = (1.5627/1.2622) CHF = 1.2381 CHF in mid. For a 2-pips spread, it gives: USD/CHF @ 1,2380–1.2382.

FURTHER READING

Richard T. BAILLIE, Patrick C. McMAHON, *The Foreign Exchange Market, Theory and Econometric Evidence*, Cambridge University Press, 1990, 276 p.

Patrick J. BROWN, *Bond Markets: Structures and Yield Calculations*, ISMA Publications, 1998, 96 p.

Frank FABOZZI, *The Handbook of Fixed Income Securities*, McGraw-Hill, 7th ed., 2005, 1500 p.

Frank FABOZZI, *Fixed Income Mathematics*, McGraw-Hill, 4th ed., 2005, 600 p.

Imad A. MOOSA, Razzaque H. BHATTI, *The Theory and Empirics of Exchange Rates*, World Scientific Publishing Company, 2009, 512 p.

Lucio SARNO, Mark TAYLOR, *The Economics of Exchange Rates*, Cambridge University Press, 2003, 330 p.

Tim WEITHERS, *Foreign Exchange*, John Wiley & Sons, Inc., Hoboken, 2006, 336 p. Also covers forwards, futures and options on foreign exchange.

Equities and stock indexes

4.1 STOCKS VALUATION

The fair (theoretical) value S of a stock can be computed in different ways, none of them being fully satisfactory, hence their results are often combined to get a final result; for example, in a prospectus for an initial public offering (IPO).

4.1.1 Discounted cash flows (DCF) method

This first method uses the same rationale as for a bond valuation: the fair price is the sum of discounted future cash flows that will be paid by the stock. But here we face a succession of n unknown future dividends instead of a fixed coupon, no final maturity, and of course no repayment of a principal. Calling d_i the dividend paid in year i, and z_i the corresponding discounting rate, the result is equivalent to the one presented for a bond price (cf. Chapter 3, Eq. 3.1):

$$S = \sum_{i=1}^{i=n} \frac{d_i}{(1 + z_i)^i}$$

with two issues:

- n is an *a priori* undetermined number of years: we cannot know how long the corporation will survive (theoretically, n goes up to ∞). Fortunately, the longer the maturity is discounted, the lower the discounted amount. So above, say, 50 years, further cash flows can be neglected in present value.
- The future dividends d_i are not known in advance.

The calculation is therefore valid only if referring to a realistic assumption about the future dividends.

Example. Let us consider a stock distributing a constant dividend of $5, with a constant discount rate of 5%. The plain line of the graph in Figure 4.1 shows that between $n = 50$ and 100 years, the stock price evaluation is established between $91.28 and $99.24.

Alternatively, if we consider the dividend of year 1 is $5, growing at a (compounded) 2% rate during the following years, the corresponding stock price is now between $127.55 and $157.28 in the same range of years.

4.1.2 The Gordon–Shapiro method

At first sight, this method looks more secure because only the next-year dividend appears in the formula:

$$S = \frac{d_1}{(r - g)}$$

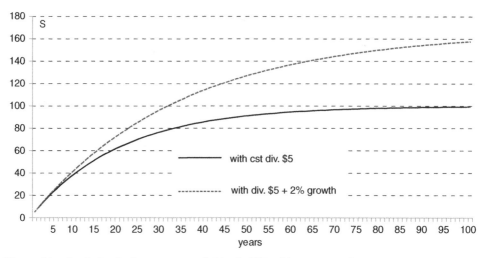

Figure 4.1 Stock distributing a constant dividend of $5, with a constant discount rate of 5%

where d_1 means $d_{+1 \text{ year}}$, but it now introduces the parameter g, as a constant growing rate estimate of the dividend, and r is now the expected stock return on the long run. So this model just shifts the problem of making assumptions on the unknown future, and its validity is conditioned to the degree of realism of these assumptions.

Because of these hypotheses,

$$d_1 = (1 + g)d_0$$

$$d_2 = (1 + g)d_1$$

$$d_3 = (1 + g)d_2 = (1 + g)^2 d_1$$

$$\rightarrow d_t = (1 + g)^{t-1}d_1$$

$$\rightarrow S = \sum_{t=1}^{\infty} \frac{(1 + g)^{t-1}d_1}{(1 + r)^t} = \frac{d_1}{1 + r} \sum_{t=1}^{\infty} \frac{(1 + g)^{t-1}}{(1 + r)^{t-1}}$$

In algebra, we can establish that a geometrical progression with 1 as the first term and q the common ratio, q^2 being <1, the (infinite) sum of the terms of the series is

$$\sum_{i=0}^{i=\infty} q^i = \frac{1}{1 - q}$$

so that, applied here,

$$S = \frac{d_1}{1 + r} \times \frac{1}{1 - \dfrac{1 + g}{1 + r}} = \frac{d_1}{1 + r} \times \frac{1}{\dfrac{1 + r - 1 - g}{1 + r}}$$

hence the Gordon–Shapiro formula. This calculation is given because of the otherwise surprising $(r - g)$ discounting rate in the formula, instead of a usual $(1 + \text{s.th.})$ term. So the formula states that the next-year dividend is discounted by the excess of an expected long-term stock return r above the expected growing rate of the dividends, which makes some economic sense, at least coherent with the hypotheses of the model.

Practically speaking, this calculation can apply to corporations presenting a stable growth rate, but not to young companies or companies expected to show a high growth rate in the next few years (called growth stocks in the market jargon).

It thus makes sense to determine the parameters of the formula by referring to the history of the stock price.

Example. If we want to reproduce the same calculation as in the previous example, we must consider a stock paying $5 in next year 1. To mimic this compounded growing rate of 2%, let us say that the history of the company fits with this view, which corresponds to a g of 2% in the formula. Using the Gordon–Shapiro formula, to obtain the same stock price of, say, $142 as a rough average of the previous results by using the DCF method, we must assess the expected return r relevant with the history of the stock prices as from

$$\frac{5}{r - 0.02} = \$142$$

that is, an implied expected $r = $ round 5.52%.

4.1.3   The case of stocks not distributing dividends

In such cases, above models are of course not applicable. Keeping the key assumption of the Gordon–Shapiro model, that is, of a constant growing rate of the company benefits in the long run (justifying the constant growth rate estimate of the dividend, in the Gordon–Shapiro model), and denoting, now, g as the constant growth rate of benefits, and considering that – because of no dividend distribution – all the benefits are reinvested in the company, we have

$$S(t) = S_0(1 + g)^t$$

or, in continuous time,

$$S(t) = S_0 e^{gt}$$

that are both the forward calculation (cf. Chapter 1, Section 1.4 and Chapter 5, Section 5.3.1) for S, given a constant growth rate g.

4.1.4   The real option method

In contrast to the Gordon–Shapiro method, the real option method may convene for start-ups or young companies, expected to grow significantly in the (near) future, but active in a very specific type of business, namely in a "reserved", identifiable, market area, such as

- energy: the company owns some fields (oil, coal, etc.);
- pharmaceuticals: the company is the owner of molecules, ready for launching new drugs;
- telecoms: the company has been granted some percentage of a (geographical) network;
- more generally, the market for a new product, technology or service, at least until competitors come out.

So this measurable *potential* asset can be viewed as the underlying of an option (cf. Chapter 10), and the company profit is an *optional* function of this underlying, according to the following reasoning.

Let us assume that the company revenue is a growing function of the benefits brought by its well-determined underlying potential. This growing rate is probabilistic, with some deterministic part and some volatility around it. These deterministic methods do not incorporate the volatility component of the growth rate, that is, the discounting is made in a deterministic environment. Here, the stock value is rather:

S = a form of discounted cash flows + the PV of growing uncertainty, that is, a call option premium on the measurable potential

Example: Tiscali

- The IPO was launched in November 1999, @ €4.60, as the result of the discounting cash flows method.
- Adding an option premium on the hypothesis that Tiscali foresees capturing 20% of the Italian e-com until 2003 (+ about 4 years), the calculation gives €6.70.
- On top of that, adding an option on cash flows brought by the third generation of cellular phones, the initial stock price goes to €30.90.

During the first few years, the Tiscali stock price moved as shown in Figure 4.2.

It is interesting to note that, first because of the dot-com bubble, then because of the dot-com crisis, the stock price moved up then down, out of proportion with the computed prices in the figure. However, during some five months in mid-2000, the price seemed to stabilize around the "full" option price, then stabilized from July 2001 to May 2002 around the first option

Figure 4.2   Tiscali stock price November 2009 to April 2004
Source: A.R. on Traderforce

price, thereafter continuing below the discounted cash flow = IPO price. Further, to the end of 2003, the market price becomes irrelevant because of this calculation hypothesis.

The limitations of the real option method validity are not negligible: even if carefully applied to company's profiles as stated previously:

- How can we determine and quantify the "potential" with a sufficient degree of precision? In particular, how do we incorporate a realistic scenario of possible competitors' involvement?
- How can we realistically determine the option parameters T, μ, σ, and K? (cf. Chapter 10 for the usual meaning of these symbols.)
- How can we justify the use of the traditional Gaussian distribution in such a case?
- The pillars of usual option pricing, namely risk neutrality and non-arbitrage condition, are not really valid in the present case.

4.1.5   The book value method

Given the uncertainties of the previous method, this may be viewed as more exempt from any assumptions, since the book value of a company is the objectively measurable difference of its assets minus its liabilities, that is, its net value if all debts were repaid and all assets sold off. Unfortunately, this boils down to a price valuation based strictly on the current situation of the company, without taking account of its future.

4.2   STOCK INDEXES

Stock indexes can be built in two ways.

Price-Weighted Index

The index I must refer to a set of involved stocks (whole market, or a sector, currency, etc.). With the exception of indexes representative of a whole market, the vast majority are based on the n most important stocks of the market, sector, and so on. For a price-weighted index, the criterion is the stock price level. So it is computed as the sum of the n stock prices S_i, divided by a coefficient c:

$$I = \sum_i \frac{S_i}{c}$$

where c is a constant, subject to periodic revisions. The constant is initially set so that the index originally starts at (usually) 100 and will evolve up or down from 100 by incorporating the fluctuations of the S_i prices over time. Because of stock price movements, the content of the index will change in the long run, some stocks going out of the index and being replaced by new stocks presenting a higher price. This may also occur in the case of a stock splitting. Usually, exchanges reset the content of the index twice a year. At each reset, the constant c must therefore be adjusted so that the new (content) index continues to move from the same level as before the reset.

Example of price-weighted indexes: DJ Industrial, MMI (US market).

Value-Weighted or Capitalization-Weighted Index

Here, the index is not weighted by the (stock) prices but by their corresponding market capitalization C_i, with

---

market capitalization or "market cap" C_i
= number of shares × share price S_i

The formula becomes

$$I = \sum_i \frac{C_i}{c}$$

and index adjustments follow the same procedure as previously.

However, today most of the market cap indexes are actually weighted by the *float* of the shares, that is, the percentage of actually traded shares on the exchange, out of permanent investors (long-term shareholders).

Example of market cap indexes: S&P 500, CAC40, DAX30, and so on.

Many stock indexes are published in several variants, including, or not, dividends reinvestment in several possible ways.

Important remark: because of the resetting process of the indexes (except for global indexes), they present a non-negligible *survivor bias* in their price level, compared to individual stocks: only the healthiest stocks remain in the index over time.

4.3 THE PORTFOLIO THEORY

4.3.1 Introduction to the Portfolio Theory

The Portfolio Theory was introduced by H. Markowitz and developed by W. Sharpe in the mid-twentieth century. Their objective was to ground portfolio management in an objective, quantitative way. More precisely, it aims to quantify the relationships between prices and corresponding return and risk measures of different assets (essentially stocks, stock indexes and bonds).

The theory involves a statistical description of stock price changes, based on *ex ante* observations. This quantitative description makes use of the first two moments of a Gaussian (normal) distribution. As such, this belongs more in the second part of this book. However, because of the anteriority of the theory with respect to the stochastic calculus and models developed in the second part, and even more because the statistical content of the Portfolio Theory does not pretend to lead to a stock prices *model*, it seems more appropriate to keep it here.

The Portfolio Theory appears to be a robust theory, although based on a simplified image of the real world. It is indeed based on several restrictive hypotheses:

- Hypotheses related to financial assets:
  - Asset returns r are modeled by a random variable, distributed as a Gaussian probabilities distribution, fully determined by its first two moments, namely its expected value E and its variance V, although instead of V, the theory makes use of the corresponding standard deviation measure STD ($STD = \sqrt{V}$).
  - Returns of different financial assets i and j are correlated by the linear correlation coefficient ρ_{ij}.

- Markets are efficient[1] – practically speaking, we observe that the more *liquid* a market, the more efficient it is.
- The theory is built on *mid* prices (average of the market quoted *bid* and *offer* (or *ask*) prices): the market *bid–offer spread* is thus not considered here.
- Various costs such as brokerage fees, taxes, and so on are not taken into account (they are too much affected by local circumstances, market features, and the investor's situation).
- Hypotheses related to investors' behavior:
  - Investors are rational.
  - Investors are characterized by some degree of risk aversion.
  - Investors' decisions are limited to the next (single) period of time.

4.3.2   Risk and return measures

Actually, the Portfolio Theory focuses on assets *returns* rather than corresponding prices. Given the above Gaussian random hypothesis, past prices observations are transformed into $r(t)$ values, which lead to some $E[r(t)]$ and $STD[r(t)]$ measures.

$E[r(t)]$ is naturally the return measure and $STD[r(t)]$ the risk measure because it quantifies the amplitude of returns fluctuations over time. The way to compute such returns and risks is presented in Chapter 14, Section 14.1, in particular how to compute them on annual percentage basis. In the following, $E[r(t)]$ is often written "E(r)" or even "r", and $STD[r(t)]$, called "volatility", is denoted "σ".

For the purpose of the Portfolio Theory, a stock is thus fully determined by its *ex post r* and σ measures, $S(r, \sigma)$, as illustrated in Figure 4.3. For example, in 2006, based on successive daily close prices, the return and risk of L'Oreal were 20% and 19% respectively.

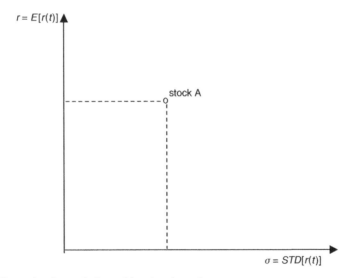

Figure 4.3   Example of a stock showed in a (r, σ) graph

---

[1] A detailed presentation of the market efficiency and its various forms (weak, semi-strong, strong) is beyond the scope of this book. See for example the seminal paper by E. FAMA, 'Efficient capital markets: a review of theory and empirical work', *Journal of Finance*, 25(1), 1970, pp. 383–417, and its sequel, E. FAMA, Efficient capital markets: II, *Journal of Finance*, 46(5), 1991, pp. 1575–1617. For a more recent state of the theory, see, for example, M. BEECHEY, D. GRUEN and J. VICKERY, *The efficient market hypothesis: a survey*, Research paper published by the Reserve Bank of Australia (January 2000).

4.3.3   The Markowitz model

Markowitz's goal was to optimize the budget allocation to a portfolio P of n stocks $S_i(r_i, \sigma_i)$, weighted by w_i, with $0 \leq w_i \leq 1$ and $\sum w_i = 1$, so that for P:

$$E(r_P) = \sum_{i=1}^{n} w_i E(r_i) \tag{4.1}$$

$$\sigma_P^2 = [w_i] \cdot \begin{bmatrix} \sigma_{11} & \sigma_{12} & \cdots & \sigma_{1n} \\ \sigma_{21} & \sigma_{22} & \cdots & \sigma_{2n} \\ & \cdots & \sigma_{ij} & \cdots & \cdots \\ \sigma_{n1} & \sigma_{n2} & \cdots & \sigma_{nn} \end{bmatrix} \cdot \begin{bmatrix} w_1 \\ w_2 \\ \cdots \\ w_n \end{bmatrix}$$

$$\Downarrow$$

variances-covariances matrix

that is,

$$\sigma_P^2 = \Sigma_i \Sigma_j w_i w_j \rho_{ij} \sigma_i \sigma_j$$

where the ρ_{ij} correlation coefficients are computed by

$$\rho_{ij} = \frac{\sigma_{ij}}{\sigma_i \sigma_j}$$

In a (r, σ) chart, it is possible, for a given past period of data to locate by a point any $S_i(r_i, \sigma_i)$, but also any possible weighted combination of up to n stocks, defining points that represent portfolios, among which the optimal ones have to be identified. Performing this graph representation shows that there is a (non-linear) "frontier" of possible portfolios presenting the highest return, for different risks. In other words, the points representing stocks or stocks portfolios are located in the hatched area of Figure 4.4 – there are no points above the frontier, which is called the "efficient frontier".

Portfolios along the efficient frontier are called efficient portfolios – indeed, they offer a maximum return for a given risk. On its extreme left side, the efficient frontier in Figure 4.4

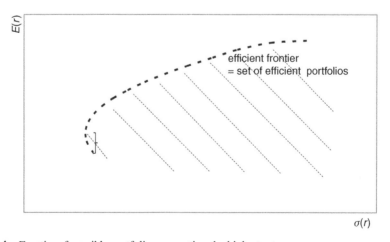

Figure 4.4   Frontier of possible portfolios presenting the highest return

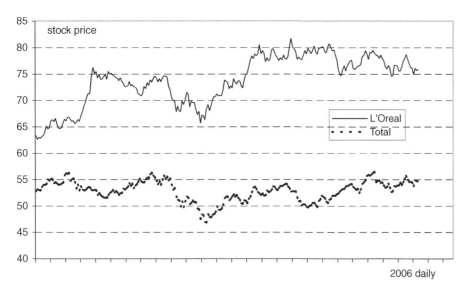

Figure 4.5   Daily close prices for L'Oreal and Total in 2006

also delimits some minimum-return portfolios called sub-optimal portfolios: for a given risk level, there exists another point of the efficient frontier that presents a higher return, due to the bending of the curve. Of course, other points – either single stocks or portfolios – in the figure, below the efficient frontier, are also sub-optimal.

The efficient frontier is actually composed of portfolios (of several stocks) only, but not of single stocks. The reason is that the diversification introduced by combining different stocks takes advantage of their relative lack of correlation. Let us illustrate this by using a portfolio of two stocks, L'Oreal and Total, using the series of daily close prices in 2006, as shown in Figure 4.5.

Calculations give:

- for L'Oreal, "L": $r_L = +20\%$, $\sigma_L = 19\%$ (on a p.a. basis);
- for Total, "T": $r_T = +4\%$, $\sigma_T = 18\%$.

Let us consider a portfolio P made up of 50% of each stock:

- P return:
    is straightforward, using Eq. 4.1: $r_P = 0.5 \times 0.2 + 0.5 \times 0.04 = 12\%$;
    that is, the weighted average of individual returns.

- P risk:
    the variance (squared risk) is affected by a covariance term:

$$\sigma_P^2 = w_L^2 \sigma_L^2 + w_T^2 \sigma_T^2 + 2 w_L w_T \mathrm{cov}_{LT} \tag{4.2}$$

    with

$$\mathrm{cov}_{LT} = \rho_{LT} \sigma_L \sigma_T$$

where ρ_{LT} is the correlation between L and T prices, computed on the whole prices series. The risk σ thus depends on this correlation value:

- Suppose the correlation is perfect, that is, $\rho_{LT} = 1$:

$$\sigma_P^2 = (0.50 \times 0.19)^2 + (0.50 \times 0.18)^2 + 2 \times 1 \times (0.50 \times 0.19) \times (0.50 \times 0.18)$$

$$= [(0.50 \times 0.19) + (0.50 \times 0.18)]^2$$

$\Rightarrow \sigma = 18.50\%$, that is, the weighted average of risks: combining fully correlated stocks does not bring any diversification. Note that perfect correlation practically never occurs, even a nearby 1 correlation is seldom seen (e.g., correlation of two closely related indexes, having some stocks in common, like Euro Stoxx 50 and DAX 30: $\rho = 0.94$ in 2006).

- Suppose the two variables (L and T prices) are independent, that is, $\rho_{LT} = 0$:

$$\sigma_P^2 = (0.50 \times 0.19)^2 + (0.50 \times 0.18)^2 + 2 \times 0 \times (0.50 \times 0.19) \times (0.50 \times 0.18)$$

$\Rightarrow \sigma = 13.09\%$, that is, a significant lowering of the risk. A further risk reduction would occur in the fully hypothetical case of the variables being negatively correlated, that is, with $-1 \leq \rho < 0$. In the extreme case of $\rho = -1$,

$$\sigma_P^2 = (0.50 \times 0.19)^2 + (0.50 \times 0.18)^2 + 2 \times (-1) \times (0.50 \times 0.19) \times (0.50 \times 0.18)$$

$$= [(0.50 \times 0.19) - (0.50 \times 0.18)]^2$$

$\Rightarrow \sigma^2 = 0.000025$ that is, $\sigma = 0.50\%$. The risk would even be 0 if both individual risks were equal, or by adjusting the weights adequately. If such a situation occurred in the real market world, it would imply strictly inverse returns, with $r_P = 0.50\, r_L + 0.50\, r_T = 0$, to achieve $\rho = -1$. So in such a hypothetical case, we would realize a riskless portfolio paying a return of 0.

- In fact, the observed correlation between the returns of these stocks was medium, that is, 0.45, as shown in Figure 4.6.

Using the same formula as above, but with $\rho = 0.45$, we obtain $\sigma = 15.75\%$, an intermediate value between 13.09 and 18.50 (respectively zero and unit correlation).

It shows that it is possible to reduce a portfolio risk by combining stocks as far de-correlated as possible. Of course, the choice of the weights has an impact also. In the case of Total and L'Oreal stocks, if we vary their respective weights, we get different combinations of $(r, \sigma)^2$, as shown in Figure 4.7.

In particular, in the case of a two-stock portfolio, it is interesting to note the one presenting the minimum variance or standard deviation (point V in Figure 4.7). From Eq. 4.2 previously, the solution is

$$w_L = \frac{\sigma_T^2 - \text{cov}_{LT}}{\sigma_L^2 + \sigma_T^2 - 2\text{cov}_{LT}} \quad \text{and } w_T = 1 - w_L$$

Applied to the above data, it gives $w_L = 0.458$ and $w_T = 0.542$, that is, not far from the initial 50/50 composition of the portfolio in this example.

---

[2] A way to select the best combination is by optimizing their ratio – see Chapter 14.

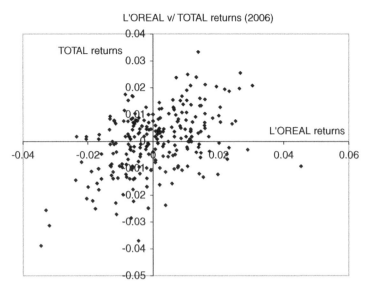

Figure 4.6 Dispersion of L'OREAL versus TOTAL returns

As a conclusion to the Markowitz model, to be optimized, an efficient portfolio must be situated on the efficient frontier, which implies it needs to be:

- diversified, by combining various stocks presenting a low pair-wise correlation;
- and optimized in weights.

Diversification has its limits, however. Understandably, more or less correlated stocks are affected by whole market movements, so that the benefit of such diversification is actually restricted to what is called the *specific*[3] *risk* (specific to each individual stock), but the global

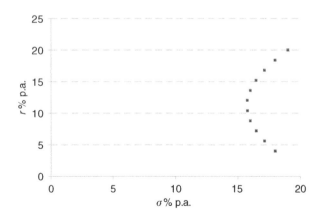

Figure 4.7 Different combinations of (r, σ) for different weights in a portfolio of L'Oreal and Total stocks

---

[3] Also called *idiosyncratic*.

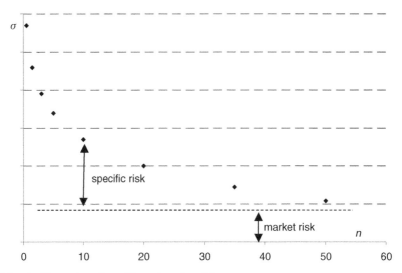

Figure 4.8   An illustration of specific and market risk

market risk remains as a whole. In other words, by increasing the number n of diversified stocks, the benefit in terms of risk reduction diminishes progressively, up to an asymptotical risk level of pure market risk (see Figure 4.8).

4.3.4   Sharpe's CAPM

Optimizing a portfolio allocation with the Markowitz methodology gives rise to the heavy computation of large variances-covariances matrix, in the real situation of a large number ($n \gg 2$) of stocks. Also, the stock returns and corresponding variances and covariances used in the Markowitz methodology are computed from historical data: they are only estimators of the actual – unknown – expected returns, variances and covariances. For large numbers of stocks, the resulting error can seriously affect the outcome of the portfolio optimization. To escape this, Sharpe has developed his CAPM or *Capital Asset Pricing Model*, based on the following principle: *stocks returns are linked together by a single common factor, F* (that will be specified later on), through a linear regression. The returns r_i and r_F are considered to be distributed as a normal distribution.

So that, for the stock $i(r_i, \sigma_i)$, the equation of the regression line of i in F is

$$r_i = \alpha_i + \beta_i r_F + \varepsilon_i(0, c^{st}) \tag{4.3}$$

assuming ε_i residuals are such as $\sigma(\varepsilon_i, \varepsilon_j) = 0$ and $\sigma(\varepsilon_i, r_F) = 0$.

Coming back to Markowitz's efficient frontier, a common case is that of a portfolio invested both in an efficient portfolio of stocks and in a risk-free instrument. If this risk-free instrument is a zero-coupon, non-defaultable T-Bond or T-Bill, for which the maturity is of a single period of time horizon, and by varying the proportions between the stocks and the risk-free bond, the corresponding portfolios are located on a straight line, as shown in Figure 4.9.

The A–B (and beyond) straight line is tangent to the efficient frontier, so that it determines the B point. It is called the *capital market line* (CML) and represents an optimal set of portfolios,

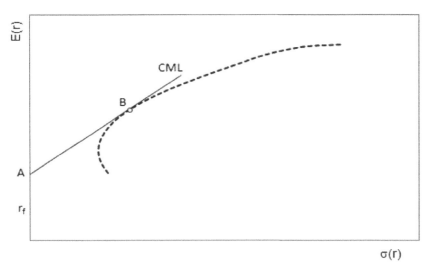

Figure 4.9   The capital market line

made of the efficient portfolio of stocks B and of risk-free instruments in various proportions. In particular:

- at A: the portfolio is 100% invested in the risk-free rate;
- at B: 100% investment in an efficient portfolio of stocks;
- between A and B: mixed portfolio, invested at $x\%$ in the risk-free rate and $(1 - x)\%$ in the efficient portfolio of stocks;
- beyond B: *leveraged* portfolio, assuming the investor has borrowed money (at the r_f rate) and has then invested $>100\%$ of his available resources in an efficient portfolio.

For a given investor, characterized by some utility function U, representing his well-being, assuming his wealth as a portfolio P,

- if the portfolio return were certain (i.e., deterministic), we would have

$$U_P = r_P$$

- but, more realistically (even if simplified, in the spirit of this theory), if the portfolio P value is normally distributed in returns, with some r_P and σ_P,

$$U_P = f(P)$$

where f is some function, often considered as a quadratic curve.[4]

So that, given the property of the CML (i.e., tangent to the efficient frontier), and some $U = f(P)$ curve, the optimal portfolio must be located at the tangent of U to CML, determining the adequate proportion between B and risk-free instrument. To illustrate this, let us compare

---

[4] For further details about utility functions, see, for example, H. GERBER, G. PAFUMI, "Utility functions: from risk theory to finance", *North American Actuarial Journal*, 2(3), 1998, pp. 74–100.

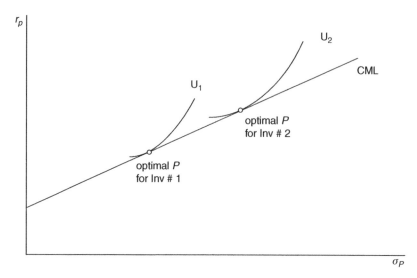

Figure 4.10   Example of two investors with different utility functions

the case of two investors, Investor #1, with utility function U_1, being more risk averse than Investor #2, with utility function U_2 (see Figure 4.10).

To specify the nature of the common factor introduced in Eq. 4.3, we need some more hypotheses:

- All (rational) investors invest in portfolios located on the efficient frontier only.
- Borrowing/lending @ r_f is possible, at no cost.
- There is a hypothesis of "homogeneous expectations": all investors agree on the same distribution of returns probabilities for each stock.
- All investors work on the same time horizon of one-period ahead.

Considering the optimal set of portfolios P that represents the CML, Sharpe defines the CML parameters as the *price of time* and the *price of risk*, as in Figure 4.11.

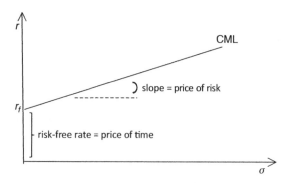

Figure 4.11   CML defined by its parameters of price of time and price of risk

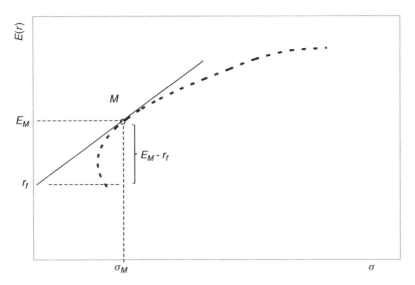

Figure 4.12 Coordinates of the weighted set of all market securities

Sharpe established that the tangency point of CML to the efficient frontier cannot be anything else than a very specific portfolio "M", namely the *weighted set of all market securities*, or "*market portfolio*", weighted by their market capitalization.[5] (The proof is based on the fact that if it was not so, stocks would be priced unsuitably, and if so, would give rise to market adjustments, to avoid arbitrages.[6]) Market practitioners usually assimilate the whole set of market stocks to a stock index: at least it should be a broad index, representative of the whole market.

Figure 4.11, which introduced the CML, thus becomes Figure 4.12 where on the ordinate axis:

- from 0 to r_f is the *price of time*, that is "pure" interest rate;
- from r_f to $E(r_M)$, further denoted E_M, is the risk price, function of the CML slope "r".

E_M and σ_M being related by

$$E_M = r_f + r_M$$

and the slope r of the CML is the *price of risk*:

$$r = \frac{E_M - r_f}{\sigma_M} \tag{4.4}$$

So Sharpe goes a step further than Markowitz: all investors, having homogenous expectations but different risk aversion levels, have the same risky component of their portfolio (although

[5] In his seminal paper, W.F. SHARPE, 'Capital Asset prices – A theory of market equilibrium under conditions of risk', *Journal of Finance*, vol. XIX, no. 3, September 1964, pp. 425–442.

[6] Actually, Sharpe's theory covers a wider range than just stocks, that is, the set of all risky assets traded on markets. However, practically speaking, the financial community restricts the market portfolio on the subset of traded stocks. Also, Sharpe's original CAPM considered only the US market, but it has been expanded to the international market.

not in the same proportion), that is, the market portfolio M. This market portfolio is made up of n stocks i, characterized by (r_i, σ_i), such as:

- $w_{i,M}$ is the portion of M invested in stock I;
- p_i is the unit price of stock I;
- q_i is the number of shares (on the exchange) of stock I;

so that

$$w_{i,M} = \frac{p_i q_i}{\sum_i p_i q_i} \text{ with } \sum_i w_{i,M} = 1$$

$$\rightarrow r_M = \sum_i w_{i,M} r_i$$

with

$$E_M = \sum_i w_{i,M} E_i$$

where E_i is the expected value $E(r_i)$. And

$$\sigma_i^2 = \sum_i \sum_j w_{i,M} w_{j,M} \rho_{i,j} \sigma_i \sigma_j$$

Sharpe also demonstrated that

$$E_i - r_f = \frac{(E_M - r_f)\sigma_{iM}}{\sigma_M^2} \tag{4.5}$$

where σ_{iM} is the covariance between i and M. Thus $E_i - r_f$, called *the risk premium* of stock i, is a linear function of its sole covariance with the market M return. This linear relationship is called the *security market line* (SML), illustrated in Figure 4.13.

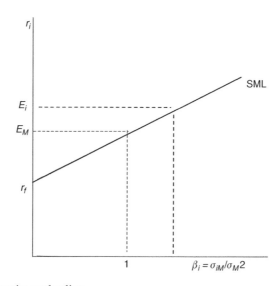

Figure 4.13   The security market line

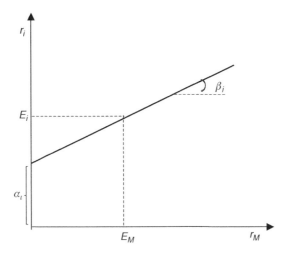

Figure 4.14   The linear relationship between the return of a stock i and the market return

Coming back to the r_F factor of the initial linear regression in Eq. 4.3, it can now be clarified as the market M return r_M:

$$r_i = \alpha_i + \beta_i r_M + \varepsilon_i \tag{4.6}$$

or, with

$$E_i = \alpha_i + \beta_i E_{M_i} \Rightarrow \alpha_i = E_i - \beta_i E_M,$$

or graphically as in Figure 4.14.

So,

$$r_i = E_i + \beta_i [r_M - E_M] + \varepsilon_i \tag{4.7}$$

And Sharpe also demonstrated that

$$\beta_i = \frac{\sigma_{iM}}{\sigma_M^2} \tag{4.8}$$

which says that the "beta" of a stock i is the ratio of the covariance between i and M, to the variance of M.

Generalizing to a portfolio P of several stocks i,

$$\beta_P = \sum_i w_i \beta_i \text{ and } \varepsilon_P = \sum_i w_i \varepsilon_i \tag{4.9}$$

It also follows that a single stock or a portfolio i having a $\beta_i < 1$ means a stock or a portfolio less volatile than the market index, and conversely. In market practice, we say that:

- a $\beta_i < 1$ stock or portfolio is "defensive" (= less volatile than the market index);
- a $\beta_i > 1$ stock or portfolio is "aggressive" (= more volatile than the market index).

An example can be found in the data for the 2009 daily closes for L'Oreal vs Euro Stoxx 50 as a market index (see Figure 4.15).

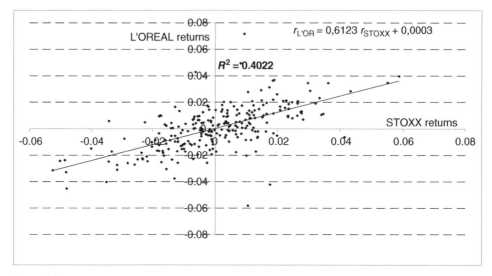

Figure 4.15   L'Oreal versus Euro Stoxx 50 as a market index (daily closes of 2009)

The regression in Figure 4.15, for the period under consideration (2009), shows that the regression line of Eq. 4.6 has an alpha of 0.0003 and a beta of 0.6123 ("defensive") towards the Euro Stoxx 50 as a proxy of the market portfolio. The quality of this regression, namely its R^2, is of 0.634, that is, the impact of the ε term of the equation. The correlation between L'OREAL and the index is of 0.4022.

Finally, the CAPM model arises from combining Eq. 4.5 and Eq. 4.8, to get Eq. 4.10:

$$E_i = r_f + (E_M - r_f)\beta_i \tag{4.10}$$

which states that the expected return of a stock is the risk-free rate plus the market portfolio excess return, in the proportion of the beta of the stock vis-à-vis the market portfolio.

Thus, for a portfolio P, with

$$r_P = \sum_i w_i r_i$$

and

$$w_i r_i = w_i(\alpha_i + \beta_i M + \varepsilon_i)$$
$$\Downarrow \quad \Downarrow \qquad\qquad \Downarrow$$

where "$w_i(\alpha_i \qquad + \varepsilon_i)$"   is the *specific* component of return
$$\Downarrow \qquad \Downarrow$$

and   "$w_i \quad \beta_i M$"   is the *systematic* component of return (i.e., related to M),

P is such that,

- using Eq. 4.6 and Eq. 4.9, its return is determined by its linear regression with M:

$$r_P = \alpha_P + \beta_P r_M + \varepsilon_P \tag{4.11}$$

and Eq. 4.10 becomes

$$E_P = r_f + (E_M - r_f)\beta_P \tag{4.12}$$

- and its squared risk is

$$\sigma^2(r_P) \ or \ \sigma_P^2 = \beta_P^2 \sigma_M^2 + \sigma_\varepsilon^2 \tag{4.13}$$

non-diversifiable risk   diversifiable risk
= systematic risk   = specific risk

so that the squared risk is the sum of systematic risk plus specific risk.

Finally, from Eq. 4.8 and the statistical formula defining the correlation coefficient, between a stock i and M,

$$\rho_{i,M} = \frac{\sigma_{iM}}{\sigma_i \sigma_M}$$

it becomes

$$\beta_i = \frac{\rho_{i,M} \sigma_i}{\sigma_M}$$

The same holds for a portfolio P instead of a stock i:

$$\beta_P = \frac{\rho_{PM} \sigma_P}{\sigma_M}$$

and thereafter Eq. 4.13 can also be expressed as

$$\sigma_P^2 = \rho_{P,M}^2 \sigma_P^2 + \sigma_\varepsilon^2 \tag{4.14}$$

4.3.5   The APT model (Roll and Ross)

Principle

The *Arbitrage Pricing Theory* (APT) is based on a multi-factors linear model explaining the return r_i of a stock i:

$r_i = f_i$ (several *systematic* factors) + *specific* factors

          determined   not determined

or, more formally, for m factors F_j, called "systematic factors":

$$r_i = E(r_i) + \sum_j \beta_{ij} F_j + \varepsilon_i \tag{4.15}$$

with

- $E(\varepsilon_i) = E(F_j) = 0$
- $E(\varepsilon_{ij}) = E(\varepsilon_i F_j) = E(F_i F_j) = 0$
- $E[\varepsilon_i^2] = 0$

Note that the β sensitivities here refer to the factors F_j, and have thus nothing to do with the CAPM's β – we will come back to this point in Section 4.3.6. In Eq. 4.15, the term

$$\sum_j \beta_{ij} F_j$$

represents

                ↙ ↘

        sensitivity to   actual return on

                  systematic factor j

so that

actual return = expected return $+\sum$ *factor sensitivity* $\times$ *factor effect + residual risk*

Why "Arbitrage" Pricing Theory?

For a portfolio P of n stocks i, weighted such that $\Sigma w_i = 0$, that is, a portfolio holding both long and short stock positions in the adequate proportion, Eq. 4.15 becomes

$$r_P = \sum_i w_i E(r_i) + \sum_i w_i \sum_j \beta_{ij} F_j + \sum_i w_i \varepsilon_i$$

and the condition $\Sigma w_i = 0$ means that building this portfolio entails no net funding cost. If n increases significantly, the three σ (.) terms in i tend to zero, hence r_P tends to zero, hence a typical "no arbitrage" situation: no cost $\Leftrightarrow$ no return.

Effect of the jth Factor on r_i

The linear regression described by Eq. 4.15 is such that, separately (by making all other Fs $= 0$), each single factor F_j affects r_i proportional to its corresponding sensitivity factor β_{ij}, as illustrated in Figure 4.16.

In particular, at point B, $F_j = 0 \rightarrow r_i = E(r_i)$.

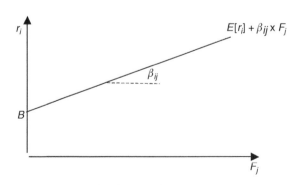

Figure 4.16   Effect of F_j on r_i, proportional to sensitivity factor β_{ij}

Choice of Factors F_j

There is no objective rule governing the choice of the factors F_j. Because of the principle of parsimony, their number m must remain small enough: the higher m, the higher the sum of estimation errors. In one of their seminal papers,[7] Roll and Ross proposed:

- $F_1 =$ change in expected inflation;
- $F_2 =$ change in expected industrial production;
- $F_3 =$ unanticipated risk premium variation;
- $F_4 =$ unanticipated yield curve move.[7]

so that the ε_i term of Eq. 4.5 would represent the impact of these factors over the period of time covered by the ex-post regression.

Practitioners (e.g., MSCI Barra) of the APT methodology work with their in-house factors. A major difficulty comes in identifying factors that actually continue to make sense over a long enough period of time. These factors may be selected because of their economic meaning, or purely statistically, through the *Principal Component Analysis* methodology.

4.3.6 CAPM versus APT

Comparing Eq. 4.7 of CAPM

$$r_i = E_i + \beta_i[r_M - E_M] + \varepsilon_i$$

with Eq. 4.15 of APT

$$r_i = E(r_i) + \sum_j \beta_{ij} F_j + \varepsilon_i$$

CAPM appears as a particular case of APT, that is, an APT with a single risk factor β_i, namely the market risk as a whole.

CAPM and APT share:

- a linear relationship with respect to factor(s);
- the goal, that, by adequate diversification, investors can reduce the specific risk (in ε), but not the systematic one (due to the common factor(s)).

But they diverge in the sense that:

- CAPM is an endogenous *market equilibrium* model (the market prices are considered in equilibrium), while APT relies on the *non-arbitrage* principle among different stock prices affected by the set of *exogenous* factors;
- in other words, APT is a *relative* pricing model (i.e., each stock price is based upon other stock prices, through the set of common factors), while CAPM is an *absolute* pricing model (i.e., stock prices relate to the whole market features of risk and return).

Finally, there is a link between the models:

- The CAPM rests upon r_M, but there is no way to clearly identify the actual content and perimeter of the market M.
- The validity of APT depends on the validity of the set of selected common factors.

---

[7] R. ROLL, S.A. ROSS, 'The Arbitrage Pricing Theory approach to strategic portfolio planning', *Financial Analysts Journal*, May/June 1984, pp. 14–26.

4.3.7   The four-moments CAPM

The CAPM being based on a somewhat restrictive Gaussian random hypothesis, it has been generalized to a more general probability distribution, which could, in some markets and circumstances, turn out to be more realistic. In this case, to determine the distribution, beyond the first two moments $M_1 = E(r)$ and $M_2 = \sigma^2(r)$, we will also need to calculate the third and fourth moments, M_3 and M_4. Usually, in the finance area further moments are not used.

Reminder

Central[8] moments M_k of order $k > 1$ are determined as

$$M_k = \frac{1}{n} \sum_{i=1}^{k} (r_i - E(r))^k$$

M_3 is a measure of asymmetry or *skewness*. Practically, we use a function of M_3 called the Fisher's coefficient for quantifying the skewness (*skew*) of a distribution:

$$skew = \frac{M_3}{3}$$

The log-normal distribution models a prices distribution, assuming their corresponding returns are normally distributed (this point will be developed in Chapter 8, Section 8.8.7) is an example of a positively or right-skewed (i.e., positive skewness) distribution, illustrated in Figure 4.17.

Note that, contrary to symmetric distribution like the normal one, where the mode is equal to the median and to the mean, if the skewness is positive, mode < median < mean, and conversely if it is negative. In Figure 4.17, these values are 0.47, 1.275, and 2.117 respectively.

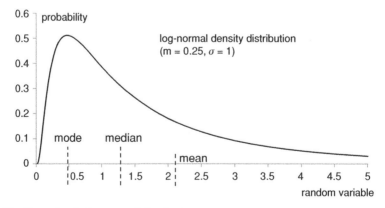

Figure 4.17   Example of a log-normal distribution

---

[8] Central moments refer to moments of higher order centered on $M_1 = E(r)$.

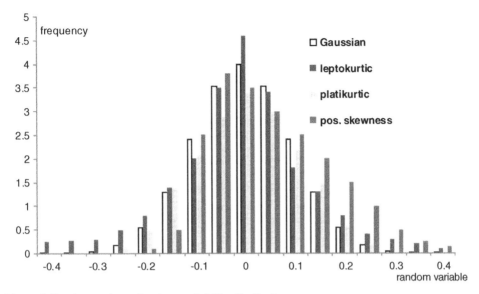

Figure 4.18   Comparison of various probability distributions

M_4, called *kurtosis*, is a measure of the "flatness" (peakedness) of a density distribution. Here, too, we use a function of M_4 called the Fisher's coefficient for quantifying the kurtosis (κ) of a distribution:

$$\kappa = \frac{M_4}{4} - 3$$

The calculation of the kurtosis for a Gaussian distribution gives $M_4/\sigma^4 = 3$, hence the "-3" in the calculation of κ, so that the Gaussian distribution presents a null kurtosis. A distribution flatter than the normal, thus $\kappa < 0$, is called *platikurtic*, and conversely, *leptokurtic*. Figure 4.18 shows an example of this typology.

The usual covariance can be generalized in a similar way. As an example, within the framework of the CAPM, considering the returns r_P of a portfolio P and r_M of a market index M, their covariance is

$$cov = \sigma_{P,M} = E[r_P - E(r_P)] \times [r_M - E(r_M)]$$

that is, with a dimension [2] in $r - E(.)$, just as $\sigma_{P,M}$ has a dimension [2] in σ, like a variance (σ^2).

Generalizing, we obtain

- co-skewness, having a dimension [3] such as M_3:

$$cosk_{PM} = E[r_P - E(r_P)] \times [r_M - E(r_M)]^2$$

- co-kurtosis, having a dimension [4] such as M_4:

$$cokur_{PM} = E[r_P - E(r_P)] \times [r_M - E(r_M)]^3$$

The four-moments CAPM

The rationale for going beyond the Gaussian distribution is mainly the observation of the "fat tails" phenomenon, namely that, at least in the short/medium term, actual returns distributions present a higher probability of large moves than described by the Gaussian distribution. It can therefore make sense to prefer modeling the returns with a distribution presenting some $M_4 > 3$. Besides, in some cases, actual returns may also present some skewness, that is null with the Gaussian. Hence, the attractiveness of a four-moments CAPM.

This generalization allows us to relax some of the hypotheses (cf. Section 4.3.1) at the base of the standard CAPM:

- the returns can be modeled by any kind of probability distribution, presenting some degree of skewness and/or kurtosis;
- investors are not necessarily rational: fat tails imply market overreactions or "herding effect", leading to market rallies or crashes.

Starting from the CAPM relationship 4.10 of Section 4.3.4, for a stock i,

$$E_i = r_f + (E_M - r_f)\beta_i$$

the $(E_M - r_f)$ term must be expanded so that the concept of riskless rate is not only riskless in terms of variance (actually, of volatility) but also in terms of skewness and kurtosis. In other words, a riskless rate must also present risk of neither skewness nor kurtosis.

To achieve this, let us denote

- $E(r_{cosk})$ as $E(r)$ of a stock of zero covariance, zero co-kurtosis and a unit of co-skewness with M;
- $E(r_{cokur})$ as $E(r)$ of a stock of zero covariance, zero co-skewness and a unit co-kurtosis with M

and expand the β concept as follows:

$$(standard\ \beta_i\ becoming:)\beta_{i1} = \frac{\sigma_{iM}}{\sigma_M^2}$$

$$\beta_{i2} = \frac{cosk_{iM}}{M_{3\ of\ M}}$$

$$\beta_{i3} = \frac{cokur_{iM}}{M_{4\ of\ M}}$$

The calculation leads to the generalized four-moments CAPM:

$$E_i = r_f + \left[E(r_M) - E(r_{cosk}) - E(r_{cokur}) - r_f\right]\beta_{i1} + \left[E(r_{cosk}) - r_f\right]\beta_{i2} + \left[E(r_{cokur}) - r_f\right]\beta_{i3}$$

or

$$r_i = \alpha_i + [\dots\dots]\beta_{i1} + [\dots\dots]\beta_{i2} + [\dots\dots]\beta_{i3} + \varepsilon_i \qquad (4.16)$$

	⇓	⇓	⇓	⇓
	"alpha"	volatility	skewness	kurtosis
	⇓	⇓	⇓	⇓
Investor:	☺	☹	☺	☹

In other words, a rational investor will favor stocks presenting the highest *odd* moments – expected value and (positive) skewness – and the lowest *even* moments – variance (volatility) and kurtosis.

Note: a similar reasoning can be made for a portfolio *P* – instead of a stock *i* – versus the market index *M*, by starting from Eq. 4.12 instead of 4.10 (from Section 4.3.4).

However, choosing to model returns with a more general distribution presents a major drawback: the successive moments are less and less stable (stationary) over time, so that the lack of stationarity of the distribution makes it more dangerous (in extrapolating past results to the future) and/or subject to more measurement errors. In other words, the two-moments CAPM is more robust than the three- or four-moments CAPM, and is mostly preferred by practitioners.

Example of lack of stationarity: expected value, standard deviation (in lieu of variance), skewness and kurtosis presented by the S&P 500 on weekly data each year from 1999 to 2009 are illustrated in Figure 4.19.

The yearly values of these measures have been deliberately reported to a common vertical scale, to show to what extent the skewness and kurtosis vary over time. Indeed, they look more

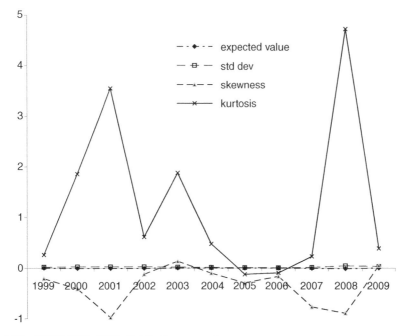

Figure 4.19   SP500 1999–2009: distribution parameters

and more dispersed as the moment order increases: on this 1999–2009 series, their standard deviation is

	Standard deviation of M_k
Expected value	0.0038
Standard deviation	0.0107
Skewness	0.3795
Kurtosis	1.5990

As an alternative, in the presence of skewness, as an intermediary step between the standard CAPM and a three- or four-moments CAPM, we can also compute a "downside beta" as a beta computed as in Eq. 4.8, but using the negative semi-variance instead of the variance.

A Look at Alternative Investment

In short, the Alternative Investment (AI) consists of investing – through hedge funds, for example – in short positions and/or in derivatives and/or in assets other than traditional ones. The rationale for looking after AI as a portion of the asset allocation is trying to improve the efficient frontier. By improvement, we mean reducing the risk and increasing the expected return together, as in Figure 4.20.

This is *a priori* possible if we assume that the returns of the AI positions are not normal, hence, by playing with the higher moments. For example, a position in a (bought or sold) option is asymmetric *per se*. Such an objective is ambitious, of course, given what has been said about the lack of stationarity of these higher moments, without mentioning other risks such as possible lack of liquidity presented by less traditional investments, higher transaction costs, and so on.

Regarding AI within the framework of the four-moments CAPM, option positions, for example, do present some skewness because of their asymmetric payoff. Going back to

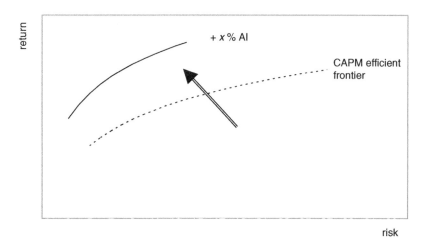

Figure 4.20   Improving the efficient frontier

Eq. 4.15, the differences between investing in traditional assets (bonds and stocks) versus investing in AI can be summarized as follows (TI means traditional investment here):

$$r_i = \alpha_i + [\ldots \ldots] \beta_{i1} + [\ldots \ldots] \beta_{i2} + [\ldots \ldots] \beta_{i3} + \varepsilon_i$$

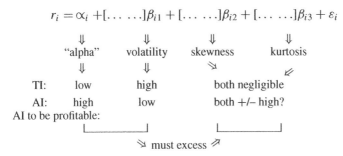

This explains why, in the case of AI, performance measures must incorporate the impact of M3 and M4 (cf. Chapter 14, Section 14.1.5), otherwise traditional performance measure, restricted to the impact of M1 and M2, will turn out to be misguided.

FURTHER READING

E. ELTON, M. GRUBER, S. BROWN, W. GOETZMANN, *Modern Portfolio Theory and Investments Analysis*, John Wiley & Sons, Inc., Hoboken, 2006, 752 p.

Robert A. HAUGEN, *Modern Investment Theory*, Prentice Hall, 4th ed., 1996, 748 p.

The author published in 2000, also with Prentice Hall, two "clones" of this book: *Modern Investment Theory – United States Edition* and *Modern Investment Theory – International Edition*.

E. JURCZENKO, B. MAILLET (eds), *Multi-Moment Asset Allocation and Pricing Models*, John Wiley & Sons, Ltd, Chichester, 2006, 233 p.

Bob LITTERMAN, *Modern Investment Management – An Equilibrium Approach*, John Wiley & Sons, Inc., Hoboken, 2003, 624 p.

William F. SHARPE, *Investors and Markets – Portfolio Choices, Asset Prices, and Investment Advice*, Princeton University Press, 2006, 232 p.

5

Forward instruments

A forward instrument is the subject of a contract, concluded today, for a transaction scheduled at a future date, but at a price fixed at the time of the contract conclusion. The object of the contract is a buy or sell transaction relative to a financial instrument called the underlying.

The difference between spot and forward operations on the same underlying, priced S at current time t_0, is straightforward, as shown in Figures 5.1 and 5.2.

Forward instruments are addressed in three chapters:

- Chapters 5 and 6 are dedicated to forward instruments traded on the OTC (interbank) market.
- Chapter 7 looks at exchange markets for forward instruments, called *futures*, to distinguish them from OTC *forward* equivalent products.

As such, forward instruments represent the simplest form of "derivative" instruments. Under their most general form, derivatives are involving a forward transaction, which can present different features (cf. further chapters, dedicated to swaps and options).

5.1 THE FORWARD FOREIGN EXCHANGE

The forward foreign exchange market has been developed to answer the following kind of problem. Consider the treasurer of a US corporation, or an investor, knowing he will receive EUR in 6 months. Today, spot EUR/USD quotes 1.3920–21. He may:

- either do nothing and wait for 6 months, to then exchange spot his EUR, at the risk that the EUR will quote higher or lower than today;
- or wish to fix today with his bank (or any qualified counterparty) the exchange rate that will be applied in 6 months on his transaction.

By opting for the second case, he covers his exchange risk by – in the present situation – selling forward his EUR against USD, at an agreed rate, called *forward exchange rate* or *forward* (fwd) – *a forward is an exchange rate fixed today for an ulterior transaction, at a given maturity date*. At maturity, the forward rate will turn out to be beneficial, or represent an opportunity loss, in the present context of hedging a forthcoming revenue. Forward rates are much more used for speculative purposes, however, resulting either in an actual profit or an actual loss.

The forward interbank market allows for buying and selling currencies at maturities ranging from 1 day to about 2 years. The case of a forward calculation above 2 years is considered at the end of Section 5.1.1.

For the bank market maker, the issue is to quote a forward currency price without taking any market risk, or involving its own view on the future evolution of the currency, that is, in a neutral way. Forward pricing results from some actuarial calculus applied on currently available *spot data only*, consisting of:

- the prevailing spot rate XXX/YYY;
- current interest rates on XXX and on YYY respectively.

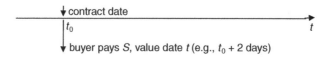

Figure 5.1   Buy spot @ S

To this extent, a forward implies a view on the future that is based only on present economic features and market data (spot currency price as well as relevant spot interest rates). Since such present market data are unquestionable, even if the forward price cannot be viewed as a best guess of the future spot currency price, at least it minimizes the error risk on it, assuming currency spot prices can be modeled by a log-normal distribution. This point will be developed in Section 8.9.

Finally, at the forward maturity, the computed forward rate $F(t)$ can be compared with the current spot rate $S(t)$ by means of the forward ratio $fr(t)$:

$$fr(t) = \frac{S(t)}{F(t)}$$

5.1.1   Forward exchange operations

A forward exchange operation (also called *outright forward*) is a contract between a bank market maker and its client/counterparty:

- to buy a currency against selling another currency;
- at a forward agreed maturity date;
- for an agreed nominal amount;
- at a price fixed in advance, that is, the forward rate "F".

Example of a 1-year forward calculation on EUR/USD:

$$\text{data}(11/15/07): \quad \text{EUR/USD spot} = 1.4625\text{–}27 \ (\text{mid}:1.4626)$$
$$\text{1Y EUR rate} \quad = 4.104\text{–}08 \quad (\text{mid}:4.106\%)$$
$$\text{1Y USD rate} \quad = 4.575\text{–}79 \quad (\text{mid}:4.577\%)$$

In Principle

To buy EUR against USD forward 1 year can be realized by buying it spot: this implies that:

- the EUR being bought 1 year too early, it will be invested during 1 year at the current EUR 1-year rate;
- the USD being not yet available for this spot transaction, it must be borrowed for 1 year at the current USD 1-year rate.

Figure 5.2   Buy forward @ F

To sell EUR against USD can be realized in a similar way, with the adequate borrowing and deposit rates.

The issue of such an operation would be affected by the impact of the bid–ask spread on the three transactions, namely the spot transaction, the deposit and the borrowing rates. This would lead to bid and ask forward prices that would present a spread that is too wide with respect to the prevailing spread on the forward market.

In Practice

To shorten the calculation time and to avoid resulting into a too wide spread, market practice uses mid-price and interest rates, so that the resulting mid-forward price can be obtained as follows:

spot price

today:		+1 year:
1€	@4.106%	$= (1 + 4.106\%) \times 1€$
$=$		
1.4626\$	@4.577%	$= (1 + 4.577\%) \times 1.4626\$$

If the above € and \$ amounts are equal today, they must also be equal 1 year later, so that

$$(1 + 4.106\%) \times 1€ = (1 + 4.577\%) \times 1.4626\$$$

$$\rightarrow 1€ = \frac{1 + 4.577\%}{1 + 4.106\%} \times 1.4626\$ = 1.4692\$$$

Hence, 1 EUR forward 1 year = 1.4692 USD in mid.

Having defined (cf. Chapter 3, Section 3.3.2) r_{ref} as the EUR interest rate here, and $r_{c/v}$ as the USD interest rate here, the formula for a forward price of maturity T (up to 1 year) is:

$$F = S \frac{1 + r_{c/v} \times T}{1 + r_{ref} \times T} \tag{5.1}$$

where $T = n_{days} / 360$ *or* 365 (depending on the day counting of the related -ibor market).

Beyond 1-year maturity, the formula must be adjusted to take into account the compounded interest above 1 year (up to 2 years), so that for $t =$ the maturity exceeding 1 year, the formula becomes

$$F = S \frac{(1 + r_{c/v})(1 + r_{c/v} \times t)}{(1 + r_{ref})(1 + r_{ref} \times t)}$$

Coming back to the calculation example, it appears that

$$\text{mid fwd} = 1.4692 = \text{mid spot } 1.4626 + \mathbf{0.0066}$$

that is, this forward being higher than the spot price, it is said to be "at premium". When market data are such that r_{ref} is higher than $r_{c/v}$, from Eq. 5.1 it results that the forward is lower than the spot, and is said to be "at discount".

To determine the bid and ask quotations for the EUR/USD 1-year forward, the premium must be adequately adjusted so that the bid–ask spread on the forward is equivalent to current market practice. Suppose that, in our 1-year forward example, the market would quote it on 3 pips, instead of on 2 pips for the corresponding spot price, it can be achieved as follows:

$$
\begin{array}{rcc}
\text{spot:} & 1.4625 - & 1.4627 \\
\text{premium/discount:} & +0.0065 - & +0.0066 \\
\hline
\text{forward:} & 1.4690 - & 1.4693
\end{array}
$$

The forward premium or discount is also called a *forward spread*, and the added premiums (here, of + 65 and + 66 pips) or discounts are called the *swap points*, to be added to the spot price for quoting the forward. Knowing that spot currency prices are adjusted on the market at a much higher pace than relative interest rates, instead of displaying the forward as such, market makers rather display the swap points to be added or deducted from the constantly changing current spot price:

$$
(\text{spot } 1.4625\text{-}27) \quad 65 - 66
$$

Note that this labeling at first sight does not show whether the swap points are to be added (forward at premium) or deducted (forward at discount). In the present example, to widen by 1 pip the spread on the spot price, it is necessary to add 1 pip more on the *ask* than on the *bid* swap points. Conversely, for forwards at discount, a similar widening of the spread needs to deduct 1 pip more on the bid than on the ask swap points, so that:

- forwards at premium: if the swap points are as above, "lower" – "higher", it implies that they have to be added;
- forwards at discount: if the swap points are presented as "higher – lower", it implies that they have to be deducted.

The above quotation is based on a strict actuarial calculation, as a theoretical, or *fair*, price. In practice, different market makers will quote slightly different prices, although not significantly different from the above calculation if the market is liquid enough (according to the no arbitrage principle, cf. Section 1.5).

Consider three final remarks:

- Looking at the earlier example, the forward ratio $fr(t)$ as defined at the end of the previous section can be computed as follows, having observed that 1 year later, the current EUR/USD spot was 1.2637 (mid):

$$
fr(t) = 1.2637/1.4626 = 0.864.
$$

- It results from Eq. 5.1 that the impact of the differential of interest rates, r_{ref} and $r_{c/v}$, on the forward price grows with the forward maturity: the swap points are increasing with maturity.
- Since longer forward maturities are normally less liquid than shorter ones, the market bid-ask spread goes slightly wider with longer forward maturities. See, for example, the market

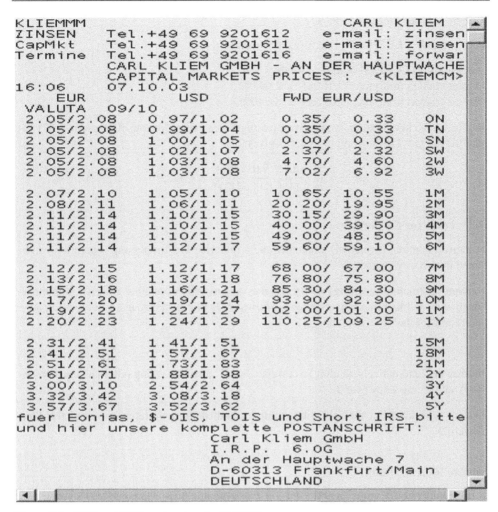

Figure 5.3   EUR and USD market data for 10/07/03
Source: Reuters

data in Figure 5.3 (data: 10/07/03). In this figure, the EUR and USD interest rates are given in the first two double columns, and the forwards, at discount, in the third double column; the maturities appear in the last column.

Forwards above 2-year maturities are actually built from CRS swaps (cf. Chapter 6). The calculation of a forward currency rate becomes:

$$F = S\frac{(1 + r_{c/v})^T}{(1 + r_{ref})^T}$$
(5.1bis)

Note that the r_{ref} and $r_{c/v}$ are actually zero-coupon rates. This is not an issue until we work with short-term, natural zero coupons, but market coupon rates have to be transformed into zero-coupon rates once we compute a long-dated forward. We looked at how to compute zero coupons from observed coupon rates Chapter 2, Section 2.3.

Example (Market Data of 05/03/11)

Let us compute a EUR/USD price forward 3 years:

- current (mid) EUR/USD spot = 1.4835;
- 3-year coupon (mid) rate EUR (ref) = 2.664%;
- 3-year coupon (mid) rate USD (c/v) = 1.240%.

By using the bootstrap method, corresponding 3-year, zero-coupon EUR *rref* is 2.6713%, and USD $r_{c/v}$ is 1.246%. Applying Eq. 5.1 gives

$$F = 1.4835 \frac{(1 + 0.01246)^3}{(1 + 0.026713)^3} = 1.422571$$

5.1.2   Forex (or FX) swaps

For a given nominal (principal) amount N and a maturity T, a forex swap[1] operation can be defined in two ways, either as

- buying (alternatively, selling) *spot* a currency against sale of another currency, simultaneously with selling (alternatively, buying) *forward* (T) this currency against buy of the other currency, for the same amount N

or

- borrowing (alternatively, lending) a currency over T, against lending (alternatively, borrowing) another currency over T.

As we will see from the following example, both definitions refer in fact to the same transaction.

Example (Data 07/13/09)

Let us consider an FX swap on USD/JPY, on $T = 6$ months (here computed as 0.5 year), for a nominal amount $N = \$1$ million. Current market data are:

- USD/JPY spot @ 93.04–06;
- 6-month USD LIBOR rate: 1.363–1.367;
- 6-month JPY LIBOR rate: 0.68–0.72.

By using Eq. 5.1, the mid forward price is 92.74, supposed here to be split as 92.72–75.

1. FX Swap Viewed as Buy Spot/Sell fwd

Counterparty:

- buys USD spot against JPY, @ 93.06;
- and sells USD fwd against JPY, @ 92.72.

---

[1] Not to be confused with swaps as developed in Chapter 6. In short, a forex swap is made up of a single exchange of cash flows, while a regular swap involves a succession of several such exchanges.

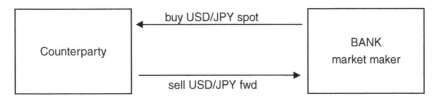

Figure 5.4   FX swap viewed as Buy spot/Sell fwd

The USD bought spot can be lent for 6 months @1.363%; at maturity, the proceeds of this deposit serve to deliver the USD forward. The JPY sold spot against the spot buying of USD have to be borrowed @ 0.72% for 6 months so that its reimbursement is made possible by the JPY received forward – see Figure 5.5.

This scheme shows that buying the USD spot and selling it forward, if completed by the corresponding lending and borrowing of the currencies, leads to the lending of USD and borrowing of JPY, which corresponds to the other view of the FX swap, as shown in Figure 5.6.

2. FX Swap Viewed as Borrow/Lend

Here, the counterparty is:

- borrowing JPY at t_0 @ 0.72% and selling spot the proceeds, against buying USD @ 93.06;
- lending the received USD from t_0 to T @ 1.363%;
- at maturity T, reimbursing the borrowed JPY and collecting the USD deposit.

So, if the operation was covered in T by selling USD against buying JPY fwd from t_0, that is, as with the first view of the forex swap, the operation is squared – see Figure 5.7.

To check that both "views" refer to the same transaction, we can see that the operations in bold characters in Figure 5.5 are written in regular font in Figure 5.7, and vice versa.

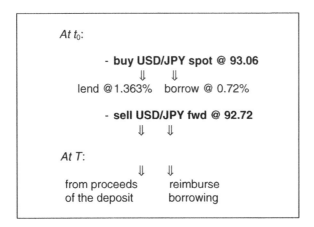

Figure 5.5   Details of a Buy spot/Sell fwd transaction

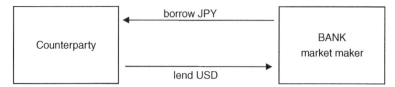

Figure 5.6   FX swap viewed as Borrow/Lend

FX swaps are commonly used in treasury operations and speculation.[2] For example, FX swaps can be used in treasury operations for a company facing scheduled mismatches in dates of cash in and cash out in a foreign currency.

A typical example of speculative trading is the carry trade. It consists of an FX swap as Borrow/Lend, without hedging it by a forward operation, as has been done here. It allows us to take advantage of the differential of borrowing and lending rates, that is, by borrowing a low interest rate currency XXX and lending a high interest rate currency YYY, but at the risk of currency spot prices fluctuations. In other words, the carry trade speculation comes to the same as speculating that at the end of the period, the current spot market of XXX/YYY will quote higher than the forward price synthesized by the borrowing and lending operations.

Example.   Using the previous data, on $N = \$1$ million: the carry trade would consist of:

- on 07/13/09:
  - borrow 6 months JPY @ 0.72%;
  - lend 6 months USD @ 1.363%;
  - buy USD/JPY spot @ 93.06 for $1m.
- 6 months later (01/13/10):
  - sell spot USD/JPY @ 91.38.

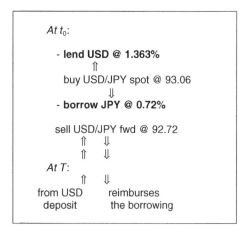

Figure 5.7   Details of a Borrow/Lend transaction

---

[2] Use in arbitrage on fwd prices is deliberately not mentioned, because the probability of taking advantage of market prices discrepancies is rather theoretical in these markets.

- The USD deposit earns $1.06815m (taking 6 months = 0.5 year), and the borrowed JPY amounts to ¥93.39502m, that needs (@ 91.38) $1.022051m. In this case, the lowered USD/JPY has lead the carry trade to a loss. To make it profitable, the final spot USD/JPY rate should have been superior to the forward price implied by the borrowing and lending, that is > 92.7684.

In practice, carry trades will associate currencies showing a wider interest rate spread, such as (at least, in 2010) JPY *vs* AUD, for example, as well as anticipating a favorable currency move.

5.1.3   Forward forex swaps or forward–forward transactions

A forward forex swaps or forward–forward transaction is a forex swap that is traded between two forward dates rather than from the spot date.

For example, using the data from Figure 5.3, on the forward swap points in EUR/USD (data 10/07/03), that is,

- T = 6 months: 59.60–59.10;
- T = 12 months: 110.25–109.25,

we can combine

Buy EUR/USD fwd 6m @ S–59.10 with *Sell* EUR/USD fwd 12m @ S–110.25

and

Sell EUR/USD fwd 6m @ S–59.60 with *Buy* EUR/USD fwd 12m @ S–109.25

to synthesize a forward 6m-forward 12m swap points quotation of

$$-110.25 - (-59.10) \text{ and } - 109.25 - (-59.60)$$
$$= -51.25 = -49.65$$

that is, a 6m/12m swap points quotation of "51.25–49.65" (remember the notation explained for swap points in Section 6.1.1).

Such an operation can be used, for example, to hedge from today a short position in EUR/USD (@ $S = 1.1777$) that is expected to exist between today + 6 months and today +12 months: by buying today a forward 6m-forward 12m EUR/USD @ S–51.25, that is $1.1777 - 0.005125 = 1.172575$.

5.1.4   The NDF market

Non-deliverable forward (NDF) operations are the alternative to forward forex for currencies of emerging markets, that is, in the absence of a regular forward market.

Principle of an NDF Operation

As in the forward market, a forward rate is computed with respect to the current currency spot and money market rates. But unlike in a forward operation, at maturity T there is no exchange in principal (nominal) amount, only the payment of a cash flow corresponding to the differential between the NDF rate and the prevailing spot rate at the NDF maturity date, for an agreed *notional* amount N. For practical reasons, the reference spot rate at maturity is a "fixing" rate, referring for example to a Reuters page:

$$NDF\ settlement = \left(1 - \frac{NDF\ rate}{fixing\ rate}\right) \times N$$

The NDF is settled by a net payment from the losing to the winning party.

Such an operation is based on the same principle of payment by difference, as in the case of FRAs on the money market interest rates (cf. Section 5.2).

Because of its reference to a notional amount, the NDF solution may seem attractive even as an alternative to the regular forward market. The drawback is not negligible, however, that is, the result of the operation being strictly linked to the fixing reference. In mature, liquid forex markets, intraday currency moves are too crucial to restrict a forward outcome to a fixing. But in the case of emerging markets, in absence of a regular forward market, an NDF solution is of course better than nothing.

Example of Operation

A US exporter will receive TWD (Taiwan dollars) 70 million in 1 year. Market data are, in mid:

- spot USD/TWD = 34 (rounded);
- NDF rate = 35.

One year later:

- if (fixing) spot = 35.30, thanks to his NDF, the exporter must receive

$$TWD\ 70\,000\,000/35\ TWD\ per\ USD = USD\ 2\,000\,000$$

instead of *70 000 000 / 35.30 = 1 983 002.83* on the prevailing spot market.

Actually, the exporter makes a spot exchange @ about 35.30 (depending at what time on the maturity day) and the bank (counterparty in NDF) pays him the balance, that is,

$$2\,000\,000 - 1\,983\,002.83 = USD\ 16\,997.17$$

If (fixing) spot = 34.70, the exporter makes a spot exchange @ 34.70:

$$TWD\ 70\,000\,000/34.70\ TWD\ per\ USD = USD\ 2\,017\,291.07$$

but because of his NDF, he must pay the balance to the bank, that is,

$$2\,017\,291.07 - 2\,000\,000 = USD\ 17\,291.07$$

If (fixing) spot = 35.00 (by chance), there is no cash flow paid/received.

5.2   FRAs

A forward rate agreement (FRA) is a forward short-term interest contract, applied on interbank rates (LIBOR or EURIBOR rates). The FRA is the equivalent on the -ibor rates of a forex forward contract but settled as an NDF.

5.2.1 Principle and calculation

Suppose today, Jan 11th, we schedule to borrow some amount of EUR @ 3M EURIBOR in 5 months. Today, the 3M EURIBOR spot is known. The aim of the FRA is to fix today the 3M EURIBOR to be applied 5 months later, hence to hedge EURIBOR fluctuations during the next 5 months (alternatively, to speculate on further evolution of the -ibor rate). The initial 5-month period is called the *intermediate period*, corresponding to the risk occurrence period, and the 3-month period of borrowing is called the *covered period*. The sum of both intermediate and covered periods is the *total period*. The FRA is noted *5X8* in this example, that is:

"intermediate period × total period"

For hedging or speculating on a borrowing rate, one talks about *buying* an FRA, and conversely, *selling* an FRA with respect to a forward deposit.

The FRA valuation is straightforward, using the forward rate calculation presented in Chapter 1, Section 1.4, calling r_{FRA} the forward rate. Based on the previous initial example, for a nominal amount of €1, denoting:

- t_{interm} and r_{interm} the intermediate period time and spot -ibor rate respectively;
- t_{tot} and r_{tot} the total period time and spot -ibor rate respectively;
- t_{FRA} and r_{FRA} the covered period time and FRA -ibor rate respectively,

we get the result shown in Figure 5.8.

$$[€1 \times (1 + t_{interm}r_{interm})](1 + t_{FRA}r_{FRA}) = €1 \times (1 + t_{tot}r_{tot})$$

For the bank counterparty, granting the FRA, the rationale is as follows: to lend forward, here on 3 months after 5 months:

- the bank borrows in the interbank market on the $3 + 5 = 8$ months total period $= t_{tot}$, @ r_{tot};
- the bank lends to its client from the fifth to the eighth month $= t_{FRA}$, as FRA period, @ r_{FRA};
- hence, the bank has to lend in the interbank market between the first and the fifth month $=$ tinterm, @ r_{interm};
- the involved nominal amounts being so that:
  - the proceeds of the lending @ must coincide with the principal of the credit to its counterparty;
  - and the credit reimbursement by its counterparty must coincide with the bank's reimbursement of its borrowing at the end of the total period.

The resulting fair (theoretical) FRA rate is thus:

$$r_{FRA} = \frac{r_{tot}t_{tot} - r_{interm}t_{interm}}{t_{FRA}(1 + r_{interm}t_{interm})}$$

Figure 5.8   Rates involved in a FRA

for time periods of maximum 1 year. The FRA market is actually working on a total period of maximum 2 years, sub-divided into any combination of sub-periods, but the majority of traded volume is involving shorter periods of some months. Of course, in case of any period exceeding 1 year, adequate compounding must be performed, in a similar way as shown in Section 1.1 above for the currency forwards.

The FRA settlement is done by payment difference – 2 business days before the end of the intermediate period:

- the current spot 3M -ibor rate is determined;
- the difference between the agreed FRA rate and this current spot 3M -ibor rate is paid by the losing party to the winning one, in present value (discounted at the current spot 3M –ibor rate).

5.2.2   Example of application

Let us price (in mid) on Nov 4, 2003 a FRA for EUR 100 million to be borrowed @ 6M EURIBOR on next Feb 4 (EURIBOR of Feb 2) 2004. EURIBOR rates are quoted on ACT/360 basis. Market data are:

- $t_{interm} = 92$ days (11/04/03 to 02/04/04), spot $r_{interm} = 2.163\%$;
- $t_{total} = 274$ days (11/04/03 to 08/04/04), spot $r_{tot} = 2.320\%$;
- $t_{FRA} = 178$ days (02/04 to 08/04/04).

The formula gives

$$r_{FRA} = \frac{0.0232 \times \dfrac{274}{360} - 0.02163 \times \dfrac{92}{360}}{\dfrac{178}{360}\left(1 + 0.02163 \times \dfrac{92}{360}\right)} = 0.024398 = 2.440\%$$

The spot 3M EURIBOR on 08/02/04 value 08/04 was actually 2.115%. In this case, supposing the market FRA rate was equal to its fair value, the forward borrower must receive the balance between 2.440% and 2.115%, discounted at 2.115% on €100M, that is

$$FV = €100M \times (0.0244 - 0.02115) = €325\,000$$

$$PV = €325\,000/(1 + 0.02115 \times 178/360) = €321\,636.49$$

5.3   OTHER FORWARD CONTRACTS

5.3.1   Forward contracts on equities

Supposing the stock does not pay any dividend, at least during the forward period, which will considered here as < 1 year, what is almost always the case in the real market. The forward price F is the future value FV of Eq. 1.7 (cf. Chapter 1, Section 1.3), in continuous or discrete time[3], where PV is the spot price S of the stock:

$$FV = PVe^{z_t t} \text{ or } FV = PV(1 + z_t t)$$

---

[3] We have omitted the subscript "c" for continuous or "d" for discrete, since the formulae are unambiguous about this feature.

Positing T the maturity date of F, and $\tau =$ time from current time t to T, we get

$$F = Se^{z_t \tau} \text{ or } F = S(1 + z_t \tau) \tag{5.2}$$

(Note that, for forward periods < 1 year, the market rates – in practice, -ibor rates – are natural zeroes.)

So that, for example, the theoretical mid-price for selling short Citigroup on September 1, 2010, maturity December 1, that is, after 91 days (ACT/360), knowing

- Citigroup on Sep 1: $S = \$3.80$;
- 3M LIBOR on Sep 1: $z = 0.396\%$

using the discrete calculation as market practice, is

$$F = 3.80(1 + 0.00396 \times 91/360) = \$3.804$$

If the stocks pays at t' a dividend d, we must consider it would have been reinvested in the stock from t' to T, that is, on τ', so that Eq. 5.2 becomes

$$F = Se^{z_T \tau} - de^{z_{t'} \tau'} \text{ or } F = S(1 + z_T \tau) - d(1 + z_{t'} \tau')$$

Coming back to the example, suppose (which was not the case, actually) Citigroup was distributing a dividend of \$0.30 on October 1. With the 1M LIBOR on September 1 at 0.258% the forward would become

$$F = 3.80(1 + 0.00396 \times 91/360) - 0.30(1 + 0.00258 \times 30/360) = \$3.504$$

Finally, it can be useful to reconsider forwards on stocks paying a dividend, as this dividend was viewed like a dividend yield $d\%$ of S, applicable on the whole period τ. Then the forward formula looks like a forward on a currency, where the reference rate becomes the dividend yield d and the counter-value rate becomes the -ibor market rate r:

$$F = Se^{(r-d)\tau} \text{ or } F = S\frac{1 + r\tau}{1 + d\tau} \tag{5.3}$$

5.3.2   Forward contracts on bonds

Forward contracts on bonds are based on the same PV $\Leftrightarrow$ FV relationships as used in the previous sub-section. Here, too, let us consider forward contracts of maturity < 1 year, which is almost always the case in the real market. In particular, Eq. 5.3 is applicable, by replacing the dividend yield d by the bond yield y (as defined in Chapter 3, Section 3.2.1). Positing B the spot price of a bond, T the maturity date of F, $\tau =$ time from current time t to T, and r the money market rate corresponding to τ, we have

$$F = Be^{(r-y)} \text{ or } F = B\frac{1 + r}{1 + y}$$

Example. On 12/10/01, the 5-year US T-Bond was quoting 96.15625% of par, with a yield of 4.46%. On the same day, the 6M LIBOR was 1.99%. The 6-month (computed here as 0.5 year) forward price of this bond is thus

$$F = 96.15625\frac{1 + 0.0199 \times 0.5}{1 + 0.0446 \times 0.5} = 94.9946$$

at t_0:

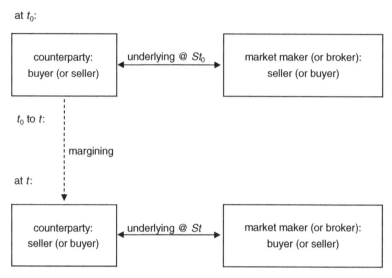

Figure 5.9   Diagram of a CFD contract

5.4   CONTRACTS FOR DIFFERENCE (CFD)

Contracts for difference (CFDs) are very popular tools for taking advantage of price moves, as an alternative to above forward contracts or to futures (cf. Chapter 7). These OTC instruments are available on a broad range of underlyings, such as stocks, stock indexes, bonds, currencies or commodities. Their common principle can be depicted as shown in Figure 5.9.

The counterparty can contract as the buyer or the seller of the CFD. There is no maturity on such a contract, even for the (short) seller. This is probably the most prominent feature of CFDs, with respect to traditional forwards and futures. CFDs contracts involve a kind of future margining system (cf. Chapter 7, Section 7.1), settled on a daily basis, that is:

- the counterparty must open an account with an initial margin, called a deposit;
- the size of the deposit depends on the underlying, that is, its volatility and liquidity, plus a commission for the market maker (or broker);
- the daily profit or loss due to the underlying daily price change is charged on the margin account;
- the counterparty must maintain a minimum margin level.

The deposit is also affected on a daily basis by the financing of the opened position. In case the counterparty is long the CFD, he is charged @ -ibor + a margin. If he is short the CFD, he will receive -ibor − a margin.

For CFDs on stocks, in case of a dividend payment, the amount of this dividend will be paid on the CFD buyer's deposit, and deducted from the deposit of the CFD seller.

To close his position, the counterparty enters a CFD in the opposite direction, and the netting of these two contracts leads to a net profit or loss.

Example. Let us consider a CFD buyer on 1000 L'Oreal stocks on 29/04/09, traded @ €52.0207. The initial deposit required by the market maker is of 3% (including his commission). At the end of the day, the market closes at 52.50–55. The CFD buyer is closing his position on the next day (30/04), when the stock is quoted 54.04–09.

The outcome of the operation is:

- on 29/04:
  - buy 1000 L'OREAL @ 52.07:   € 52 070.00
  - initial deposit: 3%:   1 562.10
- night of 29 to 30/04:
  - overnight financing on close price of 52.55,
  - 1 day on 3M EURIBOR basis @ 1.372%
  - + margin of 0.5% @ 1.872% (1000 × 52.55 × 0.01872/365 =)   2.70

                                                                      Total: 53 634.80

- on 30/04, given the rise of the stock, the buyer closes his position, @ 54.04–09:
  - sell 1000 L'Oreal @ 54.04:   54 040.00

Hence a net result of 54 040 − 53 634,80 = €405.20. That is, a return on the actually deposited amount of 1 564.80 (= 1 562.10 + 2.70) amounting to 405.20/1564.80 = 25.9%.

FURTHER READING

Peter TEMPLE, *CFDs Made Simple – A Straightforward Guide to Contracts for Difference*, Harriman House, 2009, 155 p.

6

Swaps

6.1 DEFINITIONS AND FIRST EXAMPLES

Contractually speaking, a swap contract is an agreement between two parties to exchange a series of cash flows.[1] Technically speaking, a swap is a set of successive forward transactions, involving either a fixed interest rate and a floating (or "variable") rate, or two different floating rates, or, in the case of a CRS only, two different fixed rates. Fixed rates involved in swaps are called *swap rates*. Floating rates are based on the -ibor rates, prevailing two banking days before the beginning of the period they are applied to. Both the types of cash flows, being based on a fixed or on a floating rate, are paid at their respective maturity, and netted in case of common maturity dates.

Exchanged cash flows can be assets cash flows originating from assets payments, in this case one talk about *asset swaps*, or cash flows originating from debts interest payments, hence the naming of *liability swaps*.

If the whole set of exchanged cash flows involves a common single currency, the swap is called an *interest rate swap* (IRS). If the exchange of cash flows involves two currencies, one talks of *currency rate swap* (CRS) or *cross currency rate swap* (CCRS).[2]

A swap is an *unconditional* product: the exchange of cash flows cannot depend from any kind of condition. *A contrario*, credit default swaps and similar derivatives on a default risk are not swaps, strictly speaking, because there are conditional. We will look at these in Chapter 13.

The market trades swaps on maturities from 2 to 30 years,[3] the peak of traded volumes being between 5 and 10 years. If one excludes some attempts to trade swaps on a derivative exchange (but up to now, the traded volumes are too tiny), the swap market is an OTC or interbank market, at least one of the counterparts being a bank. The success of the swap market is significantly due to the security resulting from the universally adopted standard contract documentation from the International Swaps and Derivatives Association (ISDA).

6.1.1 A first example of an IRS, on a debt (data from February 2002)

Company *A* has issued a $100 million 5-year bond, at a fixed rate (because bond investors prefer a fixed coupon) of 5% s.a. (basis: 30/360). But, for whatever reason, *A* would prefer being indebted at a floating (= variable) rate: the company may convert its fixed rate debt into a 5-year floating rate, namely, the 6-month $ LIBOR rate by entering into an IRS with the swap desk of a bank (see Figure 6.1).

---

[1] Swap contracts should be distinguished from *forex* swaps (see Chapter 5, Section 5.1.2).
[2] Some practitioners use CIRS (i.e., a "C" before "IRS"): this acronym should be banned, as in a vanilla CRS the exchanges are not limited to interest cash flows (cf. Section 6.1.2).
[3] The reason for starting from 2 years will become apparent later.

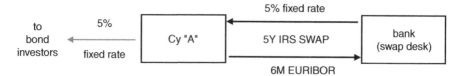

Figure 6.1   IRS between a company and a bank

The swap is made of the exchange of cash flows showed in bold on the right side of the figure. In a usual IRS, exchanged cash flows are always interest payments (above arrows are figuring interest payments). These interest payments refer to a principal amount of the swap, called the notional.

In this swap, company *A* receives the fixed rate cash flows and pays the floating rate cash flows. We can say that *A* enters into a *receiver swap* (we will see later that the fixed rate is the crucial rate in a swap). Conversely, the bank counterpart, which pays the fixed rate cash flows against receiving floating rate cash flows, is said to be entering into a *payer swap*.

The series of fixed rate payments is called the *fixed leg* of the swap, the other being the *floating leg*. An IRS can also be made of two floating legs, for example exchanging 1-year LIBOR payments against 3-months LIBOR payments, during *n* year. Such floating/floating swaps are called *basis swaps*.

The series of cash flows involved in our preliminary example are shown in Table 6.1.

Note that, in this table, the "− 6M LIBOR" are in italics, except the first one: this is the central point of swap pricing. Indeed, in a vanilla swap, floating rates interest cash flows are paid at the expiry dates, so that only the first LIBOR is known at swap inception but not the following ones (noted in italics).

Note also that in such a swap, the only cash flows exchanged are interest cash flows (the principal amount is not involved at all), hence the name *interest* rate swap.

Table 6.1   Series of cash flows

| | | Company *A* (receives fixed rate: "+", pays floating rate: "−") | | |
| | | Swap | | |
Time	Position before swap	*Floating leg*	*Fixed leg*	Position after swap
At inception	+100 000 000			+100 000 000
+6 months	−2 500 000	−6M LIBOR	+2 500 000	−6M LIBOR
+12 months	−2 500 000	*−6M LIBOR*	+2 500 000	*−6M LIBOR*
+18 months	−2 500 000	*−6M LIBOR*	+2 500 000	*−6M LIBOR*
+24 months	−2 500 000	*−6M LIBOR*	+2 500 000	*−6M LIBOR*
+30 months	−2 500 000	*−6M LIBOR*	+2 500 000	*−6M LIBOR*
+36 months	−2 500 000	*−6M LIBOR*	+2 500 000	*−6M LIBOR*
+42 months	−2 500 000	*−6M LIBOR*	+2 500 000	*−6M LIBOR*
+48 months	−2 500 000	*−6M LIBOR*	+2 500 000	*−6M LIBOR*
+54 months	−2 500 000	*−6M LIBOR*	+2 500 000	*−6M LIBOR*
+60 months	−2 500 000	*−6M LIBOR*	+2 500 000	*−6M LIBOR*
	−100 000 000			−100 000 000

6.1.2   An example of CRS liability swap (data from February 2002)

A supranational institution, here called SNL, has issued a 6-year bond of Norwegian krone (NOK) 750 million @ $6\frac{1}{2}\%$ p.a. (ACT/ACT), immediately swapped into its own EUR currency, that is, EUR 85 227 272.73, at the current EUR/NOK spot rate of 8.8000 (the rationale of this swapped issue will appear later). The whole operation involves the exchanges shown in Figures 6.2–6.4.

The following points should be noted:

1. Unlike IRSs, CRSs involve both an exchange of interest cash flows and an exchange of cash flows in the notional principal. Indeed, the whole series of (debt or asset) cash flows has here to be "converted" into the other currency, to avoid currency risk.
2. In a CRS, the initial spot exchange rate (EUR/NOK @ 8.8000) is applied to the whole set of transactions, up to the end of the operation. The reason is straightforward: the company entering into such a swap is precisely aiming to cancel out its exchange risk caused by a borrowing in a foreign currency. Actually, the currency risk is supported by the swap desk of the bank counterpart: as a market maker, it is his job to manage such a risk.
3. Since cash flows are exchanged in two different currencies, this CRS can be a fixed/fixed rates swap, where fixed interests payments in currency X are exchanged against fixed interest payments in currency Y, as in the vast majority of such transactions. Alternatively, this swap could also have been built on an exchange of a fixed NOK rate against a series of EURIBOR rates.
4. In this example, the EUR rate of 5%, paid by SNL, is actually 20bp lower than the prevailing 6-year market rate of 5.20% in EUR. Actually, SNL has got the opportunity to tap investors satisfied with a 6-year NOK return of 20bp lower than the NOK swap rate, and this 20bp saving has been "transferred" to the EUR thanks to the swap. This point will be developed later on (cf. Section 6.6), but at least it is the rationale for SNL to borrow in a currency other than its own.

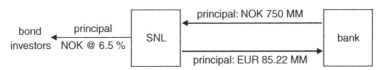

Figure 6.2   At inception (Feb 2002): forex spot operation

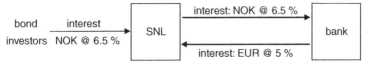

Figure 6.3   Each year, from Feb 2002 to Feb 2008: exchange of interests (fixed rates)

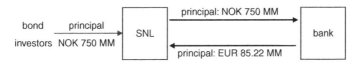

Figure 6.4   At maturity (Feb 2008): exchange of the principals:

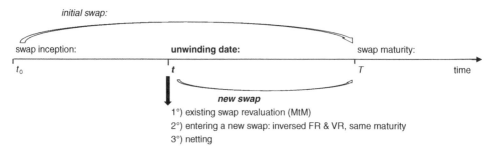

initial swap:

swap inception: **unwinding date:**   swap maturity:

t_0 t T time

new swap
1°) existing swap revaluation (MtM)
2°) entering a new swap: inversed FR & VR, same maturity
3°) netting

Figure 6.5   Diagram of an unwinding swap operation

In IRSs as well as CRSs, a swap where all cash flows are based on a unique and constant notional amount, and in absence of any other particularities (cf. Section 6.7), is called a (plain) vanilla swap. They of course form the majority of swaps traded in the market.

6.1.3   Unwinding a swap

As for any forward operation in general, if a party wants to unwind his swap before maturity, he will have to enter into a second swap, ending at the same initial maturity date but inversed (paid cash flows become received cash flows, and conversely). Since at this date the swap market has changed, the value of the new swap will differ from the MtM (cf. Section 6.4) of the initial swap. The settlement of such unwinding will be materialized by the payment of the new MtM value by the "losing" party to the other party (see Figure 6.5).

6.2   PRIOR TO AN IRS SWAP PRICING METHOD

A vanilla fixed/floating IRS can be viewed as the combination of buying a par bond and financing it at an interbank "-ibor" rate. This will be illustrated on *yearly* coupons and -ibor payments, for the sake of convenience. For example, on the $ market, consider the purchase of a 5-year bullet bond at par, offering a fixed coupon of $s\%$ p.a., for a notional amount of $100. The involved cash flows are shown in Figure 6.6. Up arrows denote received cash flows, while down arrows denote paid cash flows.

Let this investment be financed at the same 5 years @ 12-month LIBOR (see Figure 6.7).

The solid arrows denote known cash flows, while the dotted arrows are unknown at inception of the operation. Indeed, among the series of 12-month LIBOR rates, only the first one is

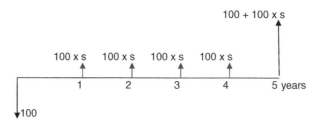

100 + 100 x s

100 x s   100 x s   100 x s   100 x s

1   2   3   4   5 years

100

Figure 6.6   Cash flows for a 5-year bullet bond at par, offering a fixed coupon of $s\%$ p.a., for a notional amount of $100

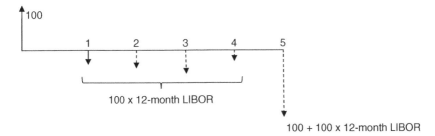

Figure 6.7   Investment financed at 5 years @ 12-month LIBOR

determined, actually 2 days in advance. The following ones will be determined later on, 2 days before their respective occurrence.

By combining both operations, we see that the principal invested and financed at inception, then recovered and reimbursed after 5 years, cancels out, so that the combination becomes the one shown in Figure 6.8, which corresponds exactly to the set of cash flows of an IRS, as presented above. So that:

---

the fixed rate of an IRS swap is equivalent to the coupon on a par bond.

Knowing the formula for the price $B = 100$ of a par bullet bond (cf. Eq. 3.1), where B is replaced here by 100, a first key relationship, for a swap on T years, is

$$100 = \sum \frac{a_t}{(1 + s_t)^t} \text{ or } = \sum a_t \times e^{-s_t t} \tag{6.1}$$

(left side: in discrete compounding – right side: in continuous compounding), where t varies from $t = 1$ to $t = T$ years, and the cash flows a_t are here $100 \times s_T$, and $100 + 100 \times s_T$ for the last a_T; s_t denotes the fixed swap zero-coupon rate for maturity or "tenor" t. In these formulae, rates are still on an annual basis. If semi-annual rates are to be used, s_t must be divided by 2, and t varies from 0.5 to T by half years. In the rest of this section, formulae will be further established on an annual basis. For application purposes, the /2 rule will be used when needed (mainly for $ fixed rates).

Also, the case of a swap with a floating leg based on < 12 month -ibor rates will be examined later.

The expression $1/(1 + s_t)^t$ or $e^{-s_t t}$ of Eq. 6.1 being the discount factors D_t, Eq. 1.5 and Eq. 1.8 become here, in discrete and continuous time:

$$D_t = \frac{1}{(1 + s_t)^t} \text{ or } = \frac{1}{1 + s_t t} \tag{6.1bis}$$

$$D_t = e^{-z_{ct} t}$$

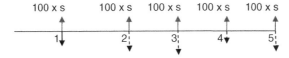

Figure 6.8   The result of combining both operations

Equation 6.1 can thus be rewritten:

$$100 = \sum D_t \times a_t \qquad (6.2)$$

Given the values of a_t in function of s_T, Eq. 6.2 can be solved in s_T, giving the first of a series of key relationships:

- s_T in function of $\{D_t\}$

  cash-flows a_1 up to $a_{T-1} = 100 \times s_T$
  last cash-flow $a_T = 100 + 100 \times s_T$
  $\rightarrow$ discounting to get the initial par value of 100:

$$100 = D_1 \times 100 \times s_T + \ldots + D_T \times 100 \times s_T + D_T \times 100$$

and dividing by 100,

$$1 = D_1 \times s_T + \ldots + D_T \times s_T + D_T$$

$$\rightarrow 1 - D_T = \sum D_t \times s_T$$

that is,

$$s_T = \frac{1 - D_T}{\sum D_t} \qquad (6.3)$$

This relationship appears to be opposite to the more useful Eq. 6.1bis, giving D_t in function of s_t.

Example.[4]   Consider the following market data (mid-market rates rounded on base of a zero-coupon Euro yield curve dated February 2001):

Year	Zero-coupon rate (%)	Discount factor
0		
0.5	4.7000	0.9770
1	4.6000	0.9560
1.5	4.6768	0.9337
2	4.7536	0.9113
2.5	4.7792	0.8900
3	4.8048	0.8687
3.5	4.8581	0.8471
4	4.9113	0.8255
4.5	4.9656	0.8042
5	5.0198	0.7828

and compute the 4-year *annual* swap rate:

$$\text{Eq. 6.3} \rightarrow s_{4y} = (1 - 0.8255)/(0.9560 + 0.9113 + 0.8687 + 0.8255) = 4.899\%$$

---

[4] In these calculations as well as throughout this chapter (unless specified otherwise) 6-month periods have been counted as 0.5 year (no particular day counting applied).

Note that this 4-year swap rate is slightly lower than the corresponding 4-year zero-coupon rate: a swap rate is a "coupon rate". For a 4-year semi-annual swap rate, using the $/2$ rule, the calculation becomes:

$$s_{4s.a} = (1 - 0.8255)/(0.9770/2 + 0.9560/2 + 0.9337/2 + 0.9113/2 + 0.8899/2$$
$$+ 0.8687/2 + 0.8471/2 + 0.8255/2) = 4.841\%$$

(given the decreasing set of discount factors, the result is lower than the s_{4y}).

- s_T *in function of* {forward rates}:

Equation 1.16 (Chapter 1) expresses the discount factors as a function of the forwards. To simplify the notations, writing f_t for $f_{t-1,t}$, that is, the forward rate ending in t, the formula becomes:

$$D_t = 1/(1 + f_1)(1 + f_2)\ldots(1 + f_t)$$

Applied to 1 and 2 periods respectively, it gives:

$$f_1 = (D_0/D_1) - 1 = (1/D_1) - 1 \text{ (because } D_0 = 1)$$

and

$$f_2 = (D_1/D_2) - 1$$

or

$$f_1 D_1 = 1 - D_1 \quad \text{and} \quad f_2 D_2 = D_1 - D_2$$
$$\rightarrow \sum f_t D_t \text{ on 2 periods} = f_1 D_1 + f_2 D_2 = 1 - D_1 + D_1 - D_2 = 1 - D_2$$

Generalizing on T periods,

$$\sum f_t D_t = 1 - D_T$$

Hence, from Eq. 6.3,

$$s_T = \frac{\sum_{t=1}^{t=T} f_{t-1,t} D_t}{\sum_{t=1}^{t=T} D_t} \tag{6.4}$$

This key relationship expresses that:

---

the swap rate is a weighted arithmetic average of the corresponding set of forward rates, the weights being the set of discount factors. In other words, *a swap may be viewed as a series of forward transactions.*

- {z_t} *in function of* {forward rates}:

Because of the discount factor relationship with forward rates (cf. again Eq. 1.16), we have:

$$(1 + z_T)^T = 1/D_T = \Pi(1 + f_t)$$

Π representing the product of the $(1 + f_t)$ terms. That is,

$$1 + z_T = \sqrt[T]{\Pi(1 + f_t)} \tag{6.5}$$

where $\sqrt[T]{\Pi}(.)$ is known as a geometric average.[5] This relationship says that one plus a zero-coupon rate is the geometric average of the series of one plus the corresponding forward rates. This result becomes more appealing if translated into continuous compounding: recalling (cf. Eq. 1.6bis) that

$$z_{cT} = \ln(1 + z_{dT})$$

with subscript "c" denoting continuous rates and "d" for discrete rates, so that

$$f_{cT} = \ln(1 + f_{dT})$$

Equation 6.5 becomes

$$z_{cT} = \frac{\sum f_{ct}}{T} \tag{6.5bis}$$

Σf_{ct} denoting the sum of T terms f_c, from $t = 1$ to $t = T$, that is,

---

the continuously compounded 0-cpn rate is the arithmetic average of the corresponding continuously compounded forward rates.

In practice, the observed data are the swap rates, quoted by the market. From these swap rates, it is possible to compute the corresponding zeroes, by use of the "bootstrap" method presented in Chapter 2, Section 2.3. In the table below, the zeroes for half years have been computed as the average obtained from nearby round years. From these zeroes, discount factors and forward rates can be computed on base of the formulae of Chapter 1, Section 1.4.

Year	(Swap) fixed rates (%)	Zero-coupon rate (%)	Discount factor	6M EURIBOR Spot/fwd (%)
0				
0.5		4.7000	0.9770	4.7000 ← spot
1	4.600 (*)	4.6000	0.9560	4.3969 ← fwd
1.5		4.6768	0.9337	4.7734 ← fwd
2	4.750	4.7536	0.9113	4.9239 ← fwd
2.5		4.7792	0.8900	4.8237 ← fwd
3	4.800	4.8048	0.8687	4.8733 ← fwd
3.5		4.8581	0.8471	5.1133 ← fwd
4	4.900	4.9113	0.8255	5.2164 ← fwd
4.5		4.9656	0.8042	5.3300 ← fwd
5	5.000	5.0198	0.7828	5.4350 ← fwd

*The so-called 1-year swap rate is actually the 12M -ibor.

---

[5] Recall that an arithmetic average is a sum divided by the number n of its components, while a geometric average is the nth root of the product of its n components.

Example of These Calculations: About the 2-Year Line

- From $s_2 = 4.75\%$, the corresponding z_2 comes from applying the bootstrap:

$$100 = 4.75/1.046 + 104.75/(1 + z_2)^2 \rightarrow z_2 = 4.7536\%.$$

- $D_2 = 1/(1 + 0.047536)^2 \rightarrow D_2 = 0.9113.$
- 6M after 1.5y forward EURIBOR: $1.047536^2 = 1.046768^{1.5} \times (1 + f \times 0.5) \rightarrow f = 4.9239\%.$

NB: for the intermediate periods (on 0.5 years), we have computed the forwards as per the zeroes, by averaging forwards of nearby round years.

Notice that, for a normal (= upward slope, cf. Chapter 2, Section 2.1) yield curve, forward rates are above zeroes, that are above swap rates. This order is inverted in the case of a downward yield curve.

6.3 PRICING OF AN IRS SWAP

A swap being an exchange of future cash flows, at inception, the deal must be equilibrated for both counterparts, in mid rates (we will clarify further how the swap market maker will take his profit). To translate this practically, using mid rates, the present value of the fixed rate cash flows must equal the present value of the floating rates cash flows, so that the total net present value *NPV* is 0.[6]

For a vanilla swap, the initial pricing calculation looks like a tautology. Indeed, the question is: for which fixed rate is the present value of fixed rate cash flows equivalent to the present value of floating rates cash flows? Since present value calculations are based on discount factors, themselves based on a yield curve composed of market swap rates, the answer is obvious: for a fixed rate equal to the swap rate of same maturity as for the swap.

However, if for the fixed rate cash flows the calculation is straightforward, it is not the case for the floating rates cash flows. Indeed, only the first floating rate is known at the inception of the swap, so how can we determine the floating rates cash flows to be discounted? To solve this, we must use the same rule as for any calculation involving market rates to be determined in the future that are unknown today: replace a presently unknown rate by its forward calculation based on the current yield curve. The reason for using the forward rates will become clear in Chapter 8, Section 8.9, with respect to the probability distribution of possible future spot prices.

Hence, at inception time t_0, for a swap having its cash flows exchanged on $t_1, t_2, \ldots, T$, one uses the current -ibor maturing at t_1, and the unknown -bor rates maturing at $t_2, \ldots, T$ are in the meantime replaced by the forward -ibors maturing in $t_2, \ldots, T$.

Example. Based on earlier set of swap rates (the available market data) and corresponding zeroes, forward and discount factors, the pricing of a 5-year IRS on EUR 100 million, with a floating leg based on the 6-month EURIBOR is shown in Figure 6.9.

In this figure, the first five columns are the ones used in the previous example. The swap calculation is made up of the four last columns:

- interest cash flows – FR: if we use the current 5-year swap rate as the fixed rate, it makes €5 million on each of the 5 years;

---

[6] That is, the present value of the cash flows paid by one counterparty must equal the one paid by the other counterparty.

year	cpn y.c. (%)	0-cpn rates (%)	discount factors	6M EURIBOR (%)	interest cash flows in EUR millions		PV of interest c.f. in EUR millions	
					FR	VR	FR	VR
0								
0.5	4.7	4.7	0.977	4.7		2.35		2.296
1	4.6	4.6	0.956	4.3969	5	2.1985	4.78	2.102
1.5	4.675	4.6768	0.9337	4.7734		2.3867		2.228
2	4.75	4.7536	0.9113	4.9239	5	2.462	4.557	2.244
2.5	4.775	4.7792	0.89	4.8237		2.4119		2.147
3	4.8	4.8048	0.8687	4.8733	5	2.4367	4.344	2.117
3.5	4.85	4.8581	0.8471	5.1133		2.5567		2.166
4	4.9	4.9113	0.8255	5.2164	5	2.6082	4.128	2.153
4.5	4.95	4.9656	0.8042	5.33		2.665		2.143
5	5	5.0198	0.7828	5.435	5	2.7175	3.914	2.127
							21.723	21.723

Figure 6.9   5-year IRS on EUR 100 million, with a 6-month EURIBOR floating leg
FR = fixed rate; VR = variable rate

- interest cash flows – VR: every 6-month period, compute €100 million × 6-month EURIBOR × $\frac{1}{2}$. Note that the right use of day count convention will be considered later;
- present value – FR flows: compute interest flows FR × corresponding discount factor;
- present value – VR flows: compute interest flows VR × corresponding discount factor.

Then, summing the last two columns results in the same value: the swap is fairly priced. Obviously, any other choice for the fixed rate would lead to a difference between the Σ PV of fixed rate cash flows and the Σ PV of floating rates cash flows, making $\Sigma NPV_{swap} \neq 0$.

The calculation methodology remains the same, even if the swap presents particular features such as:

- a nominal amount that is not the same at each step of the exchange;
- a forward swap: the exchanges of cash-flows are postponed.

Unsurprisingly, in such cases, the current market swap rate – quoted for vanilla swaps – will not convene to equalize both sums of present values. It must be adapted to a value that leads to $\Sigma NPV_{swap} = 0$.

Example.   Let us consider a forward IRS on a non-constant notional amount,[7] namely a 5-year swap against 6-month EURIBOR, starting 1 year forward from its contract date, with a notional amount that is decreasing in function of time, from €100 million to 20 million (called *amortizing* swap). The same market data are used as for the previous example. If we keep the same 5% fixed rate as before, the calculation table becomes that illustrated in Figure 6.10, showing the swap is unbalanced. Replacing the 5% fixed rate by x and solving for x (by successive approximations) so that the total of the present value of FR cash flows is equal to the total of the present value of VR cash flows, we obtain 4.01726% (see Figure 6.11).

---

[7] In a swap contract, the only restriction is that the notional amount – fixed or variable – be fully unconditionally determined at inception. If it was not the case, the operation would involve an option component.

year	national in EUR millions	cpn y.c. (%)	0-cpn rates (%)	discount factors	6M EURIBOR (%)	interest cash flows in EUR millions FR	VR	PV of interest c.f. in EUR millions FR	VR
0									
0.5	0	4.7	4.7	0.977	4.7		0		0
1	100	4.6	4.6	0.956	4.3969	5	2.1985	4.78	2.102
1.5	80	4.675	4.6768	0.9337	4.7734		1.9094		1.783
2	80	4.75	4.7536	0.9113	4.9239	4	1.9696	3.645	1.795
2.5	60	4.775	4.7792	0.89	4.8237		1.4471		1.288
3	60	4.8	4.8048	0.8687	4.8733	3	1.462	2.606	1.27
3.5	40	4.85	4.8581	0.8471	5.1133		1.0227		0.866
4	40	4.9	4.9113	0.8255	5.2164	2	1.0433	1.651	0.861
4.5	20	4.95	4.9656	0.8042	5.33		0.533		0.429
5	20	5	5.0198	0.7828	5.435	1	0.5435	0.783	0.425
					fixed rate: 5 %			13.465	10.819

Figure 6.10   An unbalanced swap

Back to the forward swap feature, besides the above swap calculation, we can express the relationship between the fixed rate s and corresponding discount factors D_t as follows, for a forward swap @ s_τ, for a constant notional amount, departing from year t and maturing in T years, with $T - t = \tau$:

- Compounding relationship between t, τ and T:

$$s_T \sum_{i=1}^{T} D_i = s_t \sum_{i=1}^{t} D_i + s_\tau \sum_{i=t+1}^{T} D_i$$

year	national in EUR millions	cpn y.c. (%)	0-cpn rates (%)	discount factors	6M EURIBOR (%)	interest cash flows in EUR millions FR	VR	PV of interest c.f. in EUR millions FR	VR
0									
0.5	0	4.7	4.7	0.977	4.7		0		0
1	100	4.6	4.6	0.956	4.3969	**4.0173**	2.1985	**3.841**	2.102
1.5	80	4.675	4.6768	0.9337	4.7734		1.9094		1.783
2	80	4.75	4.7536	0.9113	4.9239	**3.2138**	1.9696	**2.929**	1.795
2.5	60	4.775	4.7792	0.89	4.8237		1.4471		1.288
3	60	4.8	4.8048	0.8687	4.8733	**2.4104**	1.462	**2.094**	1.27
3.5	40	4.85	4.8581	0.8471	5.1133		1.0227		0.866
4	40	4.9	4.9113	0.8255	5.2164	**1.6069**	1.0433	**1.326**	0.861
4.5	20	4.95	4.9656	0.8042	5.33		0.533		0.429
5	20	5	5.0198	0.7828	5.435	**0.8035**	0.5435	**0.629**	0.425
					fixed rate: **4.01726 %**			**10.819**	10.819

Figure 6.11   Updated calculations

- Present value relationship between s_t and D_t: applying Eq. 6.3 to s_t and s_T gives:

$$s_t \sum_{i=1}^{t} D_i = 1 - D_t$$

and

$$s_T \sum_{i=1}^{T} D_i = 1 - D_T$$

leads to

$$s = \frac{D_t - D_T}{\sum_{i=t+1}^{T} D_i}$$

6.4   (RE)VALUATION OF AN IRS SWAP

The calculation follows the same steps as for the initial pricing of the swap, but it leads to a net sum of discounted cash flow that will normally be $\neq 0$: the difference indicates what the MtM of the swap is. Indeed:

- day after day, the yield curve is changing, affecting the whole calculation scheme, including the forward -ibor rates values;
- periodically, forward -ibor rates are replaced by spot rates (passing from a 1-day forward to a "0-day forward"), since the swap contract is based on actual -ibor rates.

As a consequence, the swap will turn out to be profitable to one of the counterparties and unprofitable for the other one. Such a situation will, among other things, be reflected in the case of unwinding of the swap before its maturity (cf. Section 6.1.3).

Example.   Let us take the data of the first vanilla 5-year swap previously. To illustrate the (re)valuation process, let us suppose, as a hypothetical case, that later in the same day of inception, the yield curve has changed on the 5-year rate only, by + 10bp. The advantage of this hypothesis is that it allows us to clearly exemplify the effect of one single market rate change of 10bp on the whole calculation process. The table becomes the one shown in Figure 6.12 (NB: modified values are in bold).

We see that, consecutive to the change in 5-year swap market rate, the 5-year zero-coupon rate, the 5-year discount factor and the 6-month after 4.5 year forward rate respectively have changed. Consequently, the floating leg cash flow and its present value have changed, but also the present value of the – though unchanged – fixed rate cash flow. Finally, the sums of present values of both legs are modified accordingly.

It is worth noting that the net difference between both ΣPV is due to a change in the ΣPV of the fixed leg and to a change in the ΣPV of the floating leg, although such changes can be of different sign. In the example, the ΣPV of the fixed leg has lowered, while the ΣPV of the floating leg has increased:

- Net change in the swap value:
  - change in the ΣPV of fixed leg: from 21.723 to 21.703, that is, -0.02 million EUR;
  - change in the ΣPV of floating leg: from 21.723 to 22.136, that is, $+ 0.413$;

year	cpn y.c. (%)	0-cpn rates (%)	discount factors	6M EURIBOR (%)	interest cash flows in EUR millions		PV of interest c.f. in EUR millions	
					FR	VR	FR	VR
0								
0.5	4.7	4.7	0.977	4.7		2.35		2.296
1	4.6	4.6	0.956	4.3969	5	2.1985	4.78	2.102
1.5	4.675	4.6768	0.9337	4.7734		2.3867		2.228
2	4.75	4.7536	0.9113	4.9239	5	2.462	4.557	2.244
2.5	4.775	4.7792	0.89	4.8237		2.4119		2.147
3	4.8	4.8048	0.8687	4.8733	5	2.4367	4.344	2.117
3.5	4.85	4.8581	0.8471	5.1133		2.5567		2.166
4	4.9	4.9113	0.8255	5.2164	5	2.6082	4.128	2.153
4.5	5	**5.0212**	**0.8021**	**5.82**		**2.91**		**2.334**
5	**5.1**	**5.1311**	**0.7787**	**6.0344**	5	**3.0172**	**3.894**	**2.349**
				fixed rate: 5 %			**21.703**	**22.136**

Figure 6.12   The effect of one single market rate change of 10bp on the whole calculation process

- total change $= |-0.02| + |0.413| = 0.433$ million EUR $=$ net present value of the swap $= 22.136 - 21.703 = 0.433$.

In the case of unwinding a swap, the net change is due as settlement to the "winning" party as the "unwinding fee". In the example, the 0.433 million EUR is clearly due to the payer in the swap contract (that is, paying the fixed rate).

Such a revaluation calculus is needed:

- for periodic MtM purpose: the profit or loss on the swap is accounted accordingly;
- in the case of unwinding: the "losing" party must pay the net change to the other.

In short,

at swap inception: net present value $= 0$ (in mid rates)
updated market data
→ updated set of 0-cpns, forward rates and discount factors
    → updated floating payments
    → updated PVs of fixed and of floating legs
        → determination of the net present value ≡ swap value
later on: net present value $\neq 0$

Note: remember that all above calculations are made on mid rates.

6.5   THE SWAP (RATES) MARKET

Swaps involve both a succession of fixed rate payments and of floating rates payments: even though the former rate is known (fixed in advance) unlike the latter, which is unknown in advance, the crucial rate in a swap is the fixed rate. Indeed, on the whole lifetime of the swap contract, this fixed rate remaining unchanged, it becomes more and more obsolete or inconsistent with current market conditions. That is why the (fixed) swap market rate has become a new commodity rate, along with the pre-existent fixed rates market of government bonds. Of course, the swap (rates) market is actually the interbank fixed rates market, since it is organized among banks. Therefore, market practice has, not surprisingly, developed on the following basis:

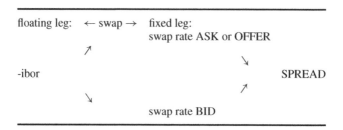

The meaning of this spread is straightforward. In a swap contracted between a bank (market maker) and a client counterparty:

- if the counterparty is paying the fixed rate, that is, is entering into a *payer* swap, it pays the higher – ask – swap rate;
- if the counterparty enters into a *receiver* swap, it receives the lower – bid – swap rate.

You will notice that there is no spread applied to the floating leg rate. A single spread is of course enough to make a market, but then, whatever the counterparty to the bank in a swap is paying or receiving the floating rate, the -ibor rate is the only floating rate used, despite the fact that, theoretically, it should be used for a (company) borrowing rate and not for a lending rate.

It is worth noting than once the bid–ask spread is added to the swap rate, the initial value of the swap is not zero any more, and the subsequent value of the swap is also affected.

As regards the day count basis, one should refer to the specific currency market conventions. For example:

- On the USD swap market:

  for the $ LIBOR floating leg: ACT/360;
  for the fixed leg: 30/360 semi-annual.

- On the EUR swap market:

  for the EURIBOR floating leg: ACT/360;
  for the fixed leg (swap rate): 30/360.

Note that the use of non-standard day count conventions will affect the swap valuation.

Finally, we can build a swap yield curve, which starts with -ibor rates on its money market portion, up to the 12-month maturity, and continues with the swap rates from 2 years[8] and beyond, the market quoting swap rates by full years. Such a yield curve reveals a homogeneous rating level, namely, a kind of "average" rating of banks active in the interbank swap market. Broadly speaking, this rating is on average the one of big OECD banks, that is, AA (S&P)

---

[8] Between 0 and 2 years, the market is quoting the FRA single forward rates (cf. Chapter 5, Section 5.2). The swap market thus relays the FRAs beyond the 2-year maturity.

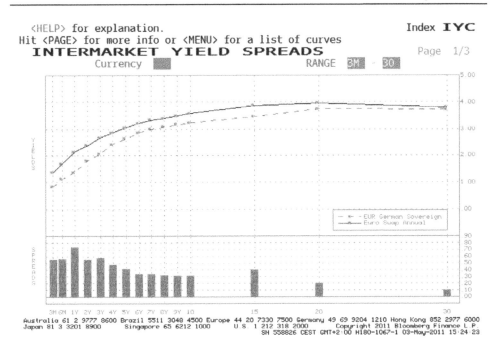

Figure 6.13   Example of the EUR market (05/03/11) curves of German government coupon rates and coupon swap rates
Source: Bloomberg

or Aa2 (Moody's). As such, the swap yield curve is based on a lower rating than the one of OECD governments. It is therefore normal that swap rates are higher than bond yields for government bonds (risk-free rates) of the same maturity, so that the swap yield curve lies above the government bonds yield curve. Example of the EUR market (05/03/11) curves of German government coupon rates and coupon swap rates respectively can be seen in Figure 6.13.

It is important to note that the spread between a swap rate and a government bond yield of same maturity (and currency) is both:

- varying with time, for multiple reasons, linked to market behavior;
- a function of liquidity. That is, of the liquidity of the government bond market, rather than the one of the swap market, by far more liquid. In other words, the spread is not equal over the maturities range.

6.6   PRICING OF A CRS SWAP

The IRS pricing methodology is still applicable, with two major differences:

1. CRS normally also involves exchange of principal notional amounts (since a currency risk is introduced, it makes sense that if one takes care to convert interest cash flows from one currency into another one, it is worth one's while to also convert the cash flows in principal).
2. The swap pricing involves two yield curves instead of one, that is, the yield curves corresponding to each of the currencies involved in the swap.

But, in this respect, the mechanics remains the same, that is:

$$\text{at inception: net PV} = 0 \qquad \text{later on: net PV} \neq 0$$

the *PV* of each leg being computed on its own yield curve. Since the sum of each of the PVs of respective cash flows will be expressed in its own currency, the condition of net PV = 0 is verified if the all series of cash flows of currency 1 is converted into currency 2 at a unique exchange rate, namely the spot rate prevailing at the swap conclusion. As a consequence, a counterparty facing a series of future revenues (in principal or in interest) in a given currency may enter into a CRS to convert them into another currency (normally, his own), in order to fully cover its currency risk. The CRS, appearing as a series of forward transactions, is actually using a single (spot) currency exchange rate and involving two series of successive interest rates (through the impact of successive discount factors). This happens to be the contrary of a set of forward operations, which will use different forward exchange rates, originated by two series of successive interest rates.

Example (Market Data as of 05/03/11)

Let us consider the case of a fund manager having invested the counter-value of EUR 100 million in a US denominated bond, and willing to swap his USD revenues (interest + principal in bullet) into EUR. He will thus enter into a 5-year CRS, EUR/USD, fixed against fixed rates; the current (mid) EUR/USD spot = 1.4835. The swap is based on a 5-year fixed USD swap rate of 2.106% and a 5-year fixed EUR swap rate of 3.057%. To simplify the presentation, the cash flows have been computed and exchanged as if they were both on an annual basis – see Figure 6.14.

The yearly interest cash flows in EUR are €100 million × 3.057%, that is, €3.057 million, and in USD, (€100 million × 1.4835 =) $ 148.35 million, × 2.106%, = $ 3.1243 million. There is nothing to add about the calculation steps, and we can verify that this CRS is indeed equilibrated (in mid rates) at inception: the counter-value of the sum of discounted EUR cash flows equals the sum of discounted USD cash flows at the contractual spot rate of 1.4835.

As mentioned before, an alternative to this CRS would consist in a series of five forward currency exchanges (but the regular forward market is actually limited to about 2 years), that

year	cpn rates (%) EUR	USD	0-cpn rates (%) EUR	USD	discount factors EUR	USD	cash flows (in 10⁶) EUR	USD	PV of cash flows EUR	USD
1	2.143	0.758	2.143	0.758	0.979	0.9925	3.057	3.1243	2.9928	3.1009
2	2.389	0.762	2.3919	0.762	0.9538	0.9849	3.057	3.1243	2.9158	3.0771
3	2.664	1.24	2.6713	1.246	0.924	0.9635	3.057	3.1243	2.8247	3.0103
4	2.883	1.681	2.8966	1.6964	0.8921	0.9349	3.057	3.1243	2.7271	2.9209
5	3.057	2.106	3.0781	2.1382	0.8593	0.8996	3.057	3.1243	2.6269	2.8106
							100	148.35	85.93	133.4557

total: 100.0173 148.3755
(c/v @ 1.4835: 100.0172)

Figure 6.14   Swap based on a 5-year fixed USD swap rate of 2.106% and a 5-year fixed EUR swap rate of 3.057%

cash flows EUR	fwd rates ——>	in USD	PV
3.057	1.4634	4.4736	4.44
3.057	1.4366	4.3917	4.3254
3.057	1.4226	4.3489	4.1902
3.057	1.4155	4.3272	4.0455
{3.057	1.4171	4.3321	3.8972
{100	1.4171	141.71	127.4823
		total:	148.3806

Figure 6.15   USD equivalent of the EUR cash flows

would be calculated by Eq. 5.1bis (Chapter 5):

$$F = S\frac{(1 + r_{c/v})^T}{(1 + r_{ref})^T}$$

Applying it to the example above, we can compute the USD equivalent of the EUR cash flows and verify (taking into account the various roundings) that the sum of their present values equals the sum of the USD cash flows of the CRS – see Figure 6.15.

In particular, a single forward exchange, at 5 years for example, can be built through a forward CRS, equivalent to the previous one, but where there is no exchange of cash flows until the fifth year, resulting in a 5-yr forward EUR/USD exchange rate of 1.4171.

Back to the beginning of the example, suppose now that the invested bond pays USD swap rate + 1%, due to its (lower) rating. If the fund manager wants to exchange the full value of his interest cash flows, he must pay USD cash flows of interests @ swap rate + 1%, that is, 2.106% + 1% = 3.106%. In exchange, he will receive EUR interests @ swap rate + something, to maintain the initial equilibrium of the swap. The precise calculation leads to a spread of 1.036% on the Euro leg, that is, almost equivalent to the $ spread of 1%, as in Figure 6.16.

					€ spread = 0.01036		0.01 = $ spread			
	cpn rates (%)		0-cpn rates (%)		discount factors		cash flows (in 10^6)		PV of cash flows	
year	EUR	USD	EUR	USD	EUR	USD	EUR	USD	EUR	USD
1	2.143	0.758	2.143	0.758	0.979	0.9925	4.093	4.6078	4.007	4.5732
2	2.389	0.762	2.3919	0.762	0.9538	0.9849	4.093	4.6078	3.9039	4.5382
3	2.664	1.24	2.6713	1.246	0.924	0.9635	4.093	4.6078	3.7819	4.4396
4	2.883	1.681	2.8966	1.6964	0.8921	0.9349	4.093	4.6078	3.6514	4.3078
5	3.057	2.106	3.0781	2.1382	0.8593	0.8996	{4.093	4.6078	3.5171	4.1452
							{100	148.35	85.93	133.4557
							total:		104.7913	155.4597
							(c/v @ 1.4835: 104.7925)			

Figure 6.16   The initial equilibrium of a CRS swap

Normally, this does not happen in the case of an IRS. Suppose an asset manager wants to swap -ibor revenues into a fixed rate, in the same currency, through an IRS. If these revenues are @ -ibor + or − some spread, the swap will be built on the exchange of (fixed) swap rate against -ibor, and the manager will altogether get (fixed) swap rate plus or minus the spread on the -ibor revenues.

6.7 PRICING OF SECOND-GENERATION SWAPS

The above IRS and CRS pricing methodology is also applicable in the case of swaps whose specifications differ from the vanilla case, that are called second-generation swaps or "exotic" swaps.

6.7.1 Zero-coupon swap

Zero-coupon swaps are widely used, for example for building "principal protected" structured products. It is the simplest swap possible, since it involves a single, particular, exchange of cash flows. The calculation is based on the PV ⇔ FV relationship (cf. Chapter 1, Eq. 1.3):

$$PV (1 + z_t)^t = FV$$

The swap cash flows can be represented as Figure 6.17.

In other words, a zero-coupon swap is actually a deposit or a borrowing at a fixed, capitalized rate. The reason to settle this operation under the form of a swap is to benefit from the ISDA documentation (particularly useful for long maturities).

Example. Let consider a 5-year zero-coupon swap in EUR (data from February 2001), on a notional of €100 million:

- 5-year (swap) coupon rate: 5%;
- corresponding 0-cpn rate: 5.02%.

→ (in € millions) : $PV = 100/1.055 = 78.28$

To come back to the case of "principal protected" structured products: if an investor is paying €100, to be invested into such a structured product, thanks to the zero-coupon swap the bank will first take €78.28 from the 100, to allow for reimbursing at maturity 100% of the investment, then allocate the balance (21.72) into the structure, most often as an option premium paid to benefit from some underlying (stock, index, etc.) price move.

Figure 6.17   Zero-coupon swap cash flows

6.7.2   EONIA and other basis swap

EONIA and OIS Swaps

EONIA stands for *Euro Over-Night Index Average*, that is, an overnight daily fixing rate, which is the very first rate of the series of EURIBOR fixings. EONIA swaps are particular IRS involving, at maturity, a single exchange of cash flows, namely:

- a swap (fixed) rate payment;
- the compounding of daily EONIA fixing rates during the lifetime of the swap.

EONIA swap maturities can be concluded for maturities ranging from a couple of days to a year.

As for the USD and other major currencies, the product is called an *overnight index swap* (OIS). EONIA swaps and OIS allow for speculating on the short-term evolution of the EONIA rates, or – for banks – to hedge daily borrowed or lend money at the EONIA rate against its fluctuations.

Pricing of an EONIA swap runs like for any swaps: at the swap inception, the net sum of present values of both cash-flows must equal 0. At contract inception, the successive daily EONIA fixing rates (except, of course, the initial one) must be replaced by corresponding forward values. The EONIA swap market is quoted on the ACT/360 basis.

Denoting r_i the EONIA fixing rate on day i, n_{di} the number of days corresponding to a r_i (i.e., $n_{di} = 1$ for week days, and $= 3$ for weekends), n_d the total number of days between t_o and T, the compounded EONIA rate r is given by

$$r = \left[\prod_{i=t_0}^{T-1} \left(1 + \frac{r_i \times n_{di}}{360} \right) - 1 \right] \frac{360}{n_d}$$

At maturity, the swap is settled by difference, and the losing party pays it, times the swap notional amount, one business day after.

Example. On Friday 08/12/11, a counterparty, anticipating stable or lowering EONIA rates in the coming days despite its low level with respect to the 1-week EURIBOR, is entering into a 7-days receiver EONIA swap for a notional amount of EUR 1 billion. The received fixed rate was settled at the current 1-week EURIBOR rate of 1.161% p.a., so that the swap was fairly priced (in mid) at contract inception. During the next 7 days, the successive EONIA were 0.88% (on the next Monday, counting from 3 days), 0.874%, 0.885%, 0.876% and 0.883%. At maturity, using the above formula, the compounded EONIA rate r is

$$r = \left[\left(1 + 0.00880 \times \frac{3}{360} \right) \left(1 + \frac{0.00874}{360} \right) \left(1 + \frac{0.00885}{360} \right) \right.$$

$$\left. \times \left(1 + \frac{0.00876}{360} \right) \left(1 + \frac{0.00883}{360} \right) - 1 \right] \times \frac{360}{7} = 0.8797696\%$$

So that

- the counterparty has to receive €1 000 000 000 × 0.01161 × 7/360 = €867 416.67;
- and to pay €1 000 000 000 × 0.008797 . . . × 7/360 = €171 066.30;
- that is, a net cash in of 867 416.67 − 171 066.30 = €696 350.36.

OIS or EONIA Yield Curves

Recently, the crucial problem of counterparty risk, and related risk-free rate, led the OTC swap market operations to be cleared by a clearing house, namely the LCH. Clearnet or London Clearing House, in a similar way as the clearing room of exchange derivatives, involving, in a similar way, a daily adjustment of collateral deposits. Such daily adjustments naturally relate to an overnight, daily fixing rate. By using EONIA swaps or OIS, it is possible to build a swap curve that is based upon forward EONIA or US (market, effective) Fed Fund overnight rates, and corresponding discounting rates, instead of -ibor rates. Indeed, one can consider that on such a very short overnight maturity, a counterparty default probability is near from 0, making these rates the best proxy for risk-free rates. This alternative to the regular swap rates yield curve seems highly promising, given the present concern about counterparty risk. The comparison between both yield curves, and the opportunity to extend the use of OIS swap curves to the case of swaps contracts that are not cleared through the LCH, is studied in a very interesting paper by Hull and White.[9]

CRS Basis Swap

In the case of a CRS basis swap, we should mention that, instead of considering that a flat LIBOR rate (USD, for example) would be exchanged against a flat EURIBOR rate, the market is quoting a LIBOR/EURIBOR spread of a couple of bps, that has become more sensitive since the financial crisis having affected the interbank market. This has lead interest rate models, such as the LIBOR market model (cf. Chapter 11, Section 11.2.3) to be adjusted for pricing of derivatives involving several -ibor curves. This approach uses the previous OIS data.[10]

6.7.3   In-arrear swap

In a vanilla swap, the floating, -ibor rates are fixed two banking days before the period they apply to, and the corresponding cash flows are paid or received at the maturity of each period – see Figure 6.18.

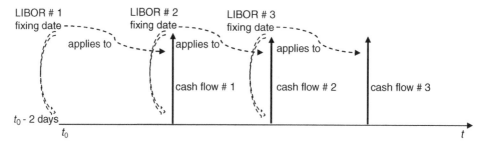

Figure 6.18   Example of a vanilla swap

[9] www.rotman.utoronto.ca/~hull/SownloadablePublications/LIBORvsOIS.pdf, March 2012.
[10] See, for example, Fabio MERCURIO, "A Libor market model with a stochastic basis", *RISK*, December 2010, pp. 84–89.

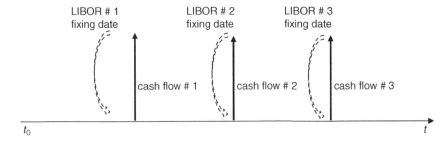

Figure 6.19   Example of an in-arrear swap

In the case of an "in-arrear swap", the -ibor rates are fixed two business days before the maturity of each period, as in Figure 6.19.

Note that if we compare these two swaps, built over n periods with respect to their floating leg, only the first and the last (nth) -ibor are not common to both the swaps, the intermediate ones applying in both cases.

Pricing an in-arrear swap is of course based on the same scheme as for a vanilla swap.

Example. On a very short maturity in order to reduce the calculation steps, namely a swap receiving 1-year fixed rate and paying two 6-month EURIBOR, for a notional of EUR 100 million, the market data (03/16/11) are:

- 6M EURIBOR @ 1.450%;
- 12M EURIBOR @ 1.745%;
- 18M rate (interpolated between 12M EURIBOR and 2-year swap rate) @ 2.417%.

For the vanilla swap, we get the result illustrated in Figure 6.20.

But for the in-arrear swap, the 6-month variable cash flow is based on the forward 6M into 6M EURIBOR of 2.0251%, that is, the one used here above for the 12-month variable cash flow, and the 12-month variable cash flow is based on forward 6M into 12M EURIBOR, that amounts to 3.7705%. For the same fixed rate leg of 1.745% (= 1 year rate), the swap cannot be equilibrated: it becomes fairly priced if one uses a fixed rate of 2.908% instead – see Figure 6.21.

year	cpn y.c. (%)	0-cpn rates (%)	discount factors	6M EURIBOR (%)	interest cash flows in EUR millions		PV of interest c.f. in EUR millions	
					FR	VR	FR	VR
0								
0.5	1.45	1.45	0.9928	1.45		0.725		0.72
1	1.745	1.745	0.9828	2.0251	1.745	1.0126	1.715	0.995
1.5	2.417	2.4275	0.4914	3.7705				
2	3.089	3.11						
							1.715	1.715

Figure 6.20   Result of a vanilla swap

year	cpn y.c. (%)	0-cpn rates (%)	discount factors	6M EURIBOR (%)	interest cash flows in EUR millions		PV of interest c.f. in EUR millions	
					FR	VR	FR	VR
0								
0.5	1.45	1.45	0.9928	**2.0251**		1.0126		1.005
1	1.745	1.745	0.9828	**3.7705**	**2.908**	1.8853	2.858	1.853
							2.858	2.858

Figure 6.21   Using a fixed price in an in-arrear swap

Note that, alternatively, this swap can be built by keeping the initial fixed rate of 1.745%, and by applying the spread (2.908–1.745%, slightly adjusted) to the EURIBOR rates instead.

6.7.4   Constant maturity swap

A constant maturity swap (CMS) is an IRS wherein the fixed rate, instead of remaining the same during the whole lifetime of the swap, is updated at each of the successive maturities of the fixed leg payments.[11] For example, a 5-year CMS will involve:

- for the first year: the current 5-year swap rate;
- for the second year: the 5-year swap rate that will be fixed by the market 1 year later;
- for the third year: the 5-year swap rate that will be fixed by the market 2 years later;
- and so on.

The other leg of the CMS may be a real fixed rate, or an -ibor rate, as usual. So a receiver 5-year CMS against either a 12M LIBOR, or a 5-year spot swap rate, will consist of the cash flows shown in Figure 6.22 (as earlier, dotted lines are for variable rates).

The swap pricing methodology remains unchanged in its principle: in the same way as, for a vanilla swap, the unknown future floating rates are meanwhile replaced by their corresponding

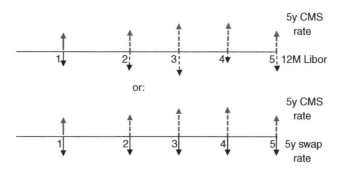

Figure 6.22   Receiver 5-year CMS against either a 12M LIBOR or a 5-year spot swap rate

---

[11] The wording "constant maturity" is unfortunately misleading: of course the maturity of this swap cannot vary over time; it rather means here that, when updating the fixed rate, one continues to use a market fixed rate of the same (initial) maturity.

forward values, in the case of a CMS, the future, updated fixed rates, unknown at the time of the swap inception, are replaced by a forward value. Continuing the example, the pricing of this 5-year CMS will use:

- for the first year: the current 5-year swap rate;
- for the second year: the 1-year forward, 5-year swap rate, in lieu of the today unknown 5-year swap rate that will be fixed by the market 1 year later;
- for the third year: the 2-year forward, 5-year swap rate, in lieu of the today unknown 5-year swap rate that will be fixed by the market 2 years later;
- and so on.

As shown in Chapter 1, Section 1.4 and applied in the above calculation, it appears that forward rates are higher than spot rates if the yield curve is a growing one, and conversely. Replacing the constant fixed rate of a vanilla swap by either higher or lower ones makes the swap unbalanced ($\Sigma NPV_{swap} \neq 0$). To restore its fair valuation, the custom is to add or subtract the adequate spread to the floating rate or spot fixed rate leg. The sum of the spot fixed rate plus this spread is called the CMS rate.

To illustrate the calculation of a CMS, let us first compute a vanilla 3-year IRS, based on the same EUR yield curve as above (data as of 16/03/11), with a notional of EUR 100 million, as in Figure 6.23.

In the case of a CMS built on this scheme, one has to replace the fixed rate basis of 2.379% for the fixed rate cash flows of years 2 and 3 by the 3-year forward 1-year and forward 2-year rates respectively. By using Eq. 1.12 from Chapter 1, the calculation of these forwards gives 3.258% and 3.693%. Compensating this by a spread on the 6-month EURIBOR basis, the equilibrium is obtained by adding a spread of 0.716% on the EURIBORs – see Figure 6.24.

It is worth mentioning that government agencies are issuing a similar product, namely, paying a fixed coupon that is updated over time. For example, one can trade "10-year treasury constant maturity" bonds on the French (TEC10) government bonds market. On the US market "constant maturity T Bonds" are rather indexes that refer to bond yields that are computed from an average of bonds yields of same maturity during the two previous weeks.

					interest cash flows		PV of interest c.f.	
	cpn y.c. (%)	0-cpn rates (%)	discount factors	6M EURIBOR (%)	in EUR millions			
year					FR	VR	FR	VR
0								
0.5	1.45	1.45	0.9928	1.45		0.725		0.72
1	1.745	1.745	0.9828	2.0251	2.379	1.0126	2.338	0.995
1.5	1.917	1.9188	0.9711	2.2544		1.1272		1.095
2	2.089	2.0926	0.9594	2.5989	**3.258**	1.2995	3.126	1.247
2.5	2.234	2.2407	0.9455	2.8154		1.4077		1.331
3	2.379	2.3887	0.9316	3.1078	**3.693**	1.5539	3.44	1.448
4	2.598							
5	2.816						8.904	6.836

Figure 6.23   A vanilla 3-year IRS

year	cpn y.c. (%)	0-cpn rates (%)	discount factors	6M EURIBOR (%)	actual floating rate	interest cash flows in EUR millions FR	VR	PV of interest c.f. in EUR millions FR	VR
0									
0.5	1.45	1.45	0.9928	1.45	**2.166**		**1.083**		1.075
1	1.745	1.745	0.9828	2.0251	**2.7411**	2.379	**1.3706**	2.338	1.347
1.5	1.917	1.9188	0.9711	2.2544	**2.9704**		**1.4852**		1.442
2	2.089	2.0926	0.9594	2.5989	**3.3149**	3.258	**1.6575**	3.126	1.59
2.5	2.234	2.2407	0.9455	2.8154	**3.5314**		**1.7657**		1.669
3	2.379	2.3887	0.9316	3.1078	**3.8238**	3.693	**1.9119**	3.44	1.781
4	2.598								
5	2.816		**float. r. = EURIBOR + 0.716 %**					8.904	8.904

Figure 6.24 A 3-year CMS swap

CMS and Convexity Adjustment

As it will appear, the previous calculation is not fully satisfying, and requires some adjustment. To explain this, let us consider the above example as a receiver 3-year CMS: as a matter of fact, the successive 3-year (spot) swap rates that will be received will not coincide with the forward calculation, that has served to price the CMS. But in the present case, successive forward periods are to be considered, to determine the 3-year swap rate forward 1 year and forward 2 years successively. We cannot consider that the equilibrium based on the initial forward curve, as per the above calculation, will be so that the successive actual values of the future 3-year (spot) swap rates will actually be randomly distributed around the series of forward values computed at the CMS contract date, so that the spirit of the fair pricing would be fulfilled.

A detailed calculation would show that the market value of a CMS rate, or how many bps must be actually added to the other leg of a CMS swap contract, happens to be systematically higher than as per the above basic calculation, and the longer the swap maturity, the higher this spread. As a consequence, market practitioners are adjusting their CMS calculation by a so-called "convexity adjustment", which is usually based on the following formula:[12]

$$convexity\ adjustment = 0.5\sigma^2 \times t \times T$$

where:

- for a given CMS rate of maturity T, forward t year;
- σ is the volatility of related to the corresponding CMS rate, for a given f and T.

Clearly, this adjustment is always positive, and proportional to the time, through the t and T parameters, and may value several dozens of bps for long enough maturities (10 years and more). It is also proportional to the volatility σ, what appears here quite abruptly. At first, we must admit that market volatility is affecting the evolution of prices or rates. To go further, we

---

[12] Further research has developed more sophisticated convexity adjustment calculation, see for example Dmitry PUGACHEVSKY, "Forward CMS rate adjustment", RISK, March 2001, pp. 125–128 and http://lesniewski.us/papers/lectures/Interest_Rate_and_FX_Models/Lecture4.pdf

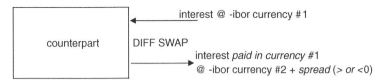

Figure 6.25   Example of a diff swap

need to be familiar with Chapter 8 and in particular with the relationship between a forward and the volatility (Section 6.8).

Finally, note that the word "convexity" may seem misguiding. But in the usual language of traders, we use the same word to qualify:

- a second order differentiation term, such as the convexity of a bond (cf. Chapter 3, Section 3.2.3), that can be viewed as a price adjustment, on the impact of the duration;
- more generally, some price adjustment or difference, needed for any reason, such as the impact of different cash flows frequency between a forward and a future price of same parameters (cf. Chapter 7, Section 7.2.4), or, here, the impact of forward calculation.

Actually, there should also be some convexity adjustment on in-arrear swaps (cf. Section 6.7.3), but to a much lesser extent, given the time differences are much shorter (between beginning and end dates of an -ibor rate).

6.7.5   Quanto or diff swap

A *quanto* or *diff* (for differential) *swap* is a particular basis swap,[13] a hybrid of an IRS and a CRS: as a CRS, it involves exchanges of interest cash flows based on the interest rates of two currencies, *but paid in one single currency*, as shown in Figure 6.25.

Example. Let us consider a 3-year diff swap on 6M EURIBOR and LIBOR, paid in EUR (data as of 05/02/11). The involved calculation of zero coupons, discount factors and forward rates are computed accordingly. Given the higher market rates in EUR than in USD, if the LIBOR cash flows are paid in EUR, the swap is unbalanced. To correct this, it needs to increase the LIBOR rates to the extent that the present value of the sum of LIBOR cash flows paid in EUR get the adequate level – see Figure 6.26.

The calculation gives a spread of +1.343% above each of the LIBOR rates. This increase is a kind of average of the successive 6-month spreads between both yield curves. Actually, such a diff swap remains however sensitive to the correlation between both yield curves, since the increase is common for all the maturities but represents a series of successive 6-month spreads.

6.7.6   Swapping other types of cash flows: performance swaps

The swap structure can also be applied to cash flows other than interest (and principal) payments. They usually consist of a single exchange, with a maturity varying from some months to several years. So that they actually refer to a single forward operation rather than

---

[13] That is, as we said earlier, a *floating/floating* swap.

year	EUR cpn y.c. (%)	USD cpn y.c. (%)	0-cpn rates		discount factors		6M EURIBOR (%)	actual LIBOR rate	interest cash flows in EUR millions		PV of interest c.f.	
			EUR	USD	EUR	USD			@ EURIBOR	@ LIBOR	@ EURIBOR	@ LIBOR
0												
0.5	1.688	0.43	1.688	0.43	0.9916	0.9979	1.688	**1.773**	0.844	**0.8865**	0.837	0.885
1	2.143	0.758	2.143	0.758	0.979	0.9925	2.5765	**2.4267**	1.2883	**1.2134**	1.261	1.204
1.5			2.2675	0.76	0.9664	0.9887	2.5015	**2.1055**	1.2508	**1.0528**	1.209	1.041
2	2.389	0.762	2.3919	0.762	0.9538	0.9849	2.7471	**2.1093**	1.3736	**1.0547**	1.31	1.039
2.5			2.5328	1.004	0.9389	0.9742	3.0747	**3.3111**	1.5374	**1.6556**	1.443	1.613
3	2.664	1.24	2.6736	1.246	0.9239	0.9635	3.3524	**3.7925**	1.6762	**1.8963**	1.549	1.827
											7.609	7.609

actual **LIBOR rates** =t= **LIBOR +1.343 %**

Figure 6.26 A 3-year diff swap on 6M EURIBOR and LIBOR

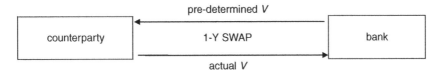

Figure 6.27   A 1-year performance swap on the underlying V

to a swap properly said, that is, a series of forward transactions. The ISDA documentation explains the swap label, which is even more justified in the case of a long term engagement. As such, these swaps are called "performance swaps" and may apply to any kind of performance, that is, a stock (under the name of "equity swap"), a stock index, the future dividends of a stock, but also a volatility or a variance measure, an inflation rate, a non-financial commodity, and so on. We will look at the case of volatility and variance swaps in Chapter 12, devoted to volatility and related instruments.

Let us call "variable" (V) the underlying of these performance swaps. They consist in exchanging a pre-determined, fixed value – often called the strike – for the variable V against its actual value at the swap maturity, for an agreed notional amount. The floating leg of the swap will somewhat naturally refer to the actual value of V, since it is unknown at the swap inception; the fixed leg will thus refer to the pre-determined value for the variable V. At maturity, the swap will be settled by difference.

As a general case, a 1-year performance swap on the underlying V can be represented as shown in Figure 6.27. This typically speculative operation implies the counterparty's trader is expecting a lowering value for V (if he is expecting the contrary, the arrows would be inversed).

To value a performance swap, the general methodology still applies. It just needs to know the equivalent of a yield curve to quantify V at futures maturity dates, in order to compute the corresponding forward values. Such curves exist for volatilities (cf. Chapter 12, Section 12.1.2), but also for inflation predictions, and so on. Existing future markets may help in other cases (e.g., for commodities or for stock indexes).

Inflation Swap

Inflation swaps valuation is at least somewhat helped by several kind of data, such as inflation adjusted rates, yields of inflation-protected bonds issued by several governments and institutions.

Example of an Operation (Data as of June 2006)

Figure 6.28   Example of an inflation swap

The product was destined to traders expecting a higher than a 2.365% inflation rate over 30 years. In this operation, both cash flows are 30-year zero coupon rates, so that:

- the fixed leg is

$$\left[(1 + 2.365\%)^{30} - 1\right] \times notional\ amount \tag{6.6}$$

where 2.365% represents a 30-year zero-coupon inflation rate of 2.295% (on 05/01/06) + a spread of 7 bp, resulting from the $\Sigma NPV_{swap} = 0$ constraint;
- the floating leg is based on the actual inflation over 30 years, measured as the difference between 05/01/06 and at maturity, of the benchmark Euro CPI, tobacco excluded (basis: 2005 = 100):

$$\left(\frac{end\ index}{start\ index} - 1\right) \times notional\ amount \tag{6.7}$$

After 3 years, at the end of June 2006, this index was = 102.53; the value of the floating leg at the end of June 2009 – current end index of 108.48 was thus, by Eq. 6.7, for a notional of €1:

$$(108.48/102.56 - 1) \times 1 = 5.772\%$$

The corresponding value of the fixed leg, by applying Eq. 6.6 on 3 years:

$$\left[(1 + 2.365\%)^{3} - 1\right] \times 1 = 7.264\%$$

Hence, the swap value at that time, for the counterparty: $(-7.264 + 5.772)\%$, or -1.492% per € of notional amount.

It is worth noting that the (re)valuation of such a swap is tricky because it is hard to assess a reasonable value to a yield curve of "real" interest rates (meaning a usual market interest rate minus the expected inflation), for example by using the market data of inflation-linked bonds (cf. Chapter 3, Section 3.2.1.4).

FURTHER READING

Gerald W. BUETOW, Frank J. FABOZZI, *Valuation of Interest Rate Swaps and Swaptions*, John Wiley & Sons, Inc., Hoboken, 2000, 248 p.

Richard R. FLAVELL, *Swaps and Other Derivatives*, 2nd ed., John Wiley & Sons, Ltd, Chichester, 392 p.

7

Futures

7.1 INTRODUCTION TO FUTURES

By definition, a future contract is an engagement between two parties – a buyer and a seller – (the seller) to deliver, respectively (the buyer) to receive;

- on a given maturity date,
- a given quantity,
- an underlying financial instrument,
- at a price agreed upfront (on the contracting day).

(The future seller will deliver the underlying, to be received by the future buyer.)

So far, such a definition should also apply to an interbank forward contract. To be qualified as a future contract, the operation must be traded on a futures exchange. This implies two key features.

Contract Standardization

Unlike the interbank market, the futures exchange operations are fully transparent, in prices, volumes and contract specifications. To ensure enough market liquidity for attracting buyers and sellers, the exchange must standardize the contract specifications as much as possible, that is:

- maturities: only 4–12 times a year;
- a nominal (notional) amount for one contract, the "contract size";
- quoted price intervals, called *tick*: one distinguishes between the:
  - tick size = minimum price movement, and the
  - tick value = tick size × nominal (notional) amount;
- settlement, at maturity: either physical, that is, in units of the underlying instrument, or in cash. The exchange imposes one of these alternatives, depending on the underlying.

Example. Euro Stoxx 50 futures: standardized contract parameters:

- underlying: Euro Stoxx 50 index;
- maturities: March, June, September, December (available contracts are usually up to about 2 years maturity);
- contract size: EUR 10 × index (cf. also Section 7.3.1);
- tick size: 1 index point;
- tick value: EUR 10;
- cash settlement.

For example, on 05/19/11, the available contracts were those of next June, September, and December, as illustrated in Figure 7.1.

<HELP> for explanation.   Index **CT**
1 <GO> to Configure Columns

| View Futures | 1) Edit Columns | 2) Chart on CCRV | Contract Table |

EURO STOXX 50   Pricing Date 05/19/11   Sort By Expiration
Eurex

                        Contracts 4/4   Tot Volume 788107   Open Int 2869474

Ticker		Last	Change	Time	Bid	Ask	Open Int	FairVal	Previous
3) SX5E	Spot	↑2905.53	+38.23	15:24					2867.30
4) VGM1	Jun11	↑2885.00	+39.00	15:24	2884.00	2885.00	2392974		2846.00
5) VGU1	Sep11	2885.00	+39.00	15:15	2883.00	2885.00	469844		2846.00
6) VGZ1	Dec11	2883.00	+42.00	14:57	2879.00	2881.00	6656		2841.00

Australia 61 2 9777 8600 Brazil 5511 3048 4500 Europe 44 20 7330 7500 Germany 49 69 9204 1210 Hong Kong 852 2977 6000
Japan 81 3 3201 8900   Singapore 65 6212 1000   U.S. 1 212 318 2000   Copyright 2011 Bloomberg Finance L.P.
                                                          SN 558826 CEST GMT+2:00 G771-1067-1 19-May-2011 15:24:54

Figure 7.1   Euro Stoxx 50 futures: June, September, and December contracts of 05/19/11
Source: Bloomberg

The column headed "Open Int" (open interest) indicates the number of contracts still "living", that is, not closed meanwhile. We see that the total is about 2.9 million, compared with the number of contracts traded on that trading day (at 3 p.m. local time) of nearly 0.8 million (for an average daily volume >1 million contracts). This gives us an idea of the importance of contracts that never reach maturity but unwind earlier. We can also notice, through this series on open interests, that the vast majority (about 80%, here) refer to the nearest maturity: there is almost no market interest for maturities which are too long.

Counterparty Risk

To eliminate counterparty risk, transactions are not concluded directly between a buyer and a seller but both contract with the *clearing house* of the exchange. At least, futures exchanges clearing houses have never faced payment default, this solves the problem with respect to the risk taken by buyers and sellers. Because the clearing house is contracting simultaneously with a buyer and a seller, the risk status of the parties appears as in Figure 7.2.

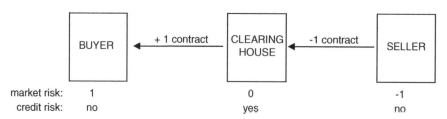

Figure 7.2   Risk status of the buyer and the seller

It is interesting to note that, through this structure:

• the buyers and sellers are exposed to a market risk, but not to credit risk;
• the clearing house is exposed to counterparties risk, but not to market risk.

The counterparty risk taken by the clearing house is that, at maturity, to what extent the buyer will actually be able to pay for receiving the underlying, and the seller to deliver it. This risk is covered by a system of collateral deposit, called the *margining* system (cf. Section 7.1.1).

For further information regarding the functioning of the future markets, see the further reading at the end of the chapter.

7.1.1 Margining system

At the contract inception, both parties must have opened a *margin account* with a bank, authorized by the exchange, and proceed with the payment of an *initial margin*, fixed by the exchange. This initial margin can be made of cash or government bonds.

At the end of each trading session, the clearing house proceeds for all contracts with the clearing of the profit and loss resulting from the session. The daily loss made by a losing party is debited from his margin account and paid on the margin account of the corresponding winning party. The debit from the losing party's margin account must be covered by the payment of a corresponding amount in cash, so that the margin account is always at least equal to the initial margin level, or, depending on the exchange rules, to a lower margin level called *maintenance margin*. As time goes by, the margin accounts of the parties reflect their successive daily profits and losses.

This can be shown through the following example, dated 01/23/03, of futures on the Euro Stoxx 50 index, maturing in March 2003.

Let us consider a speculative sale of 100 contracts, @ 2290 (expecting the index to lower). The initial margin for this contract being €3000:

• initial deposit = €300 000, that is, 100 contracts × 3000;
• the tick value of this contract being €10, each time the future price is lowering by 1 tick, the seller makes a profit of €1000 = €10 × 100 contracts;
• and if the future price is increasing by 1 *tick*, he makes a loss of €1000.

Evolution of the seller's margin account is as follows:

day	contract closing price	ticks	margin account variations	balance
23/01	2290			300 000
24/01	2231	−59	+59 000	359 000
27/01	2151	−80	+80 000	439 000
28/01	2180	+29	−29 000	410 000
29/01	2221	+41	−41 000	369 000
30/01	2218	−3	+3000	372 000

Note that in this example, the seller has never been led to add cash in his margin account.

If, on 01/30, the seller buys back his 100 contracts, his profit is:

372 000 (final margin account)
−300 000 (initial margin account)
=€72 000

that also equals the future price (initial − final), 2290 − 2218, × €10 × 100 contracts.
   We can further compute the *leverage* of the operation, through:

- the ratio of nominal amount involved in the operation,

$$2290 \times €10 \text{ per contract} \times 100 \text{ contracts} = €2\,290\,000$$

on the deposit margin of €300 000, that is, a leverage of:

$$2\,290\,000/300\,000 \approx 7.5$$

- or, per contract: the exposure was @ 2290 times €10, = €22 900, for an engaged amount of €3000, that is, a leverage of:

$$22\,900/3000 \approx 7.5$$

   The initial margin level fixed by the exchange is based on an average daily price movement of the traded future, and thus reflects its volatility. In case of unusual huge market moves, the exchange may temporarily interrupt the trading session and proceed with an *intraday margining* settlement, before resuming the trading session. Thanks to this procedure, the exchange cannot be affected by a counterparty default.

7.1.2   Settlement of the future contract at maturity

Although the vast majority of future contracts are unwound in the market before expiry, regarding the contract remaining open at maturity, the way they are settled may look somewhat puzzling at first sight.
   Let us take the case of the future buyer: at maturity, he receives the underlying from the contract seller, and pays him the *invoiced amount*. Looking to the definition, the buyer should have to pay the initially agreed future price, but the invoiced amount is actually calculated from the last future price F_{EDSP}, called the exchange delivery settlement price (EDSP). To explain this, we have to take into account what has meanwhile happened with the margin account. For example,

$$\text{at } t_0: \text{ buy } 105$$
$$\downarrow$$
$$\downarrow \text{ margin account: } + 2$$
$$\downarrow$$
$$\text{at } T: \text{EDSP } 107 \Rightarrow \text{payment of } 107$$

   Hence, the buyer is paying 107, but has got a profit of 2 on his margin account, resulting in a net payment of 105, the initially agreed price.

7.2 FUTURES PRICING

7.2.1 Theoretical price of a future

The theoretical or *fair* value of a future contract can be deducted from the following comparison: let consider A is buying an hypothetical future contract, maturing in 3 months, on a stock index @ 100, and B is buying the corresponding physical, that is, the index (constituents) @ 100.

A has nothing to pay cash, hence, to mimic this situation, let B borrowing 100 for 3 months, at the market rate of 3%. Furthermore, as B is immediately owner of the index, the benefits of the dividends paid by some of the stocks of the index, which, for convenience here, we assimilate to the pro rata of the dividend yield, lets say @ 5% during these 3 months. So that, after 3 months (assuming 1 month = 0.25 year), B pays:

$$100 + 100 \times 3\% \times 0.25 - 100 \times 5\% \times 0.25 = 99.5$$

Under the no arbitrage condition (cf. Chapter 1, Section 1.6), this should also be the theoretical future price F_{th} for investor A. Indeed, to become owner of a stock index after 3 months, becoming the owner (through having bought a future contract) of a stock index, there is no reason to have paid a different price than by the straightforward way of having bought it spot, having financed it for 3 months and having taken advantage of the accrued dividend yield.

The above example also shows that:

- with time progressively going closer to the maturity future, both the spot and the future prices will evolve, up and down, in a similar way;
- but with a reducing spread: both interest terms, on financing and on accrued interest will apply on a remaining time to maturity that will reduce progressively;
- at maturity, with 0 year to maturity, both interest terms, on financing and on accrued interest, will equal 0, and the forward 0-year future price will finally equal the spot price (S_T);
- if the financing rate is lower than the coupon rate, as in the example, the future price is lower than the spot price, and conversely.

Generalizing for any kind of financial underlying, and calling *revenue* the payment of respectively a dividend yield by a stock index, a coupon by a bond, an interest rate by a currency or by an underlying monetary rate, the relationship becomes:

$$\text{Theoretical (fair) future price} = \text{spot} + \underbrace{\text{financing cost} - \text{revenue}}_{\text{(cost of) carry}}$$

where the algebraic sum of *financing cost – revenue* is called the (*cost of*) *carry*. So that, if the carry is positive – meaning that it is globally costly to finance the underlying instrument – the theoretical future price is higher than the spot price, and conversely.

Note that for futures on non-financial commodities, this formula will be revisited (see Section 7.7.1).

7.2.2 *Theoretical* versus *market* future price

Mid futures market prices do not exactly equal theoretical prices, due to market features like liquidity, market efficiency, market pressure, and so on.

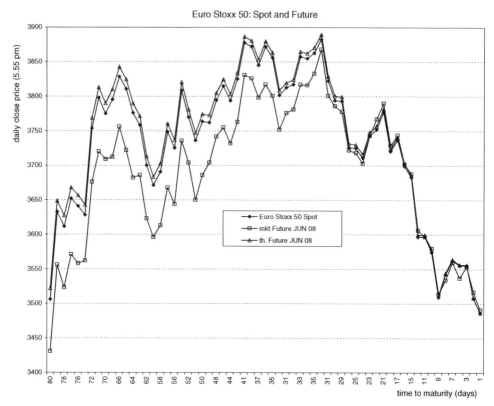

Figure 7.3   Spot price, theoretical and market prices of the JUN 2008 future on Euro Stoxx 50, from March 20, 2008 to June 19, 2008

Example. Let us consider the spot price, theoretical and market prices of the JUN (for the June maturity) 2008 future on Euro Stoxx 50, from March 20, 2008 to June 19 (last JUN trading day was at noon on June 20). The theoretical future price has been computed with an average market rate of 4.02% and an average underlying rate (index dividend yield) of 2% (see Figure 7.3).

A way to emphasize the difference between theoretical and market future prices, is to compute the future *basis b*, which is defined as:

basis = b = spot, or cash price − future price[1]

in the first example of the previous section, $b = 100 − 99.5 = 0.5$, which is >0. If and when a future price is higher than the corresponding spot price, the basis is then negative.

If we refer to the future theoretical price, the above definition determines the theoretical basis, b_{th}. In contrast, the computation of $S − F_{mkt}$ gives the *market basis, b_{mkt}*. Depending on market conditions,

$$b_{mkt} \text{ can be } > \text{ or } < b_{th}$$

---

[1] Note that in old textbooks or documentation on futures, we sometimes find the inverse relationship: basis = future − spot.

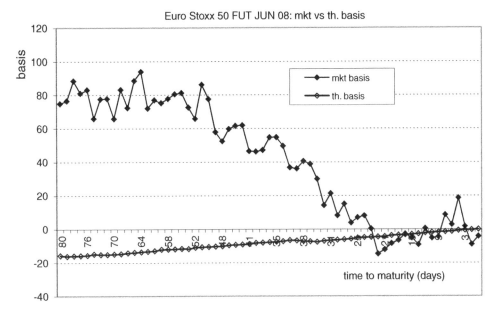

Figure 7.4   Theoretical and market basis relative to the previous Euro Stoxx 50 future

Example. Consider the theoretical and market basis relative to the previous Euro Stoxx 50 example shown in Figure 7.4.[2]

Most of the time in this example, $b_{mkt} > b_{th}$, implying that $F_{mkt} < F_{th}$ (cf. Figure 7.3), which can be the case when futures market prices are pushed down by a selling pressure, for example by stocks portfolio hedgers, or by speculators anticipating an underlying price drop.

The theoretical basis is also called *carry basis*. The difference between the basis (based on F_{mkt}) and the carry basis (based on F_{th}) is called *value basis*:

$$\text{basis} = \text{carry basis} + \text{value basis}$$

$$\Downarrow \qquad\qquad \Downarrow$$

$$\text{on } F_{mkt} \qquad \text{on } F_{th}$$

We also find the wording (for example on Bloomberg screens)

"gross basis" for "basis"
"net basis" for "value basis"

An example of basis calculations is given in Section 7.5.3.

7.2.3   The implied repo rate (IRR)

The difference between the theoretical and the market price can be formulated as follows, by adjusting the market rate to fit with the observed mid-market future price. This modified

---

[2] On the graph, the theoretical basis should appear as a straight line, but, as we said earlier, we have approximated the calculation by averaging the market rate and the underlying rate on the whole period.

market rate is called the *implied repo rate* (IRR), implied because it is the rate implied by the observed market price, and repo rate because the repo rate is the most usual money market rate used by institutions:

$$F_{th} = \text{spot} + \text{financing } cost \text{ @ } \boldsymbol{mkt\ r} - \text{revenue}$$

$$F_{th} \neq F_{mkt} = \text{spot} + \text{financing cost @ } \boldsymbol{IRR} - \text{revenue}$$

An observed market price higher than the corresponding theoretical price implies

$$IRR > mkt\ r$$

and conversely. An example of IRR calculation is given in the next section.

Observed differences between *IRR* and *mkt r* (r_{mkt} in the formulae hereafter) theoretically allow to set up "cash and carry" or "reverse cash and carry" operations, based on the following scheme.

Cash and Carry Operation:

If $F_{mkt} > F_{th}$, the arbitrageur will sell the "expensive" future and simultaneously buy the spot instrument, so that he has no net open risky position in the underlying. This leads to a net, sure arbitrage profit equal to

$$S \times (IRR - r_{mkt}) \times T$$

Indeed, buying the spot instrument can be financed at the actual market rate, which is lower than the IRR. This profit is maximized if hold until maturity, to gain the *IRR* − *mkt r* differential on the longest possible time period.

Reverse Cash and Carry Operation:

On the contrary, if $F_{mkt} < F_{th}$, that is, if *IRR* < *mkt r*, the arbitrageur will buy the "cheap" future and simultaneously sell forward the spot instrument. The corresponding arbitrage profit is

$$S \times (r_{mkt} - IRR) \times T$$

Practically speaking, actually trading such arbitrage operations is realistic only if the spread between F_{mkt} and F_{th} is wide enough, given bid–ask spreads on the spot price and on the interest rates, and if the market liquidity is sufficient to apply on a large enough nominal amount, giving enough \$ profit with respect to the actual running cost of the activity. Needless to say, for the major, most liquid futures contracts, there is little chance of such an opportunity occurring.

7.2.4   Future versus forward prices

At first, a future (mid) price should not differ from an interbank forward (mid) price, if we exclude the counterparty risk involved in the interbank forward market. There is, however, a difference, due to the different impact of treasury costs in both transaction schemes:

- the profit or loss of forward contract is brought at one time, at the contract maturity;
- the future contract gives rise to successive daily profits or losses on the margin account.

This basic difference does not seem to affect market prices in an effective way, at least on the majority of futures contracts, with a short term maturity (<1 year). But, besides, futures prices are often showing lower prices than equivalent forward prices, what can be explained by the fact that it is in practice easier to go short (to sell forward) through the sale of a future contract than on the interbank market.

Moreover, regarding the actual bid–ask prices, because of the standardization of maturity dates and subsequent market liquidity, futures are traded with a narrower bid–ask spread than forwards. To some extent, the made-to-measure has a price.

Also, the swap market rates show differences with the series of money market futures implied rates, at least for long maturities (hence, versus long dated futures contracts, of several years maturities), and such differences tend to widen with the maturity. This phenomenon is called convexity bias.[3]

7.3 FUTURES ON EQUITIES AND STOCK INDEXES

Up to now, there are only a handful of futures on (single) stocks, which are traded with too low volumes to be considered here. The following of this section is thus focused on stock index futures.

Stock index futures are cash settled, to avoid a physical transfer of many different stocks, some of them in too small quantities given the contract size.

7.3.1 Contract size versus contract value

Stock index futures are the only futures having a *variable* contract *size* (as it will appear in the further sections), namely the current underlying *spot* index value (rounded to the unit, if necessary) times some amount of money ($10 or €10, e.g., see the example in Section 7.1.1). Besides, one defines the (variable) contract *value*, as the *future price* times the same amount of money. Since it refers to the underlying *spot* value, the contract size is aimed to determine the number of futures to be bought or sold to hedge an underlying index position (cf. Section 7.3.3). By contrast, the contract value allows determining the MtM of the futures position, which of course depends on the *future* price.

Example. On the Euro Stoxx 50 (data of Feb 03):

- spot: 2140.73;
- MAR (for "March maturity") contract future: 2131.

Contract **size** : EUR 10 × underlying **spot** (rounded) value
$$= €10 × 2140.73, \text{ rounded} = €21\,407$$
Contract **value** : EUR 10 × **future** price
$$= €10 × 2131 = €21\,310$$

---

[3] For more details, see, for example, Galen BURHARDT, Bill HOSKINS, A question of bias, *Risk*, 1995, No. 8, pp. 63–70.

7.3.2   Theoretical versus market price

Applying the general relationship introduced in Section 7.2.1, that is, $F_{th} = spot + financing\ cost - revenue$, the theoretical future price at current time t is, in discrete time,

$$F_{th} = S_t \times (1 + r_\tau \tau) - FV(D)$$
$$= S_t \times (1 + r_\tau \tau) - D \times (1 + r_\tau \tau)$$

where

    S is the underlying spot index value
    τ is $T - t$, the time remaining to maturity,
    r_τ is the market rate corresponding to time τ,
    D is the weighted sum of dividends D_j of the stocks ($j = 1\ to\ n$ stocks in the index) paid
       during τ,
    $FV(.)$ is the future value of $(.)$.

If D is expressed as a *dividend yield*, the formula becomes

$$F_{th} = S_t[1 + (r_\tau - D)\tau] \tag{7.1}$$

In continuous time (with adequate equivalent continuous rates, cf. Chapter 1, Section 1.4):

$$F_{th} = S_t e^{(r_\tau - D)\tau}$$

here, D being the continuous dividend yield of the index.

Example. Take the DEC (December maturity) future on the Swiss SMI index.
    Mid-market data (of July 5, 2000):

- SMI spot $= 7866$;
- CHF LIBOR market rate between 05/07 and 15/12: 3.41%;
- SMI dividend yield: 1.53%;
- DEC future maturing on 12/15/00;
- $\tau = 163$ days on 360.

$$F_{th} = 7866\ [1 + (0.0341 - 0.0153) \times 163/360] = 7932.96$$

The market future price is implying an IRR i as follows:

$$F_{mkt} = S_t[1 + (i - D)\tau]\ or\ = S_t e^{(i-D)}.$$

Example (continued). Consider the corresponding DEC future on SMI actually quoted 7938. It implies an IRR rate of:

$$F_{mkt} = 7938 = 7866\ [1 + (i - 0.0153) \times 163/360]$$
$$\rightarrow i = 3.55\% \text{ (to be compared to CHF LIBOR of 3.41\%)}.$$

Remember that this calculation uses mid prices and rates: the spread between i and LIBOR should be much narrower by incorporating adequate bid–ask spreads, so that no arbitrage could take advantage of it.

7.3.3   Hedging calculation with index futures

Speculative trading with index futures does not involve any particular calculation, hence let us examine hedging calculations, first through an example based on the previous SMI market data.

On 07/05/00, an investor wants to cover on 3 months a position of CHF 10 million in a Swiss stocks portfolio almost replicating the SMI index, by selling DEC SMI future contracts, the next available maturity date beyond the hedge horizon:

- Number N of future contracts to be sold:

  SMI quotes 7866 and DEC future quotes 7938, in mid prices

  $\rightarrow$ 1 contract value $= 7938 \times$ CHF 10 $=$ CHF 79 380

  1 contract size $= 10 \times$ index $= 78\,660$

  $\rightarrow$ N $= 10\,000\,000/78\,660 = 127.129$ to be rounded at 127 contracts

  The general formula is:

  $$N = \text{portfolio nominal/contract size.}$$

  Until the portfolio position includes the short position in futures, the futures component of portfolio MtM is based on the contract value, that is

  $$\text{Futures MtM at time } t = 127 \times \text{CHF } 10 \times F_t$$
  $$\text{starting from } 127 \times \text{CHF } 10 \times 7938 = \text{CHF } 10\,081\,260$$

  so that the initial portfolio MtM (+ stocks – futures) $= 10\,000\,000 - 10\,081\,260 =$ CHF $-81\,260$.

  The corresponding initial margin being CHF 4000 per contract, it amounts to

  $$\text{CHF } 4000 \times 127 = \text{CHF } 508\,000$$

Unwinding the Operation:

Three months later, at the hedge horizon of 10/05, buy 127 contracts back:

SMI quotes 7967 and DEC future quotes 8024

$$\Rightarrow \textit{loss on futures} = (8024 - 7938) \times \text{CHF } 10 \times 127 \text{ contracts}$$
$$= \text{CHF } 109\,220$$
$$\Rightarrow \textit{profit on portfolio} = \text{CHF } 10\,000\,000 \times (7967 - 7866)/7866$$
$$= \text{CHF } 128\,400$$

In general, the actual hedging result will not be nil; beyond the fact that using mid prices like here is improving the hedge results, the reasons are:

- Rounding of N

  The rounding implies a slight over- or under-hedging. In this example, rounding down by 0.13 contracts somewhat reduces the loss on the futures position, by

  $$(8024 - 7938) \times \text{CHF } 10 \times 0.13 \text{ contracts} = \text{CHF } 111.80$$

- Basis risk

  This is the main source of a hedge result being $\neq 0$: by first selling and then buying back the futures, one supports twice the risk of selling and (later on) buying @ $F_{mkt} > F_{th}$ or $F_{mkt} < F_{th}$.

- Treasury cost on margin account

  The actual hedge result has also to involve the net treasury cost on the margin account, due to possible cash margin added, at some treasury cost.[4]

Further to this example, if the stocks portfolio to hedge is not almost close to the underlying index of the future contract, the way to settle the number N of future contracts has to be adjusted by the beta factor (cf. Chapter 4, Section 4.3.4) of the portfolio vis-à-vis the index, as follows:

$$N = \beta \times \text{portfolio nominal/contract size}$$

As seen in Chapter 4, Section 4.3.4, said β is the correlation coefficient – here, between the actual set of stocks constituting the portfolio, and the index – times the ratio of their covariance to the variance of the index. It is possible to somewhat refine this, by rather computing (through a linear regression) a β involving the correlation and the variances/covariance of the content of the portfolio and of the futures prices themselves:

$$\beta' = \frac{\sigma_{S,F}}{\sigma_F^2} = \rho_{S,F} \frac{\sigma_S}{\sigma_F}$$

where S refers to the spot price of the portfolio content, and F to the index future market price. This technique leads to an N called an optimal price ratio, or minimum-variance hedge ratio.

Remember, however (see Chapter 4, Section 4.3.4), that:

- the beta calculation is based on a past period, and will not necessarily be valid for the period to come (the beta varies over time);
- said in another way, an index (future) hedge is only hedging the *systematic risk* of the portfolio (not its specific risk).

7.4 FUTURES ON SHORT-TERM INTEREST RATES

7.4.1 Introduction

Futures being instruments to be bought and sold, as it is intrinsically not the case of a LIBOR or any other interbank money market rate, one must transform the underlying money market rate r into a *price*. For sake of simplicity, the industry has chosen the following transformation:

$$F \text{ (in\% of the notional amount)} = 100\% - r\%$$

to mimic the well-known relationship between bonds prices and bonds yields: here too, if the rate goes up, the price goes down (but here, in a much more simplistic way).

A LIBOR future is defined on a 3-month LIBOR rate, with an abnormally huge contract unit (because change of prices is to be prorated on a 0.25 year only, and because the underlying volatility is much lower than for a stock index future, for example) and a very small tick size. Also, the corresponding tick value takes into account the 3-month underlying maturity.

---

[4] Assuming the cash deposited on the margin account is not paid at the market rate or at the market rate paid by this cash before debiting.

Example. The leading short-term rate future is on the 3-month $LIBOR and is unfortunately called a Eurodollar future (for historical reasons, long before the creation of the Euro currency). In particular, this contract has the following specifications:

- contract size: $1 000 000;
- tick size: 0.0025%, that is, a quarter of a bp;
- → tick value: $6.25.

Indeed, the days count for this contract is a fixed 90 days per 3-month period, on a year of 360 days. So that the tick value is actually

$$\$1\,000\,000\,000 \times \frac{0.0025}{100} \times \frac{90}{360} = \$6.25$$

Short-term interest rate futures are cash settled.

7.4.2   Theoretical future price

Using the same notations as previously, the theoretical future valuation is straightforward (Eq. 7.1):

$$F_{th} = S_t[1 + (r_\tau - r_u)\tau$$

where r_u is naturally the underlying money market rate, for example a 3-month $LIBOR rate. One can see that the slope $r_\tau - r_u$ of the short end of the yield curve is directly affecting the future price.

In continuous time we have:

$$F_{th} = S_t e^{(r_\tau - r_u)\tau}$$

7.4.3   Hedging calculation with money market rate futures

Here, too, let us go through an example, that is, hedging the interest rate risk of a €100 million 3-month deposit, to be made into 6 months. Data are as of 01/06/2005, so that the deposit starts on 06/06:

- current 3-month EURIBOR: 2.150%;
- deposit rate @ EURIBOR – 45 bp;
- JUN future is today 97.66.

On the Euronext-Liffe:

- contract unit = €1 000 000;
- tick size = 0.005% (or 1/2 bp);
- tick value = €12.5.

For sake of simplicity, we take 0.5 years for the hedging time and 0.25 years for the deposit time. Hedging against lowering rates means against rising future prices, that is, selling futures. The future maturity must be the next one after hedging horizon of 06/06, hence the June maturity (expiry: 06/09).

- Number of contracts to sell, @ 97.66
  N = nominal amount to hedge/contract size

$$= 100\,000\,000 / 1\,000\,000 = 100 \text{ contracts}$$

The future price of 97.66 implies a forward 06/09 3-M EURIBOR of

$$100 - 97.66 = 2.34\%$$

to compare with the current spot rate of 2.15%.

Six months later, the position has to be unwound. 3-M EURIBOR is then quoting 2.116% and the JUN futures are bought back @ 97.885. The deposit is made @ current 3-M EURIBOR of 2.116% − 45 bp = 1.666%

- P/L on the futures transaction
  It is usually computed as follows:
  p/l = tick value of €12.50 × 100 contracts × number of ticks between opening and closing of the position,
  with number of ticks = (97.66 − 97.885) × 200 = −45 ticks
  with × 200 because 1 tick = $1/2$ bp, hence, there are 200 half bps in a (future price) percent. Hence,

$$p/l = -€12.50 \times 100 \times 45 = € - 56\,250$$

- Actual deposit rate

$$= 1.666\% - (\text{profit}) \text{ or } + (\text{loss}) \text{ on the futures}$$

Here, the loss of €56 250 on the futures represents

$$€100\,000\,000 \times 0.25 \text{ year} \times x\% = €56\,250$$
$$x = 0.225\%$$

so that the actual deposit rate is

$$1.666\% + 0.225\% = 1.891\%$$

which is nearly equal to the initial forward EURIBOR of 2.34% − 45 bp.

Remarks:

- The hedge performance is subject to the basis risk, as explained in the previous section.
- In this example, we deliberately did not discuss the opportunity to hedge by futures or not. In short, this hedge should be considered in a context of fears of lowering rates, what actually happened. Without hedging, the deposit would have been made @ 2.116 − 0.45 = 1.696%, that is, at a less attractive rate.

7.5 FUTURES ON BONDS

7.5.1 Introduction

Unlike other underlyings, bond futures are traded through a virtual, "notional" underlying government bond. The main bond futures maturity is 10 years, corresponding to the usual 10-year government (risk-free) bond benchmark used in the bonds market. Actually, a bond with ad hoc initial maturity can have a 10-year maturity only once in its lifetime. Also, care of the exchanges' attempts to assure enough liquidity led them, instead of selecting one particular bond as an underlying, to cover a range of maturities round 10 years as possible actual underlyings, and to determine a *set of deliverable bonds* associated with such a single bond future.

This single bond future is artificially created by the exchange, as a notional bond, having specific features. For example, on the Eurex futures exchange, there is a 10-year notional build with a 10-year maturity and a coupon of 6%.[5] The set of deliverable bonds is fixed by Eurex to cover bond maturities comprised between 8.5–10.5 years. Any of these deliverable bonds can be used at the future maturity, which is indeed a physical delivery contract.

The same system applies to other existing notional futures maturities (e.g., 2, 5, and 30 years).

Bond futures contracts trade on the basis of a fixed notional unit amount. For example, the Bund future, on the Bund government debt, trades on Eurex with a contract size of EUR 100 000.

7.5.2   The conversion factor

Since the future contract relates to an underlying notional bond, we need to convert the notional future traded price into its equivalent for each of the deliverable bonds. This is done through the use of a *conversion factor* (CF), such as:

notional future traded price $\times$ CF = future price on corresponding deliverable bond

The *CF* is a number not far from 1, that is computed by the futures exchange itself for each notional future contract, and is function of the notional coupon, the deliverable bond coupon and its time to maturity:

$$CF = \frac{1}{1+c} \left[\frac{C}{c} \left(1 + c - \frac{1}{(1+c)^n} \right) + \frac{1}{(1+c)^n} \right] - C(1 - f)$$

where

C = deliverable bond coupon
c = notional bond coupon
n = number of years until deliverable bond maturity
f = 1/12th of the number of full months until next coupon date of the deliverable bond.

So that, if the deliverable bond coupon is greater than the notional bond coupon, $CF > 1$, and conversely. The *CF* is set at issuance of a future contract and does not change over the lifetime of the contract.

Example. On 05/19/11, the Bund notional future maturing in June, last trading date on 06/08, delivery on 06/10 (i.e., $+2$ exchange business days) was quoting (mid closing price at 15:21:33 hour): 123.89. The set of deliverable bonds and corresponding *CF* was as shown in Figure 7.5.

We can see that the *CF*s are actually lower than 1, given the bonds coupons are lower than the 6% coupon of the notional bond. As the link between the notional bond and the various

---

[5] At the time of writing (March 2012), it amounts to 6%; this coupon rate is from time to time adjusted to correspond to the current bonds yield curve, at the launch of a new notional bond future.

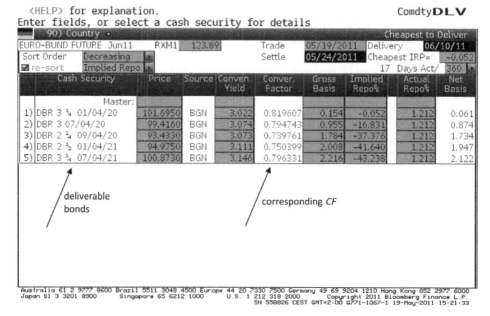

Figure 7.5   Deliverable bonds and corresponding *CF* for the Bund notional future maturing in June
Source: Bloomberg

"real" underlying bonds, the *CF* is affecting all the calculations involving bond futures, each
time a deliverable bond is concerned:

- the (cost of) carry (cf. Section 7.2.1) becomes spot bond (physical, not notional!) – notional
  future price × *CF*;
- invoiced amount: see next section;
- theoretical future price: see Section 7.5.4;
- hedging of a bonds portfolio: see Section 7.5.5.

7.5.3   The cheapest to deliver

Contractually, any of the bonds in the set of deliverable bonds can be used at the future contract
expiry. However, the price dynamics of the future market price cannot exactly be identical to the
individual market prices dynamics of each of the underlying deliverable bonds. Unavoidably,
at a given time some of the deliverable bonds are relatively cheaper than others. Contractually
again, the choice of a specific bond to be delivered is at the future *seller's* discretion. He will
naturally choice to deliver the cheapest among the deliverable bonds,[6] which is called the
cheapest to deliver (CTD).

To facilitate the traders' job, data providers are continuously determining which one of
the deliverable bonds is currently the *CTD*. Observations show that the *CTD* status remains
actually stable over long periods of time (several weeks) and changes from time to time from
one to another of the deliverable bonds. One can also observe that the notional future price is

---

[6] There is thus a free option in the hands of the futures seller, which may slightly affect the future market price.

actually tracking the current *CTD* underlying bond price behavior, just like if this *CTD* were the actual underlying bond.

Practically speaking, to determine the *CTD* it suffice, for each deliverable bond i, to compute at maturity its *bond market price* B_i / CF_i ratio: the *CTD* is the one with the lowest ratio. This looks like a receipt, but it can be easily demonstrated, by expressing the objective, for the futures seller, to maximize its return at delivery, that is, to maximize the difference between his cashed in invoice price (determined from F_{EDSP} as defined in Section 7.1.2) and the value B_i of the ith delivered bond:

$$
\begin{aligned}
MAX_{profit} &= MAX[invoice\ price - (B + accrued)_i] \\
&= MAX[F_{EDSP} \times CF_i + accrued_i - (B + accrued)_i] \\
&= MAX[F_{EDSP} \times CF_i - B_i] \\
&= MAX[F_{EDSP} \times B_i/CF_i]
\end{aligned}
$$

and the last [...] is maximized for the lowest B_i/CF_i ratio among the deliverable bonds.

Example. Working with the same data as for the above Bund future, we can verify that the Bund # 1 is the CTD:

Bund	B_i/CF_i	CTD ratio
# 1	101.695 / 0.819607	= 124.078 ← min ⇐ CTD
# 2	99.416 / 0.794743	= 125.092
# 3	93.433 / 0.739761	= 126.302
# 4	94.975 / 0.750399	= 126.566
# 5	100.873 / 0.796331	= 126.672

It could also be demonstrated that the *CTD* is the deliverable bond having the highest *IRR* (cf. Figure 7.5, Implied Repo% column).

Back to the settlement of a contract at maturity, the invoiced amount is to be adapted in the case of a bond future, in a logical way:

Invoiced amount =	EDSP of the notional	×	CF of the CTD	+	accrued interest of the CTD

7.5.4 Theoretical future price

Following the general principles set in Sections 7.2.1–7.2.3, applied with reference to any deliverable bond i with its corresponding CF_i, and taking into account the accrued interest in the full bond price calculation:

$$
F_{th\ for\ i}.CF_i + accr_{ti} = (S_{ti} + accr_{ti}).(1 + r_\tau \tau) - FV(accr_{\tau i})
$$

Where $accr_{x\ i}$ means the accrued interest paid during x (x being τ or t). Hence,

$$
F_{th\ for\ i} = [(S_{ti} + accr_{ti})(1 + r_\tau \tau) - accr_\tau(1 + r_\tau \tau) - accr_{ti}]/CF
$$

Also,

$$
F_{mkt\ for\ i} = [(S_{ti} + accr_{ti})(1 + IRR_\tau \tau) - accr_\tau(1 + IRR_\tau \tau) - accr_{ti}]/CF
$$

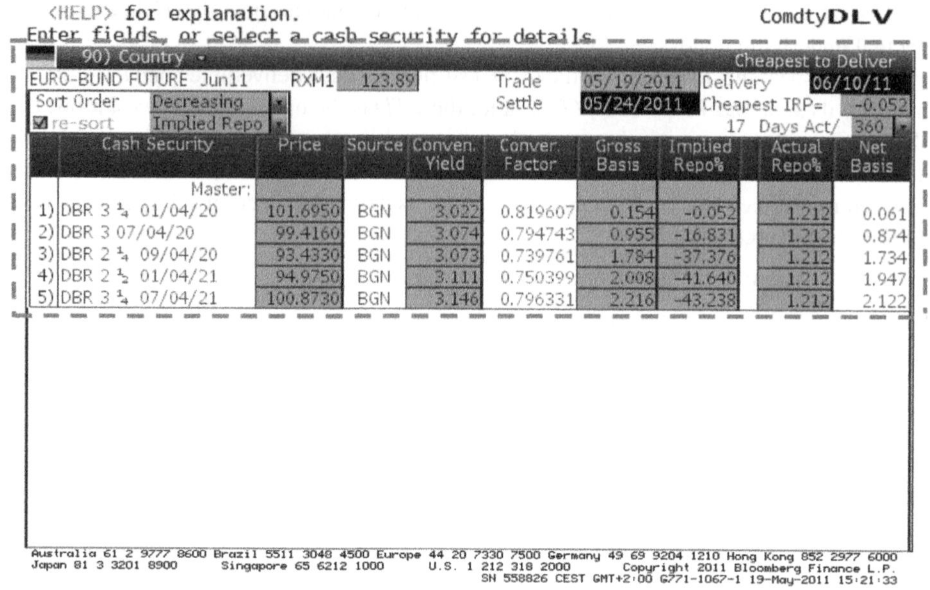

<HELP> for explanation.   ComdtyDLV
Enter fields, or select a cash security for details

90) Country ·							Cheapest to Deliver	
EURO-BUND FUTURE Jun11	RXM1	123.89			Trade	05/19/2011	Delivery	06/10/11
Sort Order	Decreasing				Settle	05/24/2011	Cheapest IRP=	-0.052
☑ re-sort	Implied Repo						17 Days Act/	360

Cash Security	Price	Source	Conven. Yield	Conver. Factor	Gross Basis	Implied Repo%	Actual Repo%	Net Basis
Master:								
1) DBR 3 ¼ 01/04/20	101.6950	BGN	3.022	0.819607	0.154	-0.052	1.212	0.061
2) DBR 3 07/04/20	99.4160	BGN	3.074	0.794743	0.955	-16.831	1.212	0.874
3) DBR 2 ¼ 09/04/20	93.4330	BGN	3.073	0.739761	1.784	-37.376	1.212	1.734
4) DBR 2 ½ 01/04/21	94.9750	BGN	3.111	0.750399	2.008	-41.640	1.212	1.947
5) DBR 3 ¼ 07/04/21	100.8730	BGN	3.146	0.796331	2.216	-43.238	1.212	2.122

Australia 61 2 9777 8600 Brazil 5511 3048 4500 Europe 44 20 7330 7500 Germany 49 69 9204 1210 Hong Kong 852 2977 6000
Japan 81 3 3201 8900   Singapore 65 6212 1000   U.S. 1 212 318 2000   Copyright 2011 Bloomberg Finance L.P.
                                                                    SN 558826 CEST GMT+2:00 G771-1067-1 19-May-2011 15:21:33

Figure 7.6   The Bloomberg screen from Figure 7.5

where $S_{ti} + accr_{ti}$ is the current dirty price of the bond (cf. Chapter 3, Section 3.2.3). These formulae look excessively heavy with the split of the accrued interest, but this allows to use a different day count on t than on τ, if necessary.

Example (continued).   The Bloomberg screen is repeated in Figure 7.6, to facilitate the reference to the data.

For example, for the # 1 bond, note (up and right of the Bloomberg screen) that there are 17 days from settlement of this day trade until delivery day, and that the current market rate (called *Actual Repo* on the Bloomberg screen) is 1.212%; the accrued interest from last coupon date of 04/01 is of 3.25% on 135 days. On the euro market, bond rates (coupons) are computed on an ACT/ACT basis, and money market rates on ACT/360 basis:

$$\overbrace{dirty\ price = 102.8971}$$

$$
\begin{aligned}
F_{th\ for_{\#1}} &= [(101.695 + 0.0325 \times 100 \times 135/365) \times (1 + 0.01212 \times 17/360) \\
&\quad -0.0325 \times 100 \times 17/360 \times (1 + 0.01212 \times 17/360) \\
&\quad -0.0325 \times 100 \times 135/365]/0.819607 \\
&= 123.9648 \\
F_{mkt} &= [(101.695 + 0.0325 \times 100 \times 135/365) \times (1 + \mathbf{IRR} \times 17/360) \\
&\quad -0.0325 \times 100 \times 17/360 \times (1 + \mathbf{IRR} \times 17/360) \\
&\quad -0.0325 \times 100 \times 135/365]/0.819607 \\
&= 123.89 \\
&\rightarrow IRR_\tau = -0.052\% \text{ (as per Bloomberg screen)}
\end{aligned}
$$

Regarding the columns Gross Basis and Net Basis (cf. Section 7.2.2),

"Gross Basis" = *"basis"* = $S - F_{mkt} \times CF = 101.695 - 123.89 \times 0.819607 = 0.15389$

"carry basis" = *basis on* $F_{th} = S - F_{th} \times CF = 101.695 - 123.9448 \times 0.819607 = 0.09257$

$\rightarrow$ *"value basis"* = *"basis"* − *"carry basis"* = *"Net Basis"* = $0.15389 - 0.09257 = 0.06132$,

as per the Bloomberg screen.

7.5.5   Hedging calculation with bond futures

Hedging a bonds portfolio means selling futures to offset potential losses on lowering bond prices of the portfolio. The determination of the hedge ratio, or number N of contracts to be sold, depends on the bonds to hedge. Going from the easiest to the most complex case, we will have to refine the basic relationship

N = bond nominal amount to hedge/nominal amount of 1 notional future contract

as follows.

The bonds portfolio contains only the current CTD (10-year, or any other):

the notional bond future behaving almost like the CTD, N becomes

$$N = \frac{nominal\ to\ hedge}{nominal\ 1\ future} \times CF_{CTD}$$

Example. On 03/10/03, Bund notional future maturing in June, last trading date on 06/06, was quoting (mid closing price): 116.25

The set of deliverable bonds and corresponding CF was:

Bund	price (*mid*)	conversion factor
#1 5% 04/01/12 − CTD	109.55	0.934130
#2 5% 04/07/12	109.51	0.931516
#3 4 1/2% 04/01/11	105.54	0.892821

On 10/03/03, hedging of €50 million for the beginning of June in Bund #1 (5% 01/04/12), as CTD of notional JUN Bund future, $CF_{CTD} = 0.93413$:

$$N = 50\,000\,000/100\,000 \times 0.93413 = 467.07 \Rightarrow 467 \text{ contracts}$$

The bonds portfolio only contains bonds of the deliverable set, out of the CTD:

Then, for each of the ith bond in the portfolio, the previous N calculation, still using the CF_{CTD}, must be adjusted by two corrective terms, namely a prices ratio and a modified durations ratio, to convert the N CTD like into a N deliverable bond i like:

$$\frac{S_{ti}}{S_{tCTD}} \ and \ \frac{MD_i}{MD_{CTD}}$$

Based on the same Bund future example, if the portfolio is made of Bund #2 (5% 07/04/12):

$$N = 50\,000\,000/100\,000 * 0.93413 * 109.51/109.55 * 7.246/7.094$$

$$= 476.89 \ or \ 477 \text{ contract}$$

The bonds portfolio contains bonds outside of (any) deliverable set:
For each ith bond in the portfolio we must:

- select the nearest (in terms of duration) deliverable bond of a notional future contract, being or not its CTD;
- apply the previous ad hoc relationship, depending on this nearest deliverable being or not the CTD;
- and finally, adjust its N by a β coefficient computed from a historical regression between some series of portfolio bond prices and of nearest deliverable bond prices; this way of determining the most adequate number of contracts and corresponding hedge ratio is similar to the one presented for stock index hedging in Section 7.3.3, as the optimal hedge ratio. Of course, such hedge ratio remains subject to further changes of the β.

Finally, in a more realistic case, the previous contract numbers must of course be computed and added for each of the portfolio bonds, depending on their status *vis-à-vis* the CTD and the deliverable bond set defined for the future contract.

7.6   FUTURES ON CURRENCIES

Currency futures do not present any particular aspects, the only source of troubles is – as always with currencies – not to make confusion in which of the two currencies, the reference one or the counter-value one, we value something. The theoretical future price is the same as for the currency forward price (cf. Eq. 5.1, but replacing here the forward maturity T by $\tau = T - t$), namely, for a τ not exceeding 1 year:

$$F_{th} = S \frac{1 + r_{c/v} \times \tau}{1 + r_{ref} \times \tau}$$

where τ is $n_{days}/360$ like on the interbank forex market.
    At first sight, this formula does not fit with the general form for F_{th},

$$F_{th} = \text{spot} + \text{financing cost} - \text{revenue}$$

The reason is of course due to the use of two currencies. Let us for example consider a future contract on the EUR/USD, that is, on a unit of EUR, quoted in dollars. Applying the general form to F_{th} on €1 gives

$F_{th} =$ current spot price of €1, expressed in some $

    $+$ financing cost, applied on these $ (i.e., @$LIBOR rate)

    $-$the *pro rata temporis* revenue on €1, that is, some quantity of €(@ EURIBOR)

Separating both currencies on each side of the "=" sign (the € on the left side and the $ on the right side), we get

F_{th} of €1 $+$ *revenue of* €1 (i.e., $1 \times r_€\tau) = S_t$ in $ \times (1 + r_\$\tau)$

    $\rightarrow$ €$1(1 + r_e\tau) = S_t(1 + r_\$\tau)$

Hence, 1 € "forward" $= S_t (1 + r_\$\tau) / (1 + r_e \tau)$, that is, conform to the above general relationship.

To illustrate the calculations, let us consider the case of a speculative trader, on 01/25/06, expecting in the weeks or months to come, a downward correction of the EUR/USD and selling accordingly JUN futures on the EUR/USD.

Such futures are quoted in USD like the corresponding spot price, the EUR being the reference currency, and are traded on the CME, with the following specifications:

- contract size: EUR 125 000;
- tick size: 1"pip"(cf. Chapter 3, Section 3.4.2), = $0.0001;
- hence tick value = $0.0001 × 125 000 = $12.50;
- settlement: cash;
- initial margin: EUR 2100 per contract.

For a nominal of; say, €4 million, the trader sells

$$N = €4\,000\,000/€125\,000 = 32 \text{ contracts.}$$

The initial deposit margin is

$$32 \text{ contracts}^*€2200 = €67\,200$$

or $82 656, @ 1.2300 (initial spot rate), that is, a leverage of about 60: 125 000 / 2100.

At inception, the (mid) spot is $1.2300 and the (mid) future is quoted $1.2385. By next 1st of March, the trader is unwinding his position, buying back the futures @ 1.2011, with a corresponding spot of 1.1950. The trading profit is

$$32 \text{ contracts} \times 125\,000 \times (\$1.2385 - \$1.2011) = \text{USD } 149\,600$$

Without taking account of possible margin call costs, the trading profit is

$$\$149\,600/\$82\,656 = 181\%,$$

or, relative to the underlying nominal of $4 290 000 (@ 1.2300):

$$149\,600/4\,920\,000 = 3.0\%.$$

7.7 FUTURES ON (NON-FINANCIAL) COMMODITIES

7.7.1 Introduction

Commodities futures, the most ancient future contracts, significantly differ by many aspects from financial futures. Historically, they were physically settled, given the nature of the underlying, but today, to facilitate the speculative trading, most of the contracts allow for a cash settlement. However, the traditional counterparties in a commodity future contract are the commodity producer and the commodity user, in a way that significantly affects the market of commodity futures. This particular relationship, specific to the commodities market, also affects the valuation of these futures. The reason is twofold:

- Non-financial commodities (precious metals, energy products, agricultural products, etc.) obviously do not pay any revenue.
- Yet they rather imply specific costs k, namely insurance and storage, which are to be added to the financing costs in the future pricing.

In the spirit of Section 7.2.1 and notations already used in Section 7.3.2, the theoretical future price thus becomes, in discrete time

$$F_{th} = S_t(1 + r_\tau \tau) + k$$

where k_τ is the costs incurred over τ. Or, by considering the present value of k over τ,

$$F_{th} = [S_t + PV(k_\tau)](1 + r_\tau)$$

In continuous time, these formulae become

$$F_{th} = S_t e^{r_\tau \tau} + k_\tau \ or \ F_{th} = [S_t PV(k_\tau)]e^{r_\tau \tau}$$

Finally, if, as often, k is quoted in dollar terms and paid up front, the formulae, in discrete and in continuous time, become

$$F_{th} = (S_t + k)(1 + r_\tau \tau) \ or \ F_{th} = (S_t + k)e^{r_\tau \tau} \tag{7.36}$$

7.7.2   Contango versus backwardation

Given the above relationships, F_{th} is naturally $>S_t$, a situation called contango, and the more the future maturity is remote, the more the contango (as measuring to what extent the future price is greater than the spot) – see Figure 7.7.

For example (January 2000), on the LME,

- spot copper price $= \$1800$ (/ton);
- 6M market rate $= 4\%$;
- copper storage cost $= \$2.20$ per month.

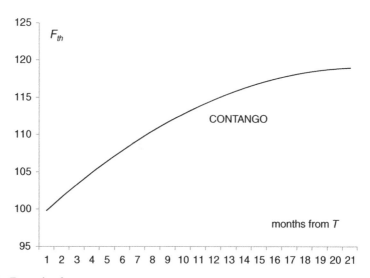

Figure 7.7 Example of contango

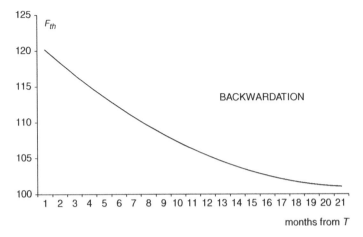

Figure 7.8   Example of a backwardation

For a 6M future contract:

$$F_{th} = 1800 \times (1 + 0.04 \times 0.5) + 6 \times 2.2 = 1849.20$$

Conversely, if F_{th} is $<S_t$, it is called a backwardation situation; the backwardation normally increases with maturity – see Figure 7.8.

It is typically the case of futures on (financial) assets offering a higher return than the financing rate, that is, with a negative carry. For example, bond futures, with a normal yield curve (i.e., such as higher bond yields than the corresponding money market rates).

7.7.3   Market price of a commodity future

To cope with commodities futures market prices, for historical reasons the market price is viewed in a different way than for financial futures. It is based on the traditional antagonism between a commodity producer = commodity seller and a commodity user = commodity buyer. From the commodity user viewpoint, if he expects lowering commodity prices, he will prefer buy (later @) spot than (today @) forward, and conversely if he expects rising commodity prices. This must be understood in the real case of producers and users selling and buying the commodity in a recurrent way, whatever the periodicity of the transactions. So, schematically,

	market expects S ↗:	market expects S ↘:
producers:	do not want sell F	want sell F (hedge)
users:	want buy F (hedge)	do not want buy F
	⇓	⇓
	users accept to pay more for hedging:	users will only buy fwd if @ more attractive price
	⇓	⇓
	$F_{mkt} > F_{th}$	$F_{mkt} < F_{th}$

The observed F_{mkt} price is actually the theoretical price, corrected by a factor called convenience yield y, that has been set as an implied revenue yield, *reducing*[7] the future price accordingly:

$$F \text{ market price} = F \text{ theoretical price} - \text{term of convenience yield } y$$

Equation 7.2 becomes:

$$F_{mkt} = F_{th \ corr} = (S_t + k)[1 + (r_\tau - y_\tau)\tau] \ or \ = (S_t + k)e^{(r_j - y_e)}$$

and can easily be adapted for the other ways to consider k.

Example. Using data from April 1989:

- spot copper $= \$1.41$, or ¢ 141 (per copper pound);
- market future price DEC (8 months $= 240$ days) $= 120.5$;
- market rate $= 12\%$;
- storage $=$ ¢ 0.5 (per copper pound and per month).

$$F_{mkt} = 141(1 + 0.12 \times 240/360) + 0.5 \times 8 - y = 120.5$$
$$\rightarrow y = ¢35.78$$

which can be converted in yield (based on spot price% p.a.):

$$y = 35.78/141 \times 360/240 = 38.06\%$$

A *positive* convenience yield thus means a *lower*, that is, *more attractive* future market price for the commodity *user*, and a *negative* convenience yield a *more attractive* future market price for the commodity *producer*. It therefore measures the possible impact of market pressure resulting from producers' wishes versus users' wishes. Today, with the increasing role of pure speculators (hedge funds, etc.), the behavior of the convenience yield over time is less straightforward. But at least this convenience yield conveys a lot of useful information.

Indeed, another way to view the convenience yield is that it is measuring the spread between the theoretical and the market price of the future. As such, we can view the standard deviation of y as the volatility of the spread between market and theoretical future prices over time.

Now, if $y < 0$, the future market price is de facto in contango, while if y goes more and more positive, it can even become high enough to induce a future market price lower than the corresponding spot price, leading to an a priori "abnormal" backwardation situation.

---

[7] From the right side of the table, it can be translated as it becomes convenient to buy forward at a reduced (market) cost.

To come back to the scheme of engaged market forces, completed by the speculative traders' role:

	market expects S ↗:	market expects S ↘:
producers:	do not want sell F	want sell F (hedge)
users:	want buy F (hedge) ⇓ users accept to pay more for hedging: ⇓ $F_{mkt} > F_{th}$ ⇓ y ↘ ⇓ contango ↗	do not want buy F ⇓ users will only buy fwd if @ more attractive price ⇓ $F_{mkt} < F_{th}$ ⇓ y ↗ ⇓ contango ↘ ⇒ backwardation
speculators:	*sell F*	*buy F*

Speculators are willing indeed to sell expensive / buy cheap, or put another way, they expect y to go back to an earlier level. As such, the speculative trading issue lies in the risk of change in the contango/backwardation regime over time.

For example, consider the WTI Crude Oil futures, quoted on the NYSE-ICE exchange, in 2011. A short time after a peak of spot price @ \$113.90 on April 29, the market had corrected somewhat, with a spot price on May 16 @ 98.71. The resulting futures prices curve presented some combination of first a contango pattern, followed by a backwardation pattern, then contango again (all with a narrow amplitude) – see Figure 7.9.

Altogether, through the role of y, the current F_{mkt} price can be viewed as the *expected value* of the spot price in T:

$$F_{mkt} = E_t(S_T)$$

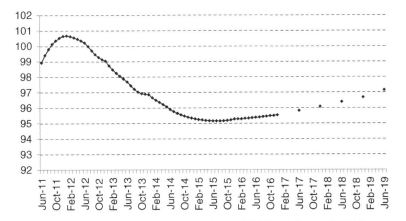

Figure 7.9   The WTI Crude Oil futures, quoted on the NYSE-ICE exchange, in 2011

In conclusion, the market price of commodities futures must be considered as significantly different from financial futures prices:

- The yield curve plays a less important role, as well as any long-term market expectation.
- More important is the current supply/demand balance and its impact, combined with speculative pressures, on $y(t)$.

7.7.4   Trading calculations with commodities futures

Let us present trading calculations through an example on the crude oil market (quoted on the NYMEX): On this market, the contract specifications are:

- contract size: 1000 barrels;
- contract value: 1000 × future price, corresponding to the price for 1 barrel;
- tick size: 1 ¢ of USD;
- →tick value = 1000 × \$0.01 = \$10;
- initial margin: \$8100;
- cash settlement.

On 10/01/08, a trader, anticipating the continuation of decreasing oil prices begun in July 2008, sells 100 MAR 09 contracts, @ 1000 × \$98.41. His initial margin is 100 × 8100 = \$810 000. After having noticed oil prices have bottomed on 12/24/08 at a price of 38.23 and initiated a correction phase from 26/12, he buys his contracts back on 01/06/09, @ 53.13. Out of possible treasury costs on his margin account, his profit is

$$100 \text{ contracts} \times 1000 \times (98.41 - 53.13) = \$4\,528\,000.$$

FURTHER READING

Galen BURGHARDT, Terry BELTON, *The Treasury Bond Basis*, McGraw-Hill, 3rd ed., 2005, 320 p. (on bond futures)

Frank J. FABOZZI, Roland FUSS, Dieter G. KAISER, *The Handbook of Commodity Investing*, John Wiley & Sons, Inc., Hoboken, 2008, 986 p.

Desmond FITGERALD, Financial futures, *Euromoney*, 1993.

Helyette GEMAN, *Commodities and Commodity Derivatives: Modelling and Pricing for Agricultural, Metals and Energy*, John Wiley & Sons, Ltd, Chichester, 2005, 416 p.

Donna KLINE, *Fundamentals of the Futures Market*, McGraw-Hill, 2000, 256 p.

Raymond M. LEUTHOLD, Joan C. JUNKUS, Jean E. CORDIER, *The Theory and Practice of Futures Markets*, Stipes Publishing, 1999, 410 p.

Part II
The Probabilistic Environment

8

The basis of stochastic calculus

8.1 STOCHASTIC PROCESSES

Stochastic is equivalent to *random*, hence the stochastic calculus develops rules of calculus to be applied if the problems to be handled are of a random (probabilistic) nature, in contrast with a *deterministic* one. As an example, unlike many physical phenomena (such as, for example, the trajectory of a bullet), the evolution of the prices or returns of financial products should intuitively not be considered as certain (deterministic). To be more realistic, their study should rather incorporate some random feature.

The deterministic or non-deterministic character of these financial products can be detected during the course of the time. It will thus concern forward products. The deterministic approach leads to the valuation of products such as vanilla swaps and futures, for which the forward value is obtained independently from the further evolution of their underlying instrument. The non-deterministic approach allows for taking into account a random evolution of the underlying spot instrument, which is necessarily the case for valuing products conditioned by such an evolution, that is, for options or any products presenting a conditional feature (for example, credit default swaps).

The evolution of the prices or returns of a financial instrument is to be represented by a mathematical *model* describing, at best, how prices or returns behave. It is important to distinguish between a *forecasting* model and an *ex post* – or *explanatory* – model. Here, we consider only *ex post* models. In the most general case, a process can be either deterministic or stochastic, or combining both features.

Strictly speaking, we should distinguish a *model* from a *process*: a prices or returns *process* is the reality, which "quants" aim to *model* in the most satisfying way. However, later in this chapter and in the following ones, we will follow the common way of saying, such as "modeling s.th. by a Wiener (for example) process".

Some Theoretical Reminder in Probability

Random variables, such as prices or returns, must be carefully related to the notion of *probability*. In the most general case, we must distinguish:

- data *samples*, or experimental outcomes, usually represented by ω; the set of all possible outcomes is represented by Ω;
- *events*, that are sets of one or several outcomes ω;
- the set of all *possible* events, represented by $\mathcal{F}$;
- $\Rightarrow$*probabilities* are assigned to events belonging to $\mathcal{F}$ (noted "$\in \mathcal{F}$"). A probability is a kind of measure, here denoted by P, so that for a possible event $A \in \mathcal{F}$, there is a $0 \leq P(A) \leq 1$ (note that $P(\Omega) = 1$);
- finally, the triplet $(\Omega, \mathcal{F}, P)$ is called a *probability space*.

Example. Let us suppose, in a simplistic way, that on a given day, the S&P 500 price would depend on a key speech to be delivered on that day by the Fed's President. The speech will contain several points, or outcomes ω. As a whole, it will be considered as favorable or unfavorable to the stock market: a favorable speech is an event, which may content several ωs, or features of the speech. The analyst will try to assess some probability to this event, namely, to the release of a speech that will be favorable to the stock market. In this example, $\mathcal{F}$ represents the set of all kinds of Fed's message that can be considered as realistic, while Ω would be the broader set of all possible messages, including oddities (but in the present case, we can assume that $\Omega = \mathcal{F}\ldots$).

Once this framework has been laid down, we can define a random variable X as a function defined on $\mathcal{F}$ so that for some event $A \in \mathcal{F}$, X has some numerical value. X is thus measurable, as a real number, in the sense that we can compute the probability that X has some values in some intervals of the set of real numbers $\mathbb{R}$.

Given probabilities are relative to events, the (cumulated probability) distribution function $F(x)$ associated to the random variable X can be defined by

$$F(x) = P(X \leq x)$$

where x represents some real number. For example, see Figure 8.1 for the case of a cumulative normal distribution.

In this example of a normal distribution ($\mu = 0$, $\sigma = 0.40$), $F(x) = P(X \leq x) = 0.7734$.

Provided $F(x)$ is continuously differentiable, we can determine the corresponding density function $f(x)$ associated to the random variable X as

$$f(x) = \frac{dF(x)}{dx}$$

Stochastic Processes

A stochastic process can be defined as a collection of random variables defined on the same probability space $(\Omega, \mathcal{F}, P)$ and "indexed" by a set of parameter T, that is, $\{X_t, t \in T\}$. Within the framework of our chapter, t is the time.

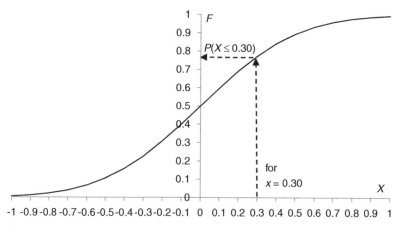

Figure 8.1   A cumulative normal distribution

For a given outcome or sample ω, $X_t(\omega)$ for $t \in T$ is called a sample path, realization or trajectory of the process. The space containing all possible values of X_t is called the state space.

Further in this chapter, we will only consider a one-dimension state space, namely the set of real numbers $\mathbb{R}$, that refers to T, and random variables X_t involved in stochastic processes $\{X_t, t \in T\}$ will be denoted by

$$\tilde{X}(t)$$

where "$\sim$" indicates its random nature over time t; these random variables will be such as a price, a rate or a return. Series of such prices or returns $\tilde{X}(t)$ in different (successive) times t of the state space

$$\{\tilde{X}(t), t\}$$

are called *time series*.

Discrete or Continuous?

This question must be raised in two aspects:

- by referring to the random variable $\{X_t, t \in T\}$, that can be either discrete or continuous: in the first case, the state space is discrete, and continuous in the second case;
- by referring to the set of parameter T: if T is discrete, we are dealing with a discrete parameter process, and if T is continuous, a continuous parameter process.

This leads to four alternatives, as follows:

	discrete parameter set:	continuous parameter set:
discrete state space:	discrete parameter chain	continuous parameter chain
continuous state space:	random sequence	random function, or **stochastic process**

In our time series, t may be considered as discrete or continuous. Most liquid financial instruments may look to be traded continuously in time, but their very nature remains discrete: there is always a time interval, as small as it may be, between two quotations, or between two consecutive traded prices. For convenience, these highly liquid instruments may, in a first approximation, be considered as continuously traded. In a continuous time environment, the $\tilde{X}(t)$ variable takes a specific value instantaneously, unlike the discrete case, where the $\tilde{X}(t)$ variable changes after a very small but measurable time interval. The hypothesis of continuous time greatly favors the mathematical treatment of the processes. Moreover, we will consider that, in such a continuous time framework, the random variable of prices or returns will change continuously as well. So that the processes we will consider relate to "stochastic processes" properly said.

Stationary or Non-Stationary Processes

A random process may also be considered as *stationary* or *non-stationary*. Broadly speaking, a process is stationary if the moments – practically, the first two to four moments, namely at least the mean and the variance – of the probability distribution characterizing this process are constant over time. Said more simply, a stationary process may be defined as a process that, as such, doesn't modify in the course of the time.

But defining precisely the stationarity would go beyond the scope of this book: indeed, if we work on a specific time series, we refer to a specific sample path or trajectory $X_t(\omega)$ of a process, given rise to a specific mean and variance of an $F(x)$, computed from the successive values of x over time. This does, however, not necessarily imply that these mean and variance would be the same for other sample paths in the state space (problem of "ergodicity"). So that, when computing a mean or a variance on a time series, to what extent can we consider that these values represent the mean and variance of the distribution $F(x)$ of the random variables of a given stochastic process?

For sake of simplicity, let us further consider that it is the case. In particular, stationarity implies that the probability P that a random variable reaches two given values on two different moments of time only depends on the time interval and not the two given moments of time:

$$P\left\{\tilde{X}(t_i) \leq x_i; \tilde{X}(t_{i+1}) \leq x_{i+1}\right\} \text{ depends on } t_i - t_{i-1} \text{ but not on } t_i, \text{ nor on } t_{i-1}.$$

Markovian Processes

A random process is said to be *Markovian* if the probability that a random variable $\tilde{X}(t_i)$ reaches a given value at a given time t_i only depends on its value reached on t_{i-1}, the previous moment of time only, and not on earlier values. It is therefore a *memory-less* process:

$$P\left\{\tilde{X}(t_i) \leq x_i | \tilde{X}(t_{i-1}) = x_{i-1}; \tilde{X}(t_{i-2}) = x_{i-2}; \ldots\right\} = P\left\{\tilde{X}(t_i) \leq x_i | \tilde{X}(t_{i-1}) = x_{i-1}\right\}$$

For $\tilde{X}(t)$, the probability of passing from a given value on t_{i-1} to a given value on t_i is called the *probability of transition*:

$$P\left\{\tilde{X}(t_i) \leq x_i | \tilde{X}(t_{i-1}) = x_{i-1}\right\}$$

In the case of a *stationary Markovian* process, the probability of transition does not depend on t_i and t_{i-1}, but on the time interval $t_i - t_{i-1}$ only.

Diffusion Processes

A *diffusion process* is a stationary Markovian process where both the time and the random variable are *continuous*. The term of *diffusion* suggests the analogy between the random behavior of our variables and the random nature of physical processes like the moving of a chemical material in a fluid. In the case of financial processes, the stochastic calculus is essentially developed within the framework of diffusion processes, considered as conveniently describing their behavior.

8.2 THE STANDARD WIENER PROCESS, OR BROWNIAN MOTION

The simplest diffusion process is a random process $\tilde{Z}$ whose values of a random variable $\tilde{y}$ in function of the time t follow a probabilistic distribution proportional to t. On a discrete time interval Δt, this process may be described by

$$\tilde{Z}(t + \Delta t) - \tilde{Z}(t) = \Delta \tilde{Z}(t) = \tilde{y}(t)\sqrt{\Delta t} \tag{8.1}$$

(The presence of "$\sqrt{\ }$" will be explained later.) Also, for $t = 0$, $\tilde{Z}(t)$ is such as $\tilde{Z}(0) = 0$.

For the sake of mathematical tractability, most financial diffusion processes assume that their random nature is fairly described by a Gaussian (or normal) probability distribution (or bell curve), fully determined by its mean μ and its variance σ^2. Hence

$$\tilde{y}(t) \sim \mathcal{N}(\mu, \sigma^2)$$

where the « $\sim$ » sign means that $\tilde{y}(t)$ "follows" a certain distribution probability law, and $\mathcal{N}(.)$ is the Gaussian distribution of probabilities.

In the case of the $\tilde{Z}$ process, $\mathcal{N}[y(t)]$ actually follows a « unit normal distribution », noted $\mathcal{N}(0,1)$, of mean $E = 0$ and variance $V = 1$ (hence, a standard deviation $STD = \sqrt{V} = 1$ as well).

In discrete time, Eq. 8.1 means therefore that the change of $\tilde{Z}(t)$ during Δt is following a Gaussian distribution with parameters $E = 0$ (because $0 \times \sqrt{\Delta t} = 0$), $STD = \sqrt{\Delta t}$ (because $1 \times \sqrt{\Delta t} = \sqrt{\Delta t}$) and $V = \Delta t$.

Passing from discrete to continuous time, and thus from discrete time (or "finite") intervals Δt to infinitely short, « infinitesimal » or « instantaneous » time intervals noted dt, Eq. 8.1 becomes

$$d\tilde{Z}(t) = \tilde{y}(t)\sqrt{dt} \qquad (8.2)$$

called a *standard Wiener process*, or a *Brownian process* or *Brownian motion*.[1] This process is also called (although improperly[2]) *white noise*, by analogy with the very light but permanent scratching behind a sound produced electronically.

From Eq. 8.2 we may deduct that the $d\tilde{Z}(t)$s are independently distributed and stationary. They are normally distributed, with $E = 0$, $V = dt$ (or $STD = \sqrt{dt}$).

Furthermore, $\tilde{Z}(t)$ is distributed according to a Gaussian distribution of parameters $E = 0$, $V = t$ (or $STD = \sqrt{t}$). We see now the reason of the presence of a $\sqrt{\ }$ in Eq. 8.1 and 2: the process allows us to consider that it is the variance V of the process that is proportional to time.

Formally speaking, a process $(X(t), t \geq 0)$ is a standard Wiener or Brownian motion if:

- $P[X(0)] = 0$: the Brownian motion starts from the origin, in $t_0 = 0$;
- $\forall s \leq t$, $X(t) - X(s)$ is a real variable, normally distributed, centered on its mean, and with a variance equal to $(t - s)$: the successive increases of the process are stationary;
- $\forall n, \forall t_i, 0 \leq t_1 \ldots \leq t_n$, the variables $X(t_n) - X(t_{n-1}), \ldots, X(t_1) - X(t_0), X(t_0)$, are independent: the successive increases of the process are independent.

Some statistical calculus[3] lead to the following properties of $\tilde{Z}(t)$:

$$1°) \, d\tilde{Z}^2(t) = dt \qquad (8.3)$$

---

[1] In the nineteenth century, a biologist named Brown had observed that an extremely light vegetal particle laid down on a perfectly quiet surface of water, instead of keeping still, was actually moving randomly. Several decades later on, this phenomenon has been explained by the random movement of the water molecules under the light particle, which affected its position.

[2] A true continuous, Gaussian, white noise is defined by

$$P[X(t)|x(\tau)] = P[X(t)] \text{ for } t > \tau \in T$$

where the $X(t)$ are mutually independent and normally distributed for any $t \in T$, in continuous time. But this is a "mathematic fiction", that is not workable in practice.

[3] For information purpose, the proof of Eqs. 8.3–8.6 is given in Annex 8.1, at the end of this chapter.

Therefore, $d\tilde{Z}^2$ is actually not random.

$$2°) \, d\tilde{Z}(t) \times dt = 0 \tag{8.4}$$

Hence, $d\tilde{Z}(t) \times dt$ is also not random.

With respect to the expected value of the product of $d\tilde{Z}(t)$ at two different points of time t_1 and t_2,

$$3°) \, E\left[d\tilde{Z}(t_1) \times d\tilde{Z}(t_2)\right] = 0 \tag{8.5}$$

Finally, the product of two different standard Wiener processes Z_1 and Z_2, is not random:

$$4°) \, d\tilde{Z}_1(t) \times d\tilde{Z}_2(t) = \rho_{1,2}(t) \times dt \tag{8.6}$$

where $\rho_{1,2}$ is the correlation coefficient between the two processes.

These relationships constitute the core of the stochastic calculus, together with the more general hypothesis that

$$5°) \, dt^2 = 0 \tag{8.7}$$

as a reasonable assertion.

A more general diffusion process is:

8.3   THE GENERAL WIENER PROCESS

This process describes a random variable $\tilde{X}$ combining a deterministic process – the μdt term – with a standard Wiener process in $d\tilde{Z}$

$$d\tilde{X}(t) = \mu dt + \sigma d\tilde{Z}(t) \tag{8.8}$$

In the general Wiener process, the μ and σ coefficients are posited *constant* and are called the *drift* and the *volatility* of the process. The drift can be defined as the instantaneous expected value of change in $\tilde{X}(t)$ per time unit and the volatility is the instantaneous *STD* of change in $\tilde{X}(t)$ per time unit. It follows that the expected value and variance of the general Wiener process are

$$E\left[d\tilde{X}(t)\right] = \mu dt$$
$$V\left[d\tilde{X}(t)\right] = \sigma^2 dt \rightarrow STD[.] = \sigma\sqrt{dt}$$

Finally, applying the Eqs. 8.3–8.5 to $\tilde{X}(t)$, we obtain:

$$(\mu dt + \sigma d\tilde{Z})^2 = \sigma^2 dt \tag{8.9}$$

8.4   THE ITÔ PROCESS

The most generalized form of the general Wiener process is called the *Itô process*, where the drift and volatility are functions of the stochastic variable and of the time:

$$d\tilde{X}(t) = \mu\left[\tilde{X}(t), t\right] dt + \sigma\left[\tilde{X}(t), t\right] d\tilde{Z}(t) \tag{8.10}$$

So that the expected value and the variance of the Itô process are also functions of $\tilde{X}(t)$ and t.

8.5 APPLICATION OF THE GENERAL WIENER PROCESS

General Wiener processes[4] are widely used to describe the behavior of financial products. In practice, we actually model the *returns* (rather than the prices) of financial time series by a general Wiener process. Long time series can indeed present large prices variations, while returns are more stable over time, as can be viewed in the example next.

If we define the instantaneous return in a continuous series of (spot) prices S, as

$$instantaneous\ return : X(t) = \frac{dS(t)}{S(t)}$$

from Eq. 8.8 we have

$$\frac{dS(t)}{S(t)} = \mu dt + \sigma dZ \tag{8.11}$$

giving

$$dS(t) = \mu S(t)dt + \sigma S(t)dZ \tag{8.11b}$$

which implies that S also follows a general Wiener process, but where the drift and volatility are proportional to the price level. This particular case of Wiener process is called *geometric* Wiener (or Brownian) process (geometric, because in a geometric average, numbers are not added but multiplied, like here μ and σ are multiplied by S). This process particularly fits well with the reality, since drifts and volatilities are actually proportional to the prices levels.

As an example, let us consider the time series of 395 5-minute prices of the S&P 500 from 09/08/09 to 09/14/09, as shown in Figure 8.2.

We have thus 395 times of observations $\{1, 2, \ldots, T\}$ with $T = 395$, and observations S_n, for $n = 1, 2, \ldots, T$.

Figure 8.2   Time series of 395 5-minute prices of the S&P 500

---

[4] NB: from now on, we will abandon the "~" subscripts on functions and variables since we will no longer question whether they are random or not.

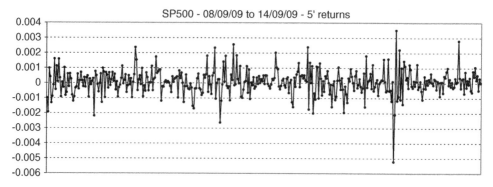

Figure 8.3   Corresponding 5' returns, computed as $r = \Delta S/S$

The corresponding 5' returns, computed as $r = \Delta S/S$, are shown in Figure 8.3.
In this example:

- the average of the series of 395 returns is $\mu = 0.00005934$; it corresponds to a return of 117.20% on a p.a. basis (i.e., × 395/5 on a day × 250, counting for 250 trading days a year[5]). To appreciate this value, it happens that the overall return $(S_T − S_1)/S_1$ on the whole 5-day period was 2.4736%, which, × 50 for a year, leads to the same order of magnitude;
- the standard deviation, or volatility of the returns is $\sigma = 0.000838$, or 11.77% on a p.a. basis, that is, $0.000838 \times \sqrt{(250 \times 395/5)} = 0.1177$.

Although 5 minutes is hardly an approximation for dt, discretizing dt by a $\Delta t = 5'$, the general Wiener process (by discretizing Eq. 8.11 and by omitting "(t)" in $S(t)$, to simplify the notations) is:

$$\frac{\Delta S}{S} = r = \mu \Delta t + \sigma \Delta Z = 0.00005934\Delta t + 0.000838\Delta Z$$

where Δt is the unit time interval and ΔZ is a standard Wiener process such as $\Delta Z \sim N(0,1)$, or

$$\Delta S = 0.00005934 S \Delta t + 0.000838 S \Delta Z$$

with $\Delta S = S_{t+1} − S_t$, so that

$$S_{t+1} = S_t + \mu S_t \Delta t + \sigma S_t \Delta Z$$

So that, computed *ex post*, on the whole time series, the trend applied on the prices series is $S \times \mu$ on the 5' data, which gives:

$$S_{t+1} = S_t \times (1 + 0.00005934) \ from \ t = 1 \ to \ t = 395$$

as the dotted line shows in Figure 8.4.

In our example, selecting a particular 5' time interval where the S&P 500 price is $S_t = 1040$ and assuming – what is actually not fully true – the returns distribution is Gaussian,

---

[5] For this convention, and further about the p.a. value of volatility, see Chapter 14, Section 14.1.2.

Figure 8.4   Trend applied on the SP500 prices series

there are 68% chances that, 5 minutes later, S_{t+1} will be comprised between $+1$ and -1 standard deviation:

$$S_t + \mu S_t + \sigma S_t \times (-1) \ and \ S_t + \mu S_t + \sigma S_t \times (+1)$$

that is, between

$$1040 + 1040 \times 0.00005934 - 1040 \times 0.000838 = 1039.19$$

and

$$1040 + 1040 \times 0.00005934 + 1040 \times 0.000838 = 1040.93$$

The drift and the volatility of the time series can be viewed as the measure of its return (profit) and risk respectively. Indeed, supposing that the computed drift and volatility are – will remain – constant over time, in average, such an investment in the S&P 500 would have:

• earned an average profit or return of 117.20% p.a.
• with a risk (of fluctuations around this average profit) of 11.77% p.a.

8.6   THE ITÔ LEMMA

The problem with working on financial time series is that, while the above processes are defined by differential equations, successive prices and returns are actually not continuous in time. This prohibits differentiating or integering them in function of the time, as if they were continuous in time. To overcome this difficulty, instead of working directly on the returns or on the prices, we can use a continuous function of the time and of the financial variable (return or price), that becomes differentiable. Let y be such a continuous function of a financial variable $X(t)$, X being, for example, a return or a price:

$$y(t) = y\,[X(t), t]$$

If we consider $X(t)$ as modeled by an Itô process (as the most general case among those presented in Sections 8.2–8.4), that is, by Eq. 8.10

$$dx(t) = \mu\,[X(t), t]\,dt + \sigma\,[X(t), t]\,dZ(t)$$

the Itô lemma consists in the calculation of the subsequent derivative of $y = y[X(t),t]$, that is, $dy(X,t)$:

$$dy(X,t) = \left[\frac{\partial y}{\partial t} + \frac{\partial y}{\partial X}\mu + \frac{1}{2}\frac{\partial^2 y}{\partial X^2}\sigma^2\right]dt + \frac{\partial y}{\partial X}\sigma \, dZ \qquad (8.12)$$

Equation 8.12 results from the development of the differential dy up to terms of order-2 (higher powers being considered as negligible), then applying Eq. 8.3, Eq. 8.4, Eq. 8.7 and Eq. 8.9 of the stochastic calculus on each of the partial differentials of dy. Its proof is given in Annex 8.2, at the end of this chapter.

It is worth mentioning that the above Itô lemma is the particular case of the more general presentation of this lemma, where μ and thus X are n-dimensional vectors, and dZ is an m-dimensional vector (cf. the references at the end of this chapter).

8.7 APPLICATION OF THE ITÔ LEMMA

Let us consider that the (spot) price S of a stock follows the geometric Wiener process of Eq. 8.11b:

$$dS(t) = \mu S(t)dt + \sigma S(t)dZ$$

and let us take as a continuous function y of time and price:

$$y(t) = \ln S(t)$$

(The reason for choosing the $\ln$ function will become clear later.) By applying the Itô lemma (Eq. 8.12), and taking into account that

- $\partial y(t)/\partial t$ does not exist, since S is actually not derivable by t, because of its stochastic component;[6]
- $\partial y(t)/\partial S(t) = 1/S(t)$ (classical result of algebra);
- $\partial^2 y(t)/\partial S(t)^2 = -1/S(t)^2$ (idem),

the result is

$$dy(t) = \left(\mu - \frac{1}{2}\sigma^2\right)dt + \sigma \, dZ$$

By integrating this relation from $t = 0$ to current time t,

$$y(t) = y(0) + \int_0^t \left(\mu - \frac{1}{2}\sigma^2\right)ds + \int_0^t \sigma \, dZ$$

with $y(t) = \ln S(t)$, and remembering the relationship defining $Z(t)$ as a random variable multiplied by $\sqrt{t}$ (cf. Eq. 8.2 defining the standard Wiener process), we obtain

$$y(t) = \ln S(t) = \ln S(0) + \left(\mu - \frac{1}{2}\sigma^2\right)t + [Z(t) - Z(0)]\sqrt{t}$$

with $Z(0) = 0$ (cf. Section 8.2). Notice that, in the previous equation, the notations $Z(t)$ and $Z(0)$ are used for convenience. They actually represent the observed values of $y(t)$ in t and in

---

[6] Actually, S is not derivable by t in the sense of the classical analysis, since it is modeled by a Wiener process, in continuous time, but with a non-continuous real argument.

$t = 0$, given the process $Z(t)$ as defined by Eq. 8.2. So that $y(t) = \ln S(t)$ follows a normal distribution of

- mean $= \ln S(0) + \left(\mu - \frac{1}{2}\sigma^2\right) t$;
- variance $= \sigma^2 t$.

This relationship can be re-written as

$$\ln \frac{S(t)}{S(0)} = \left(\mu - \frac{1}{2}\sigma^2\right) t + \sigma \sqrt{t} Z(t) \tag{8.13}$$

Having defined the return of S between $t - 1$ and t under its usual form by $(S_t - S_{t-1})/S_{t-1}$, or $S_t/S_{t-1} - 1$, we can see that the $\ln$ of this expression gives a nearby result and can also be considered as a "return", more specifically called the $\ln$ of the return or the "log return", that is,

$$\ln \frac{S_t}{S_{t-1}}$$

Example. With $S_{t-1} = 100$ and $S_t = 101$, the classical return is 0.01 or 1% and the log return is $\ln 101/100 = 0.00995$. Actually, log returns are extensively used in quantitative finance, due to the pertinence and usefulness of Eq. 8.13.

Equation 8.13 thus models the log returns of $S(t)$, that are normally distributed (because of the term in $Z(t)$). Furthermore, from Eq. 8.13 we can model the prices themselves:

$$S(t) = S(0)e^{\left(\mu - \frac{\sigma^2}{2}\right)t + \sigma \sqrt{t} Z(t)} \tag{8.14}$$

meaning that while the log returns of $S(t)$ are normally distributed, the prices themselves are "log-normally" distributed (the log-normal distribution is defined as the probability distribution of a variable of which the distribution of its $\ln$ is normal).

If the integration was made without taking care of the rules of the stochastic calculus, the differential Eq. 8.10 of the process would be integrated without passing through the Itô lemma and would give

$$\ln \frac{S(t)}{S(0)} = \mu t + \sigma \sqrt{t} Z(t)$$

instead of Eq. 8.13, that is, without the term in $-\frac{1}{2}\sigma^2 t$, as well as in its price variant:

$$S(t) = S(0)e^{\mu t + \sigma \sqrt{t} Z(t)} \tag{8.14'}$$

And one more step "earlier", if the integration was made in a purely deterministic world, that is, without taking into account the stochastic term of the differential integration of the process Eq. 8.10, it would give

$$\ln \frac{S(t)}{S(0)} = \mu t \text{ and } S(t) = S(0)e^{\mu t} \tag{8.14''}$$

Let us look after the effect of these three "levels" of integration through the following example:

The price S of a stock follows a geometric Wiener process Eq. 8.10, with S valuing presently $\$100$, its μ equal to 10% p.a. and its σ, 10% p.a. Let us consider these parameters would remain constant in the future price evolution of S over the next 5 years. In a purely deterministic world,

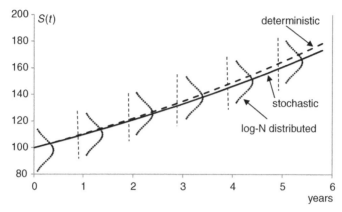

Figure 8.5   Comparison between three "levels" of integration

based on Eq. 8.14", $S(1)$, $S(2)$, ... and $S(5)$, that is prices after 1, 2, ... and 5 years would be:

$$S(1) = 100e^{0.10*1} = 110.52$$
$$S(2) = 100e^{0.10*2} = 122.14$$

...

$$S(5) = 100e^{0.10*5} = 164.87$$

Now, by using Eq. 8.14', in a random world but without following the rules of the stochastic calculus, it would lead to ranges of prices distributed according to a log-normal curve centered around each of the previous results.

Finally, by strictly applying the stochastic calculus with Eq. 8.14, the result is:

$S(1)$ range log-normally distributed around $100 \times exp[0.10 - \frac{1}{2}\, 0.10^2) \times 1]$
$S(2)$ range log-normally distributed around $100 \times exp[0.10 - \frac{1}{2}\, 0.10^2) \times 2]$

...

$S(5)$ range log-normally distributed around $100 \times exp[0.10 - \frac{1}{2}\, 0.10^2) \times 5] = 160.8$,

which is less than the value of 164.87 calculated in the deterministic hypothesis. These three ways can be worked out as in Figure 8.5.

We can see the importance of the term $-\frac{1}{2}\sigma^2 t$, which may be viewed as an effect of turbulence in a water flow. The volatility indeed plays such a role, that is, an effect of slowing down, in the prices evolution: like in a turbulent flow, where a part of the water is whirling around itself, and thus, despite the general move ahead, causing some slowing down proportional to the amplitude of the turbulence (that is, here, of the volatility).

Also, notice that on the above schematic graph, it is not possible to show that the successive log-normal distributions actually present a variance increasing with t (cf. Eq. 8.14 and 14').

8.8   NOTION OF RISK NEUTRAL PROBABILITY

The diffusion processes presented here have all in common a probabilistic $dZ(t)$ component based on the normal distribution. Researchers have proposed alternative probabilistic distributions (cf. Chapter 15, Section 15.1), to try to better capture some aspects of the actual probabilistic behavior of financial time series, but beyond the complexity of such models, none has actually been accepted as working better in general.

It is nevertheless the case that the normal distribution is oversimplifying the reality. It should be emphasized that the whole material developed within the framework of the usual stochastic calculus being based on the use of the normal distribution, its results are restricted on such a specific hypothesis.

Among others, because of the symmetry of the normal distribution, the probability of positive returns is equal to the probability of negative returns, which implies neither expectation of any unequal probability of up- nor down-trend in returns. Moreover, with mixed processes, combining a deterministic and a probabilistic component, a questionable parameter is the value of the μ parameter: like for the σ parameter,[7] it can only have been determined *ex post*, or posited quite arbitrarily for the future.

In particular, μ can be set equal to the market risk-less rate r, as a way to escape to any kind of opinion about it: the normal probability distribution, centered on a mean $= r$, is therefore called "risk neutral probability" (if $\mu \neq r$, we talk of "physical probability"). And the calculations based on $\mu = r$ in addition to our initial set of hypotheses and consequences of the choice of the normal distribution, are said to be made in a "risk neutral world". In the same way, a "risk neutral" investor is the one considering $\mu = r$, making thus no assumption about possible $\mu <$ or $> r$. Any other value for μ implies some degree of *risk aversion*, which can be defined as

$$\frac{\mu - r}{\sigma} \tag{8.15}$$

This measure recalls – despite somewhat different notations – the price of risk measure within the framework of the CAPM (cf. Chapter 4, Section 4.3.4, Eq. 4.4).

8.9 NOTION OF MARTINGALE

The geometric Wiener process applied on the returns of a stock price S (Eq. 8.1),

$$\frac{dS}{S} = \mu dt + \sigma dZ$$

has been built by using a physical probability measure, given the μ drift, associated with the stochastic standard Wiener process dZ. By assuming $\mu = r$, this equation can be rewritten with the risk neutral probability measure, called Q. Defining dZ^Q as

$$dZ^Q = dZ - \frac{\mu - r}{\sigma} dt$$

we obtain

$$\frac{dS}{S} = rdt + dZ^Q \tag{8.16}$$

---

[7] The case of the σ will be considered in Chapter 12.

that is, a geometric Wiener process involving a standard Wiener process under Q^8. Integrating Eq. 8.16 in the same manner as in Section 8.7, instead of obtaining (Eq. 8.14)

$$S(t) = S(0)e^{\left(\mu - \frac{\sigma^2}{2}\right)t + \sigma\sqrt{t}Z(t)}$$

we obtain a similar relationship, but with r instead of μ:

$$S(t) = S(0)e^{\left(r - \frac{\sigma^2}{2}\right)t + \sigma\sqrt{t}Z(t)}$$

Therefore, by integration, the realization of $S(t)$ on T will involve a (log-normal) risk neutral probability distribution, centered on the objective, "neutral" value of r, instead of on an arbitrary value μ. To further explain the word "centered", let us refer to the statistic theory, establishing the following correspondence between normal and log-normal parameters:

	normal distribution (returns):	log-normal distribution (prices):
mean:	m	$e^{m + \frac{\sigma^2}{2}}$
median:	m	e^m
variance:	σ^2	σ^2

In particular, there is an equal probability that S_T will actually turn out to be higher or lower than the median. Since the median of a log-normal distribution is of the form of e^m, it corresponds to the forward value F_T as expected value for S_t, at T. For a maturity T, while the traditional forward is $F_T = S_t e^{\mu T}$ (in continuous time, cf. Eq. 1.7), the forward "under Q" becomes

$$F_T^Q = S_t e^{rT} \qquad (8.17)$$

Under Q, there is thus an equal probability that S_T actually turns out to be higher or lower than the median $F_T^Q = S_t e^{rT}$, as shown in Figure 8.6.

Thus, under Q, the actual realization of $S(t+1)$ *only* depends on the previous value of $S(t)$ *and nothing else* (no more of an arbitrary μ). It thus corresponds to a no-arbitrage valuation (there is no more possibility of arbitrage between two valuations based on two different μ values).

In particular, since our process is Markovian (cf. Sections 7.1 and 7.2), neither does $S(T)$ depend on earlier values of S at previous times t. With this respect, the geometric Wiener process under Q, of Eq. 8.16, using the risk neutral probability measure, is called a *semimartingale*, That is, a variant of a "martingale". A martingale is a Markovian (memory-less) stochastic process such as, at t, the conditional expected value of S_{t+1}

$$E(S_{t+1}|S_t, \ldots, S_1) = S_t$$

is S_t. In our case, we talk of a *semimartingale*, that is, a martingale completed by a finite variation, of the e^{rt} form here. Indeed, in our case, $E(S_{t+1}|S_t, \ldots, S_1)$ does not equal S_t, but the forward value $F_{t+1}^Q = S_t e^{r(t+1)}$.

These notions will play a major role in the option pricing theory, see Chapter 10, in particular Section 10.2.4.

---

[8] This can be more formally stated by use of the Girsanov's theorem (cf., e.g., NEFTCI in the further reading at the end of the chapter).

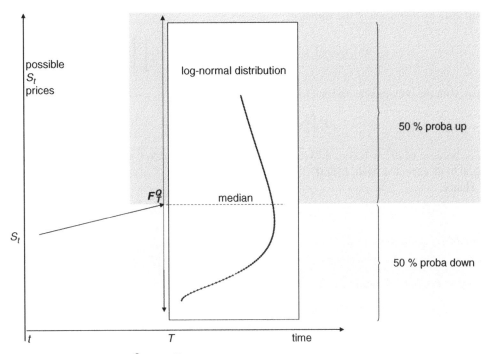

Figure 8.6   Property of $F_T^Q = S_t e^{rT}$

Finally, let us come back to the relationship 8.17, valuing a forward or future under Q, the risk neutral probability measure: as a consequence, the geometric general Wiener process (Eq. 8.16) under Q, applied to a forward or a future, comes down to

$$dF_T^Q = \sigma F_T^Q dZ^Q \tag{8.18}$$

ANNEX 8.1: PROOFS OF THE PROPERTIES OF $dZ(t)$

(see Section 2) These proofs are given for information purpose only, the calculations bringing no useful concept or more insight about stochastic calculus. Most of these proofs are based on the variance definition, and on the fact that a variable having a null variance is not stochastic and is equal to its expected value.

NB: for convenience, the "$\sim$" symbol is omitted hereafter.

Proof of Eq. 8.3 – Square of the Standard Wiener Process

$$dZ(t)^2 = dt$$

By definition of the variance,

$$V[dZ(t)] = E[dZ(t) - E(dZ(t))]^2$$

knowing that $V[dZ(t)] = dt$, since $E[dZ(t)] = 0$,

$$V[dZ(t)] = dt = E[dZ(t)]^2$$

And also, by definition of the variance,

$$V\left[dZ(t)^2\right] = E\left\{\left[\left(y\sqrt{dt}\right)^2 - E\left(dZ(t)^2\right)\right]^2\right\}$$

here, with the previous result for $E[dZ(t)]^2$,

$$E\left\{\left[y^2dt - dt\right]^2\right\} = dt^2 E\{\ldots\}$$

$= 0$, because of $dt^2 = 0$ (Eq. 8.7). Since its variance is null, $dZ(t)^2$ is not stochastic, and is equal to its expected value $E[dZ(t)^2]$.

Hence,

$$dZ(t)^2 = E\left[dZ(t)^2\right] = dt$$

And $dZ(t)^2$ is not stochastic.

Proof of Eq. 8.4 – Product $dZ(t) \times dt$

Let us again start from the variance definition:

$$V[dZ(t)dt] = E\left\{[dZ(t)dt - E(dZ(t)dt)]^2\right\} = dt^2 E\{\ldots\} = 0$$

Since its variance is null, $dZ(t)dt$ is not stochastic, and is equal to its expected value $E[dZ(t)dt]$. With

$$E[dZ(t)dt] = dtE[dZ(t)]$$

and given $E[dZ(t)] = 0$,

$$E[dZ(t)dt] = 0$$

and $dZ(t) \times dt$ is not stochastic.

Proof of Eq. 8.5 – Expected Value of the Product of Two dZ(t) at Two Different Moments of Time

For $t_i \neq t_j$, by definition of the $y(t)$ process, $y(t_i)$ and $y(t_j)$ are independent hence $cov[y(t_i), y(t_j)] = 0$; moreover,

$$E[y(t_i)] = E\left[y(t_j)\right] = 0$$

Hence,

$$E\left[dZ(t_i)\,dZ(t_j)\right] = dt\left\{cov\left[y(t_i),\, y(t_j)\right] + E[y(t_i)]\,E\left[y(t_j)\right]\right\} = 0$$

In other words, $dZ(t_i)$ is not correlated with $dZ(t_j)$.

It can be further shown that $dZ(t)$ is a stationary process:

- first-order moment: $E[dZ(t)] = 0$
- second-order moment: $V[dZ(t)] = dt$
- second-order moments: negligible because they contain dt^n with $n > 2$.

Proof of Eq. 8.6 – Product of Two Standard Wiener Processes

$$dZ_1(t)dZ_2(t) = \rho_{12}(t)dt$$

The expected value of the product of two stochastic variables is

$$E\left[dZ_1(t)dZ_2(t)\right] = E\left[dZ_1(t)\right] E\left[dZ_2(t)\right] + cov\left[dZ_1(t), dZ_2(t)\right]$$

which introduces the covariance. Here, both $E[dZ_i(t)] = 0$, hence

$$E\left[dZ_1(t)dZ_2(t)\right] = cov\left[dZ_1(t), dZ_2(t)\right]$$

From the relationship between covariance and correlation

$$cov\left[dZ_1(t)dZ_2(t)\right] = \rho_{12}(t)STD\left[dZ_1(t)\right] STD\left[dZ_2(t)\right]$$

since both $STD[dZ_i(t)] = \sqrt{dt}$,

$$cov\left[dZ_1(t)dZ_2(t)\right] = \rho_{12}(t)dt$$

hence,

$$E\left[dZ_1(t)dZ_2(t)\right] = \rho_{12}(t)dt$$

The variance of the product of these stochastic variables is

$$V\left[dZ_1(t)dZ_2(t)\right] = E\left[dZ_1(t)^2dZ_2(t)^2\right] - E\left[dZ_1(t)dZ_2(t)\right]^2 = dt^2 - \rho_{12}(t)^2dt^2 = 0$$

Since its variance is null, $dZ_1(t)dZ_2(t)$ is not stochastic, and is equal to its expected value:

$$E\left[dZ_1(t)dZ_2(t)\right] = cov\left[dZ_1(t)dZ_2(t)\right] = \rho_{12}(t)dt$$

ANNEX 8.2: PROOF OF THE ITÔ LEMMA

(cf. Section 6) To prove the Eq. 8.12, let us start from the full differential of $dy(X,t)$, omitting here and after the writing of "(t)" in $X(t)$ and "(X,t)" in $dy(X,t)$ to simplify the notations:

$$dy = \frac{\partial y}{\partial x}dx + \frac{\partial y}{\partial t}dt + \frac{1}{2}\frac{\partial^2 y}{\partial x^2}dx^2 + \frac{1}{2}\frac{\partial^2 y}{\partial x\partial t}dxdt + \frac{1}{2}\frac{\partial^2 y}{\partial t^2}dt^2 + terms\ of\ higher\ order$$

Given Eq. 8.10,

$$dx = \mu dt + \sigma dZ$$

and Eq. 8.9, that is,

$$(\mu dt + \sigma dZ)^2 = \sigma^2 dt$$

so that in dy, $dx^2 = \sigma^2 dt$, dy becomes:

$$dy = \frac{\partial y}{\partial x}(\mu dt + \sigma dZ) + \frac{\partial y}{\partial t}dt + \frac{1}{2}\frac{\partial^2 y}{\partial x^2}\sigma^2 dt + \frac{1}{2}\frac{\partial^2 y}{\partial x\partial t}(\mu dt^2 + \sigma dZdt) + \frac{1}{2}\frac{\partial^2 y}{\partial t^2}dt^2$$

$$\Downarrow \quad \Downarrow \quad \Downarrow$$
$$= 0 = 0 = 0$$

by Eq. 8.7, 8.4 and 8.7 respectively.
    Rearranging the terms in dt and in dZ leads to Eq. 8.12.

FURTHER READING

Darrell DUFFIE, *Security Markets: Stochastic Models*, Academic Press Inc., 1988, 250 p.

L.C.G. ROGERS, David WILLIAMS, *Diffusions, Markov Processes and Martingales, vol. 1: Foundations, vol. 2: Itô Calculus*, Cambridge University Press, 2nd ed., 2000, 406 and 494 p.

A.G. MALLIARIS, W.A. BROCK, *Stochastic Methods in Economics and Finance*, North-Holland, 2nd ed., 1981, 324 p. Interestingly broadening the field of applications of stochastic calculus.

Salih N. NEFTCI, *An Introduction to the Mathematics of Financial Derivatives*, Academic Press, 2nd ed., 2000, 527 p. In my opinion, the most convenient book to enter the stochastic calculus theory. Half of it is devoted to the topics of this chapter; the balance can be used to deepen Chapters 11 and 12.

## 9

Other financial models: from ARMA to the GARCH family

The previous chapter dealt with *stochastic* processes, which consist of (returns) models involving a mixture of deterministic and stochastic components. By contrast, the models developed here present three major differences:

- These models are *deterministic*; since they are aiming to model a non-deterministic variable such as a return, the difference between the model output and the actual observed value is a *probabilistic* error term.
- By contrast with stochastic processes described by differential equations, these models are built in *discrete time*, in practice, the periodicity of the modeled return (daily, for example).
- By contrast with usual Markovian stochastic processes, these models incorporate in the general case a limited number of previous return values, so that they are not Markovian.

For a time series of past observations on the variable x up to $t - 1$, all these processes are of the form

$$x_t = deterministic\ f\ (1\ or\ several\ past\ values\ of\ x(t)) + probabilistic\ error\ term$$

where $f(.)$ is linear.

9.1 THE AUTOREGRESSIVE (AR) PROCESS

Let us consider a series of past returns $\{r_0, \ldots, r_{t-1}\}$ or, in short, $\{r_t\}$, of 0 mean, such as:

$$r_t = r_t\ forecast + \varepsilon_t$$

where ε_t is the error term, also called "innovation",[1] or "white noise". In practice, ε_t is supposed to be normally distributed: $\varepsilon_t \sim \mathcal{N}(0, \sigma_t^2)$.

Let further be the r_t *forecast* defined as the previous return r_{t-1}, times a constant a: the autoregressive process $AR(1)$ is defined by:

$$r_t = ar_{t-1} + \varepsilon_t$$

where r_t is thus depending on the previous value (r_{t-1}) of r only. Generalizing, if $\{r_t\}$ has a mean $\mu \neq 0$, actually, a positive or negative trend:

$$r_t - \mu = a\ (r_{t-1} - \mu) + \varepsilon_t$$

---

[1] Actually, there is some nuance between the "error" and "innovation" terms; but it goes beyond the scope of this book. See for example, Chapter 1 of F.J. FABOZZI, S. FOCARDI, P. KOLM, *Trends in Quantitative Finance*, CFA Institute: regarding forecasting models, the authors distinguish between errors as innovation and errors containing some residual forecastability.

Figure 9.1 Computing an AR(1) forecasting

Example. On a past series of 21 daily closing prices of S&P 500 (10/13 to 11/09/09), let us forecast the returns (and corresponding prices) from 11/10 to 11/17 by an AR(1), as in Figure 9.1.

This example results in a rather poor forecast. It is given for exemplifying the process implementation only. Practically speaking, the number of previous terms of the series (here, arbitrarily, 18 terms) should have to be optimized, and the parameter a updated for the successive forecasts. Moreover, if the data present irregularities in their succession (changes of trends, mean reversion, etc.), the AR process is unable to incorporate such phenomena and works poorly.

The generalized form of the previous case, in order to forecast r_t as a function of more than its previous observed value, can be represented as follows:

$$r_t - \mu = a_1 (r_{t-1} - \mu) + a_2 (r_{t-2} - \mu) + \ldots + a_p (r_{t-p} - \mu) + \varepsilon_t$$

This is called an $AR(p)$ process, involving the previous p values of the series. There is no rule for determining p, provided it is not excessive (by application of the "parcimony principle"). The above relationship looks like a linear regression, but instead of regressing according to a series of independent variables, this regression uses previous values of the dependent variable itself, hence the "autoregression" name.

9.2 THE MOVING AVERAGE (MA) PROCESS

Let us consider a series of returns consisting in pure so-called "random numbers" $\{\varepsilon_t\}$, i.i.d., generally distributed following a normal distribution. These ε_t are generated such as

- $E[\varepsilon_t] = 0$
- $V[\varepsilon_t] = \sigma^2$
- $\text{cov}[\varepsilon_t, \varepsilon_{t'}] = 0$, that is, the ε_t are mutually independent.

An *MA*(1) process is defined as

$$r_t = \varepsilon_t + b\varepsilon_{t-1}$$

where b is a constant. r_t is a "random walk" built from the successive random numbers.
Generalizing, a MA(q) process, involving the q previous values of the series, is defined by

$$r_t = \varepsilon_t + b_1\varepsilon_{t-1} + b_2\varepsilon_{t-2} + \ldots + b_q\varepsilon_{t-q}$$

It results that

- $E[r_t] = 0$
- $V[r_t] = \sigma^2 \Sigma b_k{}^2$ (since the ε_t are independent)
- for $|t - t'| \leq q$, $cov[r_t, r_{t'}] = \sigma^2 \Sigma b_t b_{t'}$ and $= 0$ for $|t - t'| > q$.

This process is stationary, given $E[.]$ is constant and $cov[.]$ is independent of t. We say
that the process has a "memory" of q, to express that the resulting r_t is computed from the q
previous values of the data series.

Example. Let us start from a series of 20 randomly selected numbers ε_t, normally distributed
as a $\mathcal{N}(0, 1)^2$ and compute an MA(1) and an MA(5), with $b_1 = b_2 = \ldots = b_5 = 0.5$:

$$r_t = \varepsilon_t + 0.5\varepsilon_{t-1}$$
$$r_t = \varepsilon_t + 0.5\varepsilon_{t-1} + 0.5\varepsilon_{t-2} + 0.5\varepsilon_{t-3} + 0.5\varepsilon_{t-4} + 0.5\varepsilon_{t-5}$$

On Excel, we can use the *NORMSINV (Rand())* function to generate the ε_ts from a $\mathcal{N}(0, 1)$
(see Figure 9.2).

We notice that the variance is reducing with the length of the process memory. By contrast,
the AR process has an infinite memory, since each r_t depends on the previous one.

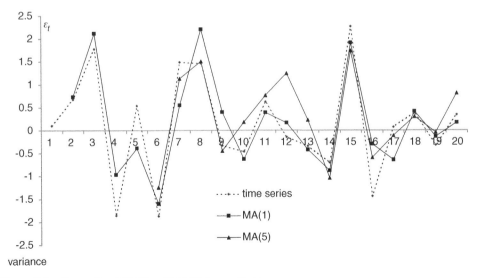

Figure 9.2   Computing MA(1) and MA(5) forecastings

---

[2] The mean and σ of the 20 data in the following table are not exactly 0 and 1 because of the small size of the sample.

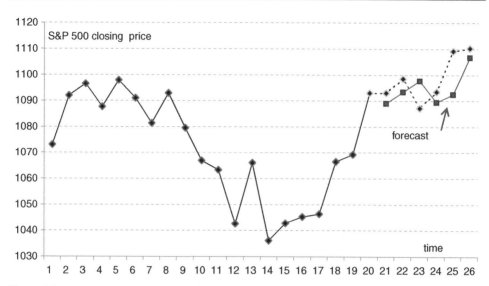

Figure 9.3   Computing an ARMA(1,1) forecasting

9.3   THE AUTOREGRESSION MOVING AVERAGE (ARMA) PROCESS

The autoregression moving average (ARMA) process is a combination of both AR and MA processes before. In its more general form, that is, combining an AR(p) and an MA(q), we obtain an ARMA(p,q):

$$r_t - \mu = a_1 (r_{t-1} - \mu) + a_2 (r_{t-2} - \mu) + \ldots + a_p (r_{t-p} - \mu) + \varepsilon_t + b_1 \varepsilon_{t-1} + b_2 \varepsilon_{t-2}$$
$$+ \ldots + b_q \varepsilon_{t-q}$$

Example.   Let us go back to our earlier AR(1) example which has been applied to S&P 500 data sets, in order to compute an ARMA(1,1) forecasting for the last 6 days of the sample data shown in Figure 9.3.

As we can see, there is no significant difference between ARMA(1,1) and AR(1) results from Section 9.1. The accuracy and the difference between AR and ARMA forecasting models depends on the degree of their stationarity[3] of the time series data. Actually, there is no stationarity in financial data series.

9.4   THE AUTOREGRESSIVE INTEGRATED MOVING AVERAGE (ARIMA) PROCESS

The above stationarity problem is worth investigating further: indeed, the series of data can present some autocorrelation, or autocovariance, that is, an internal correlation between terms of the series. The autocovariance of the terms x_t of a series of n data with mean $\mu(t)$ and

---

[3] Stationarity has been defined in Chapter 5, Section 1.

variance $\sigma^2(t)$, and its corresponding terms *lagged* by 1 is

$$cov(x_t, x_{t+1}) = \frac{1}{n-1} \sum_{i=1}^{n-1} (x_i - \mu(t))(x_{i+1} - \mu(t+1)) = E[(x_i - \mu(t))(x_{i+1} - \mu(t+1))]$$

and the autocorrelation is

$$\rho(x_t, x_{t+1}) = \frac{cov(x_t, x_{t+1})}{\sigma^2}$$

Generalizing with a lag L,

$$cov(x_t, x_{t+L}) = \frac{1}{n-L} \sum_{i=1}^{n-L} (x_i - \mu(t))(x_{i+L} - \mu(t+L)) = E[x_i - \mu(t))(x_{i+L} - \mu(t+L))]$$

$$\rho(x_t, x_{t+L}) = \frac{cov(x_t, x_{t+L})}{\sigma^2}$$

Example. Let us use the same series of returns corresponding to the daily closing prices of the S&P 500 from 10/13/09, used in the previous sections (for the sake of simplicity, $\mu(t)$ and $\sigma^2(t)$ have been supposed constant, on the whole series of data). Applied on the series of prices, with $L = 1, 3, 5, 10,$ *and* 20, we get the result shown in Figure 9.4.

We notice that these prices are significantly autocorrelated: it needs a lag of about 20 to observe no more autocorrelation. But if we work on the returns, these present no autocorrelation from $L = 1$, as we can see in Figure 9.5 (a part of the table has been hidden).

Hence, the autoregressive integrated moving average process (ARIMA) aims to transform the original data (x_t) into *stationarized* ones, by removing autocorrelation. This can be obtained by working on lagged prices differences y_t, z_t, and so on:

$$y_{t+1} = x_{t+1} - x_t$$
$$z_{t+2} = y_{t+2} - z_{t+1} = x_{t+2} - 2x_{t+1} + x_t$$

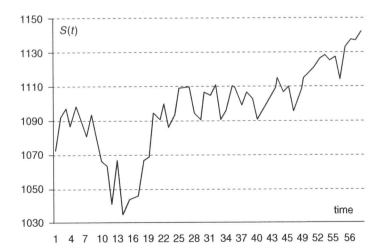

Figure 9.4   Computing an ARIMA forecasting on prices

						L=1:	L=3:	L=5:	L=10:	L=20:	
variance:	585.8107298	0.000100587				-2.43345E-05	4.83079E-07	2.95669E-05	-9.10855E-06	-2.72898E-05	<-- autocovariance
mean:	1096.760833	0.001048714				-4.15399E-08	8.24633E-10	5.04718E-08	-1.55486E-08	-4.65847E-08	<-- autocorrelation
			S_t			$(x_i - \mu)(x_{i+L} - \mu)$:					
13/10'09			1073.19								
14/10'09			1092.02	0.017393671	59						
15/10'09			1096.56	0.004148815	58	5.0671E-05					
16/10'09			1087.68	-0.008131019	57	-2.84581E-05					
19/10'09			1097.91	0.009361385	56	-7.63081E-05	2.42625E-06				
20/10'09			1091.06	-0.006258672	55	-6.07439E-05	-4.11884E-07				
21/10'09			1081.4	-0.008893203	54	7.26494E-05	1.69008E-06	-0.0001625			
22/10'09			1092.91	0.010587366	53	-9.48325E-05	1.49607E-06	2.95708E-05			
23/10'09			1079.6	-0.012253261	52	-0.000126883	1.86928E-06	0.000122109			
26/10'09			1066.95	-0.011786491	51	0.000170734	2.50209E-06	-0.000106695			
27/10'09			1063.41	-0.003323385	50	5.61168E-05	-8.34079E-07	3.19486E-05			
28/10'09			1042.63	-0.019734359	49	9.08556E-05	5.64196E-06	0.000206624	-0.000339698		
29/10'09			1066.11	0.022270143	48	-0.000441046	-5.67461E-06	0.000202424	6.57886E05		
30/10'09			1036.19	-0.028465985	47	-0.000626344	2.74556E-06	0.000392604	0.000270937		
02/11'09			1042.88	0.006435592	46	-0.000158992	-2.43388E-06	-6.91417E-05	4.47794E-05		
03/11'09			1045.41	0.002423036	45	7.40331E-06	6.48113E-07	-6.00867E-06	-1.00427E-05		
04/11'09			1046.5	0.00104211	44	-9.07549E-09	4.42963E-09	1.37243E-07	6.56525E-08		
05/11'09			1066.63	0.019052883	43	-1.18892E-07	2.25549E-06	0.000382074	0.000171736		
06/11'09			1069.3	0.002500083	42	2.61307E-05	4.74917E-08	-4.28367E-05	-1.93061E-05		
09/11'09			1093.08	0.021995171	41	3.04011E-05	-3.37371E-09	0.000112836	-0.000268852		
10/11'09			1093.01	-6.40413E 05	40	-2.33083E-05	-5.00856E-07	-1.52928E-06	4.86507E-06		
11/11'09			1098.51	0.005019358	39	-4.41835E-06	1.47766E-07	-2.62206E-08	-8.25222E-05	6.49E-05	
12/11'09			1087.24	-0.010312341	38	-4.51107E-05	-6.26247E-06	-0.000204546	-0.000241098	-3.52204E-05	
13/11'09			1093.48	0.005722896	37	-5.31036E-05	-1.40573E-07	6.78397E-06	-0.000137957	-4.29077E-05	
...			...		...						
05/01/10			1136.52	0.003110806	3	3.06579E-05	-5.86587E-07	2.15815E-07	9.82427E-06	9.16736E-06	
06/01/10			1137.14	0.000545376	2	-1.03793E-06	2.80588E-06	1.23352E-06	-4.73147E-06	1.77183E-06	
07/01/10			1141.69	0.003993283	1	-1.48211E-06	4.3778E-05	-2.51285E-06	7.38653E-06	-3.34301E-05	

Figure 9.5 Computing an ARMA(1,1) forecasting on returns

So that an ARIMA(p,d,q) denotes an AR(p) combined with an MA(q), on prices differences lagged d times (in the previous equation, using z_t implies $d = 2$). Such a process is less useful with respect to financial markets data, since we model the returns rather than the prices, and as shown in Figure 9.5, these usually present no autocorrelation.

9.5   THE ARCH PROCESS

Let us come back[4] to the AR(1) with 0 mean[5] process:

$$r_t = ar_{t-1} + \varepsilon_t \tag{9.1}$$

where ε_t is $\sim \mathcal{N}(0, \sigma_t^2)$.

Before going further, we need to establish a distinction between "unconditional" and "conditional" moments, namely mean and variance here. For a time series $\{x_t\}$:

- the *unconditional mean* and *variance* of a variable x_t are the usual ones, defined by $E(x_t)$ and $V(x_t) = E[x_t - E(x_t)]^2$ respectively, on the whole set of data of the series;
- the *conditional mean* and *variance* are mean and variance measures conditioned to the way previous information is affecting the next x_t: calling ϕ_{t-1} the information about the market available at $t - 1$, it comes: $cond\ E(x_t) = E(x_t|\phi_{t-1})$ and $cond\ V(x) = E[x - E(x|\phi_{t-1})]^2$ respectively.

The process described by Eq. 9.1 can now be generalized as follows:

$$r_t = E\left(r_t|_{t-1}\right) + \varepsilon_t \tag{9.2}$$

such as $E\left(r_t|_{t-1}\right)$ is the conditional mean of r_t, that is, the expected value of r_t conditional on the information available up to now: it is the *predictable* variable component of r_t. On the other hand, by nature of this process, its conditional variance – like its unconditional variance – is fixed, that is, not depending from available information ϕ_{t-1}, since ε_t has been posited $\sim \mathcal{N}(0, \sigma_t^2)$:

$$V\left(r_t|r_{t-1}\right) = E\left[(r_t - E\left(r_t|r_{t-1}\right))^2 |r_{t-1}\right] = E\left[\varepsilon_t^2 |r_{t-1}\right] = E\left(\varepsilon_{t-1}^2\right) = \sigma_t^2$$

The *unpredictable* component of r_t, or innovation ε_t, represents the impact of current ϕ_t causing the forecast error at t. Coming back to Eq. 9.2

$$r_t = E\left(r_t|_{t-1}\right) + \varepsilon_t,$$

the first term of this relationship, $E\left(r_t|_{t-1}\right)$, is the conditional mean of r_t, and is predictable. It values ar_{t-1} if it is modeled by an AR(1) process. The second term, ε_t, is the innovation term, that is unpredictable. To go a step further, it makes thus sense to now model ε_t, to (try to) reduce this forecast error. There are two ways: either, by a stochastic equation (stochastic volatility model, cf. Chapter 12, Section 12.2), or, similarly as for the conditional mean, by a linear (auto)regression, that is, by an ARCH model:

Autoregressive conditional heteroskedastic or ARCH processes – developed by R. Engle[6] – aim to model the error term ε_t, responsible for the volatility of the returns, by considering that

---

[4] This section and the following one are partly inspired by an anonymous textbook edited by the HEC Montreal (Canada).
[5] Actually, the following reasoning is also valid with $\mu \neq 0$, and in the more general case of an ARMA(p,q): the choice of this particular version is for simplicity and clarity.
[6] R. ENGLE, "Autoregressive conditional heteroskedasticity with estimates of the variance of U.K. inflation", *Econometrica*, 50 (1982), pp. 98–1008.

the variance – that is, the squared volatility – of the process is also conditional to the available information, through a specific function h_t. To formulate this in a more general way, ARCH models formalize a temporal dependence in the second moment of asset returns distributions.

Denoting by $f(r_t)$ in general, a function of the explanatory variables of the returns properly said, as in an ARMA(p,q) for example, an ARCH(p) can be defined as

$$r_t = f(r_t) + \varepsilon_t \quad where \ \varepsilon_t|_{t-1} \sim N(0, h_t)$$

ε_t is modeled as

$$\varepsilon_t = z_t \sqrt{h_t} \tag{9.3}$$

where z_t is a so-called "random number" drawn from a $\mathcal{N}(0, 1)$, and with

$$h_t = \alpha_0 + \sum_{i=1}^{p} \alpha_i \varepsilon_{t-i}^2 \tag{9.4}$$

where $\alpha_0 > 0$ and $\alpha_i \geq 0$ (because ε_t^2 ought to be positive). p is called the *memory* of the process: the higher the p, the more previous squared volatility innovations or "shocks" ε_{t-1}^2 affect ε_t (via Eq. 9.3), hence the longer the persistence of previous volatility levels in the current value of ε_t.

Note that because of Eq. 9.3, it can be proved that $E(\varepsilon_t) = E(\varepsilon_t|\phi_{t-1}) = E(\varepsilon_t, \varepsilon_{t'}) = 0$.

Equation 9.4 represents the conditional variance of r_t, namely σ_t^2, which follows an autoregressive process, as an AR(p) applied to the variance such as, in the case of $p = 1$,

$$\varepsilon_t^2 = \alpha_0 + \alpha_1 \varepsilon_{t-1}^2 + v_t \tag{9.5}$$

where v_t becomes the "ultimate" error term or innovation, or residual of the full process in r_t.

Since the variance of the returns is affected by the impact of current information ϕ_t, it will vary over time, what is called "heteroskedasticity".[7] The ARCH model, for *Autoregressive Conditional Heteroskedasticity*, is modeling the predictable, conditional variance as a linear function of p past squared forecasting errors.

9.6 THE GARCH PROCESS

It happens that in practice, to build an ARCH(p) model, we need p to be large enough, that is, to have a long enough memory, to get a satisfying result. Hence the interest of the "generalized" ARCH model developed by T. Bollerslev,[8] labeled GARCH(p,q) for *Generalized autoregressive conditional heteroskedasticity*. It consists in modeling h_t – that is σ_t^2, the conditional variance of r_t – not only by use of p previous squared volatility innovations or "shocks" ε_{t-1}^2 as in Eq. 9.4, but also by use of an AR(q) on h_t itself:

$$h_t = \alpha_0 + \sum_{i=1}^{p} \alpha_i \varepsilon_{t-i}^2 + \sum_{j=1}^{q} \beta_j h_{t-j} \tag{9.6}$$

with $\beta_j \geq 0$ and $\alpha_i + \Sigma \beta_j < 1$.

---

[7] By contrast, in the AR and MA models, having no requirement about the variance of the error term, the series of returns is supposed to be *homoskedastic*.

[8] Tim BOLLERSLEV, "Generalized autoregressive conditional heteroskedasticity", *Journal of Econometrics*, 31(3), (1986), pp. 307–327.

As such, a GARCH(p,q) model can be viewed as an ARMA on the squared errors ε^2: referring to a GARCH(1,1), from Eq. 9.4 (for $p = 1$) and (5) we have

$$h_t = \varepsilon_t^2 - v_t$$

and substituting in Eq. 9.6 for $p = 1$,

$$\varepsilon_t^2 = \alpha_0 + \alpha_1 \varepsilon_{t-1}^2 + \beta_1 \varepsilon_{t-1}^2 - \beta_1 v_{t-1} + v_t$$

that is, an ARMA(1,1) in ε^2:

$$\varepsilon_t^2 = \alpha_0 + (\alpha_1 + \beta_1)\, \varepsilon_{t-1}^2 - \beta_1 v_{t-1} + v_t$$

which emphasizes the impact of previous volatility shocks on the current volatility. In particular, if ε_{t-1} was large (small), it will tend to make subsequent h_t large (small). This feature more or less fits with market observations about volatilities. Indeed, that is, huge (low) shocks in returns (and prices) are often followed by further huge (low) shocks in returns, leading to successive periods of higher and lower volatilities, what is called "GARCH effect". This important feature will be revisited in Chapter 12.

Finally, in practice it appears that a GARCH(p,q) is preferable to an ARCH(p,q), because it requires smaller p,q terms, proving to be a more robust and parsimonious process.

In conclusion, the GARCH(p,q) model presents several advantages:

- Besides a constant unconditional (variance or) volatility, it allows for a variable conditional volatility, that better fits with market observation.
- The residuals remain low.
- It may allow for a non-Gaussian returns distribution, also more in line with market observations.

But there is a significant drawback – as generally encountered each time we go beyond simple, robust models – namely, a lack of stationarity, the p,q parameters being subject to changes over time.

9.7   VARIANTS OF (G)ARCH PROCESSES

The EWMA Process

Let us start from a GARCH(1,1), using Eq. 9.6:

$$h_t = \alpha_0 + \alpha_1 \varepsilon_{t-1}^2 + \beta_1 h_{t-1}$$

If we consider the simplified case of $\alpha_0 = 0$, and $\alpha_1 + \beta_1 = 1$, and by calling "λ" the β_1 coefficient (≤ 1), and also by recalling that h_t is σ_t^2, the conditional variance of r_t, it becomes

$$\sigma_t^2 = \lambda \sigma_{t-1}^2 + (1 - \lambda)\varepsilon_{t-1}^2$$

called the *exponentially weighted moving average* (EWMA) model. The λ factor is called "decay". By using the formula in a recursive way, it comes

$$\sigma_t^2 = (1 - \lambda)(\varepsilon_{t-1}^2 + \lambda \varepsilon_{t-2}^2 + \lambda^2 \varepsilon_{t-3}^2 + \ldots)$$

so that the lower the λ, the less is the impact of the oldest observations, weighted by λ exponent more and more. Hence, a λ close to 1 implies a slower decay, and conversely. Note that the

EWMA model, here presented as a particular, simplified case of a GARCH, is actually anterior to it.

Given its simplicity, it is used for example by RiskMetrics, a leading provider of risk management tools, with $\lambda = 0.94$ (when working on daily data).

Other Variants

There are more than 150 varieties of (G)ARCH processes, listed by Bollerslev,[9] including:

- IGARCH (integrated GARCH) is a more general case of EWMA: instead of positing $\alpha_1 + \beta_1 = 1$ in a GARCH(1,1), it involves proceeding in a similar way with a GARCH(p,q), that is, Eq. 9.6 where

$$\sum_{i=1}^{p} \alpha_i + \sum_{j=1}^{q} \beta_j = 1$$

- EGARCH (exponential GARCH) allows us to take into account asymmetric innovations, that is, by distinguishing the impact of financial/economical information (called news) viewed as positive, from the ones viewed as negative by traders.
- MGARCH (multivariate GARCH) can apply to a portfolio return, when allocation weights are varying over time: instead of starting from a unique regression of Eq. 9.1 type for example, we have to cope with a system of n such regressions, introducing beyond the above conditional variance, a conditional variance covariance matrix.

9.8   THE MIDAS PROCESS

To close this chapter, let us mention, as an example illustrative of the burgeoning research in financial modeling, the MIDAS estimator,[10] for *Mixed Data Sampling*: it consists in mixing daily and monthly data to estimate the conditional variance of *monthly* returns R_t (r_t continuing to refer to daily returns):

$$V^{MIDAS}(R_{t+1}|R_t) = 22 \sum_{d=0}^{\infty} w_d r_{t-d}^2$$

where "22" refers to the average of trading days per month, and w_d is the weight given to the squared return of day $t - d$ (for more details on the form of this weight, cf. the referenced paper).

According to the authors, as a variance estimator, MIDAS performs better than a GARCH.

FURTHER READING

R.F. ENGLE, D.L. McFADDEN (eds) *Handbook of Econometrics*, Elsevier, 1994; in particular, Chapter 49, T. BOLLERSLEV, R. ENGLE, D. NELSON, *ARCH models*, 79 p., available on the Internet.

---

[9] Tim BOLLERSLEV, *Glossary to ARCH (GARCH)*, CREATES, School of Economics and Management, University of Aarhus, Denmark, 2008, working paper.

[10] E. GHYSELS, P. SANTA-CLARA, R. VALKANOV, "There is a risk-return trade-off after all", *Journal of Financial Economics*, vol. 76, 2005, pp. 509–548.

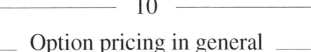

10

Option pricing in general

10.1 INTRODUCTION TO OPTION PRICING

An option is a contract granting:

- the right to its holder, the option buyer – but the obligation to its issuer, the seller,
- to negotiate, that is, either to buy (call option) or to sell (put option), if the option buyer *exercises* its right,
- at a price, fixed in advance and called the exercise price or strike price some quantity of underlying instrument (stock, currency, bond, etc.),
- at a given maturity date or until a given maturity date: in the first case, one refers to a European option, in the second, to an American option.

To some extent, this definition reminds us of an insurance contract. The insured party (the option buyer) pays an insurance premium to the insurer (the option seller), to be insured against something that could happen, and in this instance, exercises its right to be indemnified according to the contract clauses. The insurance premium is perceived by the insurer in any case, and must be sized so that the indemnification requests – that represent some probabilistic outcome – are compensated by the sum of insurance premiums. In the case of options, since the option buyer would exercise its option if such exercise implies a profit – that is, a loss for the option seller – the option seller is entitled to perceive an option premium, in the same way as the insurer.

For the beginner, dealing with options may be a source of confusion, since the human brain is mostly used to consider binary situation (buy versus sell, borrow versus lend, assets versus liabilities, etc.), while here, we are confronted with a "quaternary" situation, that is, for a party, to be:

- either the *buyer* of an option giving the right to *buy*
- or the *buyer* of an option giving the right to *sell*
- or the *seller* of an option giving the right to *buy*
- or the *seller* of an option giving the right to *sell*

and, obviously, the outcomes of these four situations are not at all comparable.

Regarding the European or American feature of an option contract, the difference will be considered later on (cf. Section 5.1). Meanwhile, let us agree that, later in this book, if it is not specified as American, the option will be supposed to be a European one.

The strike price of the option contract is contractually fixed at any price level, whatever it is, the current spot price, or the current forward price (corresponding to the option maturity), or any other price level. Of course, the choice of the strike will affect the option premium: the right to buy something @ $100 may not cost the same premium as the right to buy it @ $120 or @ $80.

In particular, if the strike corresponds to the current forward underlying price, the option is said to be at the money (ATM). Because many practitioners tend to use ATM when talking about a strike equal to the current spot underlying price, it is worth specifying ATMF (at the money forward) or ATMS (at the money spot) accordingly.[1]

Similarly, if an option strike price is more attractive (i.e., granting the right to buy cheaper, or to sell at a higher price) than the corresponding current forward price, the option is said to be in the money (ITM) and otherwise out of the money (OTM). We also use the acronyms DOTM and DITM for "deep" OTM or ITM, namely if the forward is very far from the strike price.

It is also important to notice that the meaning of *option price* does not refer to is *exercise price*, but refers to the *option contract value*, that is, the premium paid at the option contract inception, and later on, its revaluation. Given the crucial uncertainty for an option to be exercised or not, the option contract valuation is the core topic of this chapter.

As a first step in valuing an option contract, we must define its *intrinsic value*:

- At option maturity T, the contract will be exercised or not, depending on the current spot underlying price level *vis-à-vis* the option strike: for a call option, the intrinsic value IV is 0 in case of no exercise, or the positive difference between the spot S_T at T and the strike K:

$$C(T) = 0 \ or \ S_T - K$$

- If $IV = 0$, the call is said to be ending its life OTM, while it is ending ITM if $IV = S_T - K$ (>0). This can be represented, in function of S_T, and for a strike of \$100, as in Figure 10.1.

The passage to a put option is straightforward, with

$$P(T) = 0 \ or \ K - S_T$$

that is, the IV of a put option is either 0, if the put is ending OTM, or $K - S_T$ (>0) if it ends ITM. The corresponding graph of IV is shown in Figure 10.2.

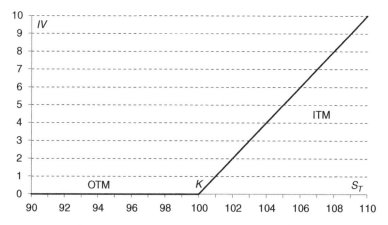

Figure 10.1   Intrinsic value of a call at maturity

---

[1] For information, Bloomberg uses this precision.

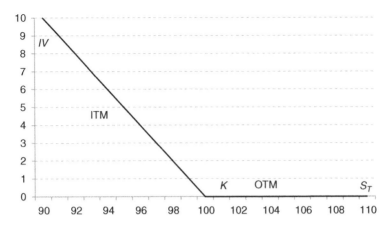

Figure 10.2   Intrinsic value of a put at maturity

At maturity, the value of the option is equal to its intrinsic value, that is, the maximum between 0 and $S_T - K$ for a call, $K - S_T$ for a put, which can be written as

$$C(T) = MAX\,(0;\, S_T - K)$$
$$P(T) = MAX(0;\, K - S_T)$$

where *MAX* means "the highest of", in this case, between either *0* or the positive difference between the spot price *S* at maturity and *K*.

- At any time $t \geq t_0$ (t_0 denoting the option contract date) before maturity, the intrinsic value of an option will still be defined as previously, but will not any more represent the (full) value of the option price:

$$IV\ of\ C\,(t) = MAX\,(0;\, S_t - K)$$
$$IV\ of\ P\,(t) = MAX(0;\, K - S_t)$$

because there is still time to maturity, so that the underlying S_t is subject to further changes. The extent of such further price changes depends on the *volatility* σ of S_t between t and T, that is, the extent of its further move, up *or* down. These further underlying price changes will occur during $\tau = T - t$. The option price component depending on these further underlying price moves is called the *time value* of the option. So that the option price can be viewed as

$$
\begin{array}{ccccc}
\text{option price} & = & \text{intrinsic value} & + & \text{time value} \\
> 0 & & = \text{or} > 0 & & > 0 \\
\text{before T} & & \text{up to T} & & \text{before T}
\end{array}
$$

In the rest of this chapter, we will present several ways of valuing an option price, that will imply how to model and to what extent its time value can be computed for a given volatility and time to maturity. The output of these methods will lead to determining the call and put price curves shown in Figures 10.3 and 10.4, where *TV* is for time value.

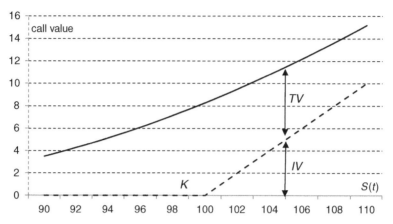

Figure 10.3   Call price curve

Finally, regarding the volatility measure used in option valuation, we must distinguish between:

- the past volatility presented by the underlying price up to t_0, that is called the *historical* volatility, and conventionally measured by the standard deviation of successive price changes ("returns");
- and the volatility that will be used in the option valuation model, called the *implied* volatility, which leads to the option price made by the market maker, and represents his "volatility market view" of what will happen to be the actual volatility that will be measured *ex post* between t_0 and T. Conversely, from a given option price, one can extract the volatility that has been used, hence the naming of "implied volatility".

The following sections of this chapter present the three major option pricing models used by practitioners. They all pursue the same objective of modeling in a more or less realistic way how the underlying spot price will move over time, to compute what should be the option fair/theoretical price accordingly.

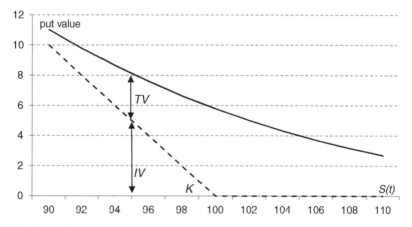

Figure 10.4   Put price curve

10.2   THE BLACK–SCHOLES FORMULA

10.2.1   Introduction

F. Black and M. Scholes were the first to publish,[2] in 1973, a well-grounded formula for computing call and put options prices. The way their formula is established is useful to better understand the underlyings of option pricing. This formula is subject to rather restrictive hypotheses, which may be questioned in some circumstances but at least it constitutes a robust pricing tool, not necessarily the case for further, more complex, pricing models (cf. Chapter 15, Section 15.1), whose sophistication is also synonymous of real difficulties to properly assess correct values to their ingredients.

The Black–Scholes formula is applicable to European options only, and provided the underlying financial instrument offers no return during the lifetime of the option: for example, a stock delivering no dividend during such period, or any non-financial commodity.

The hypotheses underlying the Black–Scholes formula are as follows:

- The underlying price is the only stochastic variable and is assumed to follow a geometric (general) Wiener process. This implies a constant drift and volatility of the underlying returns during the lifetime of the option.
- Financial markets are efficient; in other words, market prices are always perfectly reflecting all the market information and thus always updated in accordance with this market information. Efficiency also implies, practically speaking, enough market liquidity.
- Market prices are assumed to be continuous, like the Wiener process used to model the underlying (cf. Chapter 8, Sections 8.1 and 8.2).
- Market prices and interest rates are assumed to be traded at the mid: no bid–offer spread is taken into account.
- Short selling is always available, at no cost.
- There are no taxes or brokerage fees applicable to the transactions.
- The prevailing risk-free interest rate – the rate applicable to non-defaultable sovereign debt – corresponding to the maturity of the option is well determined and remains constant during the whole life of the option. Also, it is always possible to borrow at this rate.

The Black–Scholes formula will be introduced with respect of a call price C, the passage to a put P being straightforward. It is based on the following preliminary question: what is the change ΔC of a call option price when the underlying spot price S is changing by ΔS? The answer is under the form of

$$\Delta C = x \times \Delta S$$

that is, the change in option price should be in some proportion x of the change in underlying price. x is thus equal to $\Delta C / \Delta S$ that is, in continuous time, the partial derivative of the option price in S:

$$x = \frac{\partial C}{\partial S}$$

Let us now start from the process of the underlying spot price S of, say, a stock:

$$dS = \mu S dt + \sigma S dZ \tag{10.1}$$

---

[2] F. BLACK, M. SCHOLES, The pricing of options and corporate liabilities, *Journal of Political Economy*, (1973) vol. 81 no. 3, pp. 637–654.

that is, a geometric (general) Wiener process (cf. Chapter 8, Section 8.5, Eq. 8.11b). Let C be a continuous function of S and of t, and apply Itô's lemma (cf. Chapter, Eq. 8.12) to C:

$$dC = \left(\frac{\partial C}{\partial S} \mu S + \frac{\partial C}{\partial t} + \frac{1}{2} \frac{\partial^2 C}{\partial S^2} \sigma^2 S^2 \right) dt + \frac{\partial C}{\partial S} \sigma S dZ \tag{10.2}$$

Then let be a portfolio Π, of some quantity of the stock and some quantity of call options on this stock. By comparing the terms in dZ in Eq. 10.1 and in Eq. 10.2 we see that we can eliminate the stochastic term dZ from the portfolio Π if it is adequately balanced in its two components, as follows:

$$\Pi = -C + \frac{\partial C}{\partial S} S \tag{10.3}$$

that is, a portfolio comprising -1 option (i.e., a short position) and a portion $\partial C/\partial S$ (long position) of the corresponding underlying. The total instantaneous variation of the portfolio value is

$$d\Pi = -dC + \frac{\partial C}{\partial S} dS \tag{10.3b}$$

In this equation, by replacing dC by its value from Eq. 10.2 we get

$$d\Pi = \left(-\frac{\partial C}{\partial t} - \frac{1}{2} \frac{\partial^2 C}{\partial S^2} \sigma^2 S^2 \right) dt \tag{10.4}$$

We see that, indeed, $d\Pi$ does not contain dZ any more.

Equation 10.4 also shows that the portfolio variations are not anymore depending on the drift term μ either. In other words, the effect of μ on the option component is counterbalanced by its effect on the underlying component! The variations of value of such a portfolio are thus independent from both μ and dZ.

In particular, the independence from dZ means that the portfolio behavior is not stochastic. Having therefore a certain – or deterministic – behavior implies that this portfolio must necessarily offer the return r of a risk-free bond. Offering more than r would suppose that it presents some risk, linked to a stochastic behavior, what is not the case. The variation of value of this riskless portfolio must thus be such as that

$$d\Pi = r\Pi dt \tag{10.5}$$

By combining Eq. 10.3, Eq. 10.4, and Eq. 10.5 we get the following "diffusion equation":

$$\frac{\partial C}{\partial t} + rS \frac{\partial C}{\partial S} + \frac{1}{2} \frac{\partial^2 C}{\partial S^2} \sigma^2 S^2 = rC \tag{10.6}$$

Solving this partial differential equation is not easy and needs first some extra information, called "boundary conditions". In this case of a call option, the boundary conditions are

$$i)\ C\ (S = 0\ and\ t = 0) = 0$$

and

$$ii)\ C = MAX(0; S - K)$$

the second condition representing the call value at maturity (see Section 10.1), where K is the strike price. The solution of the diffusion equation can be obtained either by a technique called

"Laplace transform", or by a change of variables S and t:

$$S' = \frac{2}{\sigma^2}\left(r - \frac{\frac{1}{2}}{\sigma^2}\right)\left[ln\frac{S}{K} + \left(r - \frac{1}{2}\sigma^2\right)t\right]$$

$$t' = \frac{2}{\sigma^2}\left(r - \frac{1}{2}\sigma^2\right)^2 t$$

Then, by integration and taking account of the boundary conditions, the solution of Eq. 10.6 is the Black–Scholes formula for call options:

$$C = SN(d_1) - Ke^{-rT}N(d_2) \tag{10.7}$$

with

$$d_1 = \left[ln\frac{S}{K} + \left(r + \frac{1}{2}\sigma^2\right)T\right]\frac{1}{\sigma\sqrt{T}} \tag{10.8}$$

and

$$d_2 = d_1 - \sigma\sqrt{T} \tag{10.9}$$

where

$T =$ option maturity, expressed in (fraction of) years
$N(.) =$ cumulative normal distribution

Beyond the algebra, Eq. 10.7 means that the price of a call options is

- $+ S.N(d_1)$, namely, receiving the underlying at its current value S at maturity time T;
- $- K.e^{-rT}.N(d_2)$, namely, paying the present value of its strike price K;
- if and only if (i.e., because of the probabilities $N(d_1)$ and $N(d_2)$) at maturity, S is greater than K.

Note that, unlike the term in K, regarding $SN(d_1)$, there is no apparent term of present value in the form of e^{-rT}: this will be clarified in the next section.

For put options, a similar development leads to

$$P = -S[1 - N(d_1)] + Ke^{-rT}[1 - N(d_2)]$$

with the same d_1 and d_2 as per Eqs. 10.8 and 10.9.

Example. Let us compute a European call option maturing in 90 days (or $= 90/365 = 0.2466$ year) on L'OREAL stock quoting EUR 64.5 (data as of Jan 06), with an ATMS strike price of EUR 64.5; the risk-free interest rate is 2.514% p.a. and the stock volatility is 11.9% p.a. Equations 10.7–10.9 give:

- because $\ln(S/K) = \ln(64.5/64.5) = \ln 1 = 0$, $d_1 = (0.02514 + 0.119^2/2) \times 0.2466/0.119$ $\sqrt{0.246} = 0.134457$
- $d_2 = d_1 - 0.119\sqrt{0.2466} = 0.075363$
- hence, using the cumulative normal distribution $N(0,1)$, $N(d_1) = 0.553479$, and $N(d_2) = 0.530037$
- $\rightarrow C = 64.5 \times 0.553479 - 64.5 \times e^{-0.02514\times0.2466} \times 0.530037 = €1.72$ (rounded).

10.2.2   Variants of the Black–Scholes formula

The Black–Scholes formula can be extended to European options on any kind of underlying offering a return $\neq 0$, provided that its process can be reasonably modeled by a geometric Wiener process. This extension is valid if the underlying return can be considered as continuous in time.[3] This will be the case of a LIBOR rate of return, for example. Let precise the above r return, by calling it r_m, as the market rate of return, and calling r_u the return of the underlying, both up to the maturity T of the option. The call option price formula becomes

$$C = Se^{-r_u T} N(d_1) - Ke^{-r_m T} N(d_2) \tag{10.10}$$

with

$$d_1 = \left[\ln\frac{S}{K} + \left(r_m - r_u + \frac{1}{2}\sigma^2 \right) T \right] \frac{1}{\sigma\sqrt{T}} \tag{10.11}$$

d_2 remaining unchanged, see, for example, Eq. 10.9.

And for the put:

$$P = -Se^{-r_u T} [1 - N(d_1)] + Ke^{-r_m T} [1 - N(d_2)] \tag{10.12}$$

To some extent, such formula can be applied to bond options (cf. Chapter 11, Section 11.2 for more details on bond options), if the maturity of the option is not too close to the bond redemption. r_u will then be the yield to maturity y of the bond. With some degree of approximation, it can also apply to options on stock indexes, provided the whole of dividends paid by each constituent of the index can be reasonably assimilated to a continuous return, namely the "dividend yield" of the index.

The Case of Currency Options

Equations 10.10–10.12 can also apply for currency options, then called the *Garman–Kohlhagen*[4] formula. Of course, r_m and r_u must adequately correspond to the rates of each currency, that is,

$$r_u \rightarrow r_{ref}$$
$$r_m \rightarrow r_{c/v}$$

(for the meaning of r_{ref} and $r_{c/v}$ rates, cf. Chapter 3, Section 3.3). Indeed, logically, the market rate of Eq. 10.10 becomes here the currency counter-value rate, in which the reference currency is quoted, and the underlying rate is the currency reference rate. The Garman–Kohlhagen formula can thus be written as

$$C = Se^{-r_{ref} T} N(d_1) - Ke^{-r_{c/v} T} N(d_2)$$

And for d_1 (d_2 remaining unchanged),

$$d_1 = \left[\ln\frac{S}{K} + \left(r_{c/v} - r_{ref} + \frac{1}{2}\sigma^2 \right) T \right] \frac{1}{\sigma\sqrt{T}}$$

---

[3] This means assimilating a discrete return as continuous, like it has been done for interest rates (cf. Chapter 1, Section 1.3), which implies a high enough frequency of rates observations.

[4] From their seminal paper, Mark B. GARMAN and Steven W. KOHLHAGEN, "Foreign currency option values", *Journal of International Money and Finance* (December 1983), vol. 2, pp. 231–237.

and the corresponding put price becomes

$$P = -Se^{-r_{ref}T} [1 - N(d_1)] + Ke^{-r_{c/v}T} [1 - N(d_2)]$$

A detailed example of currency option pricing will be given in Chapter 11, Section 11.1.

The Case of Options on Futures or Forwards

Coming back to Eq. 10.10, Eq. 10.11, and Eq. 10.9, they can be re-formulated by introducing forward prices F, in continuous time. Given (cf. Chapter 5, Section 5.3.1, Eq. 5.3)

$$F = Se^{(r_m - r_u)T} \qquad (10.13)$$

we obtain the price of a call option on a forward or future instrument:

$$C = e^{-r_m T} [FN(d_1) - KN(d_2)] \qquad (10.14)$$

with

$$d_1 = \left[ln\frac{F}{K} + \frac{1}{2}\sigma^2 T \right] \frac{1}{\sigma\sqrt{T}}$$

Here, too, d_2 is the same as in Eq. 10.9. And for the put:

$$P = e^{-r_m T} \{-F[1 - N(d_1)] + K[1 - N(d_2)]\} \qquad (10.15)$$

Note that here, the present value of the first term is visible, contrary to the case of option price on a spot instrument, where it was hidden, so that both the terms of the call (or put) price are actually discounted, by $e^{-r_m T}$.

This variant of the Black–Scholes equation is also called the *Black model*.

10.2.3   Call–put parity

Comparing Eq. 10.10 with Eq. 10.12, it is not surprising that, in general, call prices will differ from put prices, for the same strike, same maturity and same underlying. However, it is possible to identify for what particular strike price, these prices must be equal. By posing C of Eq. 10.10 = P of Eq. 10.12, that is, by making (10.10) – (10.12) = 0 and solving in K, we get:

$$C - P = 0 = Se^{-r_u T} - Ke^{-r_m T}$$

which is verified with

$$K = Se^{(r_m - r_u)T} = F$$

This important result explains the crucial role of At the Money Forward options (cf. Section 10.1): for ATMF options, the call (mid) price equals the put (mid) price. This relationship is called call–put parity.

Beyond these equations, it is useful to notice why such parity: the forward price being today's best expectation of what will value the underlying at maturity (as developed in Chapter 8, Section 8.9), it must be normal that the right to buy or the right to sell the underlying at such (forward) price must be equivalent. But for any other strike price, there will always be a difference between the call and the put value: if the strike is higher than the forward, the right to buy will be cheaper (because at a less attractive strike price than the expected forward price) whilst the right to sell will be more expensive (because at a more favorable strike price), and conversely.

10.2.4   The key role of the forward price – meaning of $N(d_1)$ and $N(d_2)$

The importance of the forward is valid only within the framework of the Black–Scholes hypotheses, namely, of returns modeled as a Gaussian, and of underlying prices modeled with a log-normal distribution. Coming back to the Black and Scholes formula Eqs. 10.7–10.9 and all the subsequent formulae, we notice that such option prices do not depend on the μ drift, as already mentioned about the Black and Scholes portfolio variation in Eq. 10.4. This means that such options prices are to be considered as risk neutral (cf. Chapter 5, Sections 5.8 and 5.9), or indifferent to the risk that the today expectation of what will be the underlying price at maturity, could differ from the forward price. So that, instead of any forward price valued as $S\,e^{\mu T}$, the option price is based on a risk neutral forward (cf. Eq. 8.17) $F_T^Q = S_t e^{rT}$, r being the risk-free market rate.

Meaning of $N(d_1)$ and $N(d_2)$

As will appear in Section 10.5.1, $N(d_1)$ is the slope of the Black–Scholes call or put price curve in function of S, that is, the sensitivity of the option price to underlying price movements.

$N(d_2)$ is the probability that the option will be exercised at maturity, more precisely: the *risk-neutral* probability, *under the assumptions of the Black–Scholes model*. From Eq. 10.8 and Eq. 10.9 of the genuine Black–Scholes formula, it is easy to verify that, for a call,

- if S is $\ll K$, d_1, d_2 and therefore $N(d_2)$ tend to 0 probability of exercising;
- if S is $\gg K$, d_1, d_2 and therefore $N(d_2)$ tend to 1 probability of exercising;

and conversely for a put. In particular, if

$$K = Se^{\left(r - \frac{\sigma^2}{2}\right)T}$$

that is, the "adjusted forward" price resulting from modeling S according to the Black–Scholes formula (cf. Eq. 8.14, in a risk-neutral world with μ being replaced by the risk-free rate r), Eq. 10.8 becomes:

$$d_1 = \left[ln\frac{S}{Se^{\left(r - \frac{\sigma^2}{2}\right)T}} + \left(r + \frac{\sigma^2}{2}\right)T \right]\frac{1}{\sigma\sqrt{T}} = \sigma\sqrt{T}\, d_2 = d_1 - \sigma\sqrt{T} = 0$$

So that, for a strike equal to this "adjusted forward", $N(d_2) = 0.5$, that is a 50–50 chance that the option will be exercised.

Notion of Moneyness

The moneyness measures the "distance" between K and F: if $K = F$, the moneyness is said to value 0 (in this case, the option is ATMF). If $K \neq F$, the difference $K - F$ is measured by the corresponding number of standard deviations (hence, in σs).

Example. Consider 3M European options on L'Oreal: mid data as of 02/19/08 are

- S = €83.06
- 3M F = 82.535
- 3M implied volatility = 35.569% p.a.

The moneyness of an option (call or put) for which the strike = 82.535 is 0. A moneyness of +1 corresponds to a strike of $F + 1\sigma$. Here, with a 3M = 90 days option, we have:

$$F + 1\sigma = F(1 + 0.35569 \times 90/365) = 89.774$$

and similarly:

moneyness:	strike:
−3	60.819
−2	68.058
−1	75.296
0	82.535 = F
1	89.774
2	97.012
3	104.251

These values are shown in Figure 10.5 together with two strikes, K'' and K', respectively at:

$K' = S - €10 = 73.06$ corresponding to a moneyness of -1.31
$K'' = S + €10 = 93.06$ corresponding to a moneyness of $+1.45$.

The moneyness measure is mainly used with respect to the option smile, as developed in Chapter 12, Section 12.1.3.

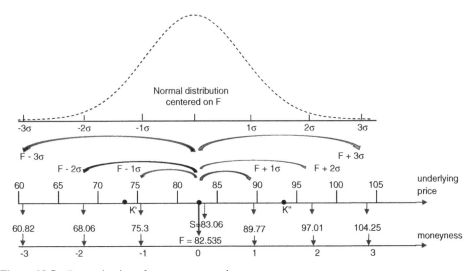

Figure 10.5 Determination of a moneyness scale

10.2.5 Beyond the Black–Scholes formula

The Black–Scholes formula is an answer to the diffusion equation (cf. Eq. 10.6, for call options) leading to an option valuation subject to the very specific assumptions as set in Section 10.2.1. This formula, and its variants, is called an "analytical" solution to option pricing, since if suffices to replace the variables of the formula by their values relating to the option to be priced.

Moreover, the fact remains that the analytic – also called "close form" or "closed-form" – Black–Scholes formula presents the advantage of allowing a straightforward calculation of options sensitivities (cf. Section 10.5).

However, in many instances, some of the Black–Scholes assumptions must be relaxed or modified, for example in the case of:

- incorporating dividend payments (options on equities);
- American options;
- options on interest rates, volatility, or other underlyings, that do not fit with the geometric general Wiener process (see Chapters 11 and 12);
- second generation options (cf. Chapter 11);
- relaxing the Gaussian framework, for taking into account observed asymmetry and kurtosis in the underlying probability distribution of returns in general (cf. Chapter 15).

In some cases, these problems can be solved by using approximate analytical solutions, derived from the Black–Scholes formula: see, for example, Chapter 11. Besides, we can use non-analytical methods, namely:

- finite difference methods, or "binomial trees", also called "lattice" methods;
- Monte Carlo simulation techniques.

In general, as it will appear from the next sections, these other pricing tools have in common that the obtained price cannot be considered as "exact": their output only gives an approximate valuation. Note that an "exact" price means exact only with respect to the assumptions having led to its valuation. Since such assumptions are basically just fixed to help the Black–Scholes diffusion equation to be established and analytically solved, we should keep in mind that a Black–Scholes option price is only exact from a mathematical viewpoint, to the extent of the validity of these assumptions . . . Other methods deliberately lead to approximate solutions, whose approximation degree must be appreciated vis-à-vis the market bid-offer spread of the option price: normally this spread must be wider than the pricing approximation error. For vanilla options, the degree of precision of these non-analytical methods may be considered as widely sufficient.

10.3   FINITE DIFFERENCE METHODS: THE COX–ROSS–RUBINSTEIN (CRR) OPTION PRICING MODEL

The CRR is not the only finite differences method available, but it is by far its main application. Note that we do not label the CRR as an option pricing "formula", but, rather, "model", since its output is no longer a pricing formula but an *algorithm*.

The underlying principle of the CRR methodology can be presented as follows, in the case of an equity option, through an example with deliberately unrealistic data (as in the spirit of the seminal paper of Cox, Ross, and Rubinstein).[5]

Let S be a stock price, currently valuing $100 at t_0. To the end of the next period of time (a day, or a month, or any period of time), ending at T, S can either go up to $150 or down to $50 only. And let us consider an "arbitrage portfolio" made of

- sale of four calls on this stock, ATMS ($K = S$), maturing at T, @ C to be determined;
- purchase of two stocks, @ S;
- borrowing of the present value of S, given an $r = 10\%$, that is, borrowing of $91.

At T, the portfolio value depends on whether S will value $50 or $150:

	S = 50	S = 150
sell 4 calls:	0	− 200
MtM of 2 stocks:	+ 100	+ 300
reimburse loan:	− 100	− 100
portfolio MtM:	0	0

Since in both cases, this portfolio is worth 0 at T, originally (at t_0) it can only be worth 0, so that:

$$+4 \times C \quad - 200 \quad + 91 \quad = 0$$

proceeds of the sale of 4 calls

purchase of 2 stocks @ 100

borrowed money

The core of this methodology is the use of the *binomial* distribution, as a first step covering a first sub-period Δt:

S_{up} with "up" probability p_u

S

S_{down} with down probability p_d

with

$$p_u + p_d = 1$$

If we repeat this first step n times, for $n \to \infty$, corresponding to an infinity of sub-periods dt, one replicates the Gaussian distribution, as used in the Wiener process for Black–Scholes for example. The CRR model is based on a set of n finite sub-periods Δt.

Hence the following CRR algorithm for pricing a (European) call or put option of strike K and maturity T, on stock worth S.

[5] J. COX, S.A. ROSS, M. RUBINSTEIN, "Option pricing: a simplified approach", *Journal of Financial Economics* (1979), no. 7, pp. 229–263.

T is divided into a finite number n of sub-periods Δt totaling T (we will revert later on a reasonable value for n). In a first step, starting from S, we build a binomial "tree" of possible stock prices $S_{t\,up}$ and $S_{t\,down}$, with their respective probabilities p_u and p_d. Note that this tree is a "recombining" tree, since an "up then down" move leads to the same S_t value than a "down then up" move.

At T, we obtain a series $\{S_t\}$ of $n+1$ possible stock prices, for what we can compute the option value (i.e., a pure intrinsic value), with respect to K. To this series of possible options values are associated the corresponding probabilities of $\{S_t\}$.

Then comes the second stage of the algorithm: by recombining backwards these option values associated to their corresponding probabilities, and applying a present value factor over each Δt, we compute step by step, at each "node" of the tree, intermediate options values for each S_t and Δt, up to the initial S, where we obtain the actual corresponding option price.

The CRR seminal paper gives the detailed calculation leading to the following parameters of the algorithm:

- Upward move u over Δt (where σ is the volatility):

$$u = e^{\sigma \sqrt{T/n}}$$

- Downward move d over Δt:

$$d = {}^1\!/_u$$

- p_u probability of an upward move:

$$p_u = \frac{e^{r\frac{T}{n}} - d}{u - d}$$

- p_d probability of a downward move:

$$p_d = 1 - p_u$$

- Present value factor on one Δt period, @ r (risk-free rate over T):

$$PV \ of \ 1 = e^{-r\frac{T}{n}}$$

These valuations allow for example to replicate the Black–Scholes result for a European option.

Let us illustrate this algorithm in the case of a put, over $n = 5$ iterations only, to allow for a graph view, with

S = 100 = K
T = 100 days = 0.274 year
n = 5
r = 3% p.a.
σ = 19% p.a.

The above formulae give:

present value factor = 0.9930
u = 1.045, d = 0.956
p_u = 0.507
p_d = 0.493.

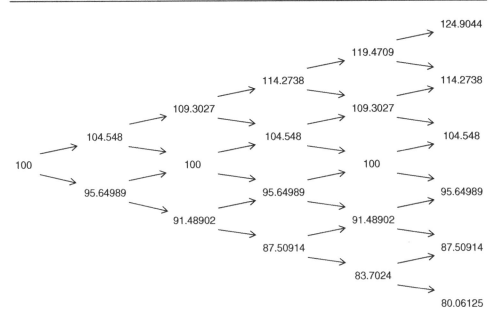

Figure 10.6   Binomial tree of S_t

Note that upward probabilities differ from downward probabilities. Indeed, because, as shown in Chapter 8, Section 8.7, a symmetric (normal) distribution of the returns leads to a log-normal distribution of the prices, which presents some asymmetry, and therefore unequal probabilities of the up and down moves.

Figure 10.6 is the binomial tree of S_t, which corresponds to the European put calculation illustrated in Figure 10.7. That is, $P = 3.75$, against 3.56 for a precise calculation, if n were large enough. In practice it is not needed to increase n above 50 to 60 periods: the obtained price is quickly converging toward a stable value. Since this convergence is oscillating around the correct value, practitioners apply the algorithm for two nearby values of n, for example 50 and 51, and take the arithmetic average of both results. Note that n does not need to depend on T, so that shorter maturities are "sliced" in smaller time intervals than longer maturities, what makes sense, for accuracy purpose.

To detail the previous calculation, let us zoom on the three S values in gray:

• if $S = 95.64989$, the intrinsic value of the put $= 100 - 95.64989 = 4.35011$; same way for $S = 87.50914$
• to move backwards to the put value one Δt earlier (hence, with 1 sub-period discounting @ 0.9984), that is, corresponding to $S = 91.48902$:

$$0.9984 \, (4.35011 \times 0.507 + 12.49086 \times 0.493) = 8.3467$$

In the case of a European option on a stock without dividend distribution over T, the algorithm of course gives almost (remember, CRR gives an approximate result) the same option valuation as the Black–Scholes formula.

The advantage of the CRR algorithm is that, by slicing the time to maturity in Δt sub-periods, it allows for pricing an American option, by adding to the above calculation the opportunity

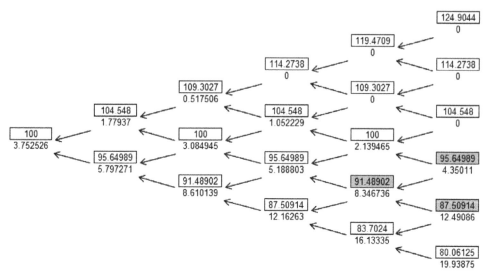

Figure 10.7   European put calculation

of earlier exercise at any node of the tree. Let us continue with the same example, but this time for pricing an American put. In addition to the re-combinations of intermediate option prices, we now have to also consider any possibility of earlier exercise at any node, and we keep for further backward move, the highest between re-combination and early exercise (in this case of a put, $K - S_t$), so that the final result is incorporating all possible early exercises.

Actually, we can have up to three possible put values at each node, resulting from:

- the recombination from intrinsic values at maturity, as in the case of European put, previously;
- early exercise at an intermediate node: shaded gray;
- the recombination of the highest result in each of the next two nodes, shown in italic

and to move backwards, we have to hold the highest value from each node, shown in bold (Figure 10.8).

In the example in Figure 10.8, we finally obtain a different (higher) price for the American put than for the equivalent European put, what is understandable ($r_m > r_u$, cf. Section 10.5.1). Of course, the obtained price of 3.82 is not precise enough, given the insufficient number of sub-periods here. The right price should be 3.63.

In short, the CRR algorithm is widely used for option pricing if events or decisions are to be taken into account during the lifetime of the option, namely

- the case of American options;
- incorporating dividends payments, or other special events (stock splits, etc.).

Example. In the above prices tree, suppose that at the third sub-period, the stock distributed a dividend of $3: the tree must be adjusted as in Figure 10.9.

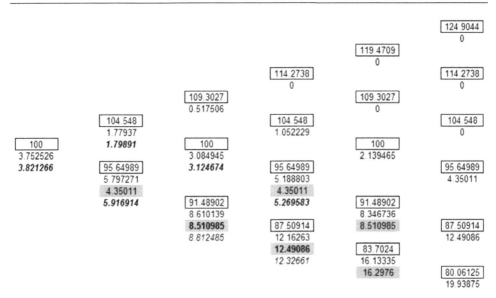

Figure 10.8   American put calculation

10.4 MONTE CARLO SIMULATIONS

This option pricing method consists in simulating a huge number of times the path followed by the successive underlying spot prices. *Per se*, the method is not required for regular European nor for American options, but rather for second generation ones. It will anyway be presented here in the case of a classic European option (the data of this example will be reused to price a second-generation option in Chapter 11, Section 11.8).

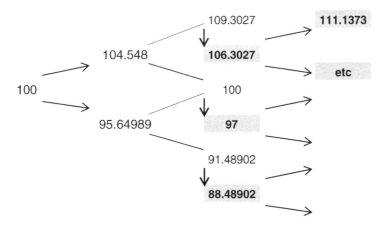

Figure 10.9   Impact of a dividend payment on the binomial tree of S_t

Let us start from an underlying spot price S, modeled by a geometric general Wiener process as used for the Black–Scholes formula (cf. Eq. 10.1):

$$dS = \mu S dt + \sigma S dZ$$

In discrete time, we have (cf. Eq. 8.1)

$$\Delta \tilde{Z}(t) = \tilde{y}(t)\sqrt{\Delta t}$$

where $\tilde{y}(t)$ is a Gaussian random variable, that can be described by draws of so-called Gaussian "random numbers" ε, so that

$$\Delta S \simeq \mu S \Delta t + \sigma S \varepsilon \sqrt{\Delta t}$$

meaning that $\Delta S/S$ is distributed as a Gaussian:

$$\frac{\Delta S}{S} \sim \mathcal{N}(\mu \Delta t, \sigma \sqrt{\Delta t})$$

To simulate the successive daily $S(t)$ prices, let us first divide T into n very small time intervals

$$t, t + \Delta t, t + 2\Delta t, \ldots, t + n\Delta t (= T)$$

in practice, n can go up to 100 000 or even more, taking into account of both the need for some accuracy level, and the computation time.

Let us continue with illustrating the method on the 3-month European call ATMS on L'Oreal stock, already used to apply the Black–Scholes formula (cf. Section 10.2.1). We have thus to *simulate* the $S(t)$ evolution over 3 months (90 days), for (data starting from Jan 06):

$$S = K = \text{€}64.50 \text{ spot}, \mu = 0.004375 (\text{annualized}), \sigma = 0.119 \text{ (annualized)},$$
$$\text{3M-EURIBOR} = 2.514\%$$

with $n = 9000$ and 250 (trading) days / year, $\Delta t = 90$ days/9000 $= 0.00004$ year. This time slicing corresponds to 100 time intervals per day (90 days $\times 100$ intervals $= 9000$). The distribution of discrete returns is here

$$\frac{\Delta S}{S} \sim \mathcal{N}(\mu \Delta t = 0.000000175, \sigma \sqrt{\Delta t} = 0.000755)$$

Let us thus simulate M times the successive 9000 $S(t + \Delta t)$ values, via an $\mathcal{N}(0,1)$ table of so-called random numbers ε. On Excel, the function is *NORMSINV(RAND())*.[6] One should recall, however, that it is impossible to produce numbers in a strictly random way: whatever is the method selected for producing them, it leads to only *quasi-randomly* distributed numbers. In practice, M is about 100 000. Depending on the stochastic variable to be simulated, there exist several techniques to reduce this number (cf., e.g., P. Jäckel, in the further reading at the end of this chapter).

---

[6] The reason why this function is mentioned is that, contrary to other functions used elsewhere in my numerical examples, it is not mentioned in the functions list (Excel 2007), although it works!

Table 10.1   Example of a simulation using the Monte Carlo method

| | "random numbers" | | | |
step	N(0,1)	adj N()	ΔS	S(t)
				64.5
1	−0.87691	−0.00066189	−0.04269	64.45731
2	0.261782	0.000197821	0.012751	64.47006
3	−0.84684	−0.00063919	−0.04121	64.42885
4	−0.75245	−0.00056792	−0.03659	64.39226
5	0.000807	7.83969E-07	5.05E-05	64.39231
6	−0.48191	−0.00036366	−0.02342	64.36889
7	0.0349	2.65244E-05	0.001707	64.3706
3	−0.52445	−0.00039579	−0.02548	64.34512
9	1.38253	0.001043985	0.067175	64.4123
10	2.488882	0.001879281	0.121049	64.53335
11	−1.06104	−0.00080091	−0.05169	64.48166
12	−0.80263	−0.00060581	−0.03906	64.4426
13	−0.56012	−0.00042271	−0.02724	64.41536
14	0.30551	0.000230835	0.014869	64.43023
...	...	...	...	...
8985	0.051195	3.88269E-05	0.002676	68.9243
8986	2.472993	0.001867284	0.128701	69.053
8987	2.118264	0.001599464	0.110448	69.16345
8988	−1.36976	−0.00103399	−0.07151	69.09193
8989	−0.35079	−0.00026467	−0.01829	69.07365
8990	0.767975	0.000579996	0.040062	69.11371
8991	1.045153	0.000789265	0.054549	69.16826
8992	−0.18882	−0.00014238	−0.00985	69.15841
8993	0.371084	0.000280343	0.019388	69.1778
8994	−1.63126	−0.00123143	−0.08519	69.09261
8995	1.178088	0.000889632	0.061467	69.15408
8996	−1.59072	−0.00120082	−0.08304	69.07104
8997	1.266683	0.000956521	0.066068	69.1371
8998	−0.00373	−2.6437E-06	−0.00018	69.13692
8999	0.262161	0.000198106	0.013696	69.15062
9000	2.123669	0.001603545	0.110886	69.2615

For the jth of these M simulations, let be a_{ij} the ith outcome of ε generated from $\mathcal{N}(0,1)$: passing from $\mathcal{N}(0,1)$ to $\mathcal{N}(0.000000175, 0.000755)$ implies

$$a'_{ij} = 0.000000175 + 0.000755 \times a_{ij}$$

a_{1j} = first ε from the $\mathcal{N}(0,1)$ generator = −0.87691 (cf. Table 10.1)

$$\rightarrow a'_{1j} = 0.000000175 - 0.000755 \times 0.87691 = -0.00066189$$

applied to ΔS: $\Delta S = €64.5 \times 0.00066189 = -0.04269$

$$\rightarrow S(t + \Delta t) = 64.5 - 0.04269 = 64.45731$$

$$\rightarrow \ldots$$

$$\rightarrow S(t + n\Delta t) = €69.26$$

$$= \text{jth simulation of } S(T)$$

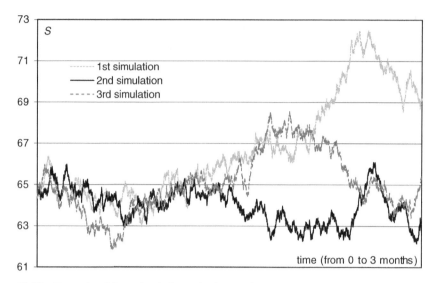

Figure 10.10   Example of three simulations of prices paths, generated by Monte Carlo

Coming back to the call price C, first simulation: the first random sample of $S(t)$ leads to the first computation of $\{S(t)\}$, that is, 100 values /day, that gives the first simulation of $S(T)$, hence the value of a first call value C_1.

A second series of n random draws (i.e., a second simulation) leads to C_2. And so on, until the Mth simulation, giving C_M. After M simulations, we can compute the arithmetic average of the Cs,

$$\hat{E}(C) = \frac{1}{M} \sum C_i = \hat{C}(S, T)$$

that is, an approximate value for the average call C.

An example of the first three simulations for the underlying spot is shown in Figure 10.10.

First simulation of $\{S(t)\}$: goes up to $S_T = 69.26 \rightarrow S_T - K = 69.26 - 64.50 = 4.76$

$$\rightarrow C_1 = 4.73$$
$$= \text{PV of } 4.76 @ 2.514\,\% \text{ on } 3 \text{ months}$$
$$= 4.76/(1 + 0.02514 \times 90/365)$$

Second simulation: $S_T = 62.86 \qquad \rightarrow C_2 = 0$

Third simulation: $S_T = 65.30 \qquad \rightarrow C_3 = 0.795$

$$= \text{PV of } (65.30 - 64.50) @ 2.514\,\% \text{ on }$$
$$3 \text{ months} = 0.80/(1 + 0.02514 \times 90/365)$$

and so on. The average of first 40 simulations leads to an average of $S_T - K = 2.055$, that is,

$$C = 2.055/(1 + 0.02514 \times 90/365) = 2.042$$

instead of 1.72, that is, the price obtained by the Black–Scholes formula (cf. Section 10.2.1), that would be obtained if the number M of simulations was big enough.

Accuracy of the Method

Let us denote σ_C the STD of the $\{C_i\}$: the standard error on $\hat{C}$ is

$$standard\ error = \frac{\sigma_C}{\sqrt{M}}$$

Note that this error measure is limited to the impact of the number M of simulations, but does not preclude the error due to the choice of the process hypothesis (Gaussian, etc.).

In short, the Monte Carlo simulation method proves useful for several second-generation options, with a complex payoff (cf. Chapter 11, Section 11.8). Although obtaining a price requires a much longer CPU time – having banned the method from front offices during years – today, with fast enough computers this is no longer an obstacle. Also, there exist some techniques (e.g., the "control variate" technique) that allow for reducing the number of simulations needed.

But the method hardly allows coping with special events, and is not adequate to apply for American options. Actually, to price an American option by Monte Carlo, we should repeat the process many times, for periods of time shorter than the actual option maturity, to look after possible early exercises... what is quicker said than properly done. Also, the Monte Carlo response to sensitivities measures (cf. next section) may dangerously lack of precision.

Altogether, it would be advisable to restrict the use of Monte Carlo to option pricing issues for which other methods fail, and to be wary of marketing points presenting this method as to be used as "the" only single multipurpose option pricing software.[7]

10.5 OPTION PRICING SENSITIVITIES

Known as the "Greeks", option pricing sensitivities are essential, mainly for options market makers, who trade options not for a particular objective, of hedging or speculation. They measure the various market risk parameters associated to a position in options. The option price sensitivities to various parameters are straightforward in the case of an analytic pricing formula: they correspond to the partial derivatives of the price, in S, t, σ and interest rate(s). It is of course useful to grasp the impact of these parameters separately, but one should not forget that in the real world, an option price is globally and simultaneously affected by the variations of each of them.

Let us present them with respect to the genuine Black–Scholes formula, Eqs. 10.7–10.9, that is, for a European option on an underlying that pays no revenue during the lifetime of the option. The main sensitivities, as presented in next Section 5.1, are useful in several aspects, including risk management (for example in VaR calculations) and are illustrated by a global numerical example in Section 10.5.2.

10.5.1 Most usual sensitivities

The Delta

The delta (Δ) is the sensitivity of a call C or put P price to a variation of the underlying spot price S:

$$\Delta = \frac{\partial C}{\partial S} = N(d_1) > 0 \quad \Delta = \frac{\partial P}{\partial S} = N(d_1) - 1 = N(-d_1) < 0$$

---

[7] For more information, see, for example, http://toolsformoney.com/monte_carlo.htm.

Although this result seems straightforward at first sight, given, for a call, Eq. 10.7

$$C = SN(d_1) - Ke^{-rT}N(d_2)$$

the variable S is also present in the d_1 and d_2 terms, so that the full derivation has to be performed. However, after many reductions, one finally comes anyway to this result. Among others, such detailed calculation necessitates the use of a formula for the partial derivative of an integral:

$$\frac{\partial}{\partial v}\int_{b_1(v)}^{b_2(v)} f(v, x)\,dx = \int_{b_1(v)}^{b_2(v)} \frac{\partial f(v, x)}{\partial v}\,dx + \frac{\partial b_2(v)}{\partial v} f(v, b_2(v)) - \frac{\partial b_1(v)}{\partial v} f(v, b_1(v))$$

and in particular:

$$\frac{\partial}{\partial v}\int_{a}^{b(v)} y(x)\,dx = \frac{\partial b(v)}{\partial v} y(b(v))$$

with here,

$$b(v) = d_1(S, \ldots) \ or \ = d_2(S, \ldots)$$

and

$$y(b(v)) = \frac{1}{\sqrt{2}} e^{-d_1^2/2 or - d_2^2/2} = N'(d_1) \ or \ N'(d_2)$$

By definition, the delta represents the slope of the option price curve in function of S. For a call, see Figure 10.11.

It non-linearly varies from 0 (or 0%) for DOTM options to 1 (or 100%) for DITM options, going through 0.5 (or 50%) around ATM options, just as the cumulative normal distribution in Figure 10.12.

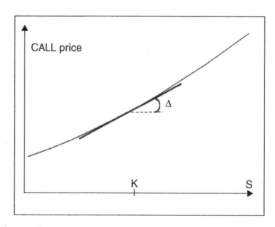

Figure 10.11 Delta for a call

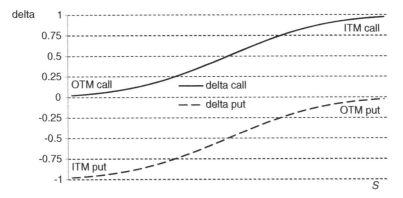

Figure 10.12   Delta of a call and a put, in function of the underlying spot price

The Gamma

The gamma (Γ) is the sensitivity of the delta of a call C or put P price to a variation of the underlying spot price S. It is thus the second derivative of a call C or put P price to a variation of the underlying spot price S. The gamma has the same value for a call as for a put:

$$\Gamma = \frac{\partial \Delta}{\partial S} = \frac{\partial^2 C}{\partial S^2} = \frac{\partial^2 P}{\partial S^2} = \frac{1}{S\sigma\sqrt{t}} N'(d_1) > 0$$

where $N'(d_1)$ is the unit normal distribution $\mathcal{N}$,

$$N'(x) = \frac{1}{\sqrt{2\pi}} e^{\frac{-x^2}{2}}$$

So that $N'(d_1)$ and thus the gamma is peaking for $d_1 = 0$, which corresponds to $N(d_1) = \sigma\sqrt{t}$ (cf. end of Section 10.2.4); it quickly goes to 0 for deep OTM and ITM situations. And because of the term in $1/\sqrt{t}$, the gamma increases dramatically when t goes to 0, that is, when the option is nearer to maturity – see Figure 10.13.

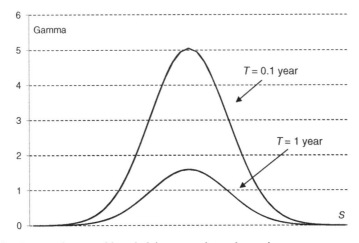

Figure 10.13   Gamma changes with underlying spot price and maturity

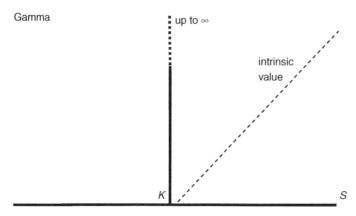

Figure 10.14   Dirac function centered on K

At maturity, indeed, the option value is restricted to its intrinsic value, so that a *dt* before, the gamma is actually a Dirac function centered on K, in case of a call for example, as in Figure 10.14.

The Delta–Gamma Neutral Management

Contrary to an option buyer or seller, who trades either for speculation or hedging, his counterpart, as a market maker, has to manage his options book in a way that his positions opened for purpose of market making, do not present any net exposure. He must therefore hedge, first on an individual basis but later on at the whole book level, his options positions. Let us illustrate this on a call C, bought by this market maker, called a "long" call position. Once the call is bought, it presents a risk in each of the variables affecting this call value, such as the volatility, time to maturity and market rate: these sensitivities will be considered hereafter. But at first, this call $C = C(S)$ also presents a market risk in the underlying price S, leading to a gain or a loss depending on whether S will go up or down. The straightforward way to neutralize this risk is by adding to its long call position the selling of $\Delta\%$ of underlying @ S ("short" position in S), so that, in the nearby range of S fluctuations, the call price variation – actually, its slope Δ – is compensated by the opposite position in ΔS. This explains why the delta is sometimes called a hedge ratio.

Of course, due to further S moves, the call Δ is changing, slower or faster depending on the Γ, leading the market maker to readjust its quantity of underlying position, up or down depending on the direction of the S move – see Figure 10.15.

This technique is called *delta–gamma neutral* options book management. In the particular case of a long call position, delta adjustments are such that, if S increases, the market maker must increase his short underlying position, by selling more and more of underlying, at a higher and higher price. Conversely, if S decreases, he must reduce his short underlying position, by buying back more and more of underlying, at a lower and lower price.

Altogether these adjustments thus give rise to a profit. If the underlying volatility (and market rate) were stable, at the end of the game, the profit caused by these adjustments must compensate for the premium paid to acquire the call. In case the market maker is selling a call,

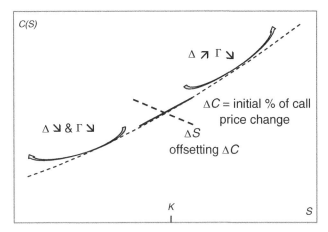

Figure 10.15   Impact of delta and gamma changes on the offsetting quantity of the underlying position

a similar reasoning leads to a global cost for delta adjustments.[8] Hence the importance of the implied volatility chosen by the market maker to price his call: if the market maker has – by means of his implied volatility – underestimated the actual volatility of S up to maturity, he will make an unexpected profit, and in case of selling the call, an unexpected loss, both caused by more underlying price moves than anticipated through the implied volatility.

Delta – gamma neutral management, also called "dynamic replication", does present limitations that should not be underestimated:[9]

- it does not preclude to adequately manage the other market risk factors (vega, theta, rho);
- in the practice, it is of course impossible to readjust *continuously* the offsetting position in underlying: beyond the bid–offer costs associated with frequent enough readjustments, discrete readjustments can present huge costs particularly if the underlying price presents important discontinuous variations;
- this technique is valid only to the extent that the underlying Gaussian process is reasonably verified.

The Theta

The "theta" (Θ) is the sensitivity of a call C or put P price to the passage of time (hence, the choice of a Greek letter for "t"). For a call,

$$\Theta = \frac{\partial C}{\partial t} = \frac{S\sigma}{2\sqrt{t}}N'(d_1) + Ke^{-rt}rN(d_2)$$

---

[8] In short, for offsetting a short call, the market maker must buy Δ times the underlying, and buy more when S goes up, selling back when S goes down.

[9] See for example, E. DERMAN, N.N. TALEB, "The illusions of dynamic replication", *Quantitative Finance* (Aug 2003), vol. 5, no. 4, pp. 323–326.

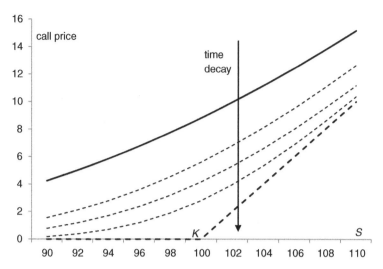

Figure 10.16   Impact of the Theta on a call price

such as

$$N(d_1) = \int\limits_{-\infty}^{d_1} N'(x)dx$$

And for a put,

$$\Theta = \frac{\partial P}{\partial t} = \frac{S\sigma}{2\sqrt{t}}N'(d_1) - rKe^{-rt}N(d_2)$$

The theta is negative (for a bought option), expressing that – other variables remaining unchanged – an option is losing value as and when it gets closer to its maturity: this phenomenon is known as "time decay". This can be displayed in two ways. Figure 10.16 shows an example for a call.

- Coming back to the graph of Section 10.1 displaying the intrinsic and time value: if we repeat the option curve in function of S at different intermediate times between the contract inception and the final result, at maturity (intrinsic value only) we get successive call prices as shown in Figure 10.16.
- Considering successive OTM call prices, from $t = t_0$ (contract inception) to $t = T$, other variables remaining unchanged. As an example, let us take an ATMS call on an underlying $S = \$100$, $T = 6$ months, implied volatility $= 25\%$ p.a., and the market rate @ 5%, which leads to a call price of $8.26: if we recomputed this price on the time to maturity period reducing from T to 0, we obtain Figure 10.17.

We notice that the time decay is accelerating. Indeed, as an OTM option, its price is pure time value, proportional to $\sigma\sqrt{t}$, let say a $C^{te} \times \sqrt{t}$: comparing the call price at inception, that is with $t = 1$ as remaining time to maturity, this price goes to half its value when it remains only 1/4th of the time to maturity because $\sqrt{0.25} = 0.5$.

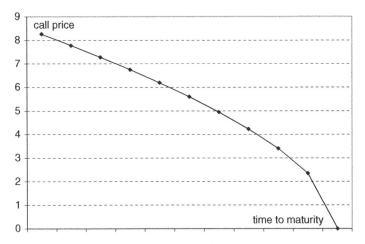

Figure 10.17   Call price decay in function of reducing time to maturity

The Vega

The Vega is the sensitivity of a call C or put P price to the volatility σ of its underlying.[10] Like for the gamma, the vega values are the same for a call as for a put:

$$vega = \frac{\partial C}{\partial \sigma} = \frac{\partial P}{\partial \sigma} = S\sqrt{t}N'(d_1)$$

and is strictly positive. Contrary to other "Greeks", the impact of the volatility is almost linear, except for very low volatility levels ($< 5\%$) that are unusual in the options markets.

As an example, let us consider the same call as previously, but keeping T $= 6$ months and letting the volatility vary between 5% and 50% – see Figure 10.18.

Unsurprisingly, the volatility level significantly affects the option price. Other features of the volatility will be developed in Chapter 12.

The Rho

Rho (ρ, equivalent to the "r" letter, for rate) is the sensitivity of the option price to the change in the market interest rate r: For a call:

$$\rho = \frac{\partial C}{\partial r} = \tau Ke^{-r\tau}N(d_2)$$

And for a put,

$$\rho = \frac{\partial C}{\partial r} = -\tau Ke^{-r\tau}N(-d_2)$$

---

[10] Vega is actually not a Greek letter (it is the name of a star), but this word has been used because it starts with a "v" as in "volatility". Alternatively, to restore the use of true Greeks, the vega is also called kappa (κ).

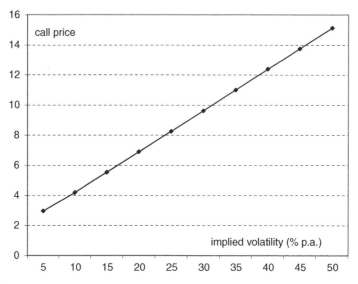

Figure 10.18 Call price in function of its implied volatility

From these formulae, it results that ρ is positive for a call, and is negative for a put. This can be understood as follows:

- for a call, if r increases, $F = S\ exp(rt)$ is increasing, making, for a given K, $F - K$ wider if $F > K$, that is, the call more ITM, and $K - F$ narrower if $F < K$, that is the call less OTM;
- for a put, if r increases, $F = S\ exp(rt)$ is increasing, making, for a given K, $F - K$ wider if $F > K$, that is, the put more OTM, and $K - F$ narrower if $F < K$, that is the put less ITM.

The impact of ρ is traditionally considered as minor by comparison with the other sensitivities. However, its impact may surprise, either in case of long maturities, or in case of dramatic rate changes.

Beyond Black–Scholes, the sensitivity to interest rates is more interesting at a broader level, that is, by considering the combined effect of both interest rates involved in option pricing, r_m and r_u (cf. Section 10.2.2): since in most cases both rates are concerned, they affect the option price in a contrary way, through their impact on the forward price.

Let us take the example of a call and a put, both of 1-year maturity, ATMS, $S = \$100$, and implied volatility of 20%, and let us consider several pairs of r_m and r_u:

rates:	F:	call price:	put price:
$r_m = 8\% - r_u = 8\%$	$= S$	7.4	7.4
$r_m = 8\% - r_u = 2\%$	105.98	10.7	5.2
$r_m = 2\% - r_u = 8\%$	94.36	5.2	10.7

Understandably, once again it is through the impact of both rates on the forward value that option prices are affected. Moreover, the role of these rates explains also why in some cases an American option is priced higher than the corresponding European one, and why in other cases, it ought to be priced equal. To show this, let us keep the same example, but complete the table by equivalent American call and put prices:

rates:	F:		call price:	put price:
$r_m = 8\% - r_u = 8\%$	$= S$	EO:	7.4	7.4
		AO:	7.4	7.4
$r_m = 8\% - r_u = 2\%$	105.98	EO:	10.7	**5.2**
		AO:	10.7	**5.8**
$r_m = 2\% - r_u = 8\%$	94.36	EO:	**5.8**	10.7
		AO:	**5.2**	10.7

The reason for these differences is as follows:

- Calls: $OA > OE$ if $r_u > r_m$: in the case of an opportunity for early exercise of an American call, acquiring the underlying offering a higher r_u improves the call holder's return, while if he wanted to take advantage of the same opportunity, but as a holder of a European call, he can only resell his option against cash @ r_m.
- Puts: $OA > OE$ if $r_u < r_m$: in the case of an opportunity for early exercise of an American put, delivering the underlying offering a lower r_u improves the call holder's return (by receiving cash in exchange), while if he wanted to take advantage of the same opportunity, but as a holder of a European put, he can only resell his option against cash @ r_m, but keeping his position in the non-delivered underlying at a lower return.

10.5.2   Numerical example

Let us illustrate the impact of the "Greeks" in the following example (data as of 01/06/12):

Option type:	European call
Underlying:	L'OREAL stock
Current spot price:	$S_0 = €82.345$
Strike:	82.5922 (i.e. ATMF)
Time to maturity:	90 days
Volatility:	23.261%
Market rate:	1.256%
Underlying return:	0 (no dividend paid during these 90 days)
→ call price C:	€3.80 (applying the B–S formula)

Let us first change the option parameters one by one:

1. by making $\Delta S = 1 \rightarrow S_1 = S_0 + 1 = 83.345$: C becomes 4.36
   → Delta $= \Delta C / \Delta S = (4.36 - 3.80)/1 = 0.56$
   NB: it is more precise to also compute this delta if $\Delta S = -1$ (cf. Eq. 10.16 in the next Section 10.5.3), and take the arithmetic average: with $S_1 = S_0 - 1 = 81.345$, $C = 3.31$
   → $(3.31 - 3.80)/1 = -0.49$
   → Δ = average between 0.56 and 0.49 $= 0.525$

2. reducing the time to maturity by 1 day, that is, 89 instead of 90 days, C becomes 3.78
   $\rightarrow$ Theta $= \Delta C / \Delta t = (3.78 - 3.80)/1 = -0.02$

3. reducing the volatility by 1%, that is 22.261% instead of 23.261%, $C = 3.64$
   $\rightarrow$ Vega $= \Delta C / \Delta \sigma = (3.64 - 3.80)/1 = -0.16$ per vol. percentage

4. increasing the market rate by 1%, that is 2.256% instead of 1.256%, $C = 3.89$
   $\rightarrow$ Rho $= \Delta C / \Delta r = (3.89 - 3.80)/1 = 0.09$ per% of interest rate

As we said at the beginning of Section 10.5, all the price parameters are moving together: starting from the previously mentioned initial market conditions, suppose that the next day, the underlying spot price is now 83.345, while the volatility has reduced by 1% and the market rate has increased by 1%. Discretizing the first order partial derivatives of the call price we get

$$\Delta C = \frac{\partial C}{\partial S}\Delta S + \frac{\partial C}{\partial t}\Delta t + \frac{\partial C}{\partial \sigma}\Delta \sigma + \frac{\partial C}{\partial r}\Delta r + terms\ of\ o. > 1$$

and the call price should now value

$$C = 3.80 + 0.525 + 0.02 - 0.16 + 0.019 = 4.24\ \text{(rounded)}$$

While its price, re-computed by using the Black–Scholes formula is now 4.26, the difference with the previous result of 4.24 is due to the discretization (using finite differences in the above Greeks calculation), and to the impact of partial derivatives of higher order. In particular, if we also want to take the Gamma into account, by using Eq. 10.17 of Section 10.5.3, to the above result, we must add

$$C = (4.36 - 2 \times 3.80 + 3.31)/1 = 0.07$$

such as $C = 4.31$, the impact of further derivatives becoming negative.

10.5.3   Other sensitivities

In theory, we could consider as much sensitivities that there are partial derivatives, to the second order practically speaking. With respect to the genuine Black–Scholes formula, the full derivative of, say, a call is

$$dC = \frac{\partial C}{\partial S}dS + \frac{\partial C}{\partial t}dt + \frac{\partial C}{\partial \sigma}d\sigma + \frac{\partial C}{\partial r}dr + \frac{\partial^2 C}{\partial S^2}dS^2 + \frac{\partial^2 C}{\partial t^2}dt^2 + \frac{\partial^2 C}{\partial \sigma^2}d\sigma^2$$
$$+ \frac{\partial^2 C}{\partial r^2}dr^2 + \mathbf{\frac{\partial^2 C}{\partial S \partial t}}dSdt + \mathbf{\frac{\partial^2 C}{\partial S \partial \sigma}}dSd\sigma + \frac{\partial^2 C}{\partial S \partial r}dSdr + \mathbf{\frac{\partial^2 C}{\partial t \partial \sigma}}dtd\sigma + \frac{\partial^2 C}{\partial t \partial r}dtdr$$
$$+ \frac{\partial^2 C}{\partial \sigma \partial r}d\sigma dr + terms\ of\ o. > 2$$

In practice, beyond the partial derivatives already reviewed, only some of second order derivative are used by option book managers (namely, the ones noted in bold here previously, that is, excluding the second derivatives involving the market rate, for the reason already explained about the rho). It appears that some higher order Greeks may well be unimportant for options around ATM, but significant for OTM (and ITM) options.[11]

---

[11] For further information, see, for example, L. EDERINGTON, W. GUAN, "Higher order Greeks", *Journal of Derivatives* (2007), vol. 14, no. 3, pp. 7–34.

Charm[12]

The charm measures the change of delta over time, so that

$$charm = \frac{\partial \Delta}{\partial t} = \frac{\partial^2 C \text{ or } P}{\partial S \partial t}$$

d Vega/d Time

There is no satisfying name for this Greek, measuring the change of volatility over time:

$$dvega/dtime = \frac{\partial vega}{\partial t} = \frac{\partial^2 C \text{ or } P}{\partial \sigma \partial t}$$

Vanna

The vanna measures the sensitivity of the vega in function of the underlying price S:

$$vanna = \frac{\partial vega}{\partial S} = \frac{\partial^2 C \text{ or } P}{\partial S \partial \sigma}$$

This measure directly implies to question about the use of a constant volatility whatever is the moneyness (cf. Section 10.2.4 previously) of an option. The problem will be dealt with in Chapter 11.

Volga

The volga (volatility gamma, sometimes also called vomma) relates to the vega in an equivalent way as of the Γ towards the Δ:

$$volga = \frac{\partial vega}{\partial \sigma} = \frac{\partial^2 C \text{ or } P}{\partial \sigma^2}$$

Moreover, given the practical importance of the second derivative Γ, market practitioners also use third derivatives involving the Γ, also introduced by M. Garman, such as the following.

Speed

The speed is the sensitivity of the gamma to the underlying price S:

$$speed = \frac{\partial \Gamma}{\partial S} = \frac{\partial^3 C \text{ or } P}{\partial S^3}$$

Color

The color is the sensitivity of the gamma to the time:

$$color = \frac{\partial \Gamma}{\partial t} = \frac{\partial^3 C \text{ or } P}{\partial S^2 \partial t}$$

---

[12] This funny name has been proposed by Mark Garman, see, for example, M. GARMAN, "Charm school", *RISK* (1992) vol. 5, no. 7, pp. 53 and 56.

10.5.4   Sensitivities and other option pricing methods

The calculus of the Greeks is of course not straightforward if we use a non-analytical pricing model, such as the binomial tree or Monte Carlo simulations.

For Options Priced With a Binomial Tree

Instead of computing the above "Greeks" partial derivatives from the analytic option formula of Black–Scholes, it is also possible to compute them as approximate differentials. These differentials naturally involve the various parameters of the tree (cf. Section 10.3), that is u, d, n, and $PV(1)$. At first sight, a good approximation for the delta would consist in re-computing the binomial tree from $S + \Delta S$ and from $S - \Delta S$ and obtain, here in the case of a call C (omitting the not concerned variables in $C(.)$)

$$\Delta = \frac{\partial C}{\partial S} \approx \frac{C(S + \Delta S) - C(S - \Delta S)}{2\Delta S} \tag{10.16}$$

and for the gamma of a call:

$$\Gamma = \frac{\partial^2 C}{\partial S^2} \approx \frac{C(S + \Delta S) - 2C(S) + C(S - \Delta S)}{\Delta S^2} \tag{10.17}$$

that may prove more accurate or realistic than going to infinitum when the option maturity becomes too near.

The theta of a call will naturally be approximated as

$$= \frac{\partial C}{\partial t} \approx \frac{C(T) - C(T - \Delta T)}{\Delta T}$$

It can be carried out in a similar way for the other Greeks.

Even combined sensitivities can be approximated, such as the delta with a change of volatility (due to a "smile" phenomenon, cf. Chapter 12, Section 10.1.3), for a call:

$$\Delta(\sigma) \approx \frac{C(S + \Delta S, \sigma_1) - C(S - \Delta S, \sigma_2)}{2\Delta S}$$

However, a satisfying solution is not straightforward.[13] Also, the choice of an adequate size for ΔS is far from easy, since the impact of a single (constant) ΔS is changing along the nodes of the tree (for more details, cf., for example, P. Jäckel, in the further reading later).

For Options Priced by Monte Carlo Simulations

The method for computing the Greeks is similar – and presents the same difficulties – as above. These difficulties are exacerbated in the normal case of using the Monte Carlo simulations for pricing second-generation options.

---

[13] See, for example, Antoon PELSSER, Ton VORST, "The binomial model and the Greeks", *Journal of Derivatives*, Spring 1994.

FURTHER READING

Darrell DUFFIE, *Dynamic Asset Pricing Theory*, Princeton University Press, 2001, 472 p.

Espen Gaarder HAUG, *The Complete Guide to Option Pricing Formulas*, Irwin Professional Publishing, 1997, 232 p.

Peter JACKEL, *Monte Carlo Methods in Finance*, John Wiley & Sons, Ltd, Chichester, 2002, 222 p.

Robert JARROW, Andrew RUDD, *Option Pricing*, Irwin, 1987, 235 p.
Although published a long time ago (and presumably available only second-hand), a simple but valuable book.

Ioannis KARATZAS, Steven E. SHREVE, *Methods of Mathematical Finance*, Springer, 2010, 430 p. Despite its title, this book focuses on the option valuation theory, developed in a sophisticated way.

Robert MERTON, *Continuous-time Finance*, Wiley-Blackwell, 1992, 752 p. A key reference book.

Nassim TALEB, *Dynamic Hedging: Managing Vanilla and Exotic Options*, John Wiley & Sons, Inc., Hoboken, 1997, 506 p.
Contains a lot of useful practical issues about options trading.

Robert TOMKINS, *Options Explained*, Macmillan Business, 1994, 597 p.

Paul WILMOTT (ed.), *The Best of Wilmott 2*, John Wiley & Sons, Ltd, Chichester, 2005, 404 p.

11

Options on specific underlyings and exotic options

The option pricing methodology has been developed in the previous chapter, exemplified with the most used – and simplest – underlying, namely stocks and stock indexes. In this chapter, particular features are considered, on other types of underlyings as well as in the case of more complex option pay offs, relative to *second-generation* or *exotic* options. To avoid cramming this chapter, there will be no references to the content of the previous one. Also, to remain within the limits of this book, as stated in the *Introduction*, since several of the topics developed hereafter are more complex, they are only outlined; that is the reason why the references in footnotes and the further reading are more abundant than in previous chapters.

11.1 CURRENCY OPTIONS

Currency options do not present particular features, and the pricing methods proposed in the previous chapter hold. We have to simply take into account the peculiar nature of the currency, as an underlying that is priced in a *relative* way: see Chapter 3, Section 3.4. Buying a reference currency against selling the counter-value currency results in the fact that a currency option is not simply a call or a put, but a call *and* a put: for example with EUR/USD, we have to consider either a call EUR/put USD (i.e., the right to buy EUR against selling USD) or a put EUR/call USD. Once this is viewed clearly, there is nothing to add to the previous chapter, Section 10.2.2. Besides regular currency options, let us consider the following variants.

NDOs (non-delivery options)

NDOs are the option equivalent of the NDFs on the OTC forward market (cf. Chapter 5, Section 5.1.4). Unlike a vanilla currency option, at maturity, if the option is exercised, there is no physical exchange, but a cash settlement by difference, that is, $| K - fixing\ rate | \times nominal\ amount$.

Example. Let us consider a Taiwanese treasurer hedging a short position of USD 1 million to be paid in 3 months against TWD (Taiwan dollar).
   Mid data (May 2006): $S = 32.12$, $(ND)F = 32.36$, implied volatility $= 4.5\%$.
   The treasurer buys a call USD/put TWD, say, ATMF$= 32.36$, @ 0.90% of the USD amount of 1 million

$\rightarrow$ *net* @ TWD 32 360 000 + ($9000 @ 32.36, *i.e.*) 291 240 = TWD 32 651 240 *or* @ 32.65

   At maturity:

- Suppose the TWD went lower: fixing USD/TWD $= 34.50$. The treasurer exercises it right to buy USD/ TWD @ 32.36. The bank counterparty will pay him

$$\$1\,000\,000/34.50 \times (34.50 - 32.36) = \$62\,028.99$$

while the Treasurer will buy $\$1\,000\,000$ @ S of 34.50 = TWD 34 500 000.

The net cost of his $ is thus

TWD 34 500 000 − ($62 028 99 @ 34.50 *or*) TWD 2 140 000 = TWD 32 360 000

achieving a USD/TWD rate @ 32.36 out of the premium (or 32.65, including the NDO premium).
- If the fixing USD/TWD < 32.36, the NDO expires worthless and the Treasurer will pay the current spot rate (corresponding to a net rate @ spot + the NDO premium).

Participating Forward Contracts

A participating forward contract (PFC) is a forward contract offering at maturity T some percentage (the "participation") of the opportunity loss, if any, arising from the difference between the agreed forward rate at the corresponding spot rate at maturity. A PFC is contractually treated as a forward operation, but it involves an embedded currency option. Let us call F' the agreed forward rate, that must be agreed at a less attractive level than the regular forward value F, S the spot rate and P (in %) the participation percentage granted, if any.

In the case of buying the reference currency (EUR against USD, for example), at maturity, the buyer of the reference currency will pay USD

$$F' - \left(F' - S\right) P \text{ if } F' > S$$

or F' if $F' \leq S$, in units of the counter-value currency.

The size of P depends on the level of F' versus F: intuitively, the less attractive is F', the higher is P. In the trivial case of $F' = F, P = 0$.

In our case of buying the reference currency, the buyer is actually like also buying a European call on the reference currency (call EUR/put USD in our example), with a strike $= F'$. The call premium P explains the difference between F' and F, as follows. Since P is valued as to be paid up front, but the operation (paying F' or less) being settled at maturity, P has to be valued forward, as

$$P'(\text{in\% of the nominal amount}) = P + \text{financing cost}(^*) = P(1 + n_{days}/36\,500).$$

(*) usually, $T < 1$ year.

The calculation gives, for the participation coefficient:

$$P = \frac{100}{1 + \dfrac{P'}{F' - F}}$$

As an example, let us refer to a call EUR/put USD (data of 02/26/08): for a PFC on 3 months = 89 days, EUR/USD mid spot = 1.4893, $r_{EUR} = 4.312\%$, $r_{USD} = 3.090\%$, F = 1.48476, F' is chosen about 5% higher, that is, 1.5590. For a strike ATMS, the premium P is 1.5416% of the nominal amount, or 0.02294 $ per EUR:

$$\rightarrow P' = 0.02294(1 + 0.03090 \times 89/365) = 0.02311$$

$$\rightarrow P = \frac{100}{1 + \dfrac{0.02311}{1.5590 - 1.48476}} = 0.7626 \text{ or } 76.26\%$$

Suppose at maturity, $S = 1.4500$: the buyer of EUR will pay

$$F'(F' - S)P = 1.5590 - (1.5590 - 1.4500)0.7626 = \$1.47588$$

instead of having paid $\$1.48476$ if he had bought the EUR forward.

To appreciate the impact of the choice of F' versus F,

- if $F' = F + 1\%$, or 1.4996 (i.e., cheaper than $F' = 1.5590$), $P = 39.10\%$;
- if $F' = F + 10\%$, or 16 332 (i.e., more expensive than $F' = 1.5590$), $P = 86.52\%$.

In the case of selling the reference currency (EUR against USD, for example), at maturity, the seller of the EUR reference currency will sell EUR against (receiving) USD @

$$F' + (S - F') P \ if \ S > F'$$

or F' if $S \leq F'$.

In this second case, the seller is buying a European put on the reference currency (put EUR/call USD in our example). The calculation of P' is the same as in the first case, and the participation coefficient becomes

$$P = \frac{100}{1 + \dfrac{P'}{F - F'}}$$

11.2   OPTIONS ON BONDS

A priori, there is no reason to devote a specific section to bond options, since they do not differ from stock options. In particular, previous pricing methods can be used, either for options on cash underlying bond, or options on bond futures. This is true, however, provided the option maturity is not too close from the bond maturity itself, given that the bond value at maturity is purely deterministic. Moreover, the credit risk impact may well affect the bond option valuation (cf. Chapter 13).

Practically speaking,

- the cash bond option strike does not amount to the price paid in case of exercise: indeed, bond option strikes are expressed as clean prices, and in case of exercise, one has to pay the corresponding dirty price (cf. Chapter 3, Section 3.2.1.2);
- bond option premiums are expressed in % of the nominal amount, not in% of the bond value;
- option volatility can be viewed in two ways: either, as computed on bond prices returns (called "price volatility", because originated by the bond prices themselves), or computed on yields (called "yield volatility"). It can be established that the relationship between the (bond price B) implied volatility σ_B and the (bond yield y) implied volatility σ_y is

$$\sigma_B = MDy_0\sigma_y$$

where MD is the modified duration of the bond at the option maturity date, and y_0 is the current forward yield corresponding to the option maturity date.

If the bond option is a European one, Eqs. 10.7–10.9 apply for cash bond options and Eqs. 10.13 and 10.14 for future bond options, both using price volatility. By doing so, we assume that bond prices are just like stock prices, reasonably distributed log-normally (corresponding to a Gaussian distribution of their returns), and the pricing is made in a risk neutral way.

In the case of American options, we usually apply the binomial tree method (cf. Chapter 10, Section 10.3) on the zero-coupon rates and determine the corresponding bond prices at each of the nodes.

Moreover, if bond options are used with respect to bond portfolio hedging, the duration D_{opt} of the option will inevitably play a key role. This concept was introduced in Chapter 3, Section 3.2.2. Let us come back to the related formula:

$$D_{opt} = \frac{B}{O_B} \times \Delta \times D_B$$

where D_B is the duration of the underlying bond, Δ is the delta of the option (i.e., the quantity of underlying used to hedge the option position – cf. Chapter 10, Section 10.5), B, the price of the underlying bond, and O_B, the price of the option (call or put). Let consider the following example of a bond portfolio made of French government bond OAT 6% 10/25/2025, quoting 97.40–53, yield 6.16–15% (market data of 01/13/00), having a modified duration of 12.65. Suppose the portfolio manager wants to reserve the possibility of reducing his portfolio duration, in case of a possible rates increase. Alternatively to "extreme" solutions such as selling the bond or selling a future, he may buy such right of selling, that is, a put on this bond, say, at 3 months.

A European put on this OAT, strike 95.40 (6.366%), 3-month maturity, with a price volatility of 11.24% was quoting 1.32% (ask), with a corresponding delta of -35%. The modified duration of this put is thus:

$$97.53 \times 0.35 \times 12.65/1.32 = 327.13!$$

It seems surprising, but this result makes itself clear if one takes into account the option leverage due to the premium (97.53/1.32) and the delta: this put will be sensitive to 35% of a bond price move. So that, the resulting MD adequately reflects the impact of this put in the MD of the combined position.

Besides straight bond options, one can encounter options that are "embedded" in bonds, such as the three following products.

11.2.1 Callable bonds

A callable bond is a bond allowing the issuer to redeem it before maturity. This implies that the bond issuer is also buying a call option on his bond:

issuer viewpoint: bond + (bought) call option on bond = callable bond

The underlying idea is of course that, during the lifetime of the bond, if market rates are going down and/or if his credit rating is improved, the issuer may early reimburse and thereafter borrow at a lower rate. The bond investor is in the situation of a call seller, receiving the premium on a p.a. basis, through a higher coupon than for a regular bond.

The callability may be offered on a discrete basis – on (semi-)annual coupon dates – or continuously, often after some initial period of time. Also, the call provision must precise at what strike it can be exercised, that is, at what bond price. This strike may or not be at bond par; it may also decline, on a yearly basis, from a higher level when starts the callability period, to end at par at maturity.

Mortgage-backed securities represent an important category of callable bonds. For more details about their specific calculation, see *Further Reading*.

Example. Here are the features of a callable UK Gilt (AAA government paper), issued on 01/26/72:

maturity:	01/26/15
isuing price:	96% of par
coupon:	$7\frac{3}{4}$% s.a., ACT/ACT
callable on	01/26/12 at par
price on 10/02/11:	106.23–106.28

Yield Calculation

Besides the usual yield calculation (cf. Chapter 3, Eq. 3.3), that is, supposing the bond is reimbursed at par, $YTM = f(B, c, T)$, we can also compute a "yield to call", by using the same formula, but applied up to the starting date of the call date, and, for the last cash flow calculation, the actual strike of the call. Both the actual yield and the yield to call, allow for a yield spread analysis, by comparison with an equivalent vanilla bond.

Example. With the above UK data, and using Eq. 3.5 (Chapter 3, Section 3.2.1.2) expressing the relationship between a bond price and the YTM out of a coupon date, and using Excel solver to determine the YTM corresponding to the market price on 02/10/11, we obtain:

- YTM = 6.01% (on 4 years minus 15 days/365)
- By comparison, the regular UK Gilt maturing nearly at the same date, that is, 01/22/15, pays a coupon of $2\frac{3}{4}$% (s.a.), with a YTM of 2.53%. The difference represents the call option premium;
- yield to call: 1.112% (on 1 year minus 15 days/365), $\approx$ current 1-year LIBOR @ 0.927%.

Callable Bond Valuation

Since the actual redemption date of a callable bond is uncertain, the deterministic bond valuation by discounting future cash flows is inadequate. A first, basic, method consists in valuing the bond at the redemption date of call exercise. If the callability is spread over some period of time, this valuation can be repeated on successive yearly dates. By retaining the lowest price obtained, the corresponding yield is called "yield to worst".

In the above example, the yield to worst coincides with the yield to call of 1.112%.

The right valuation of a callable bond actually consists in pricing the embedded call as a bond option, aside from the vanilla bond price. This leads to the OAS, for "option adjusted spread analysis".

If on 02/10/11 we value a call option on the above bond from 02/10/11 to 01/26/12, $K = 100$ (callable at par), S = 106.28, current market (price) volatility = 0.8%, $r_{mkt} = 1y$ LIBOR @ 0.927%, r_{und} = YTM of 6.01%, the theoretical premium amounts to 1.233%, and is almost pure intrinsic value (DITM option, with a delta of 94%); however, this valuation significantly differs from the actual premium resulting from the difference between the yields of both similar bonds, the callable and the vanilla ones, that is, $6.01 - 2.53 = 3.46\%$. Of course, the relevant market prices and yields are not benefitting from the market liquidity needed to have market option prices equivalent to their theoretical valuation.

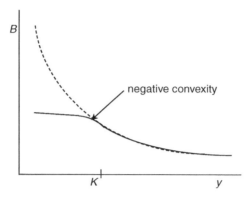

Figure 11.1   Price–yield relationship of callable and vanilla bonds

Duration

The classic formulae for duration (cf. Chapter 3, Eqs. 3.9 and 3.10) cannot apply, given the uncertainty affecting future cash flows, due to the call provision. To the extent that a price – yield $B \Leftrightarrow y$ relationship can be computed, the duration of such a bond can be approximated on this $B \Leftrightarrow y$ relationship around a given $B(y)$ reference, by computing/observing $B(y + \Delta y)$ and $B(y - \Delta y)$, where $\Delta y =$ a given number of basis points: an approximation of the tangent defines the effective duration (ED) as

$$ED = \frac{B(y - \Delta y) - B(y + \Delta y)}{2\Delta y \times B(y)}$$

Similarly, the effective convexity (EC) is (straightforward adaptation from Eq. 3.11):

$$EC = \frac{B(y - \Delta y) + B(y + \Delta y) - 2B(y)}{2\Delta y^2 \times B(y)}$$

The price–yield relationship of the callable bond (solid line in Figure 11.1) differs from the one of a vanilla bond (dotted line) due to the call provision, that becomes exercisable if $y < K$ (strike price of the call, converted into its corresponding yield). As appears from Figure 11.1, this leads to a range of prices versus yields presenting a negative convexity.

11.2.2   Putable bonds

Unlike a callable bond, an earlier redemption opportunity may be offered to the bond investor: in this case, called a putable bond, the bond investor is buying the right to resell it to the investor, namely a put on the bond:

> *Investor's viewpoint*: bond + (bought) put option on the bond = putable bond
>
> *Issuer's view point*: bond + (sold) put option on the bond = putable bond

An investor in a putable bond pays thus for having the right to sell back his bond to the issuer and reinvest in other bonds if and when interest rates rise, or if the issuer's rating is falling down. The coupon of a putable bond is therefore lower than for a vanilla bond, by deduction of the equivalent p.a. value of the premium.

Other considerations, exposed in the previous section, remain *mutatis mutandis* applicable to putable bonds. In particular, the price–yield relationship is significantly different: in the

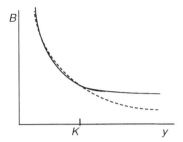

Figure 11.2   Price–yield relationship of putable and vanilla bonds

present case, if yields increase, the put value increases accordingly (from strike K, equivalent in yield), making the combined value of {bond + put} decrease at a lower pace than for a vanilla bond – see Figure 11.2.

Example of a Putable Bond

Given the decreasing rates period observed during the last decade, there has been no recent issue of putable bonds on the major sovereign bonds markets, through lack of potential interest from investors.

As an earlier example, let us consider a Belgian government issue on 03/04/03, of a 3.05%, 7-year bond, with a put maturing on 03/04/08. On 05/06/03, this bond was quoting 98.95, that is, with a YTM of 3.22%. At that date, the 7-year yield on the Belgian government yield curve was quoting 3.69%. The put premium was thus perceived by the market as the equivalent of 47 bp p.a. during 7 years.

11.2.3   Convertible bonds

A convertible bond is a bond offering the investor the opportunity, at the bond redemption, to be reimbursed in the bond issuer's stock as an alternative to a cash reimbursement. As such, a convertible bond (CB) does not relate to the previous section about bond options: the CB has actually an "embedded" option, but consisting in an equity option on the issuer's stock.[1]

This equity option is a (European) call, bought by the investor, that represents his right (but not the obligation) to decide, at the bond redemption, to be reimbursed either in cash (like for a regular bond) or in common stocks of the bond issuer. If the investor opts for the conversion, that is, for a reimbursement in stocks, this conversion will be carried out on the basis of a "conversion price" for the stock, which has been set at the bond issuance. This conversion price is the strike price K of the embedded call option. The CB can thus be viewed as the sum of

Investor's viewpoint: bond + (bought) call option on stock = convertible bond

The CB coupon is thus equivalent to the corresponding vanilla coupon, reduced by the p.a. value of the call option.

---

[1] If the embedded call refers to another company than the bond issuer, the product is called an exchangeable bond.

The CB secondary market has been for a long time not that liquid, leading to market price anomalies, all the more because adequately pricing a CB is not that simple. But more and more market participants, like hedge funds, traded these securities in a pseudo-arbitrage way, by combining for example a long position in CB with a short position in equivalent regular bond and call option, so that the market liquidity increased significantly, contributing to make disappear the price anomalies and related pseudo-arbitrage operations. So that, today, funds active on the CB market are more traditionally playing with the traditional advantages of the product, namely offering an intermediate risk/return profile between bonds and stocks, with some opportunities to play the volatility.

Before looking after CB pricing, we need to specify some typical parameters of CBs. These will be illustrated with the following CB issue, in EUR:

CB issue:	DELHAIZE 2.75% 2009 (5 years)
coupon:	2.75% (annual)
issued amount:	EUR 300 M
denomination:	EUR 250 000
issuing date:	30 April 2004
maturity date:	30 April 2009
conversion date:	24 April 2009
issuing price:	100%
redemption amount:	100%
conversion price:	EUR 57.00
conversion ratio:	4385.9649 per EUR 250 000
call protection:	Hard Call 3 years (until 15 May 2007)
stock price at issuance date:	EUR 40.50

Conversion Ratio

For a given nominal value (i.e., a portion of the issued nominal amount), conversion ratio = number of ordinary shares offered in case of conversion

$$= \text{nominal value/conversion price}$$
$$= 250\,000/57 = 4385.9649$$

"Hard" Call Protection

CBs are generally issued with a period during which the issuer cannot early redeem his bond. The longer the Hard Call, the more the investor may expect a conversion at maturity.

Let us now consider this CB on the secondary market, for example on July 18, 2008:

CB mid price:	96.90
YTM:	6.88%
stock price:	36.71
stock volatility:	29.00% p.a.
stock yield:	0%

(Stock Price) Parity

This gives the % of par if the conversion were carried out at the current spot price:

$$\text{parity} = \text{current stock price} \times \text{conversion ratio/nominal value}$$
$$= 36.71 \times 4385.9649/250\,000 = 64.404\%$$

This measure allows us to appreciate to what extent the CB can be expected to be converted at maturity, that is if, at maturity, this parity exceeds 100% (what needs a stock price of 57).

CB Premium

$$\text{Premium} = (\text{bond price} - \text{parity})/\text{parity}$$
$$= (96.90 - 64.404)/64.404 = 50.458\%$$

It says by how much more an investor has to pay for the same number of shares via the CB, rather than by buying the stock.

Bond Floor

This is the value of the CB as if it were a regular corporate bond. Given the issue data, it is possible to value such a bond, provided we compute the credit risk premium from the CB market price, which is here 213bp.

The corresponding risk-free rate at that time to maturity was 5.16%. The last cash flow on 04/30/09 is 102.75 (par + last coupon). But, given the conversion date is 6 days in advance, from this cash flow, we have to deduct 6 days @ 2.75, that is,

$$102.75 - 2.75 \times 6/360 = 102.70$$

to be discounted @ $(5.16 + 2.13 =) 7.29\%$,

so that discounting from 04/24/09 to the current 07/18/08, that is, on 276 days (30/360) leads to a bond floor of

$$\frac{102.70}{1.0729^{276/360}} = 97.306$$

With a current CB price of 96.90, we are presently slightly below this bond floor of 97.31. This difference is evidenced by the:

Risk Premium

This measures the relative percentage of the CB price over the bond floor. Its value is here:

$$\text{risk premium} = (\text{CB price} - \text{bond floor})/\text{bond floor}$$
$$= (96.90 - 97.306)/97.306 = -0.417\%$$

Outcome of the Operation

At the conversion date (04/24/09) of this CB, the spot Delhaize (closing) price was € 51.885, so that the conversion has not been exercised.

Coming back to the general case, a CB price can be evidenced in a graph such as the one in Figure 11.3 in function of the underlying stock price. In such a graph, we can distinguish different sub-areas:

- "distressed": if the corporation is facing serious financial problems, both the CB (then, a "junk" convertible) and the stock price go to 0;
- "OTM": if the parity is in the range of 40–70%, the stock price has poorly performed, well below the conversion price. It corresponds to a CB premium exceeding, say, 35%, and a

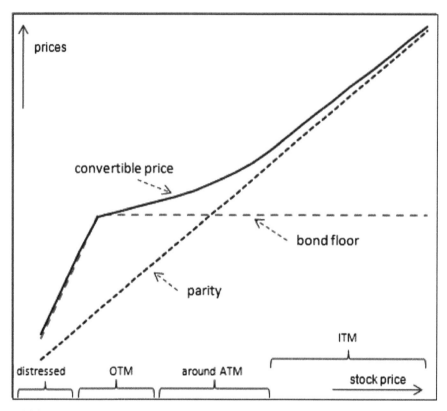

Figure 11.3   Convertible bond price as a function of its underlying stick price

very low risk premium. This situation corresponds to the Delhaize example (on the left side of this sub-area). The corresponding embedded call option is OTM, with a delta in the range of, say, 5–40%, and a corresponding time value that becomes higher and higher, leading to a CB price progressively increasing above the bond floor level, that represents the CB out of its call component;

- "around ATM": if the stock price is not far below or above the conversion price, it corresponds to the highest time value of the embedded call. Of course, in this area, the stock volatility plays the most significantly. The parity ranges from, say, 70–120%, with a CB premium reducing from about 35–10% range, and a higher risk premium, in the range of about 20–40%. The call delta is somewhat below to above 50%;
- "ITM" (actually, it should be DITM): the stock price is well above the conversion price, making the CB significantly above the bond floor. The CB premium is reduced, because DITM options (let say, with a call delta above 75%) have much less time value.

Finally, it should be mentioned that, despite a much more liquid market than a couple of decades before, CBs remain hard to price accurately: it is indeed difficult to appreciate the impact of the following factors:

- stock dilution, in case of conversion;
- stock volatility on the embedded call;

- estimate of the stock return on relatively long term (i.e., the CB maturity);
- other possible CB specs (hard call, seniority, credit risk, etc.);
- and of the CB liquidity on the secondary market.

11.3   OPTIONS ON INTEREST RATES

Bonds are of course interest rate products, but quoted in prices, so that bond options can be priced with same techniques as for equity options (provided the option maturity is not closed too much to the underlying bond redemption). But more generally, short-term and long-term interest rates option pricing has to cope with the very specific behavior of underlying interest rates, namely the *mean reversion*.

To introduce the mean reversion concept, let us come back to a comparative view of financial instruments behavior over time:

- In the very long run, stock and stock index prices can be considered to follow a positive trend. This can be explained by economic factors: a company is supposed to re-invest all or part (in case of dividend distribution) of its profits, and thus grow over time, and stock prices must also follow inflation over the long run. Of course, on a shorter horizon of time, prices may decline, even during periods lasting several consecutive years. So that, equity and index options pricing models clearly fit with the random walk hypothesis (although not necessarily strictly Gaussian).
- Currency prices do not present any global trend over time: a currency is priced relatively to another currency, and economic as well as speculative hazards comfort the random walk hypothesis.
- But over time, interest rates show the peculiar behavior of successive rising and falling phases. Unfortunately, there is no hope for anticipating both the amplitude and the periodicity of such cycles. We may carefully bound these cycles by, upwards, the "abnormally" very high (more than, say, 15% p.a.) interest rates around the 1980s (that is, before central banks learned to actually control inflation) and by 0 downwards: since the 1990s, Japan has faced interest rates at 0% or very slightly higher, but actually no negative interest rates, including inflation. Between such extreme situations, there is thus a band of interest rates wherein they evolve over time: during periods of high rates, one can expect a falling phase will follow, and conversely, periods of low rates will be followed by a rising phase, describing a mean reversion feature. Of course, the "mean" cannot be view as a constant, nor predictable.

Mean reversion processes are also called Ohrstein–Uhlenbeck processes. A quick survey over the history of successive interest rate processes attempts allows for a better understanding of the challenge. Today several process models are still competing: it means that there is still no really paradigmatic model, on the contrary to the general geometric process for most of other underlyings.

11.3.1   Single rate processes

The first and simplest attempt to model an interest rates process is due to Vasicek. The Vasicek model is a process governing a single rate r:

$$dr = a(b - r)dt + dZ \qquad (11.1)$$

Its stochastic component is same as in the traditional Wiener process. The mean reversion logically applies to its deterministic component. The b coefficient is featuring the mean objective of r, on the long run: the more r is above b, the more negative the deterministic term $(b - r)$ will be, and conversely. The a coefficient is set to quantify the strength of the reversion: the higher the a, the stronger the $(b - r)$ will affect the deterministic component, and conversely.

Note that in this process, the volatility term is under the form of $\sigma\, r^0$, that is, not proportional to the level of r.

After Vasicek, Courtadon proposed something more realistic, that is, with a stochastic term in $\sigma\, r^1$:

$$dr = a(b - r)dt + \sigma\, rdZ$$

But there was still a drawback: such a process allows for negative interest rates. Hence, Cox, Ingersoll, and Ross proposed a similar model, but with a stochastic term in $\sigma\, r^{1/2}$:

$$dr = a(b - r)dt + \sigma\sqrt{r}dZ \qquad (11.1bis)$$

However, by modeling a single interest rate process, one forgets that interest rates are belonging to a set of rates, that is, the market yield curve. Inevitably, the output of the previous models applied to interest rates of different maturities will produce independent results, not fitting the observed yield curve! Hence, the need for a second generation of more ambitious processes for yield curve modeling:

11.3.2 Modeling the yield curve

In a first approach, this was done through modeling a *set* of zero-coupon bonds, representing the yield curve. The simplest is the Ho and Lee model, which does not, however, incorporate the mean reversion feature.

For a series of zero-coupons of various maturities T_i and various zero-coupons r_i, with future value $= 1$, the corresponding prices $B_i(T_i)$ at t are

$$B_i\,(t, T_i) = e^{-r_i(T_i - t)}$$

with the r_i modeled by a generic process r such as

$$dr = \theta\,(t)\,dt + \sigma\,dZ$$

The $\theta(t)$ function is determined so that each r_i must adjust to the initial yield curve (at t_0). Note that the σ volatility is common to the all set of processes of rates r_i making up the yield curve.

In this model the zero-coupon rates r_i are Gaussian, and corresponding bond prices B_i are log-normal, allowing for an analytic solution, of the Black–Scholes type.

NB: there is an expansion of the Ho and Lee model to coupon bonds, due to Jamshidian.

Subsequently, Hull and White added mean reversion to the Ho and Lee model, as follows:

$$dr = [\theta\,(t) - ar]\,dt + \sigma\,dZ$$

Note that the mean reversion coefficient a is common for the whole set of yield curve rates r, so that with $a > 1$, the mean reversion has a stronger impact on short-term rates than on long-term rates, leading to a higher variance or volatility of short-term rates than of long-term rates, what fits with the market observation.

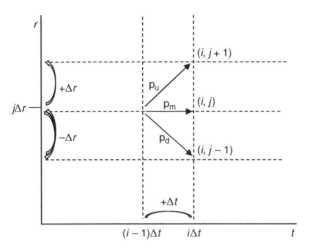

Figure 11.4   Node of a trinomial tree

Applying this model involves a finite differences technique, but rather through a *trinomial* rather than a binomial tree: in addition to the up (with probability p_u) and down (with probability p_d) moves from one node, the trinomial tree adds a probability p_m that r remains unchanged after Δt. In a first step,[2] starting from the current yield curve (at t_0), we make $\theta(t) = 0$ and $r(0) = 0$ and build the tree on $r(t)$ such as on each node, expected value and variance $E(.)$ and $V(.)$ are computed from the above process, as in Figure 11.4.

Note than from each node (i,j), we have

$$\{p_u, p_m, p_d\}_i = f(j, E, V)$$

with

$$\sum p_j = 1$$

Then, in a second step, one incorporates $\theta(t)$. The nodes of the tree are moved by quantities $f[\theta(t)]$ that are determined from the zero-coupon yield curve.

To further give an idea of the multiplicity of competing models for interest rates, let us also mention the following.

The Black–Derman–Toy (BDT) Process

It models $d \ln r$:

$$d\ln r = \left[\theta(t) - \frac{\partial\sigma(t)/\partial t}{\sigma(t)} \ln r\right] dt + \sigma(t) dZ$$

This leads to a log-normal distribution for r, restricting r to ≥ 0 values, but with such log-normal distribution of the variable, there is no analytic solution.

---

[2] For a detailed presentation of the model, see, for example, John HULL, Alan WHITE, "Numerical procedures for implementing term structure models I: single-factor models", *Journal of Derivatives* (fall 1994), pp. 7–16.

Note that the BDT process considers a variable volatility $\sigma(t)$: by making $\sigma = C^{st}$ in the BDT process, $\partial\sigma(t)/\partial t = 0$ and the process becomes the ln of the Ho and Lee process.

The Black–Karasinski Model

This can be viewed as a BDT + mean reversion:

$$dlnr = [\theta(t) - a(t)lnr]dt + \sigma(t)dZ$$

where $a(t)$ and $\sigma(t)$ have to be adjusted to the initial yield curve (at t_0). But what about the $\sigma(t)$ function? This illustrates the possible conflict between more refinement (here, with the incorporation of a mean reversion component) and less robustness and/or tractability.

11.3.3   Modeling the yield curve through forward rates

The Heat–Jarrow–Morton Model (HJM)

Besides models focused on the yield curve modeling via spot rates, there is another interesting way, that aims to model the *instantaneous, continuous* forward rates $F(t,T)$, as the Heath, Jarrow, Morton model (HJM).[3]

These $F(t,T)$ functions can be defined as follows. Starting from a discrete instead of continuous framework, between maturities T and $T+\Delta T$ we have

$$e^{r_T T}e^{F\Delta T} = e^{r_{T+\Delta T}(T+\Delta T)}$$

$$\rightarrow e^{F\Delta T} = e^{r_{T+\Delta T}(T+\Delta T)}e^{-r_T T} = \frac{1}{B_{T+\Delta T}}B_T$$

Hence,

$$F = \frac{1}{\Delta T}(-lnB_{T+\Delta T} + lnB_T) = -\frac{1}{\Delta T}(lnB_{T+\Delta T} - lnB_T)$$

or, in continuous time ($\Delta T \rightarrow dt$), between T and $T + dT$,

$$F(t, T) = -\frac{\partial lnB(t, T)}{\partial T}$$

The $F(t,T)$ function is then modeled by

$$dF(t, T) = m(t, T)dt + \sigma(t, T)dZ$$

This approach is very coherent and more realistic than the previous models, but harder to handle. Indeed, it involves a path dependent, non-Markov, process, that is much slower for

---

[3] For a detailed presentation of the model, see David HEATH, Robert A. JARROW, Andrew MORTON, "Bond pricing and the term structure of interest rates. A new methodology for contingent claim valuation", *Econometrica* (1992), vol. 60–1, pp. 77–105.

computation purpose, because it needs either Monte Carlo simulations, or a *non-recombining* tree that involves n^2 nodes for a number n of Δt periods, instead of $n + 1$ for a regular, recombining tree.

The LIBOR Market Model (LMM)

Besides its complex implementation, the HJM model involves *instantaneous* rates, which are not directly observable in the market. Hence, the interest for *discretizing* these instantaneous forwards that leads to modeling them in the form of discrete forward LIBOR (observable) rates, namely, the LMM, for *LIBOR market model*, also called the *BGM model* (for its authors, Brace, Gatarek and Musiela).[4] In particular, it is possible to implement the LMM with a regular (recombining) binomial tree, or by use of Monte Carlo simulations. This model is today the most used in practice for pricing interest rate options, such as the ones considered in the next two sub-sections.

Basically, the discretized variant of HJM is using n forward LIBOR rates that are modeled as n geometric Wiener processes,

$$\frac{dL_i(t)}{L_i(t)} = \mu_i \left(\{ L_i(t), \quad i = 1, \ldots, n \}, t \right) dt + \sigma_i(t) \, dZ_i \quad i = 1, \ldots, n \quad (11.2)$$

where

- L_i is the ith forward LIBOR rate, applying from maturity T to $T + \delta$;
- δ is the LIBOR reference, in years, for ex., 0.25 year $= 3$ months (actually, this time measure is to be based on applicable day counting convention).

These forward LIBOR rates can be directly observable, either, from the short term (market) yield curve, that is, from daily quoted spot LIBOR rates, or from the FRA (cf. Chapter 5, Section 5.2) market rates. For longer maturities, say, above 2 years, this is unfortunately not the case, they depend from the yield curve build on the IRS fixed rates.

Note that Eq. 11.2 says that these forward rates are log-normally distributed, as if they were individually priced by use of Black–Scholes formula for forward underlying (the "Black model", cf. Chapter 10, Section 10.2.2, Eq. 10.14 and next): there is no "improvement" such as a mean-reversion term. But actually, the LMM model, as a set of relationships in $L_i(t)$s, links each particular $L_i(t)$ process to the whole set of them, which allows for a more adequate modeling than a strict mean-reversion term. Moreover, by doing so, the LMM model takes into account the correlation – via covariance terms – between each of the standard Wiener processes dZ_i (cf. Eq. 8.6):

$$dZ_i dZ_j = \rho_{ij} dt \quad (11.3)$$

To calibrate the model represented by Eq. 11.2 and Eq. 11.3, we must estimate the set of σ_is and ρ_{ij}s. Both estimations are delicate issues, because these measures are not stable over time. In practice, the LMM model can be carried out either by use of a binomial recombining tree or by Monte Carlo simulations.

---

[4] As proposed in A. BRACE, D. GATAREK, M. MUSIELA, "The market model of interest rate dynamics", *Mathematical Finance* (1997), vol. 7, no. 2, pp. 127–154.

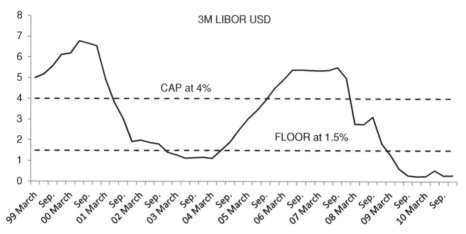

Figure 11.5   Example of a cap and a floor on the 3M LIBOR USD

11.3.4   Caps, floors, collars

Buying a *cap* consists in acquiring the right to put a ceiling to the level of an -ibor rate,[5] over some period of time (up to a maturity date *T*). The cap holder will have to exercise, or not, his option at each reset of the underlying -ibor rate, up to the end of the lifetime of the product. Conversely, a *floor* holder has the right to put a bottom to the level of this -ibor rate, as illustrated in Figure 11.5.

Caps and floors can thus be defined as series of European options on forward -ibor rates, called *caplets* and *floorlets*. Each of these caplets and floorlets are individual European options, with increasing maturities. To illustrate this, let us consider a 5-year cap on 3M LIBOR. It consists of 19 caplets, all of them having to be priced at t_0; the first one for an underlying forward LIBOR starting from $t_0 + 3$ months and maturing at $t_0 + 6$ months, the next ones applying to forwards on 3 months starting successively from $t_0 + 6$ months, $+ 9$ months, $+ \ldots , + 57$ months.

As a series of options, a cap or floor price is function of the usual variables that are the spread between spot and strike rates, maturity, volatility and the yield curve (since the underlying is a series of forward rates). These variables affect the cap or floor price as shown in Figure 11.6.

The combination of a cap and a floor is a *collar*, with the following rationale, for a borrower and for an investor, @ -ibor for a certain number of years:

- (borrower:) BUY a CAP (to limit a borrowing cost) $\Rightarrow$ pay a premium
  +
  SELL a FLOOR (to give up a lower borr. cost) $\Rightarrow$ get a premium

  _____

  = BUY a COLLAR $\Rightarrow$ @net premium

[5] There are also caps and floors on CMS swap rates (cf. Chapter 6, Section 6.7.4): this case goes outside the framework of this book (cf. *Further Reading*).

Impact of:	on Cap price:	on Floor price:
maturity ↗:	↗	↗
volatility ↗:	↗	↗
−spread K ⇔ -ibor ↗:	(-ibor ↗ − K) ↗	(K − -ibor ↗) ↗
yield curve slope ↗ [6]		
normal y.c.:	↗	↘
inverse y.c.:	↘	↗

Figure 11.6 Variables affecting the cap or floor price

- (investor:) BUY a FLOOR (to hedge ag. lowering rates) ⇒ pay a premium
  +
  SELL a CAP (to give up a higher revenue)   ⇒ get a premium
  _____
  = SELL a COLLAR   ⇒ @net premium

In normal market conditions, for a borrower, the cost of a collar is such as the whole cap ↔ floor range of -ibor rates, augmented by the collar cost on a corresponding p.a. basis, cannot be lower than the corresponding IRS rate of same maturity (for the sake of no arbitrage condition). Conversely, for an investor, the whole cap ↔ floor range of -ibor rates, reduced by the collar cost on a corresponding p.a. basis, cannot be higher than the corresponding IRS rate.

Cap and Floor Pricing

The simplest way to price a cap (floor) is by adding the premiums of each caplet (floorlet), being priced according the Black–Scholes formula for forward underlying ("Black model", cf. Eq. 10.14 and next) since the underlying is a forward rate. It will, however, need to price each caplet with the adequate volatility, coming from the related volatility curve (cf. Chapter 12, Section 12.1.2). Incidentally, this also apply for European IRGs (interest rate guarantees), that are options on FRAs, since they correspond to a single first caplet.

The call formula will apply to caps, while the put will be used for the floor. It is a pity to talk of a call or a put for these options, since we actually neither buy nor sell interest rates! But it is the underlying rationale for using the Black–Scholes formula. Note that, by doing so, the underlying "price" is an -ibor rate that is distributed log-normally, what is not that much senseless because such rates cannot go below zero.

However, we may contest the validity of modeling the LIBOR rates involved in caps and floors by individual and independent Wiener processes, hence the need for a more adapted approach. The most common way is by using the LMM model, introduced at the end of the previous section, since it is precisely aiming to model forward -ibor rates.

_____

[6] To explain the direction of the arrows, see Section 1.4 for the impact of the yield curve slope on forward rates.

Example. Let us price (using Black–Scholes, source: Bloomberg calculation) a 5-year cap on 3-month LIBOR USD. Data are of 02/23/11, strike = 2.457%, that is the current IRS 5-year rate, the current 3M LIBOR being 0.3115%:

LIBOR reset date:	caplets maturities:	3M forward:	yield volatility (p.a.):	caplet premium (in% of nominal):
05/23/11	6M	0.369%	91.40%	0.0000002%
08/23/11	9	0.459	91.40	0.0002283
11/23/11	12	0.612	91.40	0.0036822
02/23/12	15	0.871	62.74	0.0043364
05/23/12	18	1.202	62.74	0.0240690
08/23/12	21	1.567	62.74	0.0615215
11/22/12	24	1.885	62.74	0.1103009
02/21/13	27	2.166	46.32	0.1140970
05/23/13	30	2.427	46.32	0.1587796
08/22/13	33	2.667	46.32	0.2027971
11/21/13	36	2.903	46.32	0.2546354
02/21/14	39	3.115	37.52	0.2598520
05/22/14	42	3.340	37.52	0.3050609
08/21/14	45	3.567	37.52	0.3509070
11/21/14	48	3.787	37.52	0.3998023
02/23/15	51	3.889	35.70	0.4041625
05/21/15	54	4.086	35.70	0.4472726
08/21/15	57	4.276	35.70	0.4894157
11/23/15	60	4.462	35.70	0.5250344

total cap premium: 4.11596%

In accordance with the above table of cap sensitivities, we notice that, the current yield curve being "normal" (growing with maturities), 3-months forward rates are growing more and more significantly beyond the current 3M LIBOR, making the caplets more and more expensive: the first ones are still OTM (forwards < strike), but they progressively become more and more ITM (forwards > strike). This effect is dampened by a currently observed inverse volatility curve (see the third column).

Moreover, we see that, after all, the cap premium is not that expensive, given the global maturity of 5 years (on equities, the premium should be a two-digit number): this is because interest rates are much less volatile than other underlyings; the numbers in the "volatility" column seem contradict this, but these are "yield volatilities": if they were established in "price volatilities" (cf. Section 11.2), the numbers would be much lower.

11.3.5 Options on swaps, or swaptions

A *swaption* is an option to enter into a swap. As such, it corresponds to the conditional version of the forward swap (cf. end of Chapter 6, Section 6.3), and the underlying is a forward swap rate. The swaption involves two maturity steps: the maturity of the option properly said, and the maturity of the swap to be entered into, in the case of a swaption exercise (see Figure 11.7).

A swap being determined as a payer or a receiver swap, quite understandably, we will talk of *payer* or *receiver* swaptions, meaning the right to enter into a payer or a receiver swap. Here, too, we escape to the use of right to buy or right to sell (cf. the previous remark regarding

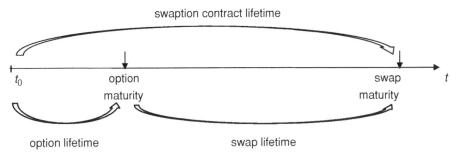

Figure 11.7   Breaking down of a swaption contract lifetime

caps and floors using the Black–Scholes formula). The strike price of a swaption is the swap (fixed) rate to be applied in case of exercise.

The swaption can be of European or American style (or even Bermudan, see further Section 11.6). In case of an American swaption, the vanilla form is such as, once an early exercise occurs, the swap is coming into force with its contractual lifetime; as an alternative, one can trade also an American swaption such as the total maturity is kept constant, so that, in case of early exercise, the swap maturity is extended accordingly.

Swaption Pricing

European swaptions can basically be valued, in the same way as for caps and floors, by use of the forward variant of the Black–Scholes formula (cf. Eq. 10.14 and next). With respect to the call or put feature, calls will apply to payer swaptions, and puts to receiver swaptions. Here, too, the underlying forward swap rate is then modeled log-normally.

But, as for caps and floors, given the nature of the underlying interest rate, other pricing methods are available, the most common one being the LMM. But, unlike for a cap premium – obtained by summing caplets premia – the swaption premium results from a single valuation, involving an adequate set of σ_is and ρ_{ij}s, that needs a calibration to swaptions market data.

Example.   Let us look at the price (using Black–Scholes, source: Bloomberg calculation) of a 1-year receiver swaption on a 5-year IRS, that would pay 3M USD LIBOR against receiving USD IRS s.a. rate. Data are of 02/22/11, strike = 3.297%, that is, ATMF, the current IRS 5-year rate forward 1 year; the current 3M LIBOR is 0.3125%. The resulting premium is 2.14795% of the notional amount.

11.4   EXCHANGE OPTIONS

An exchange option gives the right to the buyer to exchange a risky asset (a stock, for example) for another one. Such an option is both a call and a put, since in case of exercise, one asset is bought against the sale of the other one. To that extent, exchange options are similar to currency options (call and put on a currency pair, cf. Section 11.1), with the difference that, in the case of currencies, none are valued in absolute terms, while in case of exchanging two stocks for example, both are valued in some third unit ($ for example).

The valuation of a European[7] exchange option has been developed by Margrabe[8] within the framework of the Black–Scholes model, that is, a European option involving two assets paying no revenue during the lifetime of the option. In these conditions, the valuation is also valid for American options, as developed in the previous chapter.

Calling S_1 and S_2 the spot price of assets 1 and 2 respectively, both are modeled as a standard Wiener process

$$\frac{dS_i}{S_i} = \mu_i dt + \sigma_i dZ_i (i = 1, 2)$$

and the correlation between dZ_1 and dZ_2 processes is ρ_{12}, being considered as a constant, just as for σ_1 and σ_2. For a time T to maturity, the resulting exchange option price, as well a call and a put, noted w, namely the notation used by Margrabe (that is, incidentally, the notation for a call price used by Black and Scholes in their seminal paper), is

$$w(S_1, S_2, T) = S_1 N(d_1) - S_2 N(d_2)$$

with

$$d_1 = \left[\ln\left(\frac{S_1}{S_2}\right) + \frac{1}{2}\sigma^2 T \right] \frac{1}{\sigma\sqrt{T}}$$
$$d_2 = d_1 - \sigma\sqrt{T}$$
$$\sigma^2 = \sigma_1^2 + \sigma_2^2 - 2\sigma_1\sigma_2\rho_{12}$$

that presents the same look as the genuine Black–Scholes formula, with S_2 in lieu of K. If one considers asset 2 as numeraire, this exchange option price appears as a call option on asset 1, with $K = 1$ and market rate $= 0$.[9] This way of considering the price formula fits well with the main application field for exchange options, that is, in MandA operations.

Practically speaking, the hypotheses, namely μ and σ are constants, of both Wiener processes, and, more importantly, the constant correlation coefficient, express the limits of the valuation formula.

Coming back to MandA operations, the above formula justifies – and helps to quantify – the increased value of the target company between an acquisition announcement and the transaction, in normal circumstances. Let us consider[10] Company 1 is announcing its intent to acquire stocks of Company 2: considering asset 2 as numeraire, this value increase corresponds to the exchange option value.

11.5 BASKET OPTIONS

The valuation of an option on a basket of underlyings raises the question of the correlation among its constituents: the distribution of a sum of correlated log-normal random variables is anything but log-normal. At first sight, this would also affect options on (stock) indexes, but market practice does not consider it, what means that the index is considered as an underlying *per se* and not as a set of stocks. This is not too questionable inasmuch as the size of market

---

[7] For American exchange options, we need to use a binomial model.

[8] William Margrabe, "The value of an option to exchange one asset for another", *Journal of Finance*, vol. XXXIII, no. 1, March 1978, pp. 177–186.

[9] This makes sense if we notice that the market rate plays the same role for the numeraire and for asset 1.

[10] This example is developed in Margrabe, as previous.

indexes is so much prevalent vis-à-vis individual stocks, and that the index content is subject to periodic revisions (cf. Chapter 4, Section 4.2), making it heterogeneous over time.

Typically, options on indexes involve lower implied volatilities than involved in options on constituents of the index, because of the correlation between the basket constituents: generalizing Eq. 4.2 (referring to a two-stock portfolio variance), to the case of a basket B of N stocks, weighted by w_i, the basket volatility σ_B is

$$\sigma_B^2 = \sum_{i=1}^{N} w_i^2 \sigma_i^2 + 2 \sum_{i=1}^{N} \sum_{j=1}^{N} w_i w_j \rho_{ij} \sigma_i \sigma_j \tag{11.4}$$

where the correlation coefficient ρ_{ij} can be measured ex post in the same way as the standard deviation:

$$\rho_{ij} = \frac{cov_{ij}}{\sigma_i \sigma_j}$$

Assuming the market maker is able to transpose the correlation impact into a basket implied volatility, there is no obstacle to use the Black–Scholes formula or the binomial model for pricing a basket option.

Example. Let us consider a 1-year ATMS European option on a basket of equally weighted EUR/ USD and GBP/USD, say call EUR and GBP against put USD. The data (Feb 2010) are

- EUR/USD:
  - mid spot: 1.3682
  - mid vol.: 12.428%
  - r_{ref} (EUR): 1.226% annual
  - $r_{c/v}$(USD): 0.4416% annual
  - call EUR/put USD premium: 4.947% of nominal amount
- GBP/USD:
  - mid spot: 1.6158
  - mid vol.: 10.858%
  - r_{ref} (GBP): 1.2298% annual
  - $r_{c/v}$(USD): 0.4416% annual
  - call GBP/put USD premium: 4.007% of nominal amount

Applying Eq. 11.4, the basket volatility σ_B is such as

$$\sigma_B^2 = w_{EUR/USD}^2 \sigma_{EUR/USD}^2 + w_{GBP/USD}^2 \sigma_{EUR/USD}^2 + 2 w_{EUR/USD} w_{GBP/USD} \rho \sigma_{EUR/USD} \sigma_{GBP/USD}$$
$$= 0.006809 + \rho \times 0.006747$$

Based upon the correlation of 0.648, observed over a full year preceding this quotation, this gives

$$\sigma_B^2 = 0.006809 + 0.648 \times 0.006747 = 0.011181 \rightarrow \sigma_B = 10.574\%$$

that is, a lower volatility than the volatilities of each currencies, since $\rho < 1$. It corresponds to a theoretical call $BASKET\{0.5\ EUR,\ 0.5\ GBP\}$ / put USD premium of 3.783%, instead of 4.947 and 4.007% respectively for the single currency options.

The impact of correlation contributes to the vega sensitivity (cf. Chapter 10, Section 5.1) of this option. The correlation indeed varies over time: for example, if, instead of using the actual correlation of 0.648 during the full last year, we use the correlation observed during the last 3, 6, and 9 months, the resulting basket volatility would become:

- 3-month past correlation: $0.453 \rightarrow \sigma_B = 9.93\% \rightarrow$ premium $= 3.529\%$
- 6-month past correlation: $0.880 \rightarrow \sigma_B = 11.29\% \rightarrow$ premium $= 4.065\%$
- 9-month past correlation: $0.762 \rightarrow \sigma_B = 10.93\% \rightarrow$ premium $= 3.923\%$.

These results highlight the significant difference in premium due to the selected correlation level (in particular, this difference represents 15% of the premium between the two hypotheses of correlation equal to 0.453 and 0.880). The corresponding market price for such an option will thus critically depend on the basket implied volatility used by the market maker. However, the absence of any suitable correlation process can seriously affect the validity of a basket option price: there exist no grounded correlation curves to play the role of volatility curves (cf. Chapter 12, Section 12.4). For further about correlation measures in the case of a basket product, see, for example, Chapter 13, Section 13.2.3.

11.6 BERMUDAN OPTIONS

Bermudan options are somewhat intermediate between European and American options, since their exercise is possible on some dates or periods of time between the contract and maturity dates. As such, the use of a binomial model presents no particular problem. It suffices to consider possible early exercises on the set of sub-periods corresponding to the Bermudan feature of the option.[11]

11.7 OPTIONS ON NON-FINANCIAL UNDERLYINGS

Non-financial underlyings mainly refer to commodities and weather. Dealing with such non-financial commodities implies:

- first, the general pricing methodology as developed in the previous chapter, based on the possibility of going short in the underlying is not feasible in many cases: you cannot go short temperature, or energy for example;
- second, the process for non-financial commodities is not necessarily Gaussian, and, for the less liquid ones, harder to be extrapolated as a continuous process (cf. Chapter 15).

In practice, the commodities market is foremost a futures market, and commodity options are essentially options on futures. In this case, as long as the first of this remark does not hold (one can go short the future), and provided the Gaussian hypothesis holds, the valuation based on the Black–Scholes formula for forward underlying (Black model, cf. Eq. 10.14 and next) is applicable.

To better cope with the specificity of the commodities, one can use processes involving the convenience yield y (cf. Chapter 7, Section 7.7.3), either as a deterministic term associated to the market rate,

$$dS = (r - y)\,Sdt + SdZ$$

---

[11] For further details, see for example the *Product Overview* of Didier FAIVRE (Nice Sophia Antipolis university) in http://users.polytech.unice.fr/~hugues/Polytech/IMAFA/Didier%Faivre/, that also covers other topics of this chapter.

or, more sophisticated, as a stochastic, mean-reverting variable, in a two-factor process such as

$$dS = (r - y) S dt + \sigma_1 S dZ_1$$
$$dy = [a(b - y) - c] dt + \sigma_2 S dZ_2$$
$$dZ_1 dZ_2 = \rho_{1,2} dt$$

Also, in several cases, the Gaussian hypothesis seems too unrealistic, hence the recourse to processes involving a jump diffusion (Poisson) (cf. Chapter 14, Section 14.1.1).[12]

11.8 SECOND-GENERATION OPTIONS, OR EXOTICS

With respect to regular (called vanilla) options, the family of second-generation options differs by its pay-off (example: digital option), or by adding some constraints limiting the option exercise (example: barrier option). They can be grouped into two categories, according to the role played by the underlying spot price:

- path dependent option: the pay-off is depending on the "path followed" by the underlying spot price, that is, the successive spot prices during the lifetime of the option; examples: average, barrier, ladder, or lookback options;
- non-path dependent option: the pay-off differs from the one of a regular option, but not because of the impact of the successive spot prices; examples: compound, contingent, or digital options.

It is not the purpose of this book to look over each kind of exotics – this family is always subject to launching of novelties – but rather to focus on the adequate choice of a pricing model. In Chapter 10 we presented the various methods for pricing an option, and evidenced the trumps and disadvantages of each of them with respect to the nature of the option to be priced.

Also, some exotics can be decomposed into a set of vanilla and/or other exotics options so that they do not require any special valuation method: for example, the ladder options, that can be synthesized from vanilla calls and puts, and barrier options.

Let us review the option pricing methods with respect to second-generation options in general:

Applications of the Black–Scholes Formula

For some European exotic options, the valuation can be directly obtained from an ad hoc processing of the Black–Scholes formula. Let us take for example the case of a European call digital (or binary) option, of the form "cash or nothing". In the case of exercise, instead of a variable payoff equal to $(S_T - K)$, a digital call with strike K is paying a constant (cash) payoff Q, how far the call ends in the money – see Figure 11.8.

The binary option presents the peculiarity that the seller's risk is limited (to Q), contrary to the non-limited risk of a regular call seller. Needless to say, the gamma of this option makes it hard to manage, given the jump from 0 to Q at K.

---

[12] For further details, see *Further Reading* at the end of the chapter, for example, the chapter about commodity options, by Carol Alexander in Fabozzi, 2007.

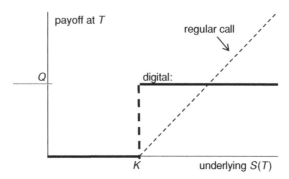

Figure 11.8   Digital call versus regular call

The valuation of this binary call, within the framework of the Black–Scholes hypotheses, and thus in a risk neutral world, translates the underlying rationale that it must be proportional to the probability that the call will be exercised. As stated in Chapter 10, Section 10.2.4, this probability is measured by $N(d_2)$, so that the price BC of a European binary call is limited to

$$BC = e^{-rT} Q \times N(d_2)$$

(cf. Eq. 10.9 for the value of d_2). Logically, the higher the payoff Q, the higher the option price.

Example.   Let us price a call option maturing in $\frac{1}{2}$ year on a non-dividend-paying stock quoted \$8, $K = \$8$, $r = 5\%$ p.a. and $\sigma = 20\%$ p.a. The vanilla European call is valuing \$0.55, with $N(2) = 0.542235$. By comparison, a digital call of same parameters, with $Q = \$8$ for example (equivalent to the current spot price), costs

$$BC = e^{-0.05 \times 0.5} \times 8 \times 0.542235 = \$4.23$$

At maturity, if exercised, this digital brings a constant net profit of $8 - 4.23 = 3.77$ (out of the premium treasury cost); by comparison, the regular call goes to break-even if S_T goes to $8 + 0.55 = 8.55$, and will bring the same profit as the digital if S_T goes to $8.55 + 3.77 = 12.32$: this profit is achieved later, but in case $S_T \geq 12.32$, the regular call will earn more than the digital.

Approximate Analytical Solutions, Derived from the Black–Scholes Formula

In several cases, it turns out it is possible to build approximate analytical solutions, for example for European average, barrier or lookback options. Such analytic models can be found, for example, in Espen Gaarder HAUG's book (cf. *Further Reading*). These approximate analytical solutions present the advantage of being based on grounded mathematical development, what is not necessarily the case with other methods, and are easy to implement.

The downside of such methods is that they need heavy maths to develop them, due to the need to model as realistically as possible – even by using simplifying hypotheses (hence, the approximation of the solution) – the particularities of the exotic form. And of course, these solutions only apply to European options.

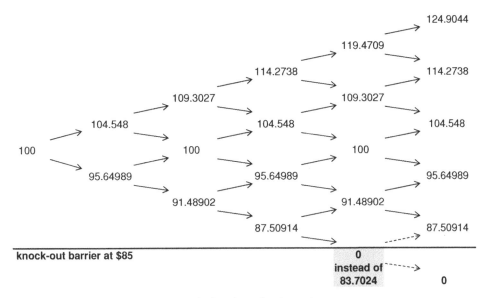

Figure 11.9 Binomial tree in the case of a knock-out barrier option

Binomial Model

In Chapter 10, Section 10.3, the advantage of this method has been emphasized in case the path to be followed by the underlying spot price is subject to events, such as a dividend payment, for example. It is also the case if the event is to be related to the feature of the exotic option, for example the touching of a barrier, in a barrier option.

Coming back to the example of binomial tree in Chapter 7, Section 7.3, that is,

$$S = 100 = K$$
$$T = 100 \text{ days} = 0.274 \text{ year}$$
$$n = 5$$
$$r = 3\% \text{ p.a.}$$
$$\sigma = 19\% \text{ p.a.}$$

regarding the pricing of a vanilla put, and let us now add a knock-out barrier struck at $85. The binomial tree has to be re-computed as in Figure 11.9.

The degree of approximation of this pricing arises from the difference between the actual barrier level and the level implied by the cut of the tree: in the above example, the resulting option price is based on an implied barrier of 83.7024 instead of 85. This problem may be circumvented by the adequate choice of nodes, so that, in the area of the barrier level, there are nodes located as much as possible at the barrier level.

For applications such as a.o., American barrier options, it is preferable to use a *trinomial* tree. A trinomial tree presents three connections from each node, instead of two for the binomial tree, as in Figure 11.10.

Starting from the current price S, and using the notations introduced for the binomial tree in Chapter 10, Section 10.3, these connections correspond to $S_u = S \times u$, S, and $S_d = S \times d$ respectively, with corresponding probabilities p_u, p_m (for the unchanged price level S) and p_d. The values for u, d, p_u, and p_d are different from the ones given in the case of the binomial

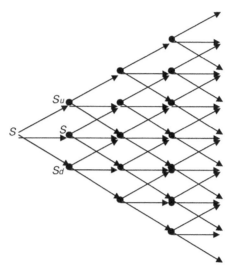

Figure 11.10   Diagram of a trinomial tree

tree, with $p_m = 1 - p_u - p_d$. For more details, see *Further Reading* (for example, Espen Gaarder HAUG). This being settled, the option valuation methodology is the same as with the binomial tree.

The advantage of the trinomial tree is that, for the same number of Δts, by increasing the number of possible intermediate prices one can increase the accuracy of the valuation (cf. also the use of a trinomial tree in the Hull and White model of options on interest rates, Section 11.3.2).

Monte Carlo Simulations

This method is the alternative to the binomial tree when the latter does not fit with specific features of second generation options, in particular:

- if a precise enough simulation of the path-dependence is required: average options, for example;
- if the payoff of the option is too complex, including, as a limit case, optional structures that are not fully replicable: "auto-call" ("auto-trigger") structures, for example.

As an example, let us compute an *average* (or Asian) call price, of the "average spot rate" type,[13] on the same data as used to illustrate the Monte Carlo simulation in Chapter 10, Section 10.4 for a vanilla option. In short, this type of average call option price must obey to the following boundary condition, at maturity T (such options are definitely European ones):

$$C = MAX\,[A\,(T) - K\,;0]$$

---

[13] Different from the average strike option, for which the strike is the average of successive spot rates, and the exercise is determined with respect to the spot rate at maturity.

where $A(T)$ – instead of S_T for a regular option – is the arithmetic average of S between t_0 and T, for example, on a daily basis (other periodicities can be agreed). To compute C, we need a value for $A(T)$, that will be estimated by Monte Carlo simulations.

Given the data used in Chapter 10, Section 10.4 (Monte Carlo example for a vanilla call), that is, a 3-month (90-day) European average call ATMS on L'OREAL stock: $S = K = €64.50$ spot, $\mu = 0.004375$ (annualized), $\sigma = 0.119$ (annualized), 3M-LIBOR = 2.514%, with $n = 9000$ time intervals, so that, for a daily average, we need the price simulations at each 100 time intervals.

- First simulation of $\{S(t)\}$: goes up to $S_T = 69.26$, with an average $A_1(T) = 66.75$

$$\rightarrow C_1 = 2.231$$
$$= \text{PV of } (66.75 - 64.50)@2.514\% \text{ on } 90 \text{ days} = 2.25/(1 + 0.0514 \times 90/365)$$

- Second simulation: to $S_T = 62.86$, with $A_2(T) = 63.98 \rightarrow C_2 = 0$
- Third simulation: to $S_T = 65.30$, with $A_3(T) = 65.05$

$$\rightarrow C_3 = 0.543$$
$$= PV \text{ of } (65.05 - 64.50)@2.514\% \text{ on } 90 \text{ days} = 0.55/(1 + 0.0514 \times 90/365)$$

and so on. With enough simulations, one obtains an average of C_i leading to a price of 0.95.

The comparison of this price with the corresponding price for a vanilla call of same parameters, that is 1.72 (cf. Chapter 10, Section 10.4) shows that an average option is cheaper, at identical parameters, than a regular option: the reason is that the volatility of an average of a series of prices is significantly lower than the volatility of these prices. The size of the option price difference is function of its time value, its maturity, and the frequency (daily, weekly, monthly) of the prices selected for the average.

FURTHER READING

Leif B.G. ANDERSEN, Vladimir V. PITERBARG, *Interest Rate Modeling*, Atlantic Financial Press, 2010. 3 volumes, 492, 376 and 546 p.; or, as a slightly shorter alternative, see BRIGO, MERCURIO below.

Kerry BACK, *A Course in Derivative Securities*, Springer, 2010, 370 p.

Tomas BJORK, *Arbitrage Theory in Continuous Time*, Oxford University Press, 2009, 512 p. In particular for its chapter on currency derivatives, exotic options, interest rates options and models.

Damiano BRIGO, Fabio MERCURIO, *Interest Rate Models – Theory and Practice*, Springer Finance, 2nd, ed., 2006, 1037 p.

Kevin B. CONNOLLY, *Pricing Convertible Bonds*, John Wiley & Sons, Ltd, Chichester, 1998, 268 p.

Frans DE WEERT, *Exotic Options Trading*, John Wiley & Sons, Ltd, Chichester, 2008, 212 p.

David F. DeROSA, *Currency Derivatives – Pricing Theory, Exotic Options, and Hedging Applications*, John Wiley & Sons, Inc., Hoboken, 1998, 387 p.

Frank J. FABOZZI, Anand K. BHATTACHARYA, William S. BERLINER, *Mortgage-Backed Securities: Products, Structuring and Analytical Techniques*, John Wiley & Sons, Inc., Hoboken, 2007, 336 p.

Frank J. FABOZZI, Roland FUSS, Dieter G. KAISER, *The Handbook of Commodity Investing*, John Wiley & Sons, Inc., Hoboken, 2008, 986 p.

See Chapter 24 – *Commodity Options*, by Carol ALEXANDER and Aanand VENKATRAMANAN.

Dariusz GATAREK, Przemyslav BACHERT, Robert MAKSYMIUK, *The Libor Market Model in Practice*, John Wiley & Sons, Ltd, Chichester, 2006, 290 p.

This book also deals with other pricing models for interest rate options.

Helyette GEMAN, *Commodities and Commodity Derivatives – Modelling and Pricing for Agricultural, Metals and Energy*, John Wiley & Sons, Ltd, Chichester, 2005, 416 p.

Helyette GEMAN, *Insurance and Weather Derivatives – From Exotic Options to Exotic Underlyings*, RISK Books, 1999, 300 p.

Espen Gaarder HAUG, *The Complete Guide to Option Pricing Formulas*, Irwin Professional Publishing, 1997, 232 p. Also covers exotic options.

Adel OSSEIRAN, Mohamed BOUZOUBAA, *Exotic Options and Hybrids*, John Wiley & Sons, Ltd, Chichester, 2010, 392 p.

Riccardo REBONATO, *Interest-rate Option Models – Understanding, Analyzing and Using Models for Exotic Interest-Rate Options*, John Wiley & Sons, Ltd, Chichester, 2nd ed., 1998, 546 p.

Amir SADR, *Interest Rate Swaps and Their Derivatives*, John Wiley & Sons, Inc., Hoboken, 2009, 247 p.

Jan de SPIEGELEER, Wim SCHOUTENS, *The Handbook of Convertible Bonds: Pricing, Strategies and Risk Management*, John Wiley & Sons, Ltd, Chichester, 2011, 400 p.

Nassim TALEB, *Dynamic Hedging – Managing Vanilla and Exotic Options*, John Wiley & Sons, Inc., Hoboken, 1997, 528 p.

Peter TANKOV, *Financial Modelling with Jump Processes*, Chapman and Hall, 2003, 552 p.

## 12

Volatility and volatility derivatives

This chapter may be viewed as a continuation of Chapter 10. As seen in Chapter 10, Section 10.1, the volatility, denoted σ, originates from processes such as the general Wiener process used to model an underlying, and appears as a key ingredient for pricing non-conditional derivatives such as options. As such, strictly speaking, options should be only used to take (or to hedge) a position on the volatility. In Chapter 10, Section 10.1, we have made the distinction between the *historical* volatility, that is, the standard deviation of (past) prices changes, and the *implied* volatility used to price an option, as a guess at what level the volatility will happen to be during the lifetime of the option. *Ex post*, we may compare the implied volatility used for option pricing, and the corresponding actual historical volatility on the same period (see below). On an *ex post* basis, the actual historical volatility is understandably also called "realized volatility", but this expression is not used here, to avoid confusion with the so-called "realized volatility" models, as presented in Section 12.3.

Strictly speaking, for a statistician, the usual formula for computing a standard deviation, hence the historical volatility, on a full[1] population of n returns r_t with a mean m, is actually the "standard estimator" of this standard deviation:

$$\sigma = \sqrt{\frac{1}{n}\sum_{t=1}^{n}(r_t - m)^2} \tag{12.1}$$

It is interesting to compare the *ex post* or historical volatility, computed as per Eq. 12.1 or using the variants of Section 12.1.5, with the implied volatility, inferred from observed option prices. As time goes by, the implied volatility usually evolves in the same way as the historical one, but in a smoother way. The following example refers to the S&P 500, showing, from March 2007 to March 2011, on a daily basis:

- the 60-day historical volatility of the index;
- the 3-months implied volatility for calls and puts round ATM (about 50% delta, cf. Chapter 10, Section 10.5.1).

The selected period includes the famous volatility peak observed by the end of 2008 (see Figure 12.1), corresponding to the dramatic index drop, linked to the Lehman Brothers bankruptcy and the banks' financial crisis.

As an alternative, for a given past period of time, the variance, as the square of the volatility, can also be computed on a weighted basis, that is, putting more weight on the more recent observations. A classical weighting scheme is the exponential one, defined via a λ coefficient valuing something between 0 and 1:

$$\sigma_t^2 = \lambda \sigma_{t-1}^2 + (1 - \lambda)(r_{t-1} - m)^2$$

---

[1] The end of Section 12.1.5 will contribute to justify this precision.

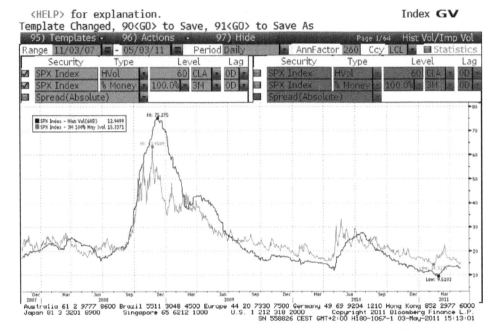

Figure 12.1 Historical and implied volatility of the SP500 (March 2007 to March 2011)
Source: Bloomberg

To recursively repeat the operation on a great enough number n of past data, we obtain

$$\sigma_t^2 = (1 - \lambda) \sum_{i=1}^{n} \lambda^{i-1} (r_{t-i} - m)^2$$

The RiskMetrics Group (MSCI Barra) is using this volatility calculation with a $\lambda = 0.97$ for the forecasting of a 1-month volatility.

12.1 PRACTICAL ISSUES ABOUT THE VOLATILITY

12.1.1 Annualized volatility

Practically, the historical volatility is computed on a discrete basis, namely, on daily, weekly or monthly data, or even at shorter time intervals (5 minutes is a wise minimum). For example, consider the first 50 daily returns of the S&P 500 in 2010, shown in Figure 12.2, that is, a volatility of 0.008151, or 0.8151%.

If a similar calculation was made on wider time intervals, the resulting standard deviation would be larger too. Hence, the usual practice is to annualize the volatility, in σ p.a., similarly as it is done with interest rates. As such,

- volatility computed on a series of yearly data is its straightforward standard deviation;
- for higher frequency data, denoting s the standard deviation and n the number of sub-periods in a year with respect to the data frequency, the formula for volatility is

$$\sigma = s \sqrt{n}$$

TIME	CLOSE	log return
31/12/10	1257.64	
03/01/11	1271.89	0.011267
04/01/11	1270.2	−0.00133
05/01/11	1276.56	0.004995
06/01/11	1273.85	−0.002125
07/01/11	1271.5	−0.001847
10/01/11	1269.75	−0.001377
...	...	...
07/03/11	1310.13	−0.008376
08/03/11	1321.82	0.008883
09/03/11	1320.02	−0.001363
10/03/11	1295.11	−0.019051
11/03/11	1304.28	0.007056
14/03/11	1296.39	−0.006068
15/03/11	1281.87	−0.011264

⌞→ standard deviation = 0.008151

Figure 12.2   Example of calculation of historical volatility

In the case of monthly or weekly data, n is of course 12 or 52. For daily data, market practice uses $n = 250$ days, which corresponds to about the actual number of trading days on exchanges.

Why the square root? In Chapter 8, Section 8.2, we have seen that the variance is proportional to the time, so that its square root, the standard deviation, is proportional to $\sqrt{t}$. Back to the previous example, the equivalent per annum of a volatility of 0.8151% is thus

$$0.8151\% \times \sqrt{250} = 12.89\% \text{ p.a.}$$

It may be useful to recall that, to avoid an excessive standard error on volatility measures, we have to use a sufficient number of data, that is, a minimum of several dozen, practically speaking. Problems arise if, because of the data frequency, such a number of data covers a too long period of time, during which the volatility cannot be reasonably considered as stationary.

Although the market practice works on this basis, a problem arises if the market data are showing autocorrelation. Remember that the covariance and related coefficient of correlation affects a variance (cf. Chapter 4, Section 4.3.3), and thus a volatility (standard deviation) calculation. In particular, if there is some covariance and therefore autocorrelation between a time series of data and the corresponding series of same but *lagged* data, this would affect the volatility calculation accordingly. Andrew Lo[2] has proposed a corrective factor η to be applied to n, which takes into account such autocorrelation factors; this corrective factor has been proposed for the calculation of an annualized Sharpe ratio (cf. Chapter 14, Section 14.1.3), but it is indeed the volatility term that is causing the correction. Adapted to the volatility, this corrective factor $\eta(n)$ is

$$\eta(n) = \frac{1}{n}\sqrt{n + 2\sum_{k=1}^{n-1}(n-k)\rho_k}$$

[2] See Andrew LO, "The statistics of Sharpe Ratios", *Financial Analysts Journal*, vol. 58, no. 4, 2002, pp. 36–45.

	lag 1	lag 2	lag 3	lag 4	lag 5
autocorrel 07/01/08 to 01/12/08:	−0.135393	0.135926	−0.288329	0.162892	−0.009967
autocorrel 08/12/08 to 16/11/09:	0.05327	−0.049379	−0.107229	−0.150429	0.189678
autocorrel 23/11/09 to 01/11/10:	−0.120874	0.088502	−0.07853	0.007597	−0.102191

Figure 12.3   Example of autocorrelations calculation

where

- k is the autocorrelation order, namely, the number of lags considered for autocorrelation; in practice, we hardly work further than with $k = 1, \ldots, 10$, that is, up to 10 first lags;
- ρ_k is the kth-order autocorrelation.

This correction sounds good, but we may question it, if, on the whole range of data of the series, the autocorrelations are non-stationary, which is not uncommon. As an example, consider the S&P 500 weekly close prices during 2008 to 2010, sub-divided into three equal subsets, as seen in Figure 12.3. The first five lags (of 1 week up to 5 weeks earlier) show the autocorrelation values in the figure, which are all but stationary.

(The results in column "lag 1" are obtained by computing the correlation between a data series and the same series, lagged by 1 week; similarly for the "lag 2" column, lagging the data by 2 weeks, etc.).

12.1.2   Volatility curve

With respect to the Black–Scholes formula for option pricing, and related pricing models, the implied volatility to be used is a constant, whatever the option maturity is. Practically speaking, the market is using different implied volatilities for different maturities: in other words, the volatility estimate (by the option market maker) is not necessarily the same for the next 3 months as for the next 3 years, for example. Hence, the use of implied volatility curves (or "volatility structure"), just as yield curves (or term structure). For example, in Figure 12.4 is the implied volatility curve of options (of ATM and near to ATM strikes) on the S&P 500, as of 05/03/2011.

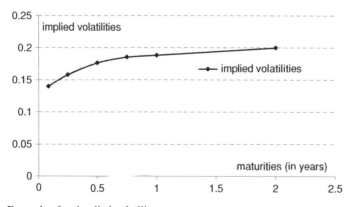

Figure 12.4   Example of an implied volatility curve

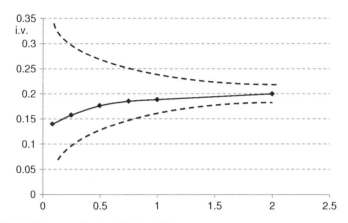

Figure 12.5   Typical shapes of an implied volatility curve

These implied volatility curves are changing over time, just as with yield curves. Contrary to yield curves, for which the curve is said to be "normal" when going upwards (cf. Chapter 2, Section 2.1), a "normal" implied volatility curve is going down with higher maturities. This can be explained by a long-term mean reversion (cf. Section 12.2) effect: the longer the maturity, the lower the volatility due to the mean reversion feature. Furthermore, shorter maturity volatilities are more volatile than longer maturity ones. So we may speak of an "implied volatility cone", involving various observed implied volatility curves for a given underlying, showing that the range of possible implied volatilities is usually broader for shorter maturities, as in Figure 12.5.

Similarly as a yield curve allows computing forward rates (cf. Chapter 1, Section 1.5), volatility curves allow the computing of forward volatilities. These forward volatilities may be used, for example, for pricing forward option products, or volatility swaps (cf. Section 12.5). The non-arbitrage principle of calculation of forward rates is used here too, as in Figure 12.6.

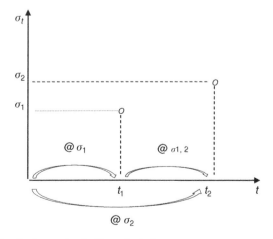

Figure 12.6   Principle of a forward volatility calculation

But on the variances and not directly on (standard deviations =) volatilities, since

$$\sigma^2 \leftrightarrow t \Rightarrow \sigma \leftrightarrow \sqrt{t}$$

as recalled in Section 12.1.1. Moreover, statistics explain that variances are additive.[3] So to compute the forward volatility $\sigma_{1,2}$ from period t_1 to period t_2, we need the (spot) volatilities σ_1 on t_1 and σ_2 on t_2:

$$t_2\sigma_2^2 = t_1\sigma_1^2 + (t_2 - t_1)\sigma_{1,2}^2$$

$$\rightarrow \sigma_{1,2} = \sqrt{\frac{1}{t_2 - t_1}(t_2\sigma_2^2 - t_1\sigma_1^2)}$$

Example. From the data used for the previous volatility curve (S&P 500, ATM options), by using the above formula, we can compute the 3-month forward implied volatility after 6 months: the data are:

- spot 6-month volatility @ 18.56%
- spot 9-month volatility @ 18.86%

giving (with 6 months and 9 months = 0.5 and 0.75 year respectively):

$$6, 9M = \sqrt{\frac{1}{0.25}\left(0.75 \times 0.1886^2 - 0.5 \times 0.1856^2\right)} = 19.45\%$$

12.1.3   The volatility smile

Stochastic models for underlyings are essentially based on the hypothesis of normal distribution of the log returns. This has proven a robust approach, and makes easier the calculations. *A contrario*, developing models based on a more general distribution presents:

- the difficulty of selecting what would be the adequate alternative distribution: this point is developed in Chapter 15, Section 15.1;
- the disadvantage that the kth moments are less and less stationary over time with k increasing (cf. Chapter 4, Section 4.3.7).

However, with respect to options valuation, the Gaussian hypothesis becomes hard to keep if and when the spot price is too far from the strike price, that is, for deep in and out of the money. Actually, the density of probability of large moves appears generally more frequent than implied by the normal distribution, what is called a "fat tails" problem. Due to the poor performance of alternative stochastic processes developed with a non-normal distribution (cf. Chapter 15, Section 15.1), the market practice generally prefers to keep the Gaussian hypothesis but to adjust the implied volatility for strikes out of some range centered around the money. Three situations may occur:

- The actual distribution remains symmetric as for the Gaussian, but presents fatter tails. This corresponds to a kurtosis feature (actually, platykurtic, as it often appears from market observations), as in Figure 12.7.

---

[3] Provided the corresponding random variables are independent.

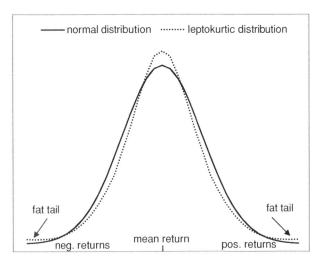

Figure 12.7   Kurtosis feature

- The actual distribution shows no fatter tails, but some dissymmetry (negative returns represent > 50% or < 50% than the positive returns), which is measured by the skewness of the distribution.
- The actual distribution shows both features together.

If we face a fat tails (kurtosis) problem, the rationale for compensating this by modifying the implied volatility value consists of locally increasing the implied volatility, so that the option price is higher, which reflects the higher probability of occurrence of corresponding moves. Of course, there is no quantitative foundation to this volatility increase, it is rather typically the role of the option market maker to quote the volatility he will use for a given strike. A convenient way to represent this step consists of putting on a chart the implied volatility in function of the *moneyness* of the option (cf. Chapter 10, Section 10.2.4), that is, practically speaking, in function of the option delta.[4] The largest returns correspond indeed to a $|\Delta|$ getting closer to 0 or to 100%, such as that in Figure 12.8.

As a consequence, quoting an option may involve the determination of an implied volatility, which not only depends on the nature of the underlying and of the maturity of the option, but also of the spread between the strike price and the underlying spot price at that moment. The shape of the relationship such as on the graph explains why this feature has been called the "volatility smile".

If the actual distribution presents no fat tails, but some asymmetry,

- first, the market may well quote different implied volatility levels for calls and for puts, implying thus a kind of market consensus for a directional trend in the underlying evolution;
- second, the market can quote different implied volatilities for DOTM calls and DITM puts on the one hand, that is corresponding to lower underlying spot prices, than for DITM calls and DOTM puts on the other hand, corresponding to higher underlying spot prices. Here, the graph would show something such as Figure 12.9, which explains why it is now called a "volatility smirk", or "sneer" (although, "grimace" would be more appropriate).

---

[4] In absolute value of the delta, this allows for a common representation for both calls and puts.

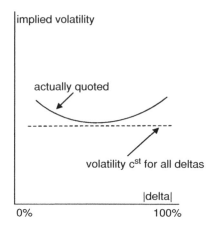

Figure 12.8   Implied volatility in function of the delta of the option

Finally, in practice, both features may well coincide, leading to patterns such as in Figure 12.10, showing the implied volatilities of calls on the S&P 500 maturing in 1 week, 1 month + 1 week, 2 months + 1 week and 3 months + 1 week (data for 04/22/11, source: Bloomberg).

We could wonder about the problem – for an options market maker – of determining an adequate implied volatility level, if such phenomena have to be taken into account. But let us not forget that, after all, to anticipate a future volatility level is in any case some delicate job: with or without smiles and the like, it will always involve some arbitrary dimension, almost impossible to reasonably model.

12.1.4   Implied volatility surface

In the previous section, we have considered different implied volatilities in function of the option delta. But looking to analytical option pricing formula such as Black–Scholes (cf. Chapter 10, Eqs. 10.7–10.9), we notice that the volatility is always associated with the (remaining) time to maturity, under the form of $\sigma \sqrt{T}$. This is the main ingredient of the option *time value*

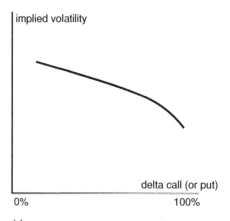

Figure 12.9   A volatility smirk, or sneer

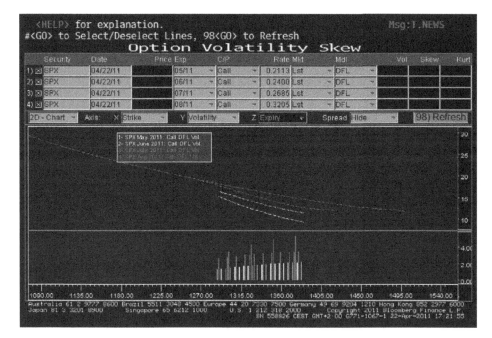

Figure 12.10   Implied volatilities of calls on the S&P 500

(cf. Chapter 10, Section 10.1). In case of a smile or a smirk, the time value may differ, through σ, in function of the option delta, but also in function of the remaining time to maturity T. Hence, the use of a three-dimensional representation of the implied volatility, in function of both the delta and the remaining time to maturity, that can present many different shapes; Figure 12.11 (source: Bloomberg) shows the volatility surface for options on the S&P 500 (data as of 04/22/11).

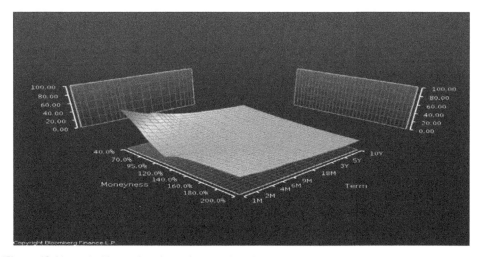

Figure 12.11   Volatility surface for options on the S&P 500

There exist numerous studies aiming to model such volatility surfaces, within the more general framework of the volatility modeling that is addressed in Section 12.2 next.

12.1.5   Intraday volatility

As said in Section 12.1.1, the volatility can be computed *ex post* from data of various frequencies (practically speaking, from 5 minutes to a month and more). In the case of high frequency measures, we can be interested in the *ex post* valuation of the volatility in the course of a trading session, or intraday volatility. At first sight, there is no reason to treat this intraday volatility in a different way to longer periods of time. However, a trading session – being an exchange trading day or a trading session in the interbank market – is to some extent affected by some local phenomena, that do not appear when using, for example, a series of close prices on a daily, weekly, and so on, basis, namely a kind of boundaries condition: there is an "open" price at the start of the session, versus the "close" price ending the session; also, market practitioners are traditionally interested by the "high" versus "low" prices of the session, that is, the highest and the lowest prices quoted during the session. This has led to several measures of an intraday volatility estimator, unfortunately without any consensus for a standard measure.

In short, these formulae propose a mixture of both the "open to close" and the "high to low" measures, in various proportions. The pioneer in this way was Parkinson, proposing a volatility measure only based on "high" and "low" prices, and related returns. For a series of $n + 1$ daily prices S_t (n returns r_t), S_{Ht} and S_{Lt} being the "high", respectively the "low" of day t, and computing "high/low returns" r_{HLt} as

$$r_{HLt} = \ln\frac{S_{Ht}}{S_{Lt}}$$

his formula is

$$\sigma_{Parkinson} = \sqrt{\frac{1}{n} \times \frac{1}{4\ln 2} \sum_{t=1}^{n} r_{HLt}^2}$$

where $1/4\ln 2 \cong 0.361$[5].

Thereafter, Garman and Klass proposed the following combination of "high", "low", "open", and "close", S_{Ot} and S_{Ct} being the "open", respectively the "close", of day t; such as

$$r_{HOt} = \ln\frac{S_{Ht}}{S_{Ot}}, \quad r_{LOt} = \ln\frac{S_{Lt}}{S_{Ot}}, \quad r_{COt} = \ln\frac{S_{Ct}}{S_{Ot}}$$

The Garman–Klass volatility is

$$\sigma_{G\&K} = \sqrt{\frac{1}{n}\sum \left[0.511(r_{HOt} - r_{LOt})^2 - 0.019\,(r_{COt}(r_{HOt} + r_{LOt}) - 2r_{HOt}r_{LOt}) - 0.383 r_{COt}^2 \right]}$$

These formulae are based on a geometric Wiener process in prices, but they do not take into account the drift of the process. Rogers and Satchell proposed the following formula, that turns out to be independent of the drift:[6]

$$\sigma_{RS} = \sqrt{\frac{1}{n}\sum [r_{HOt}\,(r_{HOt} - r_{COt}) + r_{LOt}(r_{LOt} - r_{COt})]}$$

---

[5] For an annualized value, also in the following formulae, $1/n$ has to be replaced by $250/n$.
[6] For more details about these processes, see for example D. YANG, Q. ZHANG, "Drift-independent volatility estimation based on high, low, open, and close prices", *Journal of Business*, 2000, vol. 73, no. 3, pp. 477–491.

Finally, Yang and Zhang allowed for a jump process between closes in $t - 1$ and opens in t, actually common in the real market life, based on

$$r_{HLt} = \ln\frac{S_{Ht}}{S_{Lt}}, \quad r_{OCt} = \ln\frac{S_{Ot}}{S_{Ct-1}}, \quad r_{COt} = \ln\frac{S_{Ct}}{S_{Ot}}$$

such as

$$\sigma_{Y\&Z} = \sqrt{\frac{1}{n}\sum(r_{OCt}^2 + 0.5r_{HLt}^2 - (2\ln2 - 1)r_{COt}^2)}$$

As an example of these different historical volatility calculations, let us consider the case of the S&P 500 returns, from 01/01 up to 03/31/11 (64 returns, computed from open, high, low and close daily prices). In this example, the annualized intraday volatilities (in % p.a.) obtained are very near to each other:

usual volatility:	Parkinson:	Garman–Klass:	Rogers–Satchell:	Yang–Zhang:
12.879%	10.640%	10.012%	10.208%	10.577%

It is worth noting that several researchers consider that using high frequency, intraday data means also taking into account a volatility calculation on longer periods of time (several months), considering that "high" and "low" prices – as information that is not captured by traditional series of "close" prices – are also evidencing a volatility, or *dispersion* measure. We will come back to this in Section 12.3.

12.2 MODELING THE VOLATILITY

At first, it looks strange to envisage modeling a volatility, since it is not a price or a rate of a financial instrument as such. However, even if usual models, like the Wiener process, consider the volatility of the instrument as a constant, in practice we are aware that volatility is changing over time, so why not try to model such behavior over time?

In support of this, financial markets are today widely trading the (implied) option volatilities, mainly on the S&P 500, called the "VIX", or the VXN (on the Nasdaq 100 index) and the VDAX (on the DAX index), through either futures, or options on these futures contracts. Looking at the VIX spot graph in Figure 12.12, it is understandable that such an underlying is worthy of a model just as if it was a traditional underlying.

Modeling a volatility, however, presents a pitfall; that is, advanced research tends to warn that, unlike usual stochastic models, a volatility model could actually not be built as a *Markovian* diffusion model, for the very general reason that the underlying (i.e., the volatility) does not consist of a variable as a return, but rather a *function* of such variable (i.e., of the corresponding returns). As a matter of fact, unlike market instruments prices, the volatility is not directly measurable.

Bypassing this pitfall, a volatility model will actually be associated to the corresponding model of the returns, and both processes will have to be somewhat correlated.

Not surprisingly, modeling the volatility will involve a stochastic component, as is the case in modeling returns. Furthermore, volatility presents a similar feature as an interest rate, namely a mean reversion feature: periods of high volatilities follow periods of low volatilities, both around some mean volatility level. Of course, both the length of the cycles and their amplitude

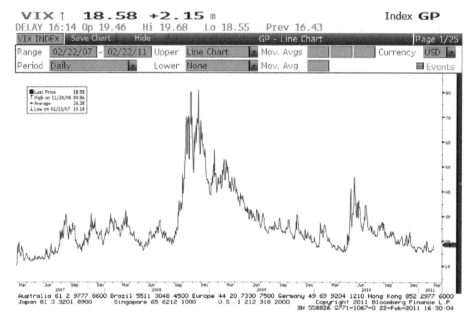

Figure 12.12   VIX graph
Source: Bloomberg

is neither regular, nor constant over time. As an example, in Figure 12.13 are the monthly historical p.a. volatilities of the S&P 500, from the beginning of 2000 to mid-2008 (further values have been deliberately excluded, because of the exceptional impact of the banks crisis on the market, from August 2008 to at least May 2009).

Volatility models may thus be advantageously designed as mean reversion processes, as described in Chapter 11, Section 11.3 (for interest rate processes). Considering the volatility σ_t of an asset of price S modeled by a geometric, general Wiener process as per Eq. 8.11b of

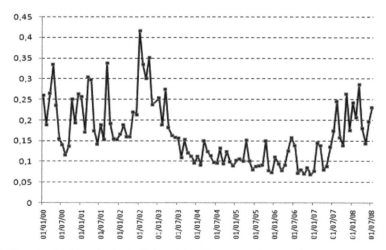

Figure 12.13   Monthly historical volatilities of the S&P 500 – 2000 to mid-2008

Chapter 8, but where the constant volatility σ is replaced by the variable σ_t, a very simplistic volatility model consists of associating the process of the underlying, involving a stochastic component dZ_1,

$$dS = \mu S dt + \sigma_t S dZ_1 \tag{12.2}$$

to a mean reverting process for its volatility, involving a stochastic component dZ_2:

$$d\sigma_t = a(b - \sigma_t) dt + \alpha \sigma_t dZ_2$$

where a and b are the mean reversion (constant) parameters of the deterministic component (cf. Eq. 11.1 and related comments in Chapter 11, Section 11.3.1), b representing the long run mean of σ_t, and α the (constant) parameter of the stochastic component, that can be viewed as the "volatility of the volatility". In such a basic model, dZ_1 and dZ_2 are linked through some correlation coefficient $\rho_{1,2}$, here considered as a constant:

$$dZ_1 dZ_2 = \rho_{1,2} dt \tag{12.3}$$

This basic model led to the most common volatility model, due to Heston, describing the stochastic component as of the corresponding variance, so that, in terms of volatility, it appears as a $\sqrt{\sigma}$ term:

$$d\sigma_t = a(b - \sigma_t) dt + \alpha \sqrt{\sigma_t} dZ_2$$

so that, like for the Cox, Ingersoll and Ross interest rate process (cf. Chapter 11, Section 11.3.1 and Eq. 11.1bis), it prevents negative values for the volatility.

But, as seen in Section 12.1.2, volatilities – again, like interest rates – are not constant for all maturities, and it is better to consider volatility curves $\sigma(T)$, where Ts are maturities. Hence, the need for modeling a σ_t variable within the framework of this volatility curve (similar to what has been done with interest rates processes, cf. Chapter 11, Section 11.3.2). That is the approach of the SABR model (SABR is for *Stochastic Alpha, Beta, Rho*, where alpha, beta and rho refer to the parameters of the model). Instead of starting from the process of the underlying spot as in Eq. 12.2, we start from a series of F_t forward underlying prices or rates, and the SABR model consists of the following system

$$dF_t = \sigma_t F_t^\beta dZ_1$$
$$d\sigma_t = \alpha \sigma_t dZ_2$$
$$dZ_1 dZ_2 = \rho_{1,2} dt$$

For a given instrument, the parameters α, β and ρ need to be calibrated on the corresponding volatility curve, that is, they must fit the market data, including observed options implied volatilities. In particular the SABR model allows for taking into account observed volatility smiles.[7]

As an alternative to the Heston and SABR models, let us also mention the one[8] consisting – instead of starting from Eq. 12.3 – in considering the following relationship:

$$dZ_1 = \rho_{1,2} dZ_2 + (1 - \rho_{1,2}^2)^{1/2} dZ_3$$

---

[7] For further details about this model, see P.S. HAGAN, D. KUMAR, A.S. LESNIEWSKI, D.E. WOODWARD, "Managing smile risk", *Wilmott Magazine*, July 2002, pp. 84–108.

[8] See A. LEWIS, *The mixing approach to stochastic volatility and jump models*, Wilmott.com, March 2002. Let us also mention the dynamic model developed by A. SEPP, which involves the VIX spot, the underlying S&P 500, and the VIX futures and options: A. SEPP, "VIX option pricing in a jump-diffusion model", *RISK*, April 2008, pp. 84–89.

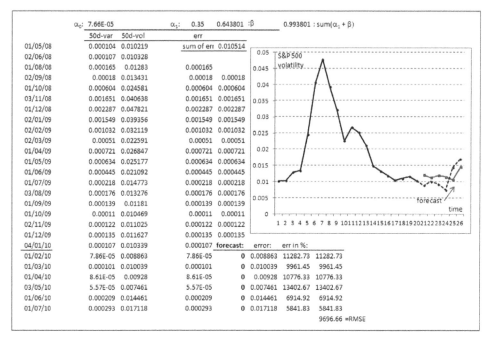

Figure 12.14   Forecasting a volatility by use of a (1,1)-type of GARCH process

that creates a third stochastic process Z_3 that is independent (uncorrelated) with Z_1. Provided some hypothesis can be reasonably made about $\rho_{1,2}$, presumably as a function of σ_t, the model allows for a Monte Carlo simulation.

Furthermore, within the broad range of volatility models, some are based on non-Gaussian models, that will be covered in Chapter 15.

Finally, another attractive and very popular way of modeling the volatility consists of using the ARCH model and its extensions (GARCH, etc.), as developed in Chapter 9, Sections 9.5–9.7. As a rather simplistic example[9] let us, for example, forecast the volatility of the S&P 500 by using a GARCH (1,1) process, by making p = q = 1 in Eq. 9.6 of Chapter 9, recalling that h_t is σ_t^2:

$$\sigma_t = \sqrt{h_t} = \sqrt{\alpha_0 + \alpha_1 \varepsilon_{t-1}^2 + \beta_1 h_{t-1}}$$

α_0, α_1 and β_1 have been (approximately) determined from observed monthly volatilities, each of them computed on the previous 50 days, from 08/01/08 to 01/04/10, and the forecasts are computed on a monthly basis from 02/01 to 07/01/10. Note in Figure 12.14 that the data involve the huge volatility peak between 08/11 and 09/01.

The (1,1)-type of GARCH is not necessarily the best choice, given the series of past data used in this example: an ARMA (1,1) computed on the same data performs better in this case, but both give, in this particular example, a better forecast than the VIX; the graph has been zoomed on the last 10 values, together with the ARMA and VIX forecasts.

---

[9] A detailed example of such a GARCH model to volatilities exceeds the framework of this book, both in size and in calculations volume: see, for example, Amit GOYAL, *Predictability of stock return volatility from GARCH models*, Anderson Graduate School of Management, UCLA, May 2000 (working paper).

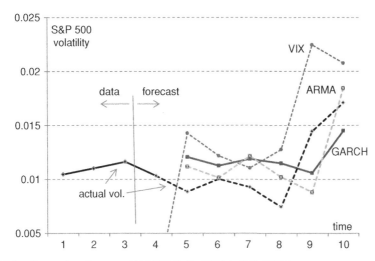

Figure 12.15 Comparison between GARCH (1,1), ARMA (1,1) VIX forecasts

and the relative error of these three models is:

	rel. Error
GARCH:	28.72%
ARMA :	23.69%
VIX:	41.60%

12.3 REALIZED VOLATILITY MODELS

As seen at the end of Section 12.1, the intraday market behavior conveys some useful information about the actual volatility of a price or rate. "Realized volatility" is the name used to refer to models of daily volatility that incorporate the sample variance of intraday returns, computed on very short time sub-intervals. In practice, even for very liquid instruments, if we want to keep constant sub-intervals of time during a trading session, it becomes dangerous to go below 5-minute time intervals, to avoid facing empty or nearly empty sub-intervals (a way to escape this problem is by considering non-constant time intervals).

For a time sub-interval of width h, a realized volatility can be modeled by starting from the following relationship, assuming a continuous sample path over h:

$$r(t+h, h) = \ln\frac{S_{t+h}}{S_t} = \int_0^h \mu_{t+s}ds + \int_0^h \sigma_{t+s}dZ(s)$$

Clearly, going further would exceed the framework of this book.[10] Entering into such time sub-intervals is relevant to the broader field of *market microstructure*, which studies how successive market prices (called *tick data*) are actually affected by the successive trading

---

[10] For further reading, see, for example, T.G. ANDERSEN, T. BOLLERSLEV, F.X. DIEBOLD, P. LABYS, "Modeling and forecasting realized volatility", *Econometrica*, 71 (2003), pp. 529–626.

orders. Market microstructure represents one of the most ambitious and sophisticated research areas in the field of modeling of the financial markets.

12.4   MODELING THE CORRELATION

It makes sense to also deal in this chapter with correlation modeling. Indeed, correlation is linked to the volatilities σ_1 & σ_2 of two different time series, 1 and 2, through the basic relationship in statistics (for data series 1 & 2)

$$\rho_{1,2} = \frac{\sigma_{1,2}}{\sigma_1 \sigma_2}$$

involving the covariance $\sigma_{1,2}$ as well.

Like volatility, correlation is not directly observable. But market practice shows that it is anything but constant over time, hence the wish for modeling it. Unfortunately, up to now (2011), there exists no (not yet a) satisfactory correlation model or process, despite extensive research. This has serious consequences on the validity of pricing of a lot of financial products, such as basket (or multi-asset) options, basket CDS and related securitization tranches, quanto options, or on the validity of the VaR calculation for a portfolio of various assets, more or less correlated. The absence of such a satisfying correlation model also raises the problem of risk management in general, in the most common case, that is, where several assets are concerned. The main problem is that, by comparison to non-stationary volatilities over time, correlations can be much more unstable, that is, time-dependent.

To illustrate this, let us take as a first example two almost not correlated instruments, namely the EUR/USD spot and the S&P 500 spot daily returns, from 01/01/2000 to 12/14/2009, and compare them with a second example of well-correlated instruments, the S&P 500 and the NASDAQ 100 spot daily returns, over the same period. Globally, calculation gives (values are not annualized here):

	EUR/USD	S&P 500	NASDAQ
volatility:	0.0068 ↘	↙ 0.0140 ↘	↙ 0.0222
correlation:	0.0547	0.8241	
covariance:	5.2070×10^{-6}	0.00026	

If we compute volatilities, correlations and covariances on successive sub-periods of 50 days (that is, somewhat more than 2-month periods), Figure 12.16 referring to uncorrelated EUR/USD and S&P 500 data shows that correlations (right scale) are significantly more unstable over time than volatilities (left scale).

This is not the case with the covariance (not shown on the graph). By contrast, referring to well-correlated S&P 500 and NASDAQ 100 data, correlations are remarkably stable over time as is shown in Figure 12.17.

The standard deviation of these 50-day series of volatilities, correlations and covariances shows a much bigger dispersion of the correlation than of the related volatilities in the case of

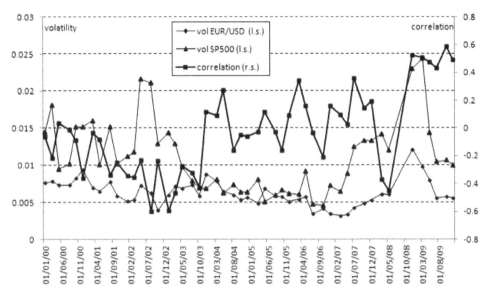

Figure 12.16   Correlation between EUR/USD and S&P 500 data (2000 to 2009)

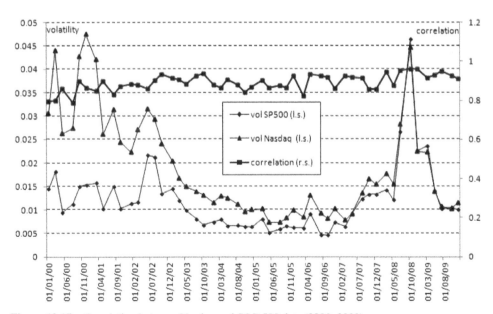

Figure 12.17   Correlation between Nasdaq and S&P 500 data (2000–2009)

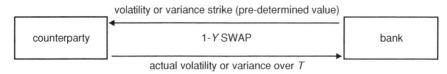

Figure 12.18 Diagram of a volatility or variance swap

the uncorrelated EUR/USD versus S&P 500, while it is of the same order of magnitude in the case of the well-correlated S&P 500 versus NASDAQ 100.

	EUR/USD		S&P 500	NASDAQ
std dev of volatilities:	0.0017		0.0049	0.0111
std dev of correlations:		0.3035		0.0418	
std dev of covariances:		3.5908×10^{-5}		0.0003	

Needless to say, the problem of a correlation model, or process, becomes even harder with respect to more than two assets, via correlation matrixes. Currently, the main trails followed by researchers consist of looking for multivariate GARCH models[11] or for a multivariate stochastic volatility model, generalizing the Heston model (cf. Section 12.2) in a matrix process of n Wiener processes, leading to a (complex) stochastic correlation model that still allows for analytic tractability.[12]

12.5   VOLATILITY AND VARIANCE SWAPS

Volatility and variance swaps belong to the family of performance swaps, presented in Chapter 6, Section 6.7.6, but are developed here, given the particular nature of the swapped commodity. Recall that performance swaps consist of a single exchange, with a maturity varying from some months to several years. In the case of a volatility or variance as the swapped commodity, the operation can be represented as in Figure 12.18.

At the maturity of a volatility swap on a given underlying, a stock index for example, the counterparty pays or receives the difference between a volatility strike and the historical volatility (= standard deviation), in percentage points, actually showed by the underlying during the lifetime of the swap, times the notional amount. In the case of a variance swap, the strike and the payout refer to the square of the volatility. Market makers prefer trading variance swaps than volatility swaps because variances are additive (cf. Section 12.1.2), which makes their hedging easier.[13] The swap contract must specify the way variances or volatilities are traded, for example – in the case of a stock index – on daily close prices of the index.

---

[11] For further reading, see for example M. CAREY, R.M. STULZ (eds), *The Risks of Financial Institutions*, more specifically, its Chapter 11, by T.G. ANDERSEN, T. BOLLERSLEV, P. CHRISTOFFERSEN, F.X. DIEBOLD, *Practical Volatility and Correlation Modeling for Financial Risk Management*, University of Chicago Press, 2007, 520 p.

[12] To go further, see for example J. DA FONSECA, M. GRASSELLI, C. TEBALDI, "A multifactor volatility Heston model", *Journal of Quantitative Finance*, 2008, vol. 8, no. 6, pp. 591–604.

[13] For further information about trading and replication of volatility and variance swaps, see for example S. BOSSU, Introduction to variance swaps, *Wilmott magazine*, March 2006, 6 p.

Let us consider the case of a variance swap and denote

- N the notional amount of the swap, called "vega notional" or "vega equivalent" ("vega" is for "volatility"), that would apply to the *volatility* change between t_0 and T;
- V_K the variance strike; it corresponds to the square of a volatility strike σ_K;
- V_{HT} the (*ex post*) historical variance, computed at the swap maturity date T, equivalent to the square of the historical volatility σ_{HT}.

The market practice is to define the "variance notional" also called "multiplier" N_V as

$$N_V = \frac{N}{2_K}$$

so that, at maturity, if σ_{HT} is one percentage point above σ_K, the payoff of the swap is approximately equal to N.

At maturity, the swap counterparty will pay or receive

$$N_V \times \left(\sigma_K^2 - \sigma_{HT}^2\right) \times 100, \quad (\sigma s \ are \ in \ volatility \ percentage \ points)$$

depending on the swap agreement (for the counterparty, to pay or to receive the strike) and the sign of the parenthesis in the formula.

Example. (Data as of end of November 2006) Let us consider a variance swap on the S&P 500, $T = 10$ year. The counterparty enters into this swap by paying the strike. The strike is of 424.36, corresponding to a volatility of 20.6%. For $N = \$1\,000\,000$ we have

$$N_V = 1\,000\,000/2 \times 0.206 = 2\,427\,184.$$

The payoff at T will be

$$2\,427\,184 \times \left(\sigma_K^2 - \sigma_{HT}^2\right) \times 100$$

Suppose at maturity the S&P 500 volatility is 1% above the strike, that is, 21.6%. The payoff would be of

$$2\,427\,184 \times \left(0.216^2 - 0.206^2\right) \times 100 = 1\,024\,272$$

that is, about N.

Variance swaps may also be used to trade the "dispersion", namely the difference between the historical variance of a stock index, and the weighted average of variances of each of its components – for example, by selling the index variance in a variance swap and buying the weighted components variance, through a set of variance swaps, restricted to the major components of the index. In such a case, the trader is actually "selling correlation": indeed, to be profitable, the operation must take advantage of a higher index variance than the weighted components variances, meaning less actual correlation between the components than implied in the index variance.

The operation must be set up on the respective variance notionals N_Vs of the constituents, so that, given the choice of two variance strikes with a net difference ΔK, its payoff will be

$$\sum_{i=1}^{n} w_i N_{Vi} \sigma_i^2 - N_{VI} \sigma_I^2 - \Delta K$$

the I subscript being for the index, other notations being straightforward.[14]

FURTHER READING

Riccardo REBONATO, *Volatility and Correlation: The Perfect Hedger and the Fox*, John Wiley & Sons, Ltd, Chichester, 2nd ed., 2004, 864 p.

Riccardo REBONATO, *Volatility and Correlation, In the Pricing of Equity, FX and Interest-Rate Options*, John Wiley & Sons, Ltd, Chichester, 1999, 360 p.

Nassim TALEB, *Dynamic Hedging: Managing Vanilla and Exotic Options*, John Wiley & Sons, Inc., Hoboken, 1997, 506 p.

Stephen J. TAYLOR, *Asset Price Dynamics, Volatility and Prediction*, Princeton University Press, 2007, 544 p.

---

[14] For more details about variance, dispersion and correlation swaps calculations, see for example Antoine JAQUIER, Saad SLAOUI, *Variance dispersion and correlation swaps*, Birkbeck University of London, Working Papers in Economics and Finance, July 2007, 25 p., and also, www.ivolatility.com/doc/VarianceSwaps.pdf and http://math.uchicago.edu/~sbossu/VarSwaps.pdf.

13

Credit derivatives

13.1 INTRODUCTION TO CREDIT DERIVATIVES

A credit derivative is a derivative product with *credit risk* as underlying. A credit risk is a risk about a *payment default*, partial or total, relative to any obligation of payments. Credit risk is also called *counterparty risk* (the counterparty to be understood as the debtor, or borrower), or *default risk*.

The major problem with credit derivatives is that, contrary to any other derivative, the underlying credit risk cannot be straight expressed as a number, nor straight measured on a spot market underlying. Hence the basic difficulty in pricing the derivative on an *a priori* "non-quantitative" underlying.

13.1.1 How to quantify a credit risk?

A non-quantitative measure as credit risk, could be *indirectly* quantified via:

- the *rating* of the debtor counterparty: at first sight, the rating attributed by rating agencies should reflect the soundness of the borrower, the risk that this debtor would default. In many cases, for a given borrower, such rating is refined for short or longer term debt maturities, even on each of specific debt issued by him.
- Unfortunately, such rating is not updated on a continuous basis, and even updates would be frequent enough, surveys indicate that the correlation is poor between the rating level and the percentage of observed defaults over time. Moreover, as usual (cf. previous chapters), such correlation is non-stationary over time;
- the interest rate paid by the borrower, practically speaking, the interest rate spread over a risk-free rate:

$$\text{interest rate} = \text{risk-free rate} + \text{risk premium paid by a borrower}$$
$$\text{in\% p.a.} \qquad \text{in\% p.a.} \quad \Rightarrow \qquad \text{in\% p.a.}$$

Here, too, unfortunately, observed risk premia are poorly correlated with the risk of defaulting: market prices of debts, and corresponding yields, are too much affected by debts market features (liquidity, market overreactions, etc.); moreover, inconsistencies may happen in terms of risk premia of different debts issued by a given borrower, due, among others, to the debt specifications (seniority, etc.).

Moreover, statistics about default occurrences and related quantitative measures (rating, spread, or any other) are hard to establish since the observed phenomenon, namely a default payment, is a *rare event*. A parallel on this can be found in statistics about natural catastrophes.

13.1.2 The two components of a default risk

As this was not enough, the situation is even worsening by the fact that, contrary to any "regular" underlying, to quantify a credit or default risk, we need two measures instead of one:

- What is, in %, the probability of occurrence of a default payment?
- And, in case of such a default, what is, in %, the value of the corresponding debt afterwards?

Both for a given maturity date?

13.1.3   Behind the underlying credit risk

A payment default, or a prospect of possible payment default, is affecting market bonds and stock price (if any[1]) of the debtor. This also applies to bank loans, if they are priced on a market. So that behind the underlying credit risk, one must look after such a market instrument. For practical reasons, in many cases, credit derivatives focus on bonds repayment risk. Further in this chapter, unless otherwise stated, the instrument behind the underlying of credit risk will be a *bond*.

Let us look after the impact of credit risk on a bond price, in the most traditional approach of discrete time, and of a single yield to maturity. For a risk-free (non-defaultable) government bond, the bond price B is (cf. Eq. 3.3):

$$B = \sum \frac{a_t}{(1 + y)^t}$$

where

- a_t are the yearly (in the case of this formula) cash-flows, made of coupons and principal repayment(s);
- y is the yield to maturity, used as the discounting rate.

For a "risky" bond, this relationship becomes (cf. Eq. 3.4):

$$B = \sum \frac{(a_t + spread)}{(1 + y + risk\ premium)^t}$$

where the spread above a_t represents a source of excess return, paid by the bond issuer to compensate for the existence of some default risk. However, the market bond price can be such as if the discounting of the cash flows were computed with a risk premium above the risk-free y.

For example, in continuous time, if a 1-year, 3% risk-free bond values

$$e^{-0.03 \times 1} = 0.9704$$

of the par, by comparison, a 1-year risky bond paying 3.5% values

$$e^{-0.035 \times 1} = 0.9656$$

that is, by comparison with the risk-free bond, at a discount of 0.496%, since

$$0.9656 = 0.9704 \times e^{-x} x = -\ln\left(\frac{0.9656}{0.9704}\right) = 0.00496$$

meaning that, by pricing this risky bond @ 0.9656, the market implies that it expects to lose 0.496% of its value because some default during the year.

---

[1] Obviously, there is no related stock price when dealing with sovereign default.

Two situations are to be considered:

1. Further to the initial bond issuance, the bond issuer is facing a worsening of his financial situation, earlier or later lowering his credit rating: at issuance – say, at par – the bond offered a coupon not significantly far from the corresponding risk-free rate. In case the market considers some possible default occurrence, the market bond price will be lowered accordingly:

$$B = \sum \frac{a_t}{(1 + y + risk\ premium)^t}$$

Since the coupon remains unchanged, there is no compensation for increasing default risk, what justifies such a lower bond price.

Example. The case of a Greece government bond is shown in Figure 13.1.

2. A low rating issuer can issue a bond at par, provided he is paying a higher coupon (hence the name of "high yield bond"), in compensation for the risk supported by the bond investor:

$$B = \sum (a_t + spread)/(1 + y + risk\ premium)^t$$

and, as long as the risk remains more or less stable, the bond price will be in line with risk-less bond prices. But if later on the credit risk presented by the issuer is changing (worsening or improving), the market bond price with move according to changes in the market view for the risk premium, since the coupon remains fixed.

NB: there exist bond issues offering a "fixed" coupon, but indexed (up or down) on the rating of the issuer, to maintain the bond market price more stable.

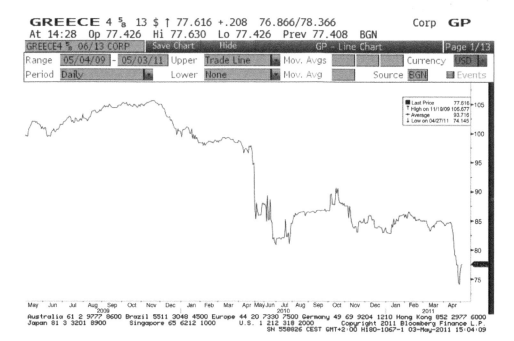

Figure 13.1   Greece government bond 2009–2011

The default probability on the further cash flows payments is also affecting the duration (cf. Chapter 3, Section 3.2.2) of risky bonds. For example, on 09/20/10, the Hellenic Republic bond $4\frac{5}{8}\%$ maturing in 13/06 was quoting 84.62 (mid), with a yield of 10.855%. Ignoring the default risk, this bond would present a duration of 2.86 years. At that time, the market quotation was implying a default probability of 45% on further cash flows payments, reducing the duration to 2.74 years.

13.1.4   Main features of a credit derivative

- Instead of taking a position (buy or sell) on credit risk, the market practice is considering to take a position by buying or selling "protection" (against default risk): Buying a protection implies paying a derivative premium, to be protected against default. Conversely, selling a protection is assuming a default risk, against receiving the derivative premium. Hedging operations mean buying protection. But a speculative trader may buy or sell protection, depending on his expectation on the future move of the derivative premium, up or down.
- As with other derivatives, trading credit derivatives does not need for funding the underlying operation: the trading refers to a notional amount (of underlying risky bond). The market value of this notional amount (that is, multiplied by its market price) is called exposure at default (ED) or credit exposure.
- As we said earlier, credit risk is measured by a couple of data,
  - the probability that a default occurs, or default rate, q, expressed in % p.a.;
  - the value of a debt after a default, v, also called recovery rate, in % of the credit exposure. So that the "loss caused by a default", or "loss given default", is $(1 - v)$.
- The credit derivatives market is OTC only. Contracts are supported by the ISDA documentation for swaps, plus a complementary documentation, specific to credit derivatives. This additional documentation is centered on:
  - specification of the actual underlying instrument, namely the bond or credit issuer (called "reference entity") and the specific bond or credit to be monitored for default risk (called "reference obligation");
  - detailed specification of what is actually a default occurrence, defined as "(credit) events": some are evident, like "bankruptcy", or "failure to pay", but others present some legal complexities, involving existence of cross default or *pari passu* clauses, without to speak about complex situations of debt restructuration or repudiation/moratorium, and many other related technical points. Despite ISDA's care, the core of the credit risk concept remains somewhat imprecise, what may affect corresponding credit valuation.
- A weak point for the credit derivative market is the extreme diversity of possible underlying bonds or bank loans, that is, a much wider range of underlyings than the corresponding number of traded stocks. As a consequence, the liquidity of most of credit derivatives, for a specific underlying (reference obligation) is insufficient. This will show crucial in credit derivative pricing.
- The credit derivative market operations extensively involve a collateral deposit, to cover the (counterparty) risk of the protection seller. This collateral secures that, in case of default, the protection seller can assume his role vis-à-vis the protection buyer (see product example).

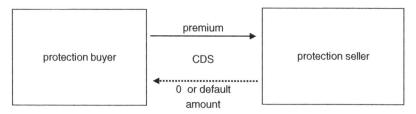

Figure 13.2   Diagram of a credit default swap

13.1.5   Example of a credit derivative

Before looking at credit derivative valuation properly said, let us present the most traded product, the *credit default swap* (CDS).

The CDS is an OTC contract between two parties (at least one is a bank, active in credit derivatives), with a contractual maturity and notional amount, on a specific underlying risky bond (reference obligation):

• The "protection buyer" can be viewed as a hedger: he holds the bond and pays for being compensated in case of default on this bond; said payment is called "premium";
• The "protection seller" receives a premium in exchange of supporting the default risk. If this occurs, under the "vanilla" form of the CDS, he pays 100% of the bond value, but receives the bond from the protection buyer. If no default occurs until the CDS maturity, nothing is paid by the seller, as illustrated in Figure 13.2.

The rationale for "indemnifying" 100% of the bond and its transfer to the indemnifying party is that at the time of a defaulted bond, its price is rather imprecise in the market, and subject to further erratic moves, given a strong lack of market liquidity during such a perturbation. As such, the CDS does not fit the needs of a speculative trader, supposed not being invested in the underlying bond: see CDS variants, hereafter.

CDS maturities can vary from a couple of months up to several years.

Example of Market Operation

Let a CDS between bank B, protection seller, and its client A, protection buyer (data as of Jan 01):

• underlying: reference entity: XXX Cy, reference obligation: YYY bond
• rating of YYY: no rating (NB: frequent on the EUR market)
• maturity: 1 year
• notional: €16 million
• premium: 22 bp

At inception, A pays to B a premium of:

$$22 \, \text{bp} \times 16\,000\,000 \times 1 \, \text{year} \, (\text{ACT}/360)$$

At maturity:

• if no default: end of the operation;
• in case of a default, that is, occurrence of one of the ISDA contract *events of default*:

- B pays to A €16 million;
- B receives from A the reference obligation, for the equivalent of the notional amount.

Although it is named swap (for marketing reasons), this contract is not a regular swap, since, except in default situation, there is no reciprocal exchange of cash flows. It is actually a *conditional* swap, the seller payment being subject to a default occurrence. Actually, a CDS should be rather viewed as an *option* contract: the protection buyer pays an option premium (as said above, the "premium" word is used in this swap contract), for having the exercise right of receiving the bond nominal value in case of default. Not surprisingly, CDS (and other similar credit derivatives) pricing involves the probabilistic dimension of option pricing, what is not the case for a regular swap.

CDS variants

The vanilla CDS as described here is based on physical settlement, since the underlying bond is transferred to the seller in case of default. To allow for a CDS to be traded by speculative traders, there is a variant involving a *cash settlement*, so that a speculative trader can trade on this market by either buying or selling protection, without being concerned by a position in the underlying bond.

The disadvantage of such cash settlement is that, now, the seller's payment in case of default must be equivalent to the "loss given default", $(1 - v)$, hard to establish at the time of a default occurrence.

Hence a further variant, the CDS with (contractually) defined recovery rate, what is preferred by speculative traders, who are focusing on the value of the premium over time. Indeed, as almost always with speculative trading on derivatives, the trader does not hold his position until the derivative maturity, he is therefore not much concerned with the recovery rate level. Moreover, the CDS premium is obviously linked to the agreed recovery rate level.

A last variant is the *CDS on basket*. In this case, instead of a single {reference entity, reference obligation}, the CDS underlying is made of a weighted sum of several reference entities and obligations. CDS on indexes as basket is the most important segment of the CDS market, just like index products on the equity market. The two leading products are called *iTraxx* (index of 125 European corporations) and its equivalent *CDX* on the US market.

Typically, CDX and iTraxx are basket CDSs, on an equally weighted set of reference entities/bonds with a defined recovery rate, and stipulate that, in case of a default on one of the entities/bonds, the seller's payment is restricted to this specific default.

Basket CDSs face a big challenge, that is, the impact of correlation among the default risks of each of the basket constituents, on the basket CDS valuation. Roughly speaking:

- if the reference entities are much heterogeneous, the correlation tends towards 0, which implies:
  - low probability of 0 defaults;
  - probability peak for a small percentage of defaults;
  - low probability of a high percentage of defaults;
- if the reference entities are much homogenous, the correlation tends close to 1, hence the basket almost behaves as a single entity, and the basket premium gets nearer to the weighted sum of individual CDS premia;
- in between, with a correlation round 0.50 we can expect:
  - a high probability of 0 defaults;
  - lowering gradually with higher percentage of defaults.

The main challenge for speculative traders in basket CDS is not only the estimation of such correlation but, even more, the evolution of this correlation over time, in different market and economic environments.

13.2 VALUATION OF CREDIT DERIVATIVES[2]

13.2.1 Useful measures and relationships

These relationships involve both dimensions of the credit risk, namely:

- the default rate q, and related exposure at default ED;
- the recovery rate v, and corresponding loss given default $(1 - v)$.

For a portfolio of N instruments subject to credit risk, the probable credit loss L is

$$L = \sum h_i \times ED_i \times (1 - v_i) \ (i = 1 \ to \ N)$$

where h_i is the variable of a Heaviside function, valuing 1 if a default occurs, 0 otherwise. Here, h_i is valuing 1 with probability q_i. Hence,

$$E\,[h_i] = q_i$$

and

$$E\,[L] = \sum E[h_i] \times ED_i \times (1 - v_i) = \sum q_i \times ED_i \times (1 - v_i) \qquad (13.1)$$

But the variance of L is critically depending on the correlation between the default occurrences, or default events, of the N instruments.

The two extreme situations of, either, the independence of defaults events, or the perfect correlation of defaults events are of course unrealistic. In the more general case, here with $N = 2$ instruments, the probability of a *joint default* $q(1 \ and \ 2)$ is

$$E\,[h_1 \times h_2] = cov\,(h_1, h_2) + E\,[h_1]\,E[h_2] = \rho\,(h_1, h_2)\,\sigma_1\sigma_2 + q_1q_2$$

Given h_i is a Heaviside variable, its standard deviation is

$$\sigma_i = \sqrt{q_i(1 - q_i)}$$

So that

$$q\,(1 \ and \ 2) = \rho\,(h_1, h_2)\,\sqrt{q_1(1 - q_1)}\sqrt{q_2(1 - q_2)} + q_1q_2$$

The absence of any satisfactory model for the correlation between probabilities of default of different instruments – despite lots of efforts leading to many more or less appropriate in-house solutions – is one of the dangers linked to credit derivatives, in this case for basket- or index products.

Example of Application

This example is adapted from a question asked at the GARP exam in 2000.

Let us take a portfolio of two risky assets of $100 million each. The risk manager considers a probability of default (over 1 year) of 10% for the first asset, and of 20% for the second one,

---

[2] This section is inspired from Ph. JORION, *Financial Risk Manager Handbook*, John Wiley & Sons, Inc., Hoboken, 5th edition, 2009, 752 p.

and a joint probability of default of 3%. Assuming a recovery rate of 40% for both assets, let us compute the expected loss on this portfolio:

There are three possible loss events, that is,

- default of asset 1: with a probability of: $0.10 - 0.03 = 0.07$;
- default of asset 2: with a probability of: $0.20 - 0.03 = 0.17$;
- joint default: with a probability of 0.03.

Using Eq. 13.1, the expected loss for the portfolio is thus

$$0.07 \times \$100\,M \times (1 - 0.40) + 0.17 \times \$100\,M \times (1 - 0.40) + 0.03 \times \$200\,M \times (1 - 0.40)$$
$$= \$18M.$$

Finally, default probabilities can also be viewed in a multi-periodic situation. Given a default rate q on a single period of time (e.g., of 1 year), what about the *cumulative* default rate c, over several periods? This can be grasped according to a binomial process, over successive years (periods) 1, 2, 3, and so on, as in Figure 13.3.

Denoting c_i the cumulative default after i years, we have

$$c_1 = q_1$$
$$c_2 = q_1 + (1 - q_1)q_2$$
$$c_3 = q_1 + (1 - q_1)q_2 + (1 - q_1)(1 - q_2)q_3$$

13.2.2 Valuation of credit derivatives

Valuing a credit derivative involves valuing both the probability q of default, and the value v of the debt after default, or recovery rate. Of course for a credit derivative based on a given, fixed, recovery rate, only q remains to be quantified. This is the case for the important segment of index products, like CDX or iTraxx. However, the price of a credit derivative with fixed recovery rate will anyway depend on the level of such contractual recovery rate.

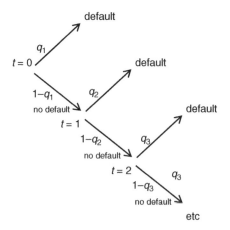

Figure 13.3 Diagram of a binomial process about default

Today, many quantitative models coexist,[3] none of them being satisfactory (except for possible "in house", undisclosed, models). The three main models are as follows.

The Merton Model (also Called "Structural Model")

Although the natural instrument underlying a default observation is a bond, the Merton model is indirectly pricing a default probability via a stock price. The reason is that stock market prices are much more liquid, thus more trustworthy, than bond prices. Remember however that for a given stock market price, there can be many more bonds prices, affected by liquidity problems, without to mention particular features like seniority and other legal clauses that may affect their valuation.

Needless to say, this model can only apply to credit derivatives relating to corporate credit risk: the vast segment of sovereign credit derivative market cannot apply since there is no stock related.

The rationale of the Merton model is twofold:

- Through its balance sheet, the stock price of a corporation reflects the company's ability to (continue to) pay its debt.
- An option pricing model: "the current stock price embodies a forecast of default probability in the same way that an option embodies a forecast of being exercised" (Jorion, op. cit.).

This first credit risk model presents the advantages of working through a very suitable observation, namely, a stock price, and of the much grounded maths of stochastic calculus developed for option pricing. However, practically speaking, the relationship between a stock level probability and a default probability for a specific debt remains too weak, given the importance of the various features of said debt, as actual underlying for the credit derivative. Without to say that, due to the fact that a default situation is a rare event, the validity of the option theory is itself questionable (see, for example, attempts, in option pricing, to take into account of non-normality, or "fat tails", and corresponding "volatility smiles", in Chapter 12).

The relationship between a stock price level and a default probability can be established as follows. Consider the simple case of a company having only two captions on the liability side of its balance sheet (total liability L at t): equity (@ S_t) and one bond (@ B_t) maturing at par $= K$ (maturity date T):

$$L_t = S_t + B_t$$

At T:

- if $L_T > K$:
  bond is repaid @ K
- if $L_T < K$:
  default (bankruptcy), and bond is repaid @ L_T, with $S_T = 0$ (bondholders are repaid before shareholders)

$$\rightarrow \ S_T = MAX(L_T - K; 0)$$

---

[3] Besides the models presented here, we could mention models (e.g., Jarrow and Turnbull) involving a "jump-diffusion" model using a Poisson process. By nature, a Poisson process allows unpredictable (in the course of the time) discontinuities in the underlying price to be incorporated. Although it may happen that some defaults appear unpredictable (e.g., the Lehman Brothers bankruptcy), a default occurrence cannot be sudden by nature: economically, it should be preceded by a certain period of worsening of the financial situation of the company, that should normally be reflected in market bonds (and stocks) prices, so that the random occurrence of (downward) jumps is hardly compatible with a developing default situation.

This was already showed by Black and Scholes (assisted by R. Merton) in their seminal paper about option pricing: a long position in a stock is equal to a long position in a call option on L with a strike (K) equal to the market value of its debt. This features the stock as a limited liability: the stockholder cannot lose more than his equity investment, viewed as his premium paid for acquiring the call.

Continuing from the previous, we also have

$$B_T = L_T - S_T = L_T - MAX(L_T - K; 0) = MIN(L_T; K)$$

and

$$B_T = L_T - S_T = K - MAX(K - L_T; 0)$$

That is, a long position in a risky bond is equal to a long position in a risk-free bond, plus a short position in a put on L.

S_t being modeled by a general geometric Wiener process, in a risk-neutral environment, we can build the distribution probabilities curve of S_t viewed for T from current t, that is, the log-normal distribution

$$S(T) = S(t)e^{\left(\mu - \frac{\sigma^2}{2}\right)(T-t) + \sigma Z(T-t)}$$

(cf. Eq. 8.14) whose cumulative distribution $N(.)$ relates to the Black–Scholes formula for a call option (cf. Section 2.1 and Eq. 10.7).

$$C = SN(d_1) - Ke^{-r(T-t)}N(d_2)$$

where $N(d_2)$ is the *risk neutral* probability that the call will be exercised at maturity (under the assumptions of the Black–Scholes formula): this probability is also that the bond will not default, therefore $(1 - N(d_2))$ or $N(-d_2)$ is the risk-neutral probability of default.

In this simplified case, the cumulative default probability thus corresponds to a $S(t)$ level such as equal to K, the value of the debt for reimbursement at maturity T, with the corresponding probability of default (the gray area of the curve in Figure 13.4).

The advantage of the Merton model, using reliable, liquid equity prices, is not negligible, but its weaknesses are considerable:

- Contrary to the simplistic example above, what becomes the valuation in the real world of the company's debt made of several different bonds, bank loans, with various maturities, seniorities, specific features?
- Since the model only looks at the default probability, it doesn't say anything about the recovery rate factor.
- What if the stock volatility is changing for other reasons (such as systematic market risk) than the ones linked to the company's ability to pay its debt? Such volatility change are in any cases affecting the probability distribution curve of the stock and thus the cumulative default probability.
- More fundamentally, one can question the validity of the Black–Scholes formula in case of dramatic moves of the stock price, what corresponds to deep OTM call situations: it is well known that in such circumstances, the call pricing model needs some adjustments, for example in terms of volatility smile (cf. Chapter 12, Section 12.1.3). Now, S_T levels corresponding to default situations are just such as corresponding to deep OTM levels.

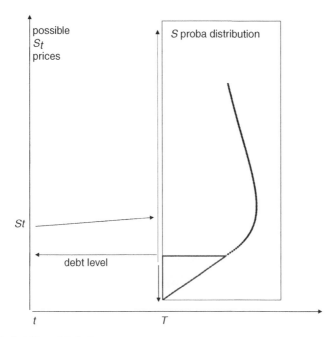

Figure 13.4   Probability of default

Finally, it seems however that the KMV's model output appears to usefully tracking changes in estimation of default probabilities in a rather global way.

The Binomial Model

Contrary to the precedent, this model directly works on bonds. To illustrate it, let us start with the simple case of a risky zero-coupon bond, with 1-year maturity, valuing B:

$$B = PV(single\ future\ cash\text{-}flow)$$
$$\llcorner\ using\ current\ z_1\ rate$$

Looking at the first step of the binomial process presented in Section 12.2.1, completed by the bond value at maturity,

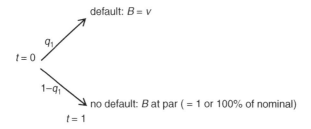

we have

$$B = PV[(1 - q) \times 1 + q \times v]$$

This relationship can be used in two ways:

- either, an observed market price B implies some (q,v) value;
- or, for any estimation of q and of v, there is a theoretical, fair value for B.

The trouble with this model is that this single relationship involves two variables. One will have either to assume a value for q and compute v for an observed market price B, or – maybe less difficult to assess – assume a value for v and compute the corresponding q.

Example. Let us take a 1-year zero-coupon @ 5%. The bond market price is 91.20, and one estimates the recovery rate at 40% (some usual benchmark):

$$PV = 100/1.05 = 95.24$$
$$91.20 = 95.24(1 - q + q \times 0.4) \quad \Rightarrow \quad implied\ q = 7.07\%$$

The calculation becomes more complicated for a 0-coupon maturing after several years: it supposes to follow the binomial path showed in Section 12.2.1. But it becomes harder for coupon bonds, because one has also to consider the coupon payment, defaulted or not, after each period.

Credit Risk Models in Practice

As stated earlier, there is unfortunately (not yet) a satisfying model for quantifying credit risk. The market players are therefore using a so-called valuation "model" that consists in a rather sophisticated statistical treatment of a wide range of any kind of useful observed market data such as:

- market prices of credit derivatives;
- credit spreads;
- prices and default correlations;
- ratings;
- recovery rates;
- and so on.

The output of this treatment is abusively called "model", because of its complexity (and cost...), but it is anything but a model, because this output is endogenous to market observations, instead of resulting from a theoretical, exogenous development. This cannot thus pretend to lead to a fair or theoretical valuation, to be confronted to an observed market value. Too often, market practitioners are using the output of this so-called practical "model" just as if it was a fair, theoretical credit risk valuation.

The main dangers linked to the "data crunching" of these pieces of information are:

- the difficulty in extrapolating from data, such as observed credit spreads, relative to debt A, to a debt B, with different features (liquidity, status, etc.);
- the lack of stationarity of the observed data and relationships among them over time;
- the validity of statistical hypothesis used in the treatment, given default are by essence rare events, and underlying "reference obligations" are so many;

- the difficulty in assessing a suitable value for the correlation between default risks, in the very important segment of basket credit derivative products (indexes, synthetic securitization tranches) – see below.

Given the very large database needed for building this "model", the staff needed to develop it, and the related costs, most of the market players are buying the output from renowned firms like CreditMetrics (J.P. Morgan), CreditRisk+ (Crédit Suisse), KMV (Moody's) or Markit. It is interesting to point out that the weight of these providers is so huge that theoreticians trying to develop models are almost forced to calibrate their models with the output of these providers. Let us also point out the presence of Moody's: unlike his major competitor Standard & Poors, ratings provided by Moody's are function of both their own quantification of a default probability and of a recovery rate, while the S&P rating is only function of the former.

Correlation Measures, in the Case of Basket Derivative Products[4]

Pricing an option – or, indirectly, a CDS for example – on a basket of several underlyings obviously requires some assumptions about the "co-dependence" among prices changes of the various items in the basket. If one restricts to market moves limited to a few standard deviations (volatility), traditional models (Wiener, etc.) almost run adequately. Beyond, market practitioners play with volatility "smiles" (or other distortions of the volatility measure), but with respect to correlation, one cannot any more work with the hypothesis of a linear relationship between the several variables. Yet, a credit default being a rare event, it corresponds to the tail of a probabilistic distribution, that is, beyond several standard deviations, where the Gaussian assumption of prices changes is not valid anymore. This can also affect the valuation of some second-generation options.

The usual, linear correlation ρ_{xy} between two variables x and y is

$$\rho_{x,y} = \frac{cov(x, y)}{\sqrt{V(x)V(y)}}$$

where the $V(.)$ are variances.

If we denote $\varphi(x,y)$ the joint density distribution of x and y, the marginal density distributions of x and y are

$$\varphi_x(x) = \int \varphi(x, y)\, dy \quad and \quad \varphi_y(y) = \int \varphi(x, y)\, dx$$

(If x and y were independent variables, we would have $\varphi(x,y) = \varphi_x(x)\varphi_y(y)$.)

If $\varphi_x(x)$ and $\varphi_y(y)$ are Gaussian, the above linear correlation is a good measure of the co-dependence of the normal variables, and the corresponding joint density distribution $\varphi(x, y)$ is a bivariate normal distribution:

$$normal\ \varphi_x(x),\ normal\ \varphi_y(y),\ \rho_{x,y} \quad \Rightarrow \quad normal\ \varphi(x, y)$$

But if their distribution is far enough from Gaussian, this measure is misleading. A famous example is if (x,y) can only value $(0,1)$, $(0,-1)$, $(1,0)$ or $(-1,0)$, with equal probability. The linear correlation of x and y is 0, although they are clearly dependent: if $x = 0$, y can only value 1 or -1, and if $x \neq 0$, $y = 0$.

---

[4] This section also concerns basket derivatives on underlyings other than credit, such as stocks or currencies. It is based on P. JACKEL, *Monte Carlo Methods in Finance*, John Wiley & Sons, Ltd, Chichester, 2002.

Coming back to the general case of $\varphi_x(x)$ and $\varphi_y(y)$ being not Gaussian, this inference

$$\varphi_x(x), \varphi_y(y), \rho_{x,y} \Rightarrow \varphi(x, y)$$

cannot be made. Typically, the classic "rank correlation" coefficient of Spearman shows the way to get round the problem: this rank correlation consists in a linear correlation coefficient of the variates,[5] now transformed in a non-linear way, by a probability transformation, that is, their respective cumulative marginal distributions:

$$\Phi_x(x) = \int_{-\infty}^{x} \varphi_x(x)dx \quad and \quad \Phi_y(y) = \int_{-\infty}^{y} \varphi_y(y)dy$$

with

$$\Phi(x, y) = \iint_{x,y=-\infty}^{x,y} \varphi(x, y)dxdy$$

The Spearman correlation is a correlation measure that can be computed from these relationships and from the general formula for $\rho_{x,y}$ above, but, as a step further, we can link above $\Phi_x(x)$, $\Phi_y(y)$ and $\Phi(x,y)$ relationships in a more general way

$$\Phi(x, y) = C(\Phi_x(x), \Phi_y(y))$$

that defines C – named a *copula* of two variables x and y – as a cumulative probability function of the marginal cumulative probabilities $\Phi_x(x)$, $\Phi_y(y)$ of x and y.[6] A copula is thus a general measure of co-dependence between two variates, which is *independent of their individual marginal distribution* – see Figure 13.5.

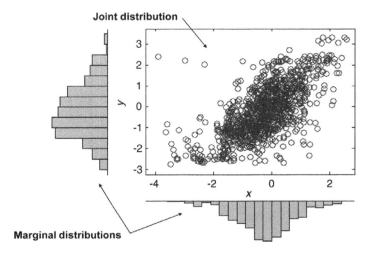

(http://www.mathworks.com/access/helpdesk/help/toolbox/stats/copula_17.gif)

Figure 13.5   Example of a copula

---

[5] The word variate designates a set of random variables that obeys a given probabilistic law, in general.
[6] Sklar's theorem states that C is unique.

The copula can be a *Gaussian copula* if it is computed from the cumulative distribution function of two marginal cumulative Gaussian probabilities. Similarly, it is possible to define many other copulas: for example, a *t*-copula, given by the cumulative distribution function of two *t*-Student marginals. Indeed, the joint probability distribution will turn out to be of the same "nature" (Gaussian, or any other) as its related marginal probability distributions.

The copula *C* function, in terms of co-dependence measurement, is much more general than a linear correlation leading to the ρ coefficient. However, the validity of this co-dependence measure is of course depending on the choice of the probability distribution chosen for the variates. Incidentally, Monte Carlo method turns out to be very appropriate to simulate bi- or multivariate copula draws with co-dependence.

Coming back to modeling credit risk, if the credit derivative is about a basket of several underlyings, the degree of co-dependence, that is, a broader measure than the traditional correlation coefficient based on a linear regression, will significantly affect the credit risk premium. Indeed, the aim is to price a multivariate product (the default probability of each of the basket constituents) in a consistent way with the prices (over time) of several univariate products.

Application to the Pricing of a CDO[7]

Basket CDSs (cf. Section 12.1.5) are also embedded into "synthetic securitizations", often called *collaterized debt obligations* (CDO), for example the C*Star 1, 1999–2001 of Citibank (data 1999), shown in Figure 13.6.

In this example, the CDO involves the lower CDS in the figure, in bold (the upper one is a regular CDS with a bank). This second CDS transfers the credit risk to an entity (*C* Star) called a *special purpose vehicle* (SPV), whose function is to pool the debts into several notes, called tranches, offered to investors. Obviously, the weighted sum of spreads (above EURIBOR, in this example) paid by the tranches must equal the one of the initial bunch of securitized debts, minus some margin (taken by the SPV).

The sharing out of the debts between the tranches occurs afterwards, in such a way that defaulted debts, if any, are allocated uppermost to the riskier tranche, paying the higher spread; if they exceed the size of this tranche, they are progressively affecting the less risky tranches. So that the most risky tranche (the BB-rated one) is the one which will suffer the first defaults (if any), thus offering the highest risk premium. Consequently, the content of each tranche being not known a priori, the crucial problem is here the relationship between the spreads of each tranche and the correlation among the set of securitized debts.

The probability of loss on a CDO tranche can be viewed as the joint distribution of loss probabilities of the underlyings in the basket. To avoid arbitrage opportunities, and even simply to make sense, the CDO tranche price must be consistent with individual risk premia of the basket content: these risk premia represent the marginal default probabilities. The choice of a copula will link the joint distribution to the corresponding marginals. Similarly to other models used, for a given choice of a copula, we can:

- either, compute the corresponding CDO tranche price by estimating the co-dependence or correlation structure from other data (see Figure 13.7).

---

[7] The following is based on M. DOREY, P. JOUBERT, *Modelling Copulas: An overview*, The Staple Inn Actuarial Society, 2005.

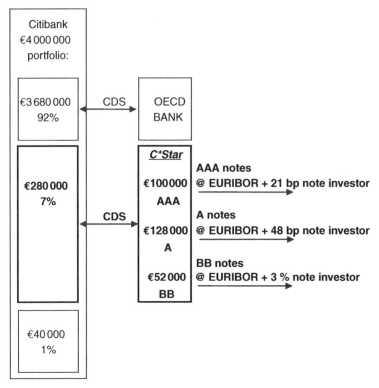

Figure 13.6   Example of a CDO

As such, a marginal distribution of default probabilities can be built from observed market data, together with pair-wise observed correlations ρ_{ij}, what leads to a joint distribution, often modeled as a Gaussian copula. In this case, the Gaussian copula is a non-linear function of the (linear) correlation matrix. Monte Carlo simulations of this joint distribution lead to the determination of the CDO price. But one must admit that the choice of a Gaussian copula is arbitrary, and the choice of constant ρ_{ij} is for want of anything better;

- or, from CDO observed prices, infer the relevant co-dependence (see Figure 13.8).
  Here, the market observed CDS premia and CDO prices leads to an "implied correlation", which is used by market practitioners like an "implied volatility", which differs from one tranche to another, and serves for correlation trading.

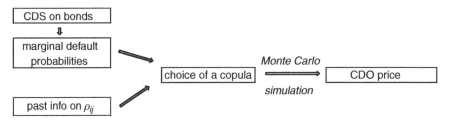

Figure 13.7   Diagram of a CDO pricing

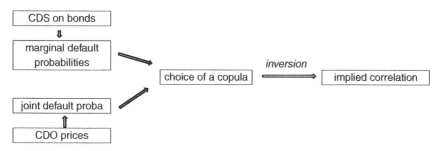

Figure 13.8   Diagram showing how to compute CDO implied correlation

13.3   CONCLUSION

Ultimately, the three major problems facing the search for a suitable credit risk valuation model are:

- the *lack of liquidity* of relevant data and underlying instruments;
- correlation problems (measure, stationarity), affecting credit derivatives built on a basket or index of underlyings: "correlation, or more generally co-movement, is one of the single greatest challenges facing quantitative analysts and risk managers today" (P. JACKEL, op. cit.);
- and, more fundamentally, an option replication problem: as a matter of fact (see Section 12.1.5), despite the credit derivatives are labeled "swaps", they are actually conditional

Figure 13.9   Graph of an iTraxx premium
Source: Bloomberg

swaps, that is, options products. Option valuation is based on the ability to build a riskless portfolio, combining some short position in underlying and some long position in a corresponding option. In the case of a credit derivative, it is impossible to take a short position on an underlying default risk, hence, no delta neutral mechanism, and the option theory is not grounded in this case, because such option is not replicable.

As a consequence, speculative trading on credit derivatives is actually very different from speculation on most other instruments, because of the absence of a grounded fair or theoretical value to be compared with observed market prices. Figure 13.9 is a graph of an iTraxx premium: how to objectively appreciate to what extent should these prices be over- or under-estimated?

Finally the credit derivative market has been developed on the OTC (interbank) market, because of their creativity and dynamism; but this market should have rather been developed by the insurance market, where, to escape to the replication problem, the risk assumed by the risk vendors is "mutualized" through the system of insurance – reassurance. Ironically, the spirit of contracts such as CDSs is of *insurance* against a default.

FURTHER READING

Antulio N. BOMFIM, *Understanding Credit Derivatives and Related Instruments*, Academic Press, 2004, 368 p.

George CHACKO, Anders SJOMAN, Hideto MOTOHASHI, Vincent DESSAIN, *Credit Derivatives*, Pearson Prentice Hall, 2006, 272 p.

Roger B. NELSEN, *An Introduction to Copulas*, Springer, 2010, 284 p.

Philipp J. SCHONBUCHER, *Credit Derivatives Pricing Models*, John Wiley & Sons, Ltd, Chichester, 2003, 600 p.

Market performance and risk measures

14.1 RETURN AND RISK MEASURES

14.1.1 Return measures

Returns relative to interest rate instruments and positions are straightforward, and have been treated in previous chapters regarding such interest rate instruments. This section is devoted to return measures for other instruments, mainly stocks. The extension to commodities products is straightforward, taking into account that in this case, there is no associated revenue like dividends for stocks.

Return on a Single Stock Position, and One Period of Time

During one period of time (i.e., 1 day, 1 month, 1 year or whatever), from $t-1$ to t, let us denote S the spot price observed in the market of stock S, S being function of t. The rate of return, in short, the return r_S "on the price" is

$$r_S = \frac{S_t - S_{t-1}}{S_{t-1}}$$

Besides, it may happen that during this single period of time, S is paying a dividend d: the return on the dividend r_d, called *dividend yield* is

$$r_d = \frac{d}{S_{t-1}}$$

Hence, the total return:

$$r = \frac{S_t - S_{t-1} + d}{S_{t-1}}$$

Example. Compute the 1-year total return (10/21/10 to 10/20/11) on L'Oreal:

- 10/21/10 close price: €87.43;
- 10/20/11 close price: €78.47;
- net dividend paid: €1.80 (not taking account the dividend payment date).

$$\Rightarrow r = (78.47 - 87.43 + 1.80)/87.43 = -8.19\%$$

Multi-periodic Return on a Single Position

Let us start with two consecutive periods:

	First period:		Second period:
S_t:	100	150	125
Single-period returns:	+50%		−16.667%

This two-period return is evidently obtained by compounding the successive one-period returns, and is called TWRR (for *Time Weighted Rate of Return*) in the funds industry:

$$\text{TWRR} = [100 \times (1 + 0.50) \times (1 - 0.1667) - 100]/100 = 25\%$$

where the portion $100 \times (1 + 0.50) \times (1 - 0.1667) = 125$ is called the NAV (for Net Assets Value).

If we want the average (return) performance on the whole two periods, *avg r*,

- the arithmetic average, $(+50\% - 17\%) = 16.5\%$ is of course wrong, because it ignores the compounding of the involved returns;
- the pro rata on one period of the global difference $(125 - 100)/100 = 25\%$ for two periods or 12.5% per period, is also wrong, for the same reason;
- the correct way is by compounding the successive returns, by using a geometric average:

$$\text{avg r} = \sqrt{[(1 + 0.5)(1 - 0.17)]} - 1 = 11.6\%$$

Generalizing on n successive periods, on a set of S(t) starting from S_0:

$$\left.\begin{array}{l} \text{TWRR} = \dfrac{S_0 (1 + r_1) \ldots (1 + r_i) \ldots (1 + r_n) - S_0}{S_0} \\[2mm] \text{NAV} = S_0 (1 + r_1) \ldots (1 + r_i) \ldots (1 + r_n) \\[2mm] \text{avg r} = \sqrt[n]{(1 + r_1) \ldots (1 + r_i) \ldots (1 + r_n)} - 1 \end{array}\right\} \quad (14.1)$$

Multi-Periodic Return of a Portfolio Involving Several Positions

In the case of a portfolio P invested in several assets, assuming the portfolio size was unchanged and has produced a series of n ($n = 1, \ldots, i, \ldots n$) periodic returns, the TWRR can be computed as

$$\text{TWRR} = \sum_{i=1}^{n} (1 + r_i) - 1$$

where the r_i are

$$r_i = \frac{P_i - P_{i-1}}{P_{i-1}}$$

P_i being the portfolio value at the end of period i.

But if, during these n periods, the portfolio (or fund) as faced cash out- and/or in-flows, these formulae actually measure the portfolio return, but do not allow for assessing the performance of the portfolio manager (not responsible for the changes in the portfolio size). A usual way to compute the performance "return" of the portfolio manager is called the Modified Dietz Method, which consists of cleaning the r_i from these cash out- and/or in-flows, denoting

- p_i the cash out- or in-flow (cash variations) during period i:
- w_i a weighting coefficient representing the fraction of period i affected by the cash variation (hence leading to an approximate result, given there may be several of such cash variations during the period);[1]

---

[1] There exist more sophisticated formulations, see, for example, E. DE BODT, P. GREGOIRE, *Le calcul a posteriori du return d'un portefeuille*, Revue de la Banque, 1997, pp. 359–369 (in French).

- r'_i the adjusted return for period i:

$$r'_i \cong \frac{P_i - P_{i-1} - p_i}{P_{i-1} + w_i p_i}$$

Expected Return

It appears from previous examples that the return is actually measured on a series of *past* data. The result is therefore an *expected* return:

$$r = E[r_t]$$

Applied on a portfolio P of n different instruments, weighted by $w_1 \ldots w_n$, the formula becomes

$$E[r_P] = \sum_{i=1}^{i=n} w_i E[r_i]$$

Return Measure, in Practice

Given the importance of stochastic calculus and most usual processes issued from it (cf. Chapter 8, Section 8.7), some market practitioners rather compute r as "log returns":

$$r = \ln\left(\frac{S_t}{S_{t-1}}\right)$$

The difference with traditional return calculation is almost negligible: for example, with $S_{t-1} = 100$ and $S_t = 101$, the classical return is 0.01 or 1% and the log return is $\ln 101/100 = 0.00995$.

From the above equation,

$$S_t = S_{t-1} . e^{r\tau}$$

that is, the deterministic forward value of S_{t-1} at $\tau = t - 1$.

Finally, to allow for comparison between different return performances, the market practice uses annualized returns, that are computed by multiplying a periodic return by the number n of periods per annum, that is, $\times n = 12$ in case of monthly returns, $\times n = 52$ in case of weekly returns, and $\times n = 250$ in case of daily returns (250 corresponds to about the actual number of days traded annually on exchanges).

14.1.2   Risk measures

NB: in this section, we consider only *market* risk (for credit risk measures, cf. Chapter 13).

Risk on a Single Position

Although risk seems rather intuitively linked to a measure of the dispersion of returns, this notion merits deeper investigation.[2] However, within the framework of this book, we will

---

[2] A very interesting study of the risk measure in its broadest approach can be found in S. RACHEV, S. ORTOBELLI, S. STOYANOV, F.J. FABOZZI, A. BIGLOVA, "Desirable properties of an ideal risk measure in portfolio theory", *International Journal of Theoretical and Applied Finance*, 2005.

restrict our approach to the usual risk measure quantified by the standard deviation, called volatility, of a series of past data, that is, a *historical* volatility (cf. beginning of Chapter 12). Because investors or traders/speculators are actually concerned with returns and not with prices, market practice actually computes the risk (volatility) on log returns rather than on prices, to avoid the impact of changes in prices levels over time.

Due to their respective calculations, it is important to keep in mind that a return is a *directional* variable (positive, if the position value goes up, and conversely), while a risk is a *non-directional* variable: risk means as well "risk of gain" as "risk of loss".

Being a standard deviation, the risk is traditionally denoted by σ, as the square root of the corresponding variance σ^2. But the obtained value is depending on the time frequency of the data: obviously the standard deviation of monthly data will be higher than for daily data, for example; indeed, the wider the time interval between the data, the more prices changes, and therefore the higher the standard deviation. Since different data frequencies on the same financial instrument should have to reflect the same volatility, that is, the one presented by the instrument, we need to adjust the calculation, referring to the year as the time unit in finance. The result is called *annualized volatility* or volatility *p.a.* For details on how to compute the annualized volatility, and the pitfalls associated with, refer to Chapter 12, Section 12.1.1.

Example. For the S&P 500, from Jan 05 to Aug 09, using daily and monthly data,

- standard deviation: daily: 1.55%   monthly: 6.25%
- annualized volatility: $1.55\% \times \sqrt{250} = 21.65\%$ $6.55\% \times \sqrt{12} = 24.56\%$

so that on a p.a. basis, the result is of the same order of magnitude.

If the returns are normally distributed, recall that

between + and − 1 σ:	$\cong$ 2/3 of cumul. probability (around the mean)
2 σ:	$\cong$ 95%
3 σ:	$\cong$ 99.8%

If the data present some skewness, it makes sense to compute a *semi-standard* deviation, that is, a standard deviation computed only on the negative or on the positive returns, or both. It comes to consider that the returns distribution is made of two distinct distributions, one for the negative returns and one for the positive ones.

Risk on Several Positions

If the risk must be computed on several positions or exposures, the correlation between the various positions values plays a significant part, which has been developed in the *Portfolio Theory* (cf. Chapter 4, Section 4.3). The variance of a portfolio P, composed of n instruments $1 \ldots i \ldots j \ldots n$, weighted by $w_1 \ldots w_n$ is

$$\sigma_P^2 = \sum_i w_i^2 \sigma_i^2 + \sum_i \sum_{j \neq i} w_i w_j \sigma_i \sigma_j \rho_{ij} \tag{14.2}$$

hence, the risk σ_P. So that, while returns are additive (see above formula for $E[r_P]$), risks are not. For an example, with two securities, see Chapter 4, Section 4.3.3.

14.1.3   Risk versus return ratios, or performance measures

Absolute Performance Measures

The Sharpe Ratio

Following the Portfolio Theory, which is elaborated on the basis of the *return – risk* paradigm, investors or traders/speculators are actually concerned by both returns and associated risks. With this respect, it makes sense to assess the attractiveness of a return by considering the risk associated with. The simplest way of doing this is by dividing the return by the risk. However, a risk-less investment, in a non-defaultable government bond, pays a risk-free rate for $\sigma = 0$. Hence, it makes sense to consider that in a risky investment (r, σ) it should be the excess return only, that is, $r - r_f$, that pays for the supported risk.

Hence the Sharpe ratio:

$$Sharpe\ ratio = \frac{r - r_f}{\sigma}$$

Practically speaking, for a given period of past data leading to r and σ measures, the r_f rate must be of a non-defaultable government bill or bond of maturity coinciding with the same period of time as used for r and σ. The data for r and r_f being usually expressed on a p.a. basis, σ must also be computed on a p.a. basis.

Example. For a fund passively invested in the S&P 500 in 2009, the computed return and risk were 17.96% p.a. and 27.04% p.a. respectively (based on daily closing prices). The corresponding 12-month T-Bill was 2.004%. The Sharpe ratio is

$$Sharpe\ ratio = \frac{17.96 - 2.004}{27.04} = 0.59$$

Note that in the fund industry, it is hard to achieve a Sharpe ratio above 1, which may be viewed as a reference level.

The Treynor Ratio

In the funds industry, the performance objective of a portfolio P is generally referring to a benchmark, typically an equity index. It makes thus sense to rate the portfolio return r_P to the index return, through its β_P (cf. Chapter 4, Section 4.3.4), hence the Treynor ratio:

$$Treynor\ ratio = \frac{r_P - r_f}{\beta_P}$$

Jensen's Alpha

With respect to the CAPM (cf. Chapter 4, Section 4.3.4), Eq. 4.11 and Eq. 4.12)

$$r_P = \alpha_P + \beta_P r_M + \varepsilon_P \quad and \quad E_P = r_f + (E_M - r_f)\beta_P$$

allow us to compute the α_P of a portfolio P from a linear regression between excess returns in P and in the market portfolio M:

$$r_P - r_f = \alpha_P + \beta_P \left(r_M - r_f\right) + \varepsilon_P$$

Jensen's α is thus

$$Jensens's\ \alpha_P = E(r_P) - r_f - \beta_P(E_M - r_f)$$

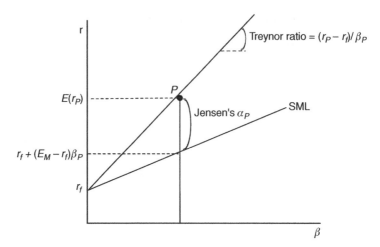

Figure 14.1   Comparing Treynor and Jensen measures, for a portfolio P

and represents the portfolio excess return versus a benchmark (theoretically, the market index). It is computed on a p.a. basis.

Figure 14.1, built from the graph showing the security market line of the CAPM in Chapter 4, Section 4.3.4, compares both Treynor and Jensen measures, for a portfolio P.

The Treynor and Jensen ratios will be illustrated below, in a global example, involving other ratios as well.

Relative Performance Measures

The following measures refer to the way a portfolio performance is achieved with respect to its related benchmark.

The Tracking Error "TE"

The TE is defined as the standard deviation of a portfolio P excess returns versus a benchmark, theoretically the market index M, but practically, versus any benchmark, to quantify up to what extent P is tracking the said benchmark in a more or less smooth way.

Considering the TE versus M, starting from Eq. 4.14

$$\sigma_P^2 = \rho_{P,M}^2 \sigma_P^2 + \sigma_\varepsilon^2$$

so that

$$\sigma_\varepsilon^2 = \sigma_P^2 - \rho_{PM}^2 \sigma_P^2$$

The TE for P is the square root of σ_ε^2, that is

$$TE_P = \sigma_P \sqrt{1 - \rho_{P,M}^2}$$

and is thus function of both the volatility of P and its correlation with the benchmark. TE may also be viewed as an "excess risk" measure, namely, the risk associated to the excess return generated by P versus if the assets were invested in the benchmark. As a risk measure, it is also computed on a p.a. basis.

The Information Ratio "IR"

The IR is defined as the excess return versus the benchmark, divided by the tracking error. It thus comes to the ratio of the Jensen's α and the Tracking Error, on a p.a. basis:

$$IR = \frac{\alpha_P}{TE_P}$$

This ratio gives an idea of the importance of the excess return obtained by a fund, considering the undergone excess risk, hence, a kind of "excess" Sharpe ratio.

Global Example of Calculation of These Ratios

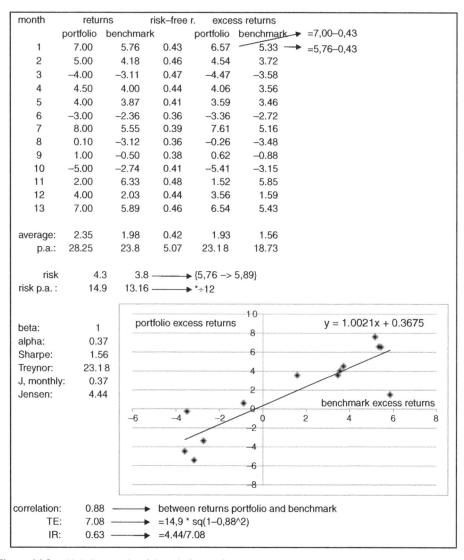

Figure 14.2 — values table and chart:

month	returns portfolio	benchmark	risk-free r.	excess returns portfolio	benchmark
1	7.00	5.76	0.43	6.57	5.33
2	5.00	4.18	0.46	4.54	3.72
3	−4.00	−3.11	0.47	−4.47	−3.58
4	4.50	4.00	0.44	4.06	3.56
5	4.00	3.87	0.41	3.59	3.46
6	−3.00	−2.36	0.36	−3.36	−2.72
7	8.00	5.55	0.39	7.61	5.16
8	0.10	−3.12	0.36	−0.26	−3.48
9	1.00	−0.50	0.38	0.62	−0.88
10	−5.00	−2.74	0.41	−5.41	−3.15
11	2.00	6.33	0.48	1.52	5.85
12	4.00	2.03	0.44	3.56	1.59
13	7.00	5.89	0.46	6.54	5.43
average:	2.35	1.98	0.42	1.93	1.56
p.a.:	28.25	23.8	5.07	23.18	18.73

=7,00–0,43
=5,76–0,43

risk	4.3	3.8 → {5,76 -> 5,89}
risk p.a. :	14.9	13.16 → *÷12

beta:	1
alpha:	0.37
Sharpe:	1.56
Treynor:	23.18
J, monthly:	0.37
Jensen:	4.44

chart: portfolio excess returns vs benchmark excess returns, $y = 1.0021x + 0.3675$

correlation:	0.88 → between returns portfolio and benchmark
TE:	7.08 → =14,9 * sq(1–0,88^2)
IR:	0.63 → =4.44/7.08

Figure 14.2   Global example of the relative performance measures

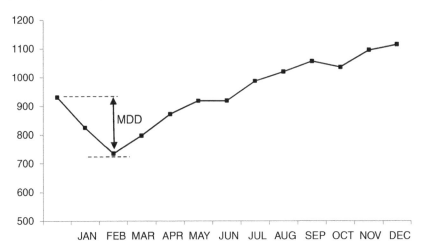

Figure 14.3   Determining the Maximum Draw Down

Maximum Draw Down (MDD); Calmar Ratio

The MDD is the highest loss over a given period. For a given series of periodic portfolio performances, it can refer to the worst periodic performance, but better on a cumulative level (if successive periodic performances are negative).

Example.   Consider the previous example related to the Sharpe ratio, of a fund invested in the S&P 500 and disclosing monthly performance (NAV): the corresponding prices data during 2009, but on a monthly basis, show a MDD of $(-)\,21.11\% = (931.8 - 735.09)/931.8$, during Jan + Feb 09 – see Figure 14.3.

   Although simplistic, this measure is significantly affecting investors in their judgement about a fund performance. Indeed, first, it may be viewed as a risk measure, further to the volatility. And second:

- from the investor's viewpoint, the deeper the MDD, the longer time can be needed to recover the incurred loss before resuming a positive performance;
- from the portfolio manager's viewpoint, the performance fee is suspended until the performance will exceed its last top level (at the inception of the MDD period).

   The Calmar ratio is associated with the absolute value of MDD measure, relatively to the p.a. return of the portfolio:

$$Calmar\ ratio = \frac{r}{|MDD|}$$

   Continuing with the same example, given a p.a. return of 17.96%, the Calmar ratio is $0.85 = 0.1796/0.2111$.

Z-score

Besides their use as a risk measure, volatilities allow us to compute a rather common measure used in proprietary trading: the *Z-score*. This measure quantifies spreads of prices or returns

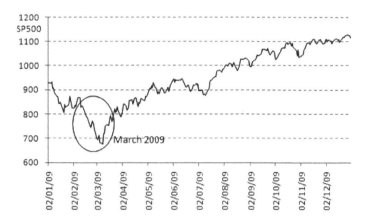

Figure 14.4   S&P 500 daily prices and log returns 2009

towards their average on a past period of time, allowing to assessing to what extent a price, for example, is abnormally cheap for a buying opportunity.

Actually, the Z-score of a random variable X (a price or a return) is the corresponding standardized normal random variable Z, assuming the variable is distributed as a Gaussian, of mean X and standard deviation ($=$volatility) σ:

$$Z = \frac{X - X}{\sigma}$$

Example.   let us consider the S&P 500 daily prices and log returns during the whole year 2009, as in Figure 14.4.

The average of returns was 0.000836 and the volatility (not annualized) was 0.01716. One sees that the market was particularly hectic in March. In Figure 14.15 we see that the Z-scores were sometimes high (corresponding to several standard deviations) during this month (data in gray).

14.1.4   Performance contribution and attribution

This sub-section aims to answer the following question: what are the explanatory factors of a performance?

Performance Contribution

The return of a portfolio P can be usefully analyzed per invested asset or, more commonly, per sub-sets, for example on a sector basis, or a country basis, or per currency. For an asset or asset class i (portfolio of assets or asset classes $1, \ldots, i, \ldots, n$) of weight w_i, having achieved a return r_i,

$$contribution\ of\ i = w_i \times r_i$$

	closes:		Z score:
03/02/09	700.82	−0.04774	−2.83
03/03/09	696.33	−0.00643	−0.42
03/04/09	712.87	0.023475	1.32
03/05/09	682.55	−0.043463	−2.58
03/06/09	683.38	0.001215	0.02
03/09/09	676.53	−0.010074	−0.64
03/10/09	719.6	0.061719	3.54
03/11/09	721.36	0.002443	0.09
03/12/09	750.74	0.039921	2.28
03/13/09	756.55	0.007709	0.4
03/16/09	753.89	−0.003522	−0.25
03/17/09	778.12	0.031634	1.79
03/18/09	794.35	0.020643	1.15
03/19/09	784.04	−0.013064	−0.81
03/20/09	768.54	−0.019967	−1.21
03/23/09	822.92	0.068366	3.93
03/24/09	806.12	−0.020626	−1.25
03/25/09	813.88	0.00958	0.51
03/26/09	832.86	0.023053	1.29
03/27/09	815.94	−0.020525	−1.24
03/30/09	787.53	−0.035439	−2.11
03/31/09	797.87	0.013044	0.71

Figure 14.5   Z-scores calculation

If we denote by r_P the global portfolio return, above contributions are such as

$$\sum contributions = r_P$$

Example. A portfolio (all in $) invested in 3-month rolled-over futures contracts, made of 45% of S&P 500, 20% of Nasdaq 100 and 35% of Nikkei 225 (in $), the performance and contributions for 2005 were as shown in Figure 14.6.

It is worth noting that such a calculation implies that the assets have been hold during the whole period (of 1 year here).

Performance Attribution

Performance attribution aims to evidence the portfolio (or fund) manager's skill about the portfolio performance track record. On the contrary to the "performance contribution", which

	PORTFOLIO		
asset	asset ret.	weight	contribution
SP 500	3.05%	0.45	1.37%
Nasdaq 100	5.65%	0.2	1.13%
Nikkei 225 (in $)	26.45%	0.35	9.26%
portfolio	11.76%	1	11.76%

Figure 14.6   Example of a *performance contribution* calculation

	PORTFOLIO		BENCHMARK	
asset	asset r.	weight	asset r.	weight
SP 500	3.05%	0.45	3.84%	0.5
Nasdaq	5.65%	0.2	2.60%	0.25
Nikkei (in $)	26.45%	0.35	22.13%	0.25
portfolio	11.76%	1	8.10%	1

Figure 14.7   Measuring excess return

is only based on portfolio data, the performance attribution needs to refer to a benchmark, to assess the portfolio manager's skill. It analyzes how and to what extent, each of the assets, or more realistically, each asset class, is representing a part of the portfolio global excess return vis-à-vis the benchmark.

The Case of Stocks Portfolios

As a first step, we have to precise things about the excess return measure. Let us consider the above portfolio, that is destined to outperform a basket of 50% of SP 500, 25% of Nasdaq 100 and 25% of Nikkei 225 (in $), as its benchmark. During the same period, because of different weights, the benchmark has realized an r_B of 8.10%, to be compared to 11.76% for our portfolio – see Figure 14.7.

The most direct (and most used) excess return measure r_{exc} is the *arithmetic* one, that is, $11.76\% - 8.10\% = 3.66\%$:

$$r_{exc} = r_P - r_B$$

This is the excess return that will be used in the continuation of this section.

Alternatively, r_{exc} may be computed in a *geometric* way,

$$r_{exc} = \frac{1 + r_P}{1 + r_B} - 1$$

that presents the advantage of being compoundable on several successive periods of time (in the same way as returns, cf. Eq. 14.1). In our example, the geometric excess return is: $1.1176/1.0810 - 1 = 3.38\%$ (instead of 3.66%).

Coming back to the performance attribution, the portfolio manager may try to "beat the benchmark" in two ways:

- by acting on the weights of the assets, in a different proportion as of the benchmark;
- by acting on the day each of assets are actually invested, which is not necessarily the last day of the period, as per the benchmark index calculation.

In practice, both actions are combining, such as we will have to consider three performance attribution components instead of two.

To make the notations more precise,

- for a portolio P of n assets (or sub-sets of the portfolio) $1, \ldots, j, \ldots n$
  with returns $r_{P1}, \ldots, r_{Pj}, \ldots, r_{Pn}$
  and weights $w_{P1}, \ldots, w_{Pj}, \ldots, w_{Pn}$

- benchmarked to B of n assets (more or less equivalent to those of P, to make sense as a benchmark)
  with returns $r_{B1}, \ldots, r_{Bj}, \ldots, r_{Bn}$
  and weights $w_{B1}, \ldots, w_{Bj}, \ldots, w_{Bn}$

let us define

- the portfolio return r_P as

$$r_P = \sum w_{Pi} \times r_{Pi}$$

- the benchmark return r_B as

$$r_B = \sum w_{Bi} \times r_{Bi}$$

$$\Rightarrow r_{exc} = r_P - r_B$$

The first component of the attribution focuses on the weights, and is called *asset allocation attribution*: the portfolio manager's skill can be quantified about this aspect, by considering the impact of the *portfolio* weights on the *benchmark* returns:

$$asset\ allocation\ attribution = \sum (w_{Pi} - w_{Bi}) \times r_{Bi} \qquad (14.3)$$

(The rationale is that this portion of the excess return brings only the weights into play, to justify for a different performance, the r_i being here the same for the portfolio as for the benchmark.)

The second component of the attribution focuses on the returns (invested at different dates than for the benchmark, the portfolio returns are different), and is called "stock selection attribution": the portfolio manager's skill can be quantified about this aspect, by considering the impact of the *portfolio* returns on the *benchmark* weights:

$$stock\ selection\ attribution = \sum (r_{Pi} - r_{Bi}) \times w_{Bi}$$

Finally, we have to add the *interaction* of both effects: a different weighting can be associated to a better or worst return, depending on the investment date:[3]

$$interaction\ attribution = \sum (w_{Pi} - w_{Bi})(r_{Pi} - r_{Bi})$$

Applied to the above example, we obtain the result in Figure 14.8, showing that the portfolio manager's skill was mainly noticeable in the stock selection in the Nasdaq and Nikkei sub-sets, and in the Nikkei asset allocation.

Impact of the Currencies on the Performance Attribution

If the portfolio in invested in one or several currencies other than the portfolio currency, in these cases the appreciation or depreciation of a currency of an asset (or a sub-set of the portfolio) is affecting the portfolio performance and therefore the performance attribution. The simplest way to incorporate this effect is by splitting the asset allocation contribution in

---

[3] This third component can be viewed as the "correlation" term, in the calculation of a variance or standard deviation for two different assets ($\sigma_P^2 = w_1^2 \sigma_2^2 + w_2^2 \sigma_2^2 + 2\rho w_1 w_2 \sigma_1 \sigma_2$), and expresses to what extent both impacts are more or less opportunely combined.

PORTFOLIO			BENCHMARK		**attribution effects:**		
asset	asset r.	weight	asset r.	weight	as. all.	stock s.	interact.
SP 500	3.05%	0.45	3.84%	0.5	−0.19%	−0.40%	0.04%
Nasdaq	5.65%	0.2	2.60%	0.25	−0.13%	**0.76%**	−0.15%
Nikkei ($)	26.45%	0.35	22.13%	0.25	**2.21%**	1.08%	0.43%
porfolio	11.76%	1	8.10%	1	**1.89%**	**1.45%**	0.32%

excess return = 3.66%

sum = 3.66%

Figure 14.8   Result of the portfolio manager's choices

two parts, one reflecting the currency performance itself, and the second reflecting the actual asset allocation contribution, that is, the original one, minus the currency effect:

actual asset allocation = original asset allocation + currency attribution

To determine the currency attribution effect, we have

- first, to define *currency returns* r_{ci}, equal to 0 for each of the portfolio lines or sub-sets quoted in the portfolio currency, and, for the other ones, equal to the appreciation or depreciation of other currencies vis-à-vis the portfolio currency; this allows to compute the global currency return r_{cB} of the benchmark, as follows:

$$r_{cB} = \sum r_{cBi} \text{ with } r_{cBi} = w_{Bi} \times r_{ci}$$

- second, to compute, for each portfolio line or sub-set, the currency attribution effect, by using the same formula as for the asset allocation attribution (Eq. 14.3), but applied here on the currency impact $r_{cBi} - r_{cB}$:

$$currency\ attribution = \sum (w_{Pi} - w_{Bi}) \times (r_{cBi} - r_{cB})$$

and deduct this amount from the original asset allocation contribution, for obtaining the actual asset allocation contribution.

Coming back to our example, the portfolio is in USD, but the Nikkei sub-set has made its performance primarily in JPY, and during the year 2005, the JPY has depreciated by 12.69% against the USD. So that, for the Nikkei portfolio subset, the actual asset allocation contribution has to be reduced by the corresponding (negative, here) currency contribution. In Figure 14.9 we see that the sum of attribution effects is unchanged, but the actual asset allocation contribution is of 3.48% instead of 2.21%: the reduction to 2.21% is due to the loss on the currency.

| | PORTFOLIO | | BENCHMARK | | currency | attribution effects: | | | |
asset	asset r.	weight	asset r.	weight	risk	as. all.	stock s.	interact.	currency
SP 500	3.05%	0.45	3.84%	0.5	0	−0.19%	−0.40%	0.04%	0.00%
Nasdaq	5.65%	0.2	2.60%	0.25	0	−0.13%	0.76%	−0.15%	0.00%
Nikkei (in $	26.45%	0.35	22.13%	0.25	0.00%	*2.21%*	1.08%	0.43%	0.00%
portfolio	11.76%	1	8.10%	1	0.00%	*1.89%*	1.45%	0.32%	0.00%

excess return = 3.66%   = r_{cB} sum = 3.66%

Figure 14.9 Impact of the currency contribution

The methodology presented here is known as the Brinson's BHB model. There exist more sophisticated methods, see the further reading at the end of the chapter.

The Case of Bonds Portfolios

Here, too, the attribution is computed from the portfolio P excess return vis-à-vis its benchmark B. Bonds being traded OTC may present less liquidity than exchange traded stocks, so that portfolio bond prices may differ from index bond prices. In such cases, for attribution computation, the portfolio excess return must first be corrected by these "price effects", if any, that is, by replacing actual bond portfolio prices by their corresponding prices such as valued in B.

It is important to notice that the following performance attribution methodology does not take into account

- the constraints of the fund or portfolio market allocation decisions rules;
- the possible trading effects, on market traded prices in case of lack of liquidity;
- the currency effect if the portfolio involves bonds quoted in several currencies: in this case, the currency attribution methodology presented in the previous sub-section applies.

The methodology can be outlined as in Figure 14.10.

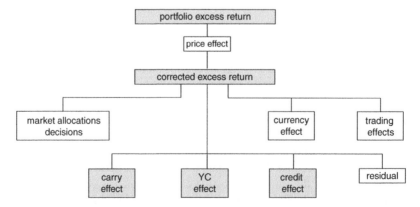

Figure 14.10 Performance attribution methodology

For an attribution calculated over a period Δt (1 month, 1 year, or whatever), the corrected excess return Δr can be broken down into the following components:

- a "carry effect" broken down into:
  - a coupon pro rata return: $c \times \Delta t$;
  - a "convergence" return, reflecting that the bond prices must converge to par: $(yield - c) \times \Delta t$;
- a "yield curve effect":
  - Given P weights w_{iP} and modified duration MD_P are different from those of B, that is, w_{iB} and MD_B, the impact of yield curve can be broken down into:
    - a "duration effect" return: by applying the w_{iB}s instead of the w_{iP}s to P and re-computing accordingly, compute a Δr due to the difference in MDs;
    - a "yield curve positioning" return: by applying a MD_B to P, compute a Δr due to the difference in weights;
- a "credit effect" made of:
  - a "swap spread" effect, resulting from changes in the spreads between risk-less and swap rates;
  - a "bond selection" effect, resulting from changes between bonds yields and swap yields.

Example. Let us consider:

- a portfolio P involving mainly corporate bonds in EUR;
- as the benchmark B, the Markit iBoxx EUR & GBP index;
- the net performance on 1 year (after deduction of management fees).

Applying the above breakdown would give, for example, the result shown in Figure 14.11.

There exist several variants of this decomposition, for example based on yield curve changes, sector breaking down, and so on,[4] but the one that is presented seems the more likely to cope with traditional bond portfolio management (given the key role of the duration), and avoids problems linked to precise yield curve changes determination.

14.1.5   Performance measures in case of non-normal returns

As seen in Chapter 4, Section 4.3.7, some circumstances justify to give up the basic hypothesis of the Portfolio Theory, namely, the normality of returns distribution. It is for example the case of exposures on derivatives, or more generally on any assets presenting some skewness and/or kurtosis. When it is the case, above performance measures cannot hold, in particular the Sharpe ratio and its variants.

The Sortino Ratio

The Sortino ratio is built in a similar way as the Sharpe ratio, except that, instead of dividing by the standard deviation of a series of past returns, the divisor is the downside semi-standard

---

[4] See for example Mathieu CUBILIE, "Fixed income attribution model", *The Journal of Performance Measurement*, Winter 2005/2006, pp. 46–63.

		P	B
return:		3.87%	3.24%
P excess return:		0.63%	
price effect:		-0.02%	
corr. excess return:		0.65%	
carry effect:		-0.045%	
coupon	-0.020%		
convergence	-0.025%		
YC effect:		0.160%	
duration	-0.020%		
YC positioning	0.180%		
credit effect:		0.520%	
swap spread	0.300%		
bond selection	0.220%		
residual:		0.01 5%	
sum:		0.650%	

Figure 14.11   Applying performance attribution to a bonds portfolio

deviation σ_d, that is, the standard deviation of the past *negative* returns. This makes sense when the portfolio is involving asymmetric instruments like options (cf. Chapter 4, Section 4.3.7):

$$Sortino\ ratio = \frac{r - r_f}{\sigma_d}$$

Example.   On the same data as for the previous Sharpe ratio example in Section 14.1.3, that is a fund invested in the S&P 500, data of year 2009, with a p.a. standard deviation of negative returns (downside semi-standard deviation) of 19.76%, the result is

$$Sortino\ ratio = \frac{17.96 - 2.004}{19.76} = 0.81$$

instead of 0.59 for the usual Sharpe ratio.

The Omega Ratio[5]

The Omega $\Omega(L)$ is the probability weighted ratio of returns above some threshold L, to returns below this threshold. Probability weighted returns above and below L can be deducted either from a given cumulative distribution F, or from the actual observation of past performances, through their histogram, what presents the advantage of escaping the problem of computing

---

[5] This ratio is also called "Gamma".

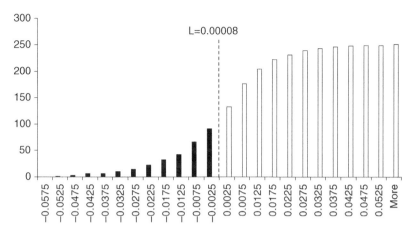

Figure 14.12   Cumulative distribution of the 251 returns

higher moments, if any. In the case of a given distribution F, and for the threshold L, $\Omega_F(L)$ is defined as

$$\Omega(L) = \frac{\int_L^\infty [1 - F(x)]dx}{\int_{-\infty}^L F(x)\,dx} \tag{14.4}$$

Usually, the threshold will be fixed at the risk-free return r_f.

As an example, based from discrete observations, let us consider the fund invested passively in the S&P 500, during year 2009, already used for the Sharpe and Sortino calculations. The 251 daily returns are not normally distributed, with a slight negative skewness of -0.063 (instead of 0 for a Gaussian) and a kurtosis of 1.976 (inferior to the value of 3 for a Gaussian, that is, a flatter distribution). Histogram intervals are of 0.005 or 0.5%, on a daily basis. The threshold L corresponds to $r_f = 2.004\%$ (cf. the Sharpe ratio example in Section 14.1.3), that is, 0.008% per day. The cumulative distribution of the 251 returns is shown in Figure 14.12.

The weighted value of F up to L (in black) $= 0.058367$, and of $(1 - F) > L$ (in white) $= 0.147251$, so that

$$\Omega = \frac{0.147251}{0.058367} = 2.52$$

If the data were distributed as a normal distribution, because its symmetry, with $L = $ its mean, from Eq. 14.4 the ratio would be $= 1$; if the distribution is not normal, the lower $[1 - F(x)]$ is below 1, and/or the higher L is above the mean, the lower the Ω, and conversely. In the example, $L = 0.008\%$ is well below the average daily return of the series, that is 0.0572%, that explains the $\Omega > 1$.

In particular, if $L = 0$, that is, if it separates positive from negative returns, the Omega ratio corresponds to what has been introduced as the "Bernardo–Ledoit gain-loss ratio".[6]

---

[6] See for example A. BERNARDO, O. LEDOIT, "Gain, loss and asset pricing", *The Journal of Political Economy*, Jan 2000, pp. 144–172.

14.2   VaR OR VALUE-AT-RISK

This section is mainly relative to a risk management tool with respect to *market* risk.[7] The last sub-section concerns the case of the *credit* risk.

The VaR is a risk measure that can be defined as the *estimated* possible *loss*, expressed as an *amount* of \$(or any other currency), that can suffer a position or group of positions in financial market instruments, over a given *horizon of time*, with respect to some given *probability level*, called *confidence level*. The VaR measure thus rests on an assessment about the probability distributions of the prices of the instruments that compose the related risky position.

Denoting c the confidence level, $1 - c = s$ the "significance level", and P a position (or exposure) value, VaR computed on this position, with a confidence level of c, and from t to a horizon of $t + \tau$, is such as

$$proba\,[P_t - P_{t+\tau} > VaR] = s = 1 - c \qquad (14.5)$$

In plain English, for a confidence level c of, for example, 99%, hence a significance level $s = 1\%$, there is 1% chance that the loss on the position is exceeding the VaR limit, and $c = 99\%$ chances that the loss is inferior to the VaR limit.

A Basic Example

Let us consider a fund having as a sole position \$100M invested in the S&P 500. From a series of 10 years past data of daily S&P 500 close prices, that is, 2510 observations, and corresponding log returns, it is possible to build the following distribution of these daily returns (data from 03/01/2000 to 02/26/2010). Histogram intervals are of 0.005 or 0.5%, on a daily basis. The data are shown in Figure 14.13 and the corresponding histogram is shown in Figure 14.14.

The answer to the question *how much this fund is likely to loss on the next day, or during 1 of the next 100 days, with a probability of 5%?* is a 1-day VaR at 95% confidence interval. From this series of 2510 data, the first 5% of losses (negative returns) represent round the cumulated first 126 observations on the left tail of the histogram. These first 126 observations approximately[8] cover the returns range of $-\infty$ to -0.0225 (between -0.025 and -0.02), see the gray data in Figure 14.13. The corresponding VaR is thus \$100M $\times$ 0.0225 = \$2.25M, corresponding to a loss of -2.25% or more. In other words, this portfolio has five chances in 100 to lose -2.25% or more, in one day.

We note from this example that

- the VaR amount being a possible loss associated to a probability level, it cannot be confused with a maximum possible loss. In practice, the determination of such a maximum loss turns out to be hard to quantify, because extreme tails of a distribution are too sensitive to the sample of data used to build the histogram;
- for the same reasons, with respect to possible higher losses beyond the VaR level, the VaR measure says nothing about the distribution of losses beyond this level;

---

[7] This section is partly inspired from Philippe JORION, *Financial Risk Manager Handbook*, 5th ed., 2009, John Wiley & Sons, Inc., Hoboken, and Moorad CHOUDHRY, *An Introduction to Value-at-Risk*, 4th ed., 2006, John Wiley & Sons, Ltd, Chichester.

[8] To make a more precise calculation, the width of the bins should be narrower than 0.5%, as used here.

bin	frequency	cumul.	bin	frequency	cumul.
				continued	
−0.1	0		0.01	342	2118
−0.095	0	0	0.015	169	2287
−0.09	3	3	0.02	97	2384
−0.085	0	3	0.025	52	2436
−0.08	0	3	0.03	23	2459
−0.075	1	4	0.035	13	2472
−0.07	0	4	0.04	17	2489
−0.065	1	5	0.045	6	2495
−0.06	2	7	0.05	4	2499
−0.055	2	9	0.055	4	2503
−0.05	6	15	0.06	0	2503
−0.045	4	19	0.065	3	2506
−0.04	6	25	0.07	2	2508
−0.035	8	33	0.075	0	2508
−0.03	20	53	0.08	0	2508
−0.025	34	87	0.085	0	2508
−0.02	56	143	0.09	0	2508
−0.015	106	249	0.095	0	2508
−0.01	183	432	0.1	0	2508
−0.005	292	724	0.105	1	2509
0	476	1200	0.11	1	2510
0.005	576	1776	*more*	0	2510

Figure 14.13   Distribution of daily returns of SP500 log returns (March 2000 to February 2010)

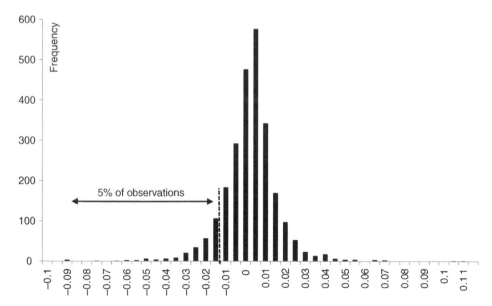

Figure 14.14   Histogram for Figure 14.13

- this procedure makes no hypothesis about the shape of the probability distribution of the returns, in this case surely not a Gaussian one;[9] it rather reflects the actual probability distribution of past returns;
- like in many comparable situations, this calculation is based on past market behavior, there is no reason to believe that the future will present the same probability distribution of returns: as it will be developed later on, there exist other VaR calculation methods, presenting various advantages and disadvantages compared with this one.

The VaR Parameters

- *Confidence level* "c": the higher confidence level, the higher the VaR: a loss that has only 1% of chances to occur, that is, a confidence level of $c = 99\%$, is of course more severe than the one having 5% chances to occur ($c = 95\%$). In the previous example, the 99% VaR is about \$4M, instead of \$2.25M, that is, 1% of the observations: 25 observations, is at the centre of the -0.04 bin on the graph.
- *Horizon of time*: the greater the horizon, the higher the VaR: for a same confidence level, the loss at risk is of course higher over a longer period of time. As it has been done for standard deviations (cf. Section 14.1.2), assuming the probability distribution of the returns is stationary;

$$\text{VaR on n days} = 1 - \text{day VaR} \times \sqrt{n}$$

The adequate choice of a time horizon mainly depends on the way the exposure remains unchanged over time: a portfolio subject to allocations changes on a very short term basis requires a 1-day VaR, while a more stationary exposure can support a 1-week or a 1-month one.

VaR Methods

In practice, VaR computation is more complicated than in the above basic example. The reasons are twofold:

- Depending on the nature of a risky instrument, one has to determine what are the *risk factors* likely to affect the instrument price; that can be a combination of interest rate, currency rate, volatility, and so on. And moreover, up to what extent one wants to refine the risk analysis: for example, in the case of a bond, restricting to the first-order derivative (duration), or going further (convexity).
- A VaR calculation applied separately to each subset of a portfolio exposure makes no sense, because of the correlation affecting the returns between these subsets. To limit the complexity of the calculation, it makes sense to keep as above risk factors a limited set of them, common to all or as much as possible different types of instruments composing the portfolio exposure, in order to compute a meaningful VaR for the entire portfolio.

There are three VaR methods, each of them having their own advantages and disadvantages:

1. Variance-covariance or delta-normal method, also called parametric or analytic method. As a preliminary step, the various ingredients of the portfolio must be decomposed into the

---

[9] The 2510 returns used for the example present a kurtosis of 7.81 and a skewness of -0.10.

selected set of risk factors, assuming a linear relationship; for a given position (or exposure) p_k, and a series of n risk factors f_i,

$$p_k = a_{k1}f_1 + \ldots + a_{ki}f_i + \ldots + a_{kn}f_n + \varepsilon(.)$$

where each of the f_i represents an amount of currency, for a given maturity. These cash flows must be discounted on the VaR calculation date. To avoid too many maturities, the calculation is grouped on a reduced set of "maturity buckets". For example, a coupon bond is decomposed into a series of 0-coupon bonds, that in turn are exposed to a series of 0-coupon rates (the yield curve), plus – in case of a portfolio involving foreign bonds – a cash position in spot forex.

This method supposes that the returns on the risk factors, computed from historical data,

- are normally distributed, with constant expectation and variance,
- and with a constant correlation between them,
- the portfolio return being a linear combination of Gaussian variables.

Hence, the portfolio risk is the square of its variance, as per Eq. 14.2:

$$\sigma_P^2 = \sum_i w_i^2 \sigma_i^2 + \sum_i \sum_{j \neq i} w_i w_j \sigma_i \sigma_j \rho_{ij}$$

As can be demonstrated, since the returns on the risk factors are posited Gaussian, so is it also for the portfolio. Therefore, the portfolio VaR calculation looks like at the end of the basic example, but instead of looking at the 5% threshold in the cumulated data – for VaR at 5% – it suffice to convert these 5% into the corresponding number of standard deviations, namely 1.645. This 1.645 σ gives the corresponding negative return (on the left tail of the Gaussian distribution for P), hence the corresponding VaR in amount of portfolio currency.

Example. For an exposure of \$100M, a portfolio returns distribution is presenting an average return μ of 10% and a standard deviation σ of 15%, on an annual basis. For a (5%, 1-year) VaR, the left hand tail of the distribution goes from $-\infty$ to:

$$\mu - 1.645\sigma = 0.1 - 1.645 \times 0.15 = -0.147$$

So that VaR $= \$100M \times -0.147 =$ a loss of \$14.7M, as shown in Figure 14.15.

Note that the constant variance hypothesis can be relaxed in favor of a GARCH model. This method is used, among others, by the J.P. Morgan's RiskMetrics tool.

1. The historical method is the one used in the initial basic example above. Instead of making assumptions on the probability distribution of the returns on the risk factors, these assumptions are replaced by statistical measures directly deducted from time series of past observations,[10] at the portfolio level: there is no use of a portfolio variance relationship as expressed here above. For a time series covering $t = 0$ to t,

$$P_t = P(f_{1,t} + f_{2,t} + \ldots + f_{n,t})$$

On the one hand, it allows escaping to hypotheses about these returns distributions (Gaussian, constant parameters) and instead captures "real" statistical features. But on the

---

[10] In the initial basic example, the only risk factor was the price change of the exposure in S&P 500.

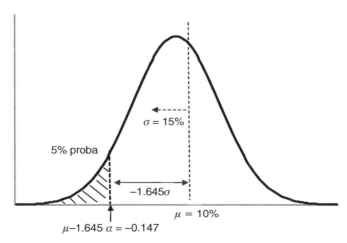

Figure 14.15   Determination of the VaR at 5%

other hand, these features are valid to the extent that the ones deducted from the series of past observations can apply to the future! Beyond this traditional stationarity problem, since the VaR is concerned with the (left-hand) extreme values of the distribution, it is even more crucial that the past observations would suit: for example the presence or the absence of previous crashes and rallies in the past data could affect the output of the method.

2. The Monte Carlo simulation method combines some of the principles of both preceding methods, plus the use of a simulation technique. From the first (variance-covariance) method, it keeps the assessment of a distribution, whatever it is, although the hypothesis of a normal distribution is prevailing in practice. But, instead of basing the calculation on a past history, it rather simulates a lot of risk factors values by Monte Carlo simulations (cf. Chapter 10, Section 10.4). Then, the VaR calculation is deducted like in the second method, but from the Monte Carlo simulations instead of from past observations.

Comparison Between the Three Methods

	variance-covariance	historical	MC simulations
P = f(f$_i$)	linear	no constraint	no constraint
proba distribution	Gaussian	no constraint	no constraint
computation	easy	medium	harder
VaR precision	excellent, but subject to validity of hypotheses	good if 1°) enough past history and 2°) if extrapolation makes sense	good, provided the number of simulations is great enough
major drawback	validity of the hypotheses, in particular at the left-hand tail level	risk of inadequacy of the past market behavior for application to the future	model risk

Note: there is an interesting variant to methods #2 and #3, although rarely used, but that makes sense for funds provided their strategy remains consistent over time: instead of determining the portfolio risk via the various instruments traded by the fund, it consists in working directly on the series of past performances of the fund. If the fund strategy is stable enough over time, the VaR calculation can be more accurate than through the traded instruments, first by avoiding the correlations problem, and second, if the composition of the fund portfolio is often modified.

Backtesting of the VaR

VaR methods presenting several weaknesses – starting with the adequate selection among several VaR methodologies – a VaR estimate needs to be tested a posteriori ("backtested"), to check to what extent it fits with actually observed losses larger than the VaR amount. As said by A. Brown[11], "*VaR is only as good as its backtest. When someone shows me a VaR number, I don't ask how it is computed. I ask to see the backtest*". The simple way to check it consists in counting the number N of times a portfolio presents losses that exceed the VaR number on a series of n successive VaR calculations. Depending on N/n, – called the "failure rate" – being higher or lower than the confidence level c associated with the VaR measures, the used VaR model is over- or underestimating the risk (the equality between N/n and c being obviously very unlikely).

The most popular backtest is the Kupiec's one, also called "POF (for *Proportion of failures*) test". In this test, the losses exceeding the VaR number are considered to be independently and identically distributed, so that N follows a binomial distribution $f(N)$ (that a loss may exceed or not the VaR number). For a confidence level c, the corresponding frequency of losses p is, repeating Eq. 14.5,

$$p = proba\,[P_t - P_{t+\tau} > VaR] = 1 - c, \tag{14.5}$$

so that the failure rate N/n could be used as an unbiased measure $\hat{p}$ of p, that would converge to $1 - c$ with n growing. $f(N)$ is therefore described by the binomial distribution

$$f(N) = C_n^N p^N (1 - p)^{n-N},$$

where C_n^N denotes the number of possible combinations of N failures and $(1 - N)$ "non-failures" on a total of n events. In algebra, one demonstrates that

$$C_n^N = \frac{n!}{N!\,(n - N)!}$$

(for example, in a simple case of $N = 2$ failures on a series of $n = 5$ observations we have $C_n^N = 120/12 = 10$).

To check if the failure rate N/n is, or not, statistically different from p, Kupiec uses a "log likelihood-ratio[12]" (denoted $log\Lambda$) test on the POF test, which consists in computing

$$log_{POF} = -2log\left(\frac{(1 - p)^{n-N} p^N}{\left[1 - \dfrac{N}{n}\right]^{n-N} \left(\dfrac{N}{n}\right)^N}\right)$$

---

[11] A. BROWN, *Private Profits and Socialized Risk – Counterpoint: Capital Inadequacy*, Global Association of Risk Professionals, June/July 08 issue. Cited by O. NIEPPOLA in his masters Thesis *Backtesting Value-At-Risk Models*, Helsinki School of Economics, 2008.

[12] See any book of statistics. This ratio is a log ratio of the likelihood that $p = \hat{p}$, divided by the likelihood that p is not $= \hat{p}$. To verify this, one must use the values of a $\chi 2$ distribution, if p is asymptotically Gaussian, which is the case of a binomial distribution.

A practical example of the Kupiec's test can be found for example in the Nieppola thesis (cf. reference in the Brown's footnote).

A test like the Kupiec test is called a test of "unconditional coverage". One can go further, by considering how the failure rate actually appears over time: do they occur in a random way, or are they clustered, or *conditioned* by some event? In such cases, one could expect that the VaR method is failing to capture some features of changes in market conditions. Hence the interest of *conditional coverage* tests. The most usual is the Christoffersen's test. This test is also based on a log-likelihood method, but extended to the probability that a failure observed on a given day (supposing daily VaR calculations) would depend on the outcome of a failure on the previous day. For more details, see Christoffersen's paper[13] and the already mentioned Nieppola thesis.

Variants of the VaR

Conditional VaR, or C-VaR

C-VaR is a measure of the *expected loss beyond the VaR level*, that is, if the VaR \$loss is exceeded. There may be some ambiguity in the word "beyond": for a VaR at a confidence level of c, noted VaR_c, on a variable loss x, one defines more precisely

- $CVaR^+$ ("upper C-VaR"), as $E(x)$ strictly exceeding VaR: also called "expected shortfall"
- $CVaR^-$ ("lower C-VaR"), as $E(x) \geq VaR$
- $\Phi(VaR)$, as the probability that loss $x \leq VaR$

because, practically speaking, the observations of x are discontinuous (cf. the previous histogram). So that *C-VaR* is a weighted average of *VaR* and *CVar$^+$*:

$$CVaR_c = \lambda VaR_c + (1 - \lambda) CVaR_c^+$$

with $0 \leq \lambda \leq 1$:

$$\lambda = \frac{(VaR) - c}{1 - c}$$

So that: $VaR \leq CVaR^- \leq CVaR \leq CVaR^+$.

Coming back to the initial basic example, having for VaR with $c = 95\%$ a value situated somewhere between the bins -0.025 and -0.02, let us simply consider that CVaR+ starts from bin -0.025 and below (down to -0.009). In such a case, $\Phi(VaR) = c$, so that $\lambda = 0$ and $CVaR_c = CVaR_c^+$. Zooming on the left-hand side of the data in Figure 14.16, we can compute the weighted average probability below the VaR level:

$$= \frac{\begin{array}{c} 3 \times 0.09 + 1 \times 0.075 + 1 \times 0.065 + 2 \times 0.06 + 2 \times 0.055 + 6 \times 0.05 + \\ 4 \times 0.045 + 6 \times 0.04 + 8 \times 0.035 + 20 \times 0.03 + 34 \times 0.025 \end{array}}{2510}$$

$$= 3.09\% \Rightarrow 1 - \text{day CVaR} = \$100M \times 3.09\% = \$3.09M,$$

that is, between the VaR of $c = 95\%$ and $c = 99\%$.

This example also enlightens the difficulty inherent in VaR calculations, inevitably linked to rare events and rare data, which are not necessarily the adequate image of a tail distribution.

---

[13] See Peter F. CHRISTOFFERSEN. Evaluating Interval Forecasts, *International Economic Review*, vol. 39, no. 4, November 1998.

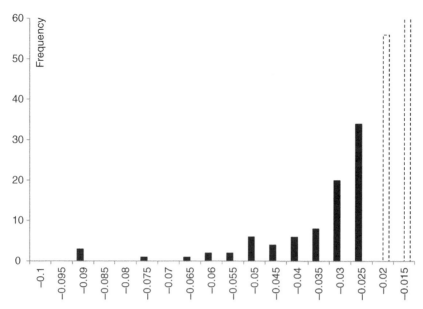

Figure 14.16   Enlargement of the left tail of the histogram, Figure 14.14

1. Relative VaR

For funds or portfolios that are clearly benchmarked to some reference index, it may be interesting to measure the following relative difference, in percent, called *relative VaR*:

$$\frac{fund\ VaR - benchmark\ VaR}{benchmark\ VaR} \times 100$$

2. Modified VaR

In a similar way as a four-moments CAPM has been developed (cf. Chapter 4, Section 4.3.7), we can consider a *modified VaR* (MVaR) involving the skewness and kurtosis of the underlying distribution of the related portfolio assets.[14] It consists in expanding the above variance-covariance method as follows: instead of quantifying the VaR as a nominal amount times the difference ($\mu - a\ number\ "n"\ of\ standard\ deviations\ corresponding\ to\ the\ selected$ *confidence interval*) or $\mu - n\sigma$, as in the above example and graph illustrating this VaR method, the difference becomes

$$\mu - \left[n + \frac{1}{6} \left(n^2 - 1 \right) skew + \frac{1}{24} \left(n^3 - 3n \right) \kappa - \frac{1}{36} \left(2n^3 - 5n \right) skew^2 \right] \sigma$$

where *sew* and κ denote the skewness and kurtosis of the distribution. Although more realistic, this MVaR is affected by the same troubles as already mentioned about the four-moments CAPM, namely the lack of stationarity of these skewness and kurtosis.

---

[14] See for example, L. FAVRE, J.GALEANO, "Mean-modified Value-at-Risk optimization with hedge funds", *Journal of Alternative Investments*, vol. 5, no. 2, 2002.

3. RaV

The Risk at Value is based on the same ingredients and methodology, but presents the problem back to front: instead of measuring the loss corresponding to a certain probability level, it measures the *probability level corresponding to a certain threshold of losses*. This threshold can be some percentage of the firm's revenue or equity, for example. To that extent, this approach is more appealing, to the extent that a fund, or a bank, is concerned by some key risk levels, or objectives in terms of loss occurrence, or a strict policy in terms of risk limits that – if exceeded – compel to adjust the exposure. However, this concept – mentioned in the risk management literature – seems not at all to be applied in practice. Besides, the RaV presents of course the same limits in the computation that the VaR.

Back to the initial basic example, let us compute what is the probability to suffer a loss of $\geq$ 5M at a 1-day horizon, supposing this threshold is crucial for the fund: 5M representing 5% of the fund, from the previous table it appears that a loss of -0.05 corresponds to a cumulated frequency of 15 observations, on a total of 2510, that is a probability of 0.60%: there is a RaV of 0.60% chance that the fund loose 5M (or more) at a 1-day horizon; this is the risk the fund may expect.

Important Remarks

- In line with its definition, the VaR amount must be carefully read, since it is function of both the horizon of time and of the probability level: a 95% VaR at + 1day has nothing in common with a 99% Var at + 1 week.
- The accuracy of VaR calculation is questionable: it is very sensitive to the number of observations on the left side of the probability distribution (effect of sampling variability). In particular, for a same number of data, a 99% VaR will obviously contain much less observations than a 95% VaR.
- In the very common case of a global VaR, that is, a VaR measure relative to a set of different positions (the case of a fund diversified into different strategies and allocations, a bank active in trading of many different instruments, etc.), the global VaR measure:
  - can be dangerously misleading if applied to instruments whom probability distribution clearly deviates from a Gaussian, such as long or short positions in options; or credit derivatives, where the crucial part of the distribution lies in the left tail;
  - is very sensitive to the changes in the underlying positions (case of active trading);
  - is very sensitive to the evolution of the correlation between different instruments, and even more if said instruments belong to the first sub-point above.

Credit VaR

Credit VaR is analogous to VaR, considering a potential loss due to a *credit default* instead of due to a market price move. Besides, the definition is the same as for VaR, that is, the maximum loss that can suffer an exposure, over a given horizon of time τ and with respect to a given probability level c. The defining formula holds:

$$proba\,[P_t - P_{t+\tau} > VaR] = c$$

provided $P_{t+\tau} < P_t$ here is due to a credit default, in lieu of a market price move.

For credit VaR, the usual horizon is $\tau = 1$ year. Indeed, modifying exposure to credit risk needs *a priori* more time than for market risk.

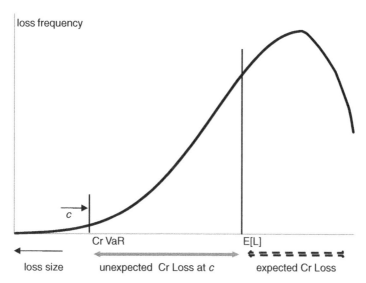

Figure 14.17   Credit VaR determination

To value a credit VaR, one can use the same methods as for VaR. However, the Gaussian distribution cannot be used here because credit losses rather show typically a left-hand or negative skewness, as in Figure 14.17.

This figure shows a typical frequency distribution of losses arising from credit default, with, first, the *expected* credit loss as presented in Chapter 13, Section 13.2.1:

$$E[L] = \sum E[h_i] \times ED_i \times (1 - v_i) = \sum q_i \times ED_i \times (1 - v_i)$$

Further to $E[L]$ is credit VaR, corresponding to an *unexpected* credit loss, at c. With respect to risk management, the expected credit loss amount should have to be lower than the profits of the bank or fund activities,[15] while the Credit VaR amount should not exceed the net asset value of the bank (or *economic capital*) or fund. A higher loss than the Credit VaR level may be viewed as likely to threaten the survival of the bank or fund, hence the tentatives to test such possibility by *stress tests*, although difficult to design properly (cf. the Nassim Taleb's "black swan").

Example. A fund has $100m of various exposures. Adequate Monte Carlo simulations allow to estimate that, over 1 year, the frequency of losses with $c = 99\%$ is 15%. For a global recovery rate (cf. Chapter 13, Section 13.1.4) of the exposure estimated at 40%, the 1-year Credit VaR is

$$credit\ VaR = \$100M \times 0.15 \times (1 - 0.40) = \$9M$$

Given the complexity of the task of modeling credit risk (cf. Chapter 13, Section 13.2.5), financial institutions generally use external systems, like CreditMetrics of J.P. Morgan for example.

---

[15] This is the rationale for pursuing these activities.

FURTHER READING

Carl R. BACON, *Practical Portfolio Performance Measurement and Attribution*, John Wiley & Sons, Ltd, Chichester, 2nd ed., 2008, 402 p.

Kevin DOWD, *Measuring Market Risk*, John Wiley & Sons, Ltd, Chichester, 2nd ed., 2005, 410 p.

Philippe JORION, *Financial Risk Manager Handbook*, John Wiley & Sons, Inc., Hoboken, 6th ed., 2010, 800 p.

Philippe JORION, *Value at Risk: The Benchmark for Controlling Market Risk*, McGraw-Hill, 3rd ed., 2007.

S.T. RACHEV, S.V. STOYANOV, F.J. FABOZZI, *A Probability Metrics Approach to Financial Risk Measures*, Wiley-Blackwell, 2011, 355 p.

15

Beyond the Gaussian hypothesis: potential troubles with derivatives valuation

This chapter has two parts:

- a review of alternatives to the Gaussian hypothesis, developed within other processes or models than the ones considered in the previous chapters;
- some views about criticisms and troubles that may arise from the various valuation methods of derivatives.

As you will see, these topics are somewhat related.

15.1 ALTERNATIVES TO THE GAUSSIAN HYPOTHESIS

The stochastic component of the processes considered up to now has always been based upon the normality of the returns distribution. Yet, several clues of non-normality may be observed from market time series, that encourage looking after alternative, more realistic hypotheses to the Gaussian distribution. The main issue will be that working on more complex distributions than the normal – requiring more than two parameters (the mean and the standard deviation) – implies quantifying the extra parameters that are themselves sources of error measurement, in such a way that the final result may well happen to be less reliable than the more simplistic, but more robust, hypothesis of normality...

The importance of the assumptions about the probability distribution of an asset price over time is evident in the case of derivatives valuation, as instruments which the value is affected by the future evolution of the underlying price. It is also relevant for spot instruments, within the framework of the Portfolio Theory (cf. Chapter 4, Section 4.3). In both cases, the main way is the hypothesis of a normal distribution of the returns, leading to a log-normal distribution of the prices. In this section we will review what are the most important alternatives to the Gaussian hypothesis.

15.1.1 Jump processes

Jump processes were developed to cope with underlyings subject to unanticipated prices changes that may occur suddenly, with some significant magnitude, such as:

- money market rates: impact of a central bank decision;
- forex: devaluations or sudden price changes;
- stocks: certain corporate actions;
- market crashes;

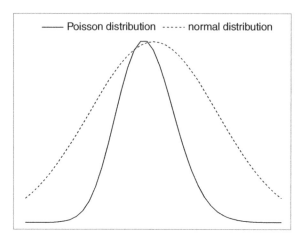

Figure 15.1   Poisson distribution compared with normal distribution

and more generally, significant, sudden market moves following the publication of unexpected market news, such as key economic statistical data. By nature, a process involving some Gaussian stochastic component, such as the usual geometric, general Wiener process, cannot involve prices jumps: starting from the discrete time form of this process (from Eq. 8.11b)

$$\Delta S = \mu S \Delta t + \sigma S \Delta Z$$

if we make $\Delta t \to 0$, changes in ΔS will become smaller and smaller. Hence, the usefulness of a specific process to describe the probability of a jump occurrence, that is typically the Poisson probability distribution Q. More specifically with respect to our topic, this distribution models the number n of random occurrences of an event – in our case, a jump – during a finite time interval of Δt, in function of a parameter λ that is the expected value (or mean) of said number of occurrences:

$$Q(n, \lambda) = \frac{1}{n!}\lambda^n e^{-\lambda}$$

In this process, λ is not only the expected value of the distribution, but also its variance. This, of course, restricts the interest of the following application. For a high enough λ (practically, >4), this distribution is bell-shaped in function of n, but distinct from a normal distribution (the approximation to a normal distribution needs a $\lambda > 1000$). In Figure 15.1, a Poisson distribution with $\lambda = 20$ (so that its standard deviation $= \sqrt{20} = 4.47$) is compared with a Gaussian with a standard distribution of 0.5.

As an application to option pricing, the "mixed jump-diffusion model" of Merton[1] is combining a general Wiener with a Poisson process:

$$\frac{dS}{S} = (\mu - \lambda k)\,dt + \sigma\,dZ + dQ$$

where Q is a Poisson process, independent from Z. Note that the σ of the Wiener process refers to the standard deviation of the returns out of the occurrence of jumps!

---

[1] See R.C. MERTON, "Option pricing when underlying stock returns are discontinuous", *Journal of Financial Economics*, 1976, 3, pp. 125–144.

Further calculations lead to European option prices that differ from the Black–Scholes. In the case of a call, for example, denoting C the Black–Scholes call price, $C = f(S, K, T, r, \sigma)$, and C_{MJD} the corresponding call price based on this mixed jump-diffusion process:

$$C_{MJD} = \sum_{j=0}^{\infty} \frac{e^{-\lambda T}(\lambda T)^j}{j!} C_j(\sigma'_j)$$

with

$$\sigma'_j = \sqrt{\sigma_{tot}^2 - \gamma_{tot}^2 + \frac{\gamma_{tot}^2}{\lambda}\left(\frac{j}{t}\right)}$$

where

σ_{tot} is the total volatility, including due to jumps: $\sigma_{tot} = \sigma + \sigma_{jumps}$
$\gamma = \sigma_{jumps}/\sigma_{tot}$.

As an example of combination between a general Wiener process and a Poisson process, let us start from one of the prices simulation of L'Oreal stock, used for the Monte Carlo simulation, in Chapter 10, Section 10.4 (on 90 days, starting from January 06). The data were

- initial stock price. €64.50
- annualized trend: 0.4375%
- annualized volatility: 11.9%

and the Monte Carlo simulation is performed on successive 9000 intervals Δts of a 1/100th of a day, by simulating a usual general Wiener process. By adding, in Figure 15.2, a random generated Poisson process of four equal jump sizes of €2 (to make them appear clearly), we obtain the result in Figure 15.3, as if the market has showed several bullish shocks.

Note that the Poisson component of the jump-diffusion process refers to the probabilistic occurrence of an event, here a jump *per se*, but cannot refer to varieties of jumps, in terms of various size and sign. Moreover, since the process is based on successive prices at time intervals of dt, the model cannot incorporate jumps that are usually observed between the close price of a trading session and the open price of the next trading session.

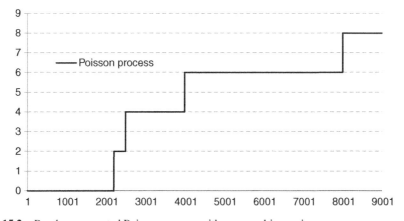

Figure 15.2   Random generated Poisson process with our equal jump sizes

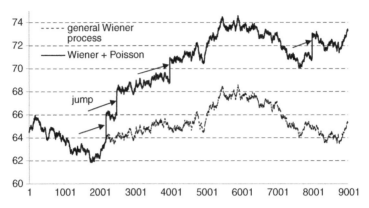

Figure 15.3   Wiener process versus Wiener + Poisson process

15.1.2   Gamma processes

Several processes call for a "gamma" process to allow for multiple jumps. The most well-known is the "variance gamma" process of Madan,[2] allowing for the recognition of kurtosis and skewness that may affect returns distributions. Applied to European option pricing, it may lead to the Black–Scholes as a particular limit case. We may introduce the model as follows:
   Starting from a general Wiener process (Eq. 8.11)

$$\frac{dS}{S} = \mu dt + \sigma dZ$$

but instead of keeping the drift μ as a constant, let us consider a process $\gamma(\mu, v, t)$, of variance v, modeling independent increments g over Δt: $g = \gamma(t + \Delta t) - \gamma(t)$. The probability density of these increments g is a function of μ, v, Δt, g and of $\Gamma(\mu^2 \Delta t/v)$, where $\Gamma(.)$ is the mathematical "gamma" function.[3] So that, in short, a variance gamma process X, involving a general Wiener process W and a $\gamma(v, t)$ process of unit mean, can be defined as

$$X(\mu, \sigma, v, t) = \mu\gamma(v, t) + \sigma W[\gamma(v, t)]$$

After integration, instead of leading to $S(t)$ as per Eq. 8.14,

$$S(t) = S(0)e^{\left(\mu - \frac{\sigma^2}{2}\right)t + \sigma\sqrt{t}Z(t)}$$

we obtain, in a risk-neutral world (with risk-less market rate r)

$$S(t) = S(0)e^{rt + X(\sigma, v, \mu, t) + \omega t}$$

where ω is a function of v, μ and σ. It appears that this model gives superior results to the Black–Scholes formula for pricing European options, but it needs for determining the variance v of the increments g – that is not easy in practice, since the skewness and kurtosis of returns are not stable over time (cf. Chapter 4, Section 4.3.7).

---

[2] See D.B. MADAN, P. CARR, E.C. CHANG, "The variance gamma process and option pricing", *European Finance Review*, 1998, vol. 2, pp. 7–105.

[3] The gamma function $\Gamma(n)$ is defined by

$$\Gamma(n) = \int_0^\infty e^{-x} x^{n-1}\, dx \quad with \quad \Gamma(n+1) = n\Gamma(n)$$

Finally, diffusion processes that involve jump discontinuities can be generalized by use of the more general class of continuous-time stochastic processes called *Lévy processes*, of which the Wiener, the Poisson and the gamma processes are particular cases (cf. *Further Reading*).

15.1.3 Other alternative processes

The search for other alternative underlying prices distribution is motivated by the observation of the smile phenomenon (cf. Chapter 12, Section 12.1.3) evidencing the unsuitability of the usual normal distribution for the returns, and the need to look after distributions fitting with observed skewness and kurtosis. Ways towards solutions explore too many directions, and present a complexity that exceeds the framework of this book. Also, we have no choice but to recognize that none such direction has succeeded in standing out in the markets.

To summarize these ways, let us mention (for more details, see the *Further Reading* at the end of the chapter):

- the use of four-moments distributions, such as the Student distribution, for example. As a matter of fact, although the Student distribution presents some skewness and kurtosis, these features, first, are function of its standard distribution, and second, cannot be adjusted to required values;[4]
- the use of a mixture of several normal distributions, to fit with a given set of observed volatilities;
- the application to the normal distribution, of *series expansions* (such as the well-known Taylor series, but specifically developed for application to probability distributions).

15.1.4 Fractional Brownian motion and non-linear models

Most of the processes considered in the previous chapters are linear, with the notable exception of the (G)ARCH family processes (cf. Chapter 9, Sections 9.5–9.7). The latter are non-linear in the sense that they involve an error term or white noise ε_t that is a non-linear function of the volatility. These (G)ARCH-type processes are modeling the conditional mean and variance of a financial time series, so that they can better be viewed as forecasting models (at least, for risk management purpose), unlike the traditional Wiener process and the models presented in the previous sections of this chapter.

Coming back to the starting point of our non-deterministic description of financial products, in Chapter 8, Section 8.2, we have defined the Brownian motion, or standard Wiener process (also called white noise) as per Eq. 8.2:

$$d\tilde{Z}(t) = \tilde{y}(t)\sqrt{dt}$$

where $y(t)$ is distributed as $\mathcal{N}(E = 0, V = 1)$, so that $Z(t)$ is distributed as $\mathcal{N}(E = 0, V = t)$, that is, with $STD = \sqrt{t}$. Because of the nature of $y(t)$, successive values of Z are independent; in discrete time, and abandoning the random subscript "~", we have

$$\Delta Z = \varepsilon\sqrt{\Delta t}$$

where ε is a so-called "random number", actually a number randomly selected from a normal density distribution. For two different times t and t', the covariance between two Brownian

---

[4] By the way, this is also the case of the log-normal distribution!

motions is necessarily 0, that is (cf. Eq. 8.5), $E[dZ(t).dZ(t')] = 0$. Now, we can generalize the Brownian motion to a fractional Brownian motion B^H, $H \in (0,1)$ having as covariance function

$$E[dZ(t) \times dZ(t')] = \frac{1}{2}(t^{2H} + t'^{2H} - |t - t'|^{2H})$$

The parameter H is called the Hurst coefficient.[5] As a particular case, if $H = \frac{1}{2}$, $cov_H(t, t') = 0$ and $B^{1/2}$ is our standard Brownian motion: the corresponding time series is (pure) random. But

- if $0 \leq H < 0.5$, the series is anti-persistent, or mean reverting: it can be shown that two successive Δts are negatively correlated;
- if $0.5 < H \leq 1$, the series is persistent or trending: two successive Δts are positively correlated.

Hence the idea of modeling financial time series by a kind of "generalized" general Wiener process (generalizing Eq. 8.11)

$$\frac{dS}{S} = \mu(t)dt + \sigma(t)dZ^H \tag{15.1}$$

that needs to significantly adapt the Itô lemma in particular, and the stochastic calculus in general (moreover, note that if $H \neq 1/2$, the time series are non-Markovian).

To illustrate the impact of H in the process described by Eq. 15.1, let us again start from one of the prices simulations of L'Oreal stock, used for the Monte Carlo simulation, in Chapter 10, Section 10.4 (on 90 days, starting from January 06). The data were:

- initial stock price. €64.50
- annualized trend: 0.4375%
- annualized volatility: 11.9%.

The Monte Carlo simulation is performed on successive intervals Δts of a 1/100th of a day, and by simulating a usual general Wiener process, that is, with $H = 0.5$ in Eq. 15.1 (in this example, μ and σ are constant). By discretizing, the stochastic term is

$$\sigma \varepsilon \sqrt{\Delta t}$$

In Figure 15.4, the corresponding prices trajectory is shown in bold, and we have recomputed the 90 daily prices with H equal to 0.2, 0.4, 0.6 and 0.8 corresponding to a stochastic term of respectively $\sigma \varepsilon \Delta t^{0.2}$, $\sigma \varepsilon \Delta t^{0.4}$, $\sigma \varepsilon \Delta t^{0.6}$ and $\sigma \varepsilon \Delta t^{0.8}$.

Note that if $H = 0$ (not shown on the graph), $\Delta Z = \varepsilon \Delta t^0 = \varepsilon$, and the simulated stock price converges to 0 (i.e., the average of the ε outcomes) after about 1/3rd of the first simulated day, that is, a strong reversion from the initial stock price. At the other extreme, if $H = 1$, $\Delta Z = \varepsilon \Delta t$, leading to too small ΔSs, so that simulated prices stay at about 64.50 (not shown on the graph for this reason). The graph is thus limited to the cases of $H = 0.2$, 0.4, 0.5 (the usual Wiener), 06 and 0.8.

---

[5] From the name of Harold E. Hurst, a hydrologist who modeled, in a similar way as our financial time series, the Nile river water levels, at the beginning of the twentieth century. For the calculation of the Hurst coefficient, see for example B. QIAN, K. RASHEED, *Hurst exponent and financial market predictability*, IASTED Conference, 2004.

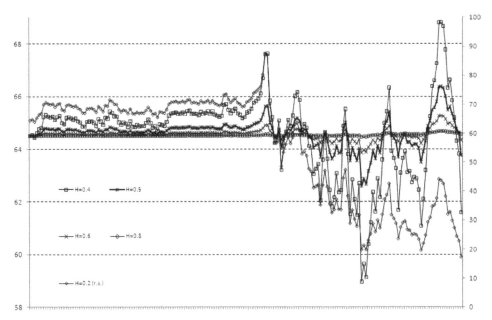

Figure 15.4   Impact of various Hurst coefficients on a Wiener process

For Hs below 0.5, the mean reversion is accompanied with the highest intermediate oscillations, so that for $H = 0.2$, the corresponding prices are on the right scale of the graph.

For Hs above 0.5 the impact of the (relatively small) trend becomes more and more effective, as shown in Figure 15.4.

Back to our initial topic, non-linearities in returns and volatilities result in different dynamics over time, caused by

- behavior of market participants failing to behave rationally (herding effects), leading to bubbles or crashes, or at least, overreactions;
- more generally, occurrence of asymmetry and kurtosis in market time series, and of some autocorrelation;
- market liquidity or restrictions problems.

These non-linearities are not questionable, although we may expect that they present variable intensity and features over time, so that their occurrence is understandably hard to model, and an adequate determination of the H coefficient is problematic. Regarding an *ex post* determination of H, practical problems are twofold:

- H undoubtedly varies over time; moreover, a precise determination needs a long enough time series of data, which is incompatible with the stability of the measure.
- We may expect that actual market behaviors are not purely persistent ($0.5 < H \le 1$), nor anti-persistent ($0 \le H < 0.5$), but rather a mixture of them, in variable proportions over time.

So altogether, for a given market and a given period of time, it is unrealistic to hope to select an adequate H value to apply a fractional Brownian motion such as per Eq. 15.1.[6]

15.1.5 Regime-switching models

The regime-switching approach is another way to build non-linear models. It consists in modeling two or more different possible processes for a given instrument behavior, each of these processes being associated with some probability of occurrence. This approach has first been developed to cope with "exogenous" causes of moving from one process to another one, for example, a central bank decision, or release of some key economic indicator, causing significant changes in a market behavior. But it has been widened to "endogenous" reasons, making so that the market behavior changes over time, resulting in a globally non-linear feature.

In its more general formulation, a stock, for example a regime-switching model, instead of determining a single process, like a general Wiener process leading to

$$\ln\frac{S(t + \Delta t)}{S(t)} \sim \mathcal{N}(\mu, \sigma)$$

one determines k process regimes p_t, $t = 1, \ldots, k$, are possible during the next Δt:

$$\ln\left(\frac{S(t + \Delta t)}{S(t)}|p_t\right) \sim \mathcal{N}(\mu_{p_t}, \sigma_t)$$

To simplify, by limiting k to 2, the above relationship means that there is some probability that the regime followed by the modeled return will be either the first or the second one:

$$\ln\frac{S(t + \Delta t)}{S(t)} \sim \begin{cases} \mathcal{N}(\mu_{1t}, \sigma_{1t}) \text{ with proba } q_1 \\ \mathcal{N}(\mu_{2t}, \sigma_{2t}) \text{ with proba } (1 - q_{1t}) \end{cases}$$

It means that the model coefficients may not be constant over some Δt. They must be of course estimated, even if both regimes are not observed, but we may determine some probabilistic statement about the likelihood of their occurrence, conditional on above-mentioned exogenous or endogenous parameters. Basically, such an approach makes more sense within the framework of a risk management concern, than a trading concern.

Existing switching processes are more often Markovian, that is, if the alternative possible processes are Markovian, but there are some researches based on non-Markovian regime-switching processes.

A similar step has been widely investigated from GARCH models (cf. Chapter 9, Section 9.6), instead of Wiener processes.

---

[6] For more details, see for example A. RUTTIENS, *Hurst coefficient, chaos theory and financial markets behavior*, Proceedings of the Conference organized by The Technical Analyst, "Automated trading 2009", London, 10/16/2009.

Regime-switching models have been developed for most of the financial instruments (currencies, interest rates, stocks, etc.), but also on volatilities, to cope with observed volatility smirks or sneers. For more details on these models, see the *Further Reading* section at the end of the chapter.

15.1.6 Neural networks

The use of so-called "neural networks", essentially as a non-parametric forecasting tool, was popular in the 1990s but did not produce convincing results. As such, this section has no "raison d'être". However, this technique seems to know a new lease of life, with some good reasons, in the successful area of high frequency ("algorithmic") trading. It is, however, hard to appraise its effectiveness, since its users, in case of positive performance, will most probably not publish on it. In short (for more details, see, e.g., *Further Reading*), neural networks (hereafter called "NN") may be defined as tools for *non-linear* forecasting.

To start from the well-known multiple linear regression, considering a series of n, $(1, \ldots, j, \ldots, n)$ data sets $\{(r_1, x_{11}, \ldots, x_{k1}, \ldots, x_{m1}), (r_2, x_{12}, \ldots, x_{k2}, \ldots, x_{m2}), \ldots, (r_j, x_{1j}, \ldots, x_{kj}, \ldots, x_{mj}), \ldots, (r_n, x_{1n}, \ldots, x_{kn}, \ldots, x_{mn})\}$, where r is the dependent variable and $x_1, \ldots, x_k, \ldots, x_m$ are the m independent variables, the corresponding multiple linear regression is the straight line

$$r = a + \sum w_k x_k + \varepsilon \tag{15.2}$$

where a is a constant, w_k are the weights and ε the residue. $\hat{a}$ and the $\hat{w}_k$ are the estimates of a and of the w_k, such as they minimize the quadratic residuals

$$\sum_{j=1}^{n} \left[r_j - \left(\sum \hat{w}_k x_k + \hat{a} \right) \right]^2$$

With the kind of display used in the NN world, the multi-linear regression can be described as in Figure 15.5, where the *transfer function* Ψ here is the linear equation 15.2. NNs involve non-linear regressions, by using a non-linear transfer function (often a sigmoid function). This scheme looks like a neuron, hence the name of "neural" network. The simplest NN, presented

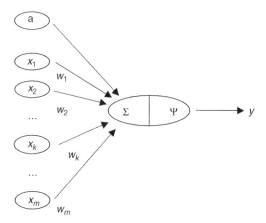

Figure 15.5   Diagram of a neural network performing a multi-linear regression

here, is made of a single "layer", to pass from the inputs to *y*. In practice, NNs include one or several intermediate (called "hidden") layers, allowing for more than one transfer function. Also, the technique often involves filtering (Kalman filters, or others). To run the NN, we determine the coefficients of the model (the regression parameters) from a subset of the data, in a "learning" phase; then the model is applied to another subset of the data, to check its validity.

The major problem with the application of NNs to forecast financial time series is that, as has already appeared in previous sections, financial time series are all but stable in their behavior over time. Hence the revival of this technique, aiming at applying it short term as a tool for market microstructure analysis.[7]

15.2 POTENTIAL TROUBLES WITH DERIVATIVES VALUATION

It's puzzling why bankers have come up
with these new ways to lose money when
the old ways were working so well.
  John STUMPF, CEO Wells Fargo[8]

Throughout this book, we have presented the main quantitative methods to value financial instruments, and outlined some more sophisticated ones, that represent the unceasing research to improve them. With respect to trading and to risk management activities, it is wise to hold on to an equilibrium point that consists in both favoring a grounded computation, and in keeping in mind that quantitative methods are limited by the hypotheses needed for building them, so that their accuracy and application area are to be considered very cautiously.

15.2.1 General

Let us start by looking over the hypotheses of the Portfolio Theory, as listed in Chapter 4, Section 4.3.1.

- Hypotheses related to financial assets:
  - *Asset returns* r *are modeled by a random variable, distributed as a Gaussian probabilities distribution, fully determined by its two first moments* – as has been shown in Section 15.1, but also in Chapters 4, 9, 11 and 12, there are many variant, non-Gaussian models, that are subject to an uneasy trade-off between, on the one hand, a more realistic description of the actual distribution, and, on the other hand, a higher degree of difficulty to adequately value – especially in the course of the time – the additional parameters needed. A contrario, the Gaussian hypothesis presents an indisputable robustness, that may be dangerously seductive.
  - *Returns of different financial assets* i *and* j *are correlated by the linear correlation coefficient* ρ_{ij} – as seen in Chapter 12, Section 12.4. Until now (2012), there is no satisfying model for the correlation. Moreover, correlation is significantly changing over time, so that coping with correlation is a serious issue, both for trading and for risk management (a.o. for VaR calculation).

---

[7] For an in-depth study of this field, see for example the PhD thesis in Applied Sciences of S. DABLEMONT, *Forecasting of high frequency financial time series*, Louvain University (Belgium), 2008 (available on the web).
[8] Quoted by Satyajit DAS, in "Tales of leverage", *RISK*, July 2009, pp. 74 and 75.

- *Markets are efficient* – well . . . at least to the extent that they are liquid enough, in particular on the secondary market; this happens not to be the case for many instruments: some narrow spot markets, exotic derivatives, structured products, and many credit derivatives. This topic is closely related to the investors' rationality hypothesis (cf. next).
- *The theory is built on mid prices; various costs such as brokerage fees, taxes, and so on are not taken into account* – there is much research about the impact of such costs, showing their importance.
- Hypotheses related to investors' behavior:
  - *Investors are rational* and *investors are characterized by some degree of risk aversion* – unfortunately, investors are not so rational;[9] in particular, kurtosis (cf. Section 15.1.3), market overreaction, and so on shows some lack of rationality. Hence the vast research area about behavioral finance[10] (cf. *Further Reading*).
  - *Investors' decisions are limited to the next (single) period of time* – although most of this book has shown that this is, in itself, an ambitious goal, the reality of financial market activities is not restricted to the next period of time. A generalization to multi-period models has long been studied, with the aim of developing an "event-tree" that allows some financial equilibrium to be determined; this approach led to consideration of a stochastic economy,[11] but we have to admit that these works lack practical issues. Hence the troubles that may occur each time traders and risk managers have to reconsider their positions and actions.

15.2.2 Continuous time versus discrete time

For the sake of tractability, the vast majority of quantitative models considered throughout this book are designed in a continuous time framework, as diffusion processes. However, the reality of financial markets and their data are definitively discontinuous. This may lead to a wide range of problems:

First, if we compare a discrete sub-sample extracted from a continuous-time process, and a sample of discrete market data observations, with the same Δt, how can we detect that one is coming from a diffusion process, but not the other? More practically, by considering discrete market data, can we conclude that the observed discontinuities may result from the discretization of a continuous-time process – which would authorize development of diffusion processes as the ones presented in the course of this book – or do we have to consider that they result from some non-diffusion behavior (such as in a jump-diffusion model)? Y. Aït-sahalia has made an interesting study about this problem, and about its consequences in derivative pricing.[12]

Second, in many cases, typically relating to the use of "tick data" in micro-structure models (cf. Section 15.1.6 and Chapter 12, Section 12.3), the market data are not following one another in equal time intervals, but in successive time intervals of *random* length. The problem of

---

[9] However, irrational expectation is not necessarily problematic, see this short but surprising paper by R. ROLL (one of the authors of the APT model), see Chapter 4, Section 4.3.5, "Rational infinitely lived asset prices must be non-stationary", *Journal of Banking & Finance*, vol. 26, no. 6, 2002, pp. 1093–1097.

[10] See a good introduction to behavioral finance can be found in M, SEWELL, *Behavioural Finance*, University of Cambridge, working paper, rev. 2010, which provides a detailed bibliography. Also, Arnold S. WOOD (Ed.), *Behavioral Finance and Investment Management*, CFA Institute, 2010.

[11] See for example, B. CORNET, A. RANJAN, *Existence of financial equilibria in a multi-period economy with restricted participation*, Paris School of Economics and University of Paris 1, working paper, 2010.

[12] Y. AÏT-SAHALIA, "Telling from discrete data whether the underlying continuous-time model is a diffusion", *Journal of Finance*, vol. LVII, no. 5, 2002, pp. 2075–2112.

"sampling randomness" has proved to be non-negligible in the estimation of the parameters of usual diffusion processes (for example, the drift and the volatility of a general Wiener process), and affects these estimations more seriously than the "sampling discreteness" considered in the previous paragraph.[13]

15.2.3 Consequences for option pricing

Option pricing models presented in Chapters 10 and 11 are based on the technique of the option replication through a riskless (@ risk-free rate r) portfolio that is continuously adjusted, as for example in the case of the Black–Scholes formula, by combining Eq. 10.3b and Eq. 10.5,

$$d\Pi = -dC + \frac{\partial C}{\partial S}dS = r\Pi dt$$

leading to the delta hedging technique (cf. Chapter 10, Section 10.5.1, the "delta-gamma neutral" management), implying a continuous, dynamic option replication. In practice, this method is subject to serious issues,[14] among others:

- it cannot apply to non-financial commodities (it is impossible to go short in them), or to financial commodities that are not liquid enough;
- dynamic replication is actually made on a discrete basis, and assumes that the underlying price is varying on a continuous basis, which is not necessarily always the case;
- it hardly applies to complex exotic derivatives and structured products.

15.2.4 Risk management issues

Generally speaking, the risk management policy of a firm (bank, fund or a corporation) can be developed on the basis of the relationship linking the occurrence of losses (represented here by their frequency) to the size of losses (expressed for example in $). This relationship is represented in Figure 15.6 as an arbitrary curve, but is realistic in its look (frequency is decreasing with higher losses).

For the sake of simplicity, let us limit our focus to market risk. We can distinguish three main subsets on this graph:

- Zone "I": up to the level of expected value of the losses, these must arguably be able to be covered by the expected profits of the market activity of the firm. If not, there is no rationale for maintaining the activity.
- Zone "II": there is some higher, unexpected, loss level corresponding to the maximum financial capacity of the firm, before going bankrupt.
- Zone III: to care for the highly improbable occurrence of losses above this maximum level, one has not found anything but "stress tests". The problem – explored by Nassim Taleb in his famous book "The Black Swan"[15] – is that it is almost impossible to guess what should have to be tested. Indeed, an abnormally huge loss cannot be caused but by a rare, unexpected event, that could have been hardly anticipated (if it was the case, it could even have resulted in a smaller loss) and tested beforehand.

---

[13] See Y. AÏT-SAHALIA, P.A. MYKLAND, "The effects of random and discrete sampling when estimating continuous-time diffusions", *Econometrica*, vol. 71, no. 2, 2003, pp. 483–549.

[14] For more about these issues, see E. DERMAN, N. TALEB, "The illusion of dynamic replication", *Quantitative Finance*, vol. 5, no. 4, 2005, pp. 323–326.

[15] Nassim N. TALEB, *The Black Swan*, 2nd ed., Random House, 2010, 480 p.

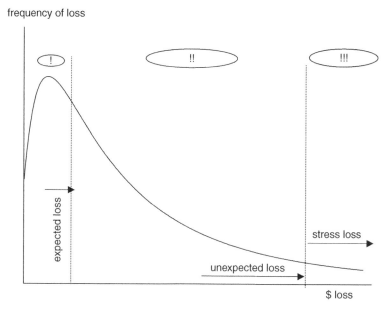

Figure 15.6   Breaking down a losses distribution in three subsets

This last consideration enlightens the crucial importance of the "fat tails" in the actual distribution of market returns or prices.

Model Risk

First, the limits of processes and quantitative models used to value financial instruments, especially derivatives, have been widely emphasized in the previous chapters of this book. They are limited in two ways:

- with respect to the validity, or applicability, of their hypotheses;
- with respect to some specific product (a pricing model for an American swaption is not necessarily applicable to Bermudan options).

Second, we must distinguish between "exogenous" models and "endogenous" models: a forward theoretical (fair) price is computed from other sources than existing forward market prices. This is not the case, practically speaking, with credit derivative pricing (cf. Chapter 13, Section 13.2). Evidently, an endogenous model is incomparably riskier than an exogenous model.

Third, for some complex options such as swaptions, for example, if we consider the case of different, competing option models, that are calibrated on the same set of existing liquid market prices, the obtained option prices will be equivalent, but not their dynamics, so that the option sensitivities may well significantly vary among them.[16]

---

[16] See M. HENRARD, Swaptions: 1 price, 10 deltas, and . . . 6 ½ gammas, *Wilmott Magazine*, April 2011, pp. 48–57.

Here is a *tentative* classification of the model risk regarding options:

risk level:	product:	causes of risk:
min	vanilla options on stocks, currencies	some model risk on - very short maturities ($<$ 1 week) - very long maturities ($>$ 2–3 years) - lack of liquidity - temporary skewness - kurtosis
↗	vanilla options on bonds	when option maturity is too much nearby bond redemption
↗	options on money market rates (« IRG »)	underlying behavior, too much affected by central banks – succession of small rate variations and sudden big moves ($\rightarrow$ not Gaussian)
↗	long term interest rate options: caps, floors	- mean reversion - usual long maturity
↗	2nd generation options on above underlyings	- lack of price accuracy, $\rightarrow$ widen the spread - in case of lack of liquidity
↗	swaptions	- no fully satisfactory model, even unsatisfactory for American or Bermudan swaptions
↗	options on baskets	- impact of (un-modeled) correlation
MAX	credit derivatives (optional component) - tranches	- lack of a satisfactory model - lack of liquidity - + impact of (un-modeled) correlation

Moreover, derivative pricing methods involving a random variable have probably become so common that most of the practitioners forget that any derivative "price" is affected by a standard error and should be associated with a confidence interval. Since a price is, in the most general case, a function $f(\mu, \sigma)$, where μ and σ are actually available as $\hat{\mu}$ and $\hat{\sigma}$ estimators, $f(.)$ is actually affected by some estimation error, that can vary in importance, depending on the kind of priced derivative and on which kind of market. Ideally, this estimation error should be within the bid–ask spread, but as a matter of fact, this is almost never checked by market practitioners ... This is a marginal aspect of the more general *model risk* problem.

More generally, Jarrow has developed some general but very useful considerations about model risk in an article devoted to risk management models, but valid for any kind of (financial) mathematical model.[17] In his article, Jarrow is distinguishing between statistical and theoretical models: the former ones refer to modeling a market price or return evolution, based on historical data, such as a GARCH model. What is usually developed as "quantitative models" by some fund or portfolio managers, also belong to statistical models. On the other hand, theoretical models aim to evidence some causality based on a financial/economic reasoning, for example the Black–Scholes formula. Both types of model imply some assumptions: Jarrow distinguishes between robust and non-robust assumptions, depending on the size of the impact when the assumption is slightly modified. The article then develops pertinent considerations

---

[17] Robert A. JARROW, Risk management models: construction, testing, usage, *Johnson School Research Paper Series* no. 38, 2010, March 15, 2011.

about testing, calibrating and using a model. Needless to say, the way models are built and applied in real financial markets activity are not necessarily fulfilling Jarrow's wise precepts . . .

Finally, it should be emphasized that the model risk, affecting the valuation of market instruments in the case of a "Marking-to-model" in lieu of a Mark-to-market, has a crucial impact on the accounting, and therefore on the equity determination, of major actors, like banks . . .

Market Liquidity Risk

This point has also been evidenced throughout this book. We must of course distinguish the structural liquidity from a temporary liquidity (impossible to continue trading). In the first case, the lack of liquidity is obviously restricting to some extent the applicability of models based on the hypothesis of market liquidity.

In the second case, a temporary lack of liquidity will affect dynamic hedging (cf. Section 15.2.3), but more dramatically, the trading of instruments priced with an endogenous model; as an example, the trading of asset backed securities linked to "subprime" credits was temporarily suspended in summer 2007, because of the lack of market prices references.

The "Position Risk" Concept[18]

What makes the difference between a $100 million exposure in a bond, a stock or a complex derivative instrument? The trader and/or the risk manager have normally done whatever is best to take care of the market risk (a.o., the volatility) of such positions. But, as has been emphasized, the liquidity risk and the model risk remain pervasive, with almost no way to value and to protect against. When quantifying is not possible, a usual statistic approach consists of replacing the quantification by a ranking. Similarly here, failing to quantify the liquidity and the model risks, we may at least weight each of them by a – even basic – coefficient, going from 0 (maximum illiquidity, or maximum model risk) to 1 (huge liquidity, or no model risk) and produce a "position risk" coefficient c globalizing both of them. For a given exposure E in $, considered ahead of both these risks, the actual position that would be actually taken would amount to $c \times E$.

By Way of Conclusion

Throughout this book, many formulae, models and quantitative techniques have been presented, without – as much as possible – dodging having to warn about their validity limitations. The reason for these warnings is well summarized by T. Coleman:[19] "Overconfidence in numbers and quantitative techniques and in our ability to represent extreme events should be subject to severe criticism because it lulls us into a false sense of security". Finally, the only wise way in trading and risk management should consist of adequately restricting exposure to associated risks, that is, the opposite of the observed trend in too many financial institutions, encouraging leverage instead (or feigning to ignore it), pushed by the dictatorship of greed and the objective of return on equity.

---

[18] See Alain RUTTIENS, *Pour contribuer à réduire le risque de pertes dans les activités de marché: la gestion d'actifs et le risque de position*, AGEFI Luxembourg, October 2008 (in French).
[19] Thomas S. Coleman, *A Practical Guide to Risk Management*, Research Foundation of CFA Institute, 2011.

FURTHER READING

H. Kent BAKER, John R. NOFSINGER, *Behavioral Finance – Investors, Corporations, and Markets*, John Wiley & Sons, Inc., Hoboken, 2010, 757 p.

Ph. H. FRANSES, D. VAN DIJK, *Non-Linear Time Series Models in Empirical Finance*, Cambridge University Press, 2000, 296 p.

E. JONDEAU, S.H. POON, M. ROCKINGER, *Financial Modeling under Non-Gaussian Distributions*, Springer, 2010, 560 p.

T. LYNCH, J. APPLEBY, *Large Fluctuation of Stochastic Differential Equations: Regime Switching and Applications to Simulation and Finance*, Lap LAMBERT Academic Publishing, 2010, 240 p.

Paul D. MCNELLIS, *Neural Networks in Finance*, Academic Press, 2005, 256 p.

Stefan ROSTEK, *Option Pricing in Fractional Brownian Markets*, Springer-Verlag, 2009, 137 p.

Wim SCHOUTENS, *Lévy Processes in Finance – Pricing Financial Derivatives*, John Wiley & Sons, Ltd, Chichester, 2003, 196 p.

P. WILMOTT, H. RASMUSSEN (eds) *New Directions in Mathematical Finance*, John Wiley & Sons, Ltd, Chichester, 2002, 256 p.

Bibliography

Leif B.G. ANDERSEN, Vladimir V. PITERBARG, *Interest Rate Modeling*, Atlantic Financial Press, 2010.

Kerry BACK, *A Course in Derivative Securities*, Springer, 2010, 370 p.

Carl R. BACON, *Practical Portfolio Performance Measurement and Attribution*, John Wiley & Sons, Ltd, Chichester, 2nd ed., 2008, 402 p.

Richard T. BAILLIE, Patrick C. McMAHON, *The Foreign Exchange Market, Theory and Econometric Evidence*, Cambridge University Press, 1990, 276 p.

H. Kent BAKER, John R. NOFSINGER, *Behavioral Finance – Investors, Corporations, and Markets*, John Wiley & Sons, Inc., Hoboken, 2010, 757 p.

Tomas BJORK, *Arbitrage Theory in Continuous Time*, Oxford University Press, 2009, 512 p.

Antulio N. BOMFIM, *Understanding Credit Derivatives and Related Instruments*, Academic Press, 2004, 368 p.

Damiano BRIGO, Fabio MERCURIO, *Interest Rate Models – Theory and Practice*, Springer Finance, 2nd, ed., 2006, 1037 p.

Patrick J. BROWN, *Bond Markets: Structures and Yield Calculations*, ISMA Publications, 1998, 96 p.

Gerald W. BUETOW, Frank J. FABOZZI, *Valuation of Interest Rate Swaps and Swaptions*, John Wiley & Sons, Inc., Hoboken, 2000, 248 p.

Galen BURGHARDT, Terry BELTON, *The Treasury Bond Basis*, McGraw-Hill, 3rd ed., 2005, 320 p.

John Y. CAMPBELL, Andrew W. LO, A. Craigh MACKINLAY, *The Econometrics of Financial Markets*, Princeton University Press, 1996, 632 p.

George CHACKO, Anders SJOMAN, Hideto MOTOHASHI, Vincent DESSAIN, *Credit Derivatives*, Pearson Prentice Hall, 2006, 272 p.

Moorhad CHOUDHRY, *Analysing and Interpreting the Yield Curve*, John Wiley & Sons, Singapore, 2004, 300 p.

Moorhad CHOUDHRY, *Yield Curve Analytics*, Butterworth-Heinemann, 2004, 352 p.

Kevin B. CONNOLLY, *Pricing Convertible Bonds*, John Wiley & Sons, Ltd, Chichester, 1998, 268 p.

Carl DE BOOR, *A Practical Guide to Splines*, Springer-Verlag, rev. ed., 2001.

Frans DE WEERT, *Exotic Options Trading*, John Wiley & Sons, Ltd, Chichester, 2008, 212 p.

David F. DeROSA, *Currency Derivatives – Pricing Theory, Exotic Options, and Hedging Applications*, John Wiley & Sons, Inc., Hoboken, 1998, 387 p.

Livingston DOUGLAS, *Yield Curve Analysis*, New York Institute of Finance, 1988, 300 p.

Kevin DOWD, *Measuring Market Risk*, John Wiley & Sons, Ltd, Chichester, 2nd ed., 2005, 410 p.

Darrell DUFFIE, *Dynamic Asset Pricing Theory*, Princeton University Press, 2001, 472 p.

Darrell DUFFIE, *Security Markets: Stochastic Models*, Academic Press Inc, 1988, 250 p.

E. ELTON, M. GRUBER, S. BROWN, W. GOETZMANN, *Modern Portfolio Theory and Investments Analysis*, John Wiley & Sons, Inc., Hoboken, 2006, 752 p.

R.F. ENGLE, D.L. McFADDEN (eds) *Handbook of Econometrics*, Elsevier, 1994.

Frank FABOZZI, *The Handbook of Fixed Income Securities*, McGraw-Hill, 7th ed., 2005, 1500 p.

Frank FABOZZI, *Fixed Income Mathematics*, McGraw-Hill, 4th ed., 2005, 600 p.

Frank J. FABOZZI, Anand K. BHATTACHARYA, William S. BERLINER, *Mortgage-Backed Securities: Products, Structuring and Analytical Techniques*, John Wiley & Sons, Inc., Hoboken, 2007, 336 p.

Frank J. FABOZZI, Roland FUSS, Dieter G. KAISER, *The Handbook of Commodity Investing*, John Wiley & Sons, Inc., Hoboken, 2008, 986 p.

Paul FAGE, *Yield Calculations*, CSFB, 1986, 134 p.

Desmond FITGERALD, *Financial Futures*, Euromoney, 1993.

Richard R. FLAVELL, *Swaps and Other Derivatives*, 2nd ed., John Wiley & Sons, Ltd, Chichester, 392 p.

Sergio M. FOCARDI, Frank J. FABOZZI, *The Mathematics of Financial Modeling and Investment Management*, John Wiley & Sons, Inc., Hoboken, 2004, 800 p.

Ph. H. FRANSES, D. VAN DIJK, *Non-Linear Time Series Models in Empirical Finance*, Cambridge University Press, 2000, 296 p.

Dariusz GATAREK, Przemyslav BACHERT, Robert MAKSYMIUK, *The Libor Market Model in Practice*, John Wiley & Sons, Ltd, Chichester, 2006, 290 p.

Helyette GEMAN, *Commodities and Commodity Derivatives – Modelling and Pricing for Agricultural, Metals and Energy*, John Wiley & Sons, Ltd, Chichester, 2005, 416 p.

Helyette GEMAN, *Insurance and Weather Derivatives – From Exotic Options to Exotic Underlyings*, RISK Books, 1999, 300 p.

Espen Gaarder HAUG, *The Complete Guide to Option Pricing Formulas*, Irwin Professional Publishing, 1997, 232 p.

Lawrence GALITZ, *Financial Times Handbook of Financial Engineering*, FT Press, 3rd ed., 2011, 480 p.

Robert A. HAUGEN, *Modern Investment Theory*, Prentice Hall, 4th ed., 1996, 748 p.

Peter JACKEL, *Monte Carlo Methods in Finance*, John Wiley & Sons, Ltd, Chichester, 2002, 222 p.

Robert JARROW, Andrew RUDD, *Option Pricing*, Irwin, 1987, 235 p.

E. JONDEAU, S.H. POON, M. ROCKINGER, *Financial Modeling under Non-Gaussian Distributions*, Springer, 2010, 560 p.

Philippe JORION, *Financial Risk Manager Handbook*, John Wiley & Sons, Inc., Hoboken, 6th ed., 2010, 800 p.

E. JURCZENKO, B. MAILLET (eds), *Multi-Moment Asset Allocation and Pricing Models*, John Wiley & Sons, Ltd, Chichester, 2006, 233 p.

Ioannis KARATZAS, Steven E. SHREVE, *Methods of Mathematical Finance*, Springer, 2010, 430 p.

Donna KLINE, *Fundamentals of the Futures Market*, McGraw-Hill, 2000, 256 p.

Tze Leung LAI, Haipeng XING, *Statistical Models and Methods for Financial Markets*, Springer, 2008, 374 p.

Raymond M. LEUTHOLD, Joan C. JUNKUS, Jean E. CORDIER, *The Theory and Practice of Futures Markets*, Stipes Publishing, 1999, 410 p.

Bob LITTERMAN, *Modern Investment Management – An Equilibrium Approach*, John Wiley & Sons, Inc., Hoboken, 2003, 624 p.

T. LYNCH, J. APPLEBY, *Large Fluctuation of Stochastic Differential Equations: Regime Switching and Applications to Simulation and Finance*, LAP LAMBERT Academic Publishing, 2010, 240 p.

A.G. MALLIARIS, W.A. BROCK, *Stochastic Methods in Economics and Finance*, North-Holland, 2nd ed., 1981, 324 p.

Paul D. McNELLIS, *Neural Networks in Finance*, Academic Press, 2005, 256 p.

Robert MERTON, *Continuous-Time Finance*, Wiley-Blackwell, 1992, 752 p.

Imad A. MOOSA, Razzaque H. BHATTI, *The Theory and Empirics of Exchange Rates*, World Scientific Publishing Company, 2009, 512 p.

Salih N. NEFTCI, *An Introduction to the Mathematics of Financial Derivatives*, Academic Press, 2nd ed., 2000, 527 p.

Roger B. NELSEN, *An Introduction to Copulas*, Springer, 2010, 284 p.

Adel OSSEIRAN, Mohamed BOUZOUBAA, *Exotic Options and Hybrids*, John Wiley & Sons, Ltd, Chichester, 2010, 392 p.

Pamela PETERSON-DRAKE, Frank J. FABOZZI, *Foundations and Applications of the Time Value of Money*, John Wiley & Sons, Inc., Hoboken, 2009, 298 p.

S.T. RACHEV, S.V. STOYANOV, F.J. FABOZZI, *A Probability Metrics Approach to Financial Risk Measures*, Wiley-Blackwell, 2011, 355 p.

Riccardo REBONATO, *Volatility and Correlation: The Perfect Hedger and the Fox*, John Wiley & Sons, Ltd, Chichester, 2nd ed., 2004, 864 p.

Riccardo REBONATO, *Volatility and Correlation, in the Pricing of Equity, FX and Interest-Rate Options*, John Wiley & Sons, Ltd, Chichester, 1999, 360 p.

Riccardo REBONATO, *Interest-Rate Option Models – Understanding, Analyzing and Using Models for Exotic Interest-Rate Options*, John Wiley & Sons, Ltd, Chichester, 2nd ed., 1998, 546 p.

L.C.G. ROGERS, David WILLIAMS, *Diffusions, Markov Processes and Martingales, Vol.1: Foundations, Vol. 2: Itô Calculus*, Cambridge University Press, 2nd ed., 2000, 406 and 494 p.

Stefan ROSTEK, *Option Pricing in Fractional Brownian Markets*, Springer-Verlag, 2009, 137 p.

David RUPPERT, *Statistics and Finance, An Introduction*, Springer, 2004, 482 p.

Amir SADR, *Interest Rate Swaps and Their Derivatives*, John Wiley & Sons, Inc., Hoboken, 2009, 247 p.

Lucio SARNO, Mark TAYLOR, *The Economics of Exchange Rates*, Cambridge University Press, 2003, 330 p.

Philipp J. SCHONBUCHER, *Credit Derivatives Pricing Models*, John Wiley & Sons, Ltd, Chichester, 2003, 600 p.

Wim SCHOUTENS, *Lévy Processes in Finance – Pricing Financial Derivatives*, John Wiley & Sons, Ltd, Chichester, 2003, 196 p.

William F. SHARPE, *Investors and Markets – Portfolio Choices, Asset Prices, and Investment Advice*, Princeton University Press, 2006, 232 p.

Jan de SPIEGELEER, Wim SCHOUTENS, *The Handbook of Convertible Bonds: Pricing, Strategies and Risk Management*, John Wiley & Sons, Ltd, Chichester, 2011, 400 p.

Dan STEFANICA, *A Primer for the Mathematics of Financial Engineering*, FE Press, 2011, 352 p.

Robert STEINER, *Mastering Financial Calculations*, FT Prentice Hall, 1997, 400 p.

Nassim TALEB, *Dynamic Hedging: Managing Vanilla and Exotic Options*, John Wiley & Sons, Inc., Hoboken, 1997, 506 p.

Peter TANKOV, *Financial Modelling with Jump Processes*, Chapman and Hall, 2003, 552 p.

Stephen J. TAYLOR, *Asset Price Dynamics, Volatility and Prediction*, Princeton University Press, 2007, 544 p.

John L. TEALL, *Financial Market Analytics*, Quorum Books, 1999, 328 p.

Peter TEMPLE, *CFDs Made Simple – A Straightforward Guide to Contracts for Difference*, Harriman House, 2009, 155 p.

Robert TOMKINS, *Options Explained*, Macmillan Business, 1994, 597 p.

Tim WEITHERS, *Foreign Exchange*, John Wiley & Sons, Inc., Hoboken, 2006, 336 p.

Paul WILMOTT (ed.), *The Best of Wilmott 2*, John Wiley & Sons, Ltd, Chichester, 2005, 404 p.

P. WILMOTT, H. RASMUSSEN (eds) *New Directions in Mathematical Finance*, John Wiley & Sons, Ltd, Chichester, 2002, 256 p.

Index

Printed and bound by CPI Group (UK) Ltd, Croydon, CR0 4YY

16/04/2025

14658506-0002